Klaus Dieter Petz
mit Gruß und Dank
22. 11. 1997

Harald

Wissenschaftliche Untersuchungen
zum Neuen Testament

Herausgegeben von
Martin Hengel und Otfried Hofius

102

Lars Hartman

Text-Centered
New Testament Studies

Text-Theoretical Essays
on Early Jewish and
Early Christian Literature

edited by

David Hellholm

Mohr Siebeck

Die Deutsche Bibliothek – CIP-Einheitsaufnahme:

Hartman, Lars:
Text-Centered New Testament studies: text-theoretical essays on early Jewish and
early Christian literature / Lars Hartman. Ed. by David Hellholm.
– Tübingen: Mohr Siebeck, 1997
  (Wissenschaftliche Untersuchungen zum Neuen Testament; 102)
  ISBN 3-16-146836-8

© 1997 J. C. B. Mohr (Paul Siebeck), P.O. Box 20 40, D-72010 Tübingen.

This book was typeset by Progressus Consultant KB in Karlstad (Sweden) using Palatino,
SymbolGreek and Hebraica typefaces, printed by Gulde-Druck in Tübingen on non-aging
paper from Papierfabrik Niefern and bound by Heinr. Koch in Tübingen.

ISSN 0512-1604

Preface

When the articles of this collection are presented as "text-theoretical studies," this may sound somewhat presumptuous, both to professional text theorists and to colleagues in exegesis who are more proficient in theory of literature, text linguistics, etc. than I am. Nevertheless the papers here gathered reflect a growing conviction on their author's part that exegesis can gain a good deal from what is done in these fields. Our task as historians and as theologians is furthered, I believe, if we pay more regard to such literary aspects as these disciplines teach us to focus on, for example taking seriously that the texts present themselves to their readers in a given shape; they also can make us realize that, when we exegetes concentrate our attention on the contents of the texts, the understanding of these contents can be improved, if we pay greater respect to their pragmatic aspects.

Had the articles of this volume been arranged according to the dates of their first publication, the reader could rather easily have observed a certain development on my part. Without being very advanced, the more recent contributions hopefully reveal that I have learnt a little since the publication of the earliest one in 1975. The articles which are here published for the first time were originally prepared for particular occasions and have not been revised before publication. But, as is also the case in almost all of the other chapters of this book, I have supplemented their bibliographies with some more recent literature. The abbreviations of periodicals etc. follow S. Schwertner's *Abkürzungsverzeichnis* in the *Theologische Realenzyklopädie* (2nd ed., Berlin/New York: de Gruyter 1994).

Lastly I want to express my sincere gratitude to Professor David Hellholm, friend and colleague, who has spent so much time and energy on this book sparing no pains in editing it. The reader will easily realize that he is an adroit editor; that he is also an expert text linguist may already be known. Thus I have felt being in reliable hands during the production of this volume.

Uppsala, December 1996   Lars Hartman

Table of Contents

I.

Narrative Texts

Gospels and Apocalypses

1. Some Reflections on the Problem of the Literary Genre of the Gospels[1]

1. *The Problem of the Literary Genre*

Let us imagine that we are taking part in the ceremonial conferment of degrees which takes place at the end of the academic year in the University Hall. When the Vice Chancellor of the University has opened the ceremony, the professor who has been assigned the task of delivering the festival lecture comes to the *cathedra*. After the obligatory introductory ceremonial addresses to the honourable guests the lecturer begins his presentation: "Once upon a time there was a poor shoemaker who lived in a little cottage at the edge of the forest ...." The learned professor continues on the same line, giving the main part of his treatment of, say, a sociological topic, in the form of a children's story.

It is not hard to guess that a lecture of this kind would provoke wholly different reactions. Some would find the approach original, others eccentric, daring, or unworthy of the situation. The reasons are obvious. The situation and the normal way of shaping an academic discourse have established a convention so that the audience has certain expectations of a conferment lecture. An expert on literary criticism or linguistics might be prepared to regard the phenomenon as a kind of "reader's expectation".[2] In our example two systems of such expectations collide, and the collision causes delighted smiles or dissatisfied grimaces.

I have made up this example in order to point to an essential aspect of the problem which I shall discuss in this paper. Mostly without thinking, we distinguish between different types of literature, or genres, and connect them with particular contents and usages. Do the Gospels belong to a type of literature which their first readers/listeners associated with a specific function; and did they then have certain expectations of their content in a way which may be suggestive of how we spontaneously react to examples of the genres of the academic lecture and of the children's story?

---

[1] A slightly revised translation of Hartman 1978, a paper read in the Royal Academy of Arts and Sciences, Uppsala, February 1977.
[2] See, e.g., Weinrich 1971, 30f., 140.

However, scrutiny of the literary genre of the Gospels raises several issues. Already the designation "genre" is problematic: it is not always used in the same manner, and some people are even sceptical of using it at all.[3] Furthermore, "Gospel" is actually a label which was affixed to these New Testament books long after they were written; moreover a couple of centuries later it was also applied to documents which look very different from those which we are wont to call Gospels.[4] (Yet I disregard modern phenomena like Levi Dowling's "The Gospel of the New Age".) As a matter of fact most of the scholars who have dealt with the history of Early Christian writings maintain that the Gospels represented a new type of literature.[5] Then one may wonder whether it is fair to speak of a reader's expectation or of any conventions which Mark and his colleagues followed. But it is also suggested that there are far-reaching similarities between, on the one hand, some sources and earlier stages of the Gospels, and, on the other, other kinds of literature from Antiquity. From such similarities conclusions are drawn as to the background and function of these sources. This means that also the pre-history of the Gospels belongs to the problems which are raised by our topic. Thus, discussing the question of the genre of the Gospels means to enter a scholarly underground. Yet I dare do so, albeit with some simplifications and leaving aside many suggestions and theories.[6]

Why, however, ask the question at all? In our days we are not much concerned about the rules for different types of literature. In Antiquity people seem to have been more prone to adhere to literary conventions when they sought to express themselves in writing.[7] They were not free in their choice of such vehicles, but nor are we, really, because the conventions which we share with our culture dictate that the form of expression we use is normally connected with a particular type of contents and with a certain function or usage.[8] Therefore, an academic lecture in the form of a children's story would make a strange impression. But this adherence to literary conventions also makes parody and burlesque possible, whether an author is writing a political satire using the form of a traveller's report (like Jonathan Swift) or gives a speech to the Opposite

---

[3] A fine survey which was instructive for the composition of this paper is Doty 1972. See also the discussion in Knierim 1973. Among writers on literary criticism see, e.g., Wellek/Warren 1949, chap. 17, and Weisstein 1968, chap. 6.

[4] See below, footnote 16.

[5] See, e.g., Kümmel 1973, 12f.; Vielhauer 1975, 349-354.

[6] See the surveys and discussion in Schmidt 1923, 50-134; Theißen 1971; Vielhauer 1975, *loc. cit.*

[7] E.g., Gunkel 1917, 2ff.; Rahn 1969.

[8] See, e.g., Fowler 1970-71, 201; Jauß 1970-71, 12f.

Sex lending it, say, the appearance of the minutes of a committee meeting, using the form, style and vocabulary of such a document.

The conventional linkage of genre with usage and contents influences our approach to an unknown text. Thus, when we examine its possible sociolinguistic function, we note features of its contents, style etc. and look for parallels in other texts, the function of which we know. The similarities lead us to the conclusion that the unknown text has the same sociolinguistic function as those from which we collected the "parallels". Thus some scholars have maintained, for example, that Mark is a literary relation of the "biographies" (*vitae, bioi*) of Antiquity, the heroes of which are philosophers or popular wandering preachers; often Philostratos' work on *Apollonios* (the first half of the 3rd century C.E.) is adduced as an example[9]. From this similarity they draw, *inter alia*, the following conclusions: in some Early Christian circles Jesus was regarded as a popular charismatic preacher, who, like other wandering preachers, performed miracles which testified to his authority.[10] The Gospel of Mark was intended to be a piece of religious propaganda written in and for a so-called "Hellenistic" environment, i.e. the sort of milieu in which such "proofs" were highly esteemed.[11] There is a slightly more complicated form of this theory, according to which the generic similarity is rather to be sought between the philosophers' *vitae* and pre-Marcan collections.[12] Then the editing hand of the evangelist has firmly grasped the material and Mark has changed, indeed rejected, its tendencies to represent Jesus as mainly a performer of miracles.[13]

Accordingly, New Testament scholars have been interested in the question of the genre of the Gospels not least because they have assumed that also in this case there is a correlation between genre and sociolinguistic function.[14] In addition, when the genre of a text is known, this immediately determines the possibilities of using it as a historical source. Thus, for example, you cannot use Aristophanes' comedy *The Clouds* as a

---

[9] Schulz 1964, 143f. Cf. Petzke 1970.

[10] The term θεῖος ἀνήρ is often used of such figures. Cf. Bieler 1967 and von Martitz 1969, 338f.

[11] In the light of modern research "Hellenistic" cannot be used to designate some sort of cultural contrast to "Palestinian" or "Jewish". See, e.g., Hengel 1973.

[12] See Robinson 1965, 131ff. [= 1971, 46ff.] (there more lit.); Koester 1968, 230ff. [= 1971, 187ff.]; Achtemeier 1970.

[13] Weeden 1968. See also the preceding note.

[14] Since the beginning of the century, they, as well as their Old Testament colleagues, have been wont to speak of the "Sitz im Leben" (viz. of Israel and of the Early Church, respectively) of different types of texts and traditions. Of course, this is much the same as defining their sociolinguistic function.

source when studying Socrates without taking into account that the play is a comedy, viz. it mocks at the great philosopher.

I shall refrain from mentioning other suggestions as to which genre the Gospels might represent, or to which genre they might be mostly akin, although there is no lack of such suggestions.[15] But one who does not daily run in and out of the exegetes' workshops may naturally wonder, "is it so difficult, after all?". Why not simply register a number of characteristics of relevant texts, compare them and draw some conclusions? Hopefully, Biblical scholars are no more insensible in their literary studies than their colleagues in other departments, but the difficulties in arriving at precise results in literary research of this kind, including the ambiguities of the material, are so many and so great as to explain why the suggestions differ so widely. Some of the sensitive questions are: what constitutes a genre?, to what extent is a genre bound to be used with specific functions in specific situations?, which comparative material is relevant? More specific questions run as follows: is it significant that the ancient philosophers' "biographies" are about 150 years younger than the oldest Gospel, and the ancient romances of the same age? — they have also been adduced for elucidation. Does it matter that most of the material of the Gospels has a probable pre-history in the form of traditions, viz. traditions which have obviously been used, in written and/or oral form, in the Early Church? Does the earlier usage have a bearing when these traditions appear as elements in a Gospel? Does it, e.g., cause any tension vis-à-vis the associations or the ideological perspective which are present when the Gospel is a literary whole? Here the assessment is complicated by the circumstance that the evangelists are not simply authors who conceive and shape a work on their own, but rather should be regarded as redactors who select, combine and edit material which to a very great extent already exists and is used in their environment. But nonetheless they moulded the material in a form which after some time acquired the name "Gospel".

2. Remarks on the Concept of Gospel

In what follows, I shall begin with a few remarks on the concept of "Gospel" (2.1.), then define how I shall use the word "genre" (2.2.). These considerations lead to the discussion of the main problem of this paper, viz. can the Gospels be assigned to a "genre" of any kind, or are they at least so similar to texts belonging to a given genre that the similarity is instructive? (3) In order to avoid undue complication, I shall concentrate on the Synoptic Gospels, disregarding John and other, later Gospels.

---

[15] See, instead, Schmidt 1923 and Theißen 1971.

2.1. First, "Gospel" as a term. In any textbook on Early Christian literature we find the information that its usage of a script is considerably younger than the New Testament Gospels.[16] Thus, the first indisputable example is found in the passage of St. Justin's Apology from the mid-second century, where he reports that at the Christian worship they read from the "memories (ἀπομνημονεύματα) of the apostles, which are called Gospels" (1.66.3).[17] Before Justin, but also in his days and later, the term is used with another meaning, the earliest example of which is in Paul. He, however, did not invent it, but took over an already established Christian usage, according to which the term stands for the Christian preaching about Jesus. In the oldest Gospel, Mark, it has precisely this meaning, and we encounter it already in the first verse: "the beginning of the Gospel of Jesus Christ, the Son of God".[18] The verse becomes a sign on a meta-level in relation to that which follows and tells the reader that the book contains good news about Jesus Christ. Mark's usage elsewhere in his book supports the opinion that the term does not refer to the book as such; cf. e.g., 8:35: "he who loses his life for my sake and for the sake of the Gospel will save it". Here the readers are not expected to risk their lives for a book but for a message which determined their lives in a definitive manner.

Now, when we encounter the word "Gospel" in the first verse of Mark's Gospel, it represents the earliest Christian usage and is not a genre designation. But nevertheless it says something about the purpose, usage and perspective of the following text, i.e. it served the Christian message about Jesus. His death and resurrection have been a kernel topic in Early Christian faith and preaching, and have also been crucial among the events denoted by the term "Gospel". But being crucial does not imply that there was nothing outside the centre, on the contrary. The Gospel of Mark is a good example. In a classical formulation it has been called "a passion narrative with a long introduction" (M. Kähler). The narrative of the passion of Jesus begins in the fourteenth of the sixteen chapters. The narrative of the preceding chapters steers towards the passion narrative *via* some previews of how the whole story will end. Thus, the first notice to this effect is at the beginning of the third chapter, where the narrator tells his readers: "the Pharisees went out and conspired with the Herodians against him, how to destroy him" (3:6). In chapters 8, 9

---

[16] See, e.g., Kümmel 1973, 11f.; Vielhauer 1975, 252ff.

[17] 2 *Clem.* 8:5 is of more or less the same age: "The Lord says in the gospel". — When Justin calls the Gospels ἀπομνημονεύματα this may be intended to help non-Christian readers to have some associations to contemporary literature, in which, on the basis of personal memories, anecdotes and sayings of renowned people were gathered. See Schwartz 1896.

[18] We need not discuss the fact that there may be some hesitation how to assess the manuscript attestation: a shorter reading lacks "the Son of God".

and 10 we encounter three solemn statements of Jesus on his death and resurrection, each followed by passages which develop the theme of adversities and passion as applied to the disciples. Moreover the geographic line of the narrative has a similar function: from Galilee to Jerusalem; from Jerusalem come the enemies who confront the hero in the beginning of the story, and there he is to be executed.[19] In other words, to the Early Christian "Gospel" did not belong only that which Paul called "a crucified Messiah" (1 Cor 1:23) and his resurrection, but also material which dealt with his acts and his preaching, including his ethical teaching on, e.g., marriage and property.[20] This religious perspective gives a particular sociolinguistic dimension to that which a reader encounters in a Gospel. They have to do with human fundamentals and with ways of understanding human existence and the aim and meaning of human life.

2.2. The deliberations above, concerning the "Gospel" concept, have bearing on my main interest in this paper, because overarching expectations concerning contents and their relevance often pertain to genre. My example of the story-telling conferment lecturer is an illustration hereof, as the form of the children's story has not normally the kind of contents encountered in a scholarly lecture, nor has it the function of such a text.

Thus, I assume that there really is something which may be called a literary genre. I am not thinking of Plato's and Aristotle's distinctions between lyrics, epics, and drama, nor of genre in the sense of sets of strict rules to which an author must conform.[21] But I have in mind vaguer but nevertheless distinguishable literary conventions, visible in so many texts that we may speak of a type of literature.

Such conventions are common to readers and author, and somehow function with both parties: the author adopts them more or less faithfully, and the attitudes and expectations of the readers are determined by them. They may manifest themselves in several properties of the text, and it can be a matter of discussion whether a text must necessarily have this or that property in order to belong to a particular literary genre. Among these conventions, however, are also such as are not visible in the text but pertain to its usage in the group or society, and its function in the life of this social entity.

I suggest that we gather the possible genre constituents in the following four groups:[22]

---

[19] For older and newer discussions concerning the composition of Mark, see Pesch 1976, 15-63.

[20] See, e.g., Roloff 1969; idem 1970.

[21] With, e.g., Cicero and the Neo-classicists; see e.g., Weisstein 1968, 143f.

[22] The features I shall discuss are of course treated in the literature mentioned in note 3 above. But I have arranged the elements more systematically and have also tried to be more precise.

C. 1. On the *linguistic surface* of the text: its style, vocabulary, sentence structure, phraseology; e.g. the "once upon a time" of the children's story, the turns of phrase typical of the old German scholarly prose, the standing epithets of the epic hexameter ("Athene of the shining eyes" etc.).

C. 2. Concerning the *contents of the text*, or, in other words, its locutionary level:[23] on the one hand, this group of constituents has to do with characteristics of the text as a whole, such as the structure of its presentation, main motifs, kind of "plot", themes, choice of topics. For example, the typical construction of a detective story with its culmination in a scene where the hero presents the solution; furthermore, the topics of the articles and items on athletic competitions in the newspapers. On the other hand, these constituents have to do with the same sort of properties in parts of the work: the structure of episodes or other portions thereof, their motifs, ways of organizing and presenting the material in shorter narrative units or in pieces of another literary kind. For example, the feature of the short interviews which may be part of articles on athletic or other events. Or the structure and motifs in the anecdotes used in some homiletic traditions, the so-called *exempla*.

C. 3. Whereas the constituents of C. 1 and C. 2 above, can be found in a text whether this text functions within a communication or not, the following ones all envisage an *addressee of the text*.

First, characteristics which are connected with the illocution of the text,[24] viz. what its author wants to say through that which he says, or, using another word, his "message". As in the case of C. 2, we can expect this constituent to be found both in minor parts of the text and in the work as a whole; for example, a part of a scholarly paper, in which the author argues against suggestions or results presented by other scholars — the "message" is that in the controversy in question the author is right and the others are wrong. This in turn is a part of the "message" of the paper as a whole, which, hopefully, sheds light on a scholarly issue. In this connection we should also take into account that parts of the text as well as the texts as a whole have semantic functions of some kind or other. Thus, e.g., I have demonstrated that so-called apocalyptic time-tables which are found in Jewish apocalyptic texts have a semantic function which is not primarily informative or descriptive, but rather exhortative.[25]

C. 4. A text of a particular genre is normally used in a particular way, and mostly this usage is also located to a *particular type of audience*, which

---

[23] Of course, the expression is inspired by J. L. Austin. Cf. Urmson 1967, 213.

[24] See the preceding note.

[25] Hartman 1975-76 [No. 6 in this volume].

is determined by features belonging to C. 1–3, above. As an example, let us return to the hypothetical case of the conferment lecture. It is part of the convention, shared by lecturer and audience, that the children's story and the academic paper, as well as the football game report, are used in different ways. They belong to different types of situation, and have different sorts of audiences with different expectations (notwithstanding the circumstance that, say, a professor may belong to different audiences on different occasions).

There are not always sharp borderlines between the different linguistic aspects which I have collected in these groups of genre constituents. Thus, for example, it is difficult to make a clear distinction between form and contents. Furthermore, even though we may list features which may be typical of a genre, it is by no means necessary that all are represented in every individual case of a given genre. Nor is it necessary that features from all the possible groups of constituents are present in a text in order that we may discern a genre or a literary convention. Thus, for example, the academic lecture nowadays rarely has a particular style, including sentence constructions and phraseology, but very often it only represents a general, rather faded, everyday language. Nevertheless certain features which could be listed under C. 2–4 must be present before it can be called an academic lecture.

We may ask ourselves whether any of these constituents are weightier than others, when it comes to deciding what is typical of a genre. I am inclined to believe that in those cases where stylistic properties are a typical feature, this plays an important role (C. 1). But then it must be combined with a particular type of contents on what I have called a locutionary level (e.g., the type of "plot", C. 2) and with a specific sociolinguistic function (C. 4). Once, for example, the Swedish writer of children's books, Astrid Lindgren, wrote an article which questioned a bizarre effect of the Swedish taxation system, choosing to use the form of a children's story of a witch by the name of Pomperipossa. The style was there, together with the construction of the plot, but its usage was alien and so was its type of illocution or its message, but the odd stylistic and formal features strengthened the political effect. (Actually the taxation rules were changed eventually.) For some genres certain "illocutionary" characteristics are presumably obligatory (C. 3) and normally these are also connected with a particular usage and sociolinguistic function (C. 4), as well as with specific "locutional" properties, such as topics and types of motif (C. 2). Take, for example, the sort of speeches politicians give in election campaigns: they hardly deserve to be characterized as such if they do not address presumptive voters, do not touch on political issues at stake, and do not contain some sort of "message" concerning these issues (even if the "message" is only "vote for me"!).

3. The Synoptic Gospels and the Concept of Genre

I shall now apply these constituents to the Synoptic Gospels and do so in comparing them with other kinds of literature from Antiquity.

Let us, however, first remind ourselves of the fact that there is some confusion as to the usage of the terms "form", "genre", and "Gattung", not least among Biblical scholars. Thus, Germans often use the word "Gattung" of minor textual units like proverbs, riddles, laments, miracle stories or parables. But they can also speak of the Gospel "Gattung" as well as of the Gospel "Form", meaning the same thing. Among English-speaking scholars, there is a tendency to employ the term "genre" of whole literary works, e.g. epics, Gospels, or oracle collections, whereas "form" is used concerning minor units. In addition, "form" may also refer to, say, particular and general form. By "particular" form I mean the specific shape of a given text, and by "general" form I mean a structure which we encounter in several pieces of literature of a similar sort and which becomes manifest in the shape of the text.[26]

Let us begin by considering the overall construction of the Synoptic Gospels, viz. one of the features of the "locutionary" surface level (C. 2). The Synoptic Gospels are composed of a number of minor units, linked together like pearls on a string. The "string" consists of short, temporal, spatial, or summarizing notices such as, "then he said ...", "and it occurred that ...", "and he came to ...". Thus, the overarching pattern becomes a narrative of a journey, the main personage of which is a wandering teacher who begins his work in Galilee and finishes his life one year later in Jerusalem. By so saying I have also mentioned a typical feature of the Synoptics, viz. their "plot". It should also be noted in this context that material of similar content is collected into larger units, resulting, for example, in collections of miracle stories or of teaching such as the parables gathered in Mark 4.

If we compare this feature of the Synoptic Gospels with other literature, we find the journey motif in the romances of Antiquity,[27] in which the hero must travel far and wide before being able to join the heroine. We also come across this pattern in the "biographies" (*vitae, bioi*) of wandering "philosophers" and miracle workers. Precisely these *vitae* have also been adduced as closely akin to the Gospels concerning genre. The

---

[26] One may for the same distinction use the one between *parole* and *langue*, so that the particular form is defined as belonging to the *parole* level.

[27] See Söder 1932; Hägg 1971.

common features are the travel pattern and a few motifs, viz. the wandering prophet or teacher who receives divine authorization through the miracles he performs. These similarities fall under C. 2, above. I have already mentioned one difficulty, viz. that the "biographies" of this kind date from a time some 150 years later than Mark. But it might well be that they build on traditions to which we no longer have access.

Another kind of literature deserves to be compared with Mark in this respect, viz. the Old Testament narratives on patriarchs and prophets. They, and similar Old Testament texts, seem to have been of a greater importance for the development of the Gospel genre than has been realized. Their major structure on the locutional level (C. 2) is worthy of note. Abraham, Jacob, Moses, Elias, and other Old Testament heroes are presented as wandering characters. Certainly, neither Abraham nor Jacob are described as teachers, but to some extent this holds true of Eliah, and of course, and much more so, of Moses. In addition, both Moses and Elias are made to confirm their divine mission through miracles.[28]

The comparison with the Old Testament narratives may also be extended to another detail on the surface of the text, viz. the short linking notices — the "string" which I mentioned above (they belong to both C. 1 and C. 2). Here, the comparison with most of the *vitae* gives a negative result. Lucian, who has also written a satirical biography of a wandering preacher and miracle maker (*De morte Peregrini*) gives the following advice on how to write:

> He (the writer) will make everyting distinct and eomplete and when he has finished the treatment of the first (topic), he will present the second, cleaving to it and linked to it like a chain, so that there are no breaks nor many stories beside each other , but always the second not only is adjacent to the first but also holds together with it and the borders merge (κοινωνεῖν καὶ ἀνακεκρᾶσθαι τὰ ἄκρα). [Luc., hist. conscr. 55].[29]

If, however, we take into account an author like Diogenes Laertios, his biographies can hardly be said to fulfil Lucian's requirements, since in his portraits of Greek philosophers we often encounter a collection of short stories which are linked together in a rather unsophisticated manner.

Moreover the joints with which Mark binds the episodes of his Gospel together, represent a technique found also in Matt and Luke, even in passages unparalleled in Mark. This particular style cannot be explained as being, e.g, Judeo-Greek, for we do not find it in other Jewish and Chris-

---

[28] The comparison is also made by Brown 1971, and intimated by Schweizer 1967, 11.
[29] Vielhauer 1975, 351, refers to the passage and discusses it.

tian Greek literature. Nor can it be said to represent some kind of vulgar style, for the description "vulgar" does not apply to the language of the Gospels.[30] But similar modes of expression appear in precisely the mentioned texts of the Greek Old Testament. Consider, for example, the following seams in the narrative on Jacob in Gen 28f. (LXX): "and Jacob left the Oath-well and wandered towards Haran ..."(28:10), "and Jacob lifted his feet and wandered toward the land of the east to Laban" (29:1), "... and while he was still speaking, Rachel, Laban's daughter, came ..." (29:9).

Another phenomenon can be added to these narrative devices which we find on the textual surface of the Gospels, viz. a large number of phraseological features (belonging to C. 1). Indeed they seem to be rather typical. I am not thinking of the religious technical terminology (although this too may be taken into account and is, to a great extent, also inspired by the Greek Bible translation). But I have in mind a whole series of neutral turns of phrase like: "he answered and said", "and it came to pass that ...", "he arose and ...", "and behold ...", "when he saw ...", "he stood and ...". [31] The frequent occurrence of such phrases in a text indicates which literary convention has inspired the author, and which, supposedly, has also come to the mind of his Early Christian readers/listeners, viz. the convention is established by the Biblical texts about patriarchs and other holy men. They were read in the Jewish synagogue and at Christian services as well. The importance of a locutionary detail like this is emphasised by the simple circumstance that if an author wishes to write a parody of a Gospel story, he almost certainly inserts many phrases like "and he answered and said ...", "and he stood and said ...", "verily, verily, I say unto you ...". The reader or listener of course catches what is going on and laughs — or frowns.

I now come to the surface structure of the minor units of the Gospels, viz. the "pearls" which are threaded on the "string". We are still in the realm of C. 2. Here, the Synoptic Gospels differ from the Old Testament narratives. The "string", i.e. the linking notices, were parallel to similar items in Old Testament narratives, but the Gospel passages thus joined are as a rule much shorter than those of the Old Testament. Instead, the literary structure of the Gospel stories has its closest parallel elsewhere. One typical example is the following, so-called controversy story of Mark 2:16f.:

When the scribes among the Pharisees saw him eating with tax-collectors and sinners, they said to his disciples: "How can he eat with tax-collectors and sinners?"

---

[30] See Rydbeck 1967.
[31] See, e.g., Filson 1946, 41f.; Tabachovitz 1956; Hartman 1963, 50f. (there more lit.)

When Jesus heard it, he said to them: "The healthy do not need a physician, but the sick. I came not to call the righteous but sinners".

We can compare this Marcan example with a rabbinic story:

An apostate said to some rabbis: "Your words are lies. You have said that God gives his commandments and does after them. Why does he then not observe the Sabbath (viz. since he is always active)?" They answered him: "You are the worst scoundrel of the world; may one not carry anything on one's own yard?" He answered: "Yes." They answered him: "The world above and the world below (i.e., the whole universe) is the yard of God."[32]

This rabbinic example also has counterparts in narratives of other teachers in Antiquity, viz. short stories which begin by presenting a problem and lead up to a decisive answer by the main personage, which solves the problem and is often witty.[33]

Another, also rabbinic, example of a short story concerns a miracle (*bBer* 33a):

In a place there was a water snake which caused much harm to people. They came and told Rabbi Hanina ben Dosa about it. He said: "Show me its hole." Then they showed him its hole. He put his heel over the mouth of the hole. Then it came out and bit him. But then the water snake died. He took it on his shoulders and carried it to the house of teaching. He said to them (i.e. to the disciples): "Behold, my sons, the water snake does not kill, but sin does." In that hour it was said: "Woe unto the man who meets a water snake, and woe unto the water snake which Rabbi Hanina ben Dosa meets".

There are several parallels to anecdotes of this kind in Antiquity and we find them also in the above-mentioned *vitae*.[34]

The similarities between the minor units of the Synoptic Gospels and non-Biblical material from the surrounding world concern both structure and contents, and belong to the constituents of C. 2, above. These features in particular have prompted scholars to maintain that the Synoptics should be regarded as belonging to the same literary genre as the *vitae*.[35] Or, they take a step backwards, suggesting that the similarities originate in earlier phases of the history of the Gospel traditions, when they were steeped in forms resembling those of the *vitae*.[36] Such suggestions derive from a principal presupposition which is typical of the so-called form-criticism, which, in its turn, learnt it from the folklore scholarship at the beginning of this century, viz. that a particular literary

---

[32] The passage is from *ExR* 30 (84d) and quoted in [Strack-]Billerbeck 1926, 462.

[33] Cf. Georgi 1972.

[34] Georgi 1972, *loc. cit.*

[35] Schulz 1964 and Georgi 1972.

[36] See above, note 12.

"form", e.g., the miracle story, is connected to, and has its original function ("Sitz im Leben") in, a particular grouping and its specific needs. Thus, it was assumed that the original function of the miracle stories was to supply the propaganda needs of Early Christian groups; stories of this kind were thought to provide their hero with some prestige in the eyes of the non-Christian "Hellenistic" world.[37] Nowadays we rightly question this presupposition that the original situation and needs behind a "form" are always principally the same.[38]

A critical reader may now accuse me of cutting off my nose to spite my face. Have I not stressed above how we normally tend to couple literary genre and sociolinguistic function? I maintain, however, that I am acquitted since when I discuss this combination, I take into account a wider spectrum of criteria and constituents, and not only the structure of the contents of the smaller textual units. Thus, although it should certainly not be assumed that there is a one-to-one relation between "form" and sociolinguistic function, my main criticism of the *vitae* explanation consists in its foundation on too simple a genre concept.

Let us return to the Synoptic Gospels as we now have them. On the one hand, we have noted that language and *larger* narrative structures of the Synoptics are similar to those in the Old Testament and, on the other, that the *smaller* units of the Gospels are constructed in a way reminiscent of other non-Biblical literature. We may ask, then, whether the evangelists inherited pieces from Early Christian tradition which had a neutral style and made them more "Biblical" by their way of binding them together. The answer is almost certainly in the negative, because the Old Testament style and phraseology were also present in the traditions which the evangelists took over. The miracle stories, controversy stories, etc., which they transmit had already been coloured by the above-mentioned Biblical style, and the evangelists merely continued in the same track as their predecessors.[39]

Themes and motifs also belonged to the possible genre constituents on a locutionary level (C. 2, above). Both in many of the minor units and in the larger whole, the Gospels present Jesus as the wandering teacher who is endowed with divine authority in teaching and action. The motifs, on both a larger and a lesser scale, can remind us of how Greek and Jewish personalities were presented in the *vitae* of philosophers or in the anecdotes about rabbis.[40] In the Eliah and Elisha cycles of 1 – 2

---

[37] Bultmann 1931, 254ff.

[38] E.g., Knierim 1973.

[39] Cf. Wifstrand 1940.

[40] Yet the stories about the rabbis do not appear in cohesive, organized narratives like the Gospels or the *vitae*, but here and there in *midrashim* or in talmudic discussions.

Kings[41] similar motifs certainly occur, although there the stories are longer. But it seems that the original authors stand relatively close to their Hellenistic world (to which Judaism belonged!) also in terms of several motifs contained in the material.[42] I shall return to what this means for the assessment of the genre problem.

I now turn to the "illocutionary" features of our texts (C. 3). Apropos the first verse of Mark ("The beginning of the Gospel of Jesus Christ, the Son of God"), I indicated that this sheds a particular light on that which follows: it should be read/heard as related to "the good message". Matt and Luke have the same outlook, and, as the texts now present themselves, also particular, partial texts elaborate on different aspects of this good message.

When I considered some Gospel elements of the C. 1 and C. 2 groups, it appeared meaningful to compare them with Old Testament material. Can such a comparison also be made concerning the "illocution"? Indeed it can, insofar as the evangelists seem to be of the opinion that the events which they reported were a fulfilment of promises contained in the Old Testament. Two examples: when Jesus is about to begin his public work, Mark introduces him in this way: "Jesus came to Galilee and preached the Gospel of God, saying: 'The time is fulfilled and the kingdom of God is at hand. Repent and believe in the Gospel'" (Mark 1:14f.).

The other example is from the so-called Sermon on the Mount: "Do not think that I have come to abolish the law and the prophets. I have not come to abolish but to fulfil" (Matt 5:17). Thus, these two evangelists regard the activity of Jesus as a goal towards which the preceding history and the old Biblical texts had led. But also the preaching and teaching of the Early Church, to which also their own work as traditionists and writers belonged, were parts of this fulfilment. The old texts were understood as containing a "message" of a future salvation, a "message" which was now repeated with reference to that which they were saying of Jesus.

We may ask whether the pieces of tradition had the same illocution, or "message", before the evangelists took them over. Of course, any answer must be uncertain. Was, for example, the function of the miracle stories in the tradition more to present Jesus as a miracle worker than is the case in the present compositions? Certainly there have existed different ways of interpreting the person of Jesus in the Early Church. In other words, there have been different Christologies. But nevertheless there are good reasons to assume that also the traditions before the evangelists were dominated by the "message" that Jesus represented the Kingdom

---

[41] See Brown 1971.
[42] See, e.g., Kertelge 1970.

of God in some way, and that with him a new, long expected situation was established.[43] In my opinion, such a view is supported by the fact that also the traditions which are older than the Gospels seem to have been steeped in the Biblical style to which I referred above.

When we now turn to the sociolinguistic function (C. 4, above) of the Synoptic Gospels, it becomes meaningful to compare with the Old Testament texts again. On every Sabbath in the Jewish synagogues one passage from the Torah and one from the Prophets were recited. To the latter were also counted the historical books in which heroes like Joshua, Gideon, and Eliah appeared. The reading from the prophets was followed by an exposition. The same Old Testament was also read in the services of the Early Church, and the divorce from Judaism did not bring any changes in this respect. The Christians read the same texts in principally the same way as the Jews, although they held that the eschatological hope had been realized through Jesus. This was to them "the good message". Almost certainly the Gospels were also used in worship as well as in Christian catechism.[44] Thus, the Old Testament and the Synoptic Gospels were used in similar ways. Such a similarity does not exist between the Gospels and the *vitae* which have so often been adduced as the closest literary relatives of the Gospels.

It is more difficult to determine the earlier use of those traditions which the evangelists gathered and edited in the Gospels. On the one hand, there were probably variations as to how they were used. But at any rate, it seems to me that there is no solid theoretical basis under the classical form-critical way of concluding from the "form" of the transmitted material (i.e., the structure and the types of motifs encountered on a locutional level) to its "Sitz im Leben".[45] On the other hand, also in this respect I tend to assume that the "Bible style" of the traditions intimates that they had a function reminiscent of the use of the Old Testament.

The comparison with the Old Testament may also be extended to the implied expectations of the readers or listeners. There is little risk in assuming that they were not too different from the intention of the author as he indirectly presents himself through his text (cf. C. 4, above). Thus, it seems that Mark intended to create something which was to be used in a way similar to that in which the Old Testament texts were read in the Early Church. He was writing on the subject which "Moses and

---

[43] See Kertelge 1970.

[44] In this connection it may be suitable to mention another stylistic particularity of the Gospels, viz. that the text is made up of short phrases, *cola*, which make it suitable for reciting. See Schütz 1922; Kleist 1936, 91ff.; Hartman 1963, 49.

[45] See Knierim 1973.

the prophets" had also treated, rightly understood, and he wrote about it in order that the addressees should take it to themselves and let it affect their lives. One illustrative example from another New Testament writer: when Luke in Acts tells his readers of Paul's participation in a synagogue service in Antioch of Pisidia, he lets the president invite Paul to preach. He addresses Paul as if he were a visiting Rabbi, saying, "if you have a word of consolation to tell the assembly, please, say it" (Acts 13:15). "A word of consolation" — this is what should be the semantic and sociolinguistic function of the Biblical text, made visible in its exposition (cf. also Rom 15:4). Paul responds to the invitation by proclaiming the Christian message. I do not without reservations take Luke's narrative as a historically reliable report, but it is instructive to note the close parallelism which he establishes between Jewish and Christian expectation vis-à-vis the Bible.

Having reviewed the four groups of constituents, it is time to ask again: is there anything that can reasonably be called a Gospel genre? If so, do the Gospels represent a new genre or do they fall within an already existing one? It seems to me that, from a literary point of view, the Synoptic Gospels are the first examples of a genre, which then, as genres can, undergoes certain changes during the first centuries C.E. During this period different — and differing! — texts are labelled "Gospels", such as, e.g., The Gospel of Thomas, The Gospel of Nicodemus, and The Gospel of Truth. But the Synoptic Gospels evidently follow literary conventions which must have been shared by their addressees. Thus, there are similarities between the Gospels and some other types of text; I have mentioned the *vitae* of the philosophers, and have pointed to different forms of short texts which are structured in a way reminiscent of some Synoptic passages. However, it seems to me that the greatest number of similarities is to be found in the Old Testament narrative cycles dealing with the patriarchs and the early prophets. Yet, there are also dissimilarities. One such is so evident that it is easy to overlook it, viz. that each of the Gospels is a narrative unit, even if they have been used, passage by passage, in worship and catechism. But the patriarchal cycles and, e.g., the Elijah-cycle are not independent works but portions of larger units, like the Book of Genesis or the Book of Kings. Possibly we might dare a comparison with the Pentateuch as a whole. At least it seems that Matthew built his Gospel in five parts, in which the teaching of Jesus might be a counterpart to the laws of Moses. But taking the Pentateuch as representing a genre seems to stretch the genre limits a little too far.

Instead, I would suggest that we adopt the following view. As literary documents, the Synoptic Gospels represent a new genre. The greater and smaller features which are typical of this genre are determined by the circumstance that the Early Church gathered around the good message which it regarded as something decisively new. Such a statement is by no means original and corresponds to a great extent to what is found in normal text-books. But I would add a few points: the new is not wholly new, because it has grown organically out of the Old Testament-Jewish heritage of the Early Church; it determined much of the Church's way of thinking, but was also re-interpreted with regard to the Christians' understanding of the Christ event. Therefore, I believe, the first Christians naturally took over the literary conventions which were established by precisely the usage of the Old Testament texts, simultaneously shaping the smaller units according to other, contemporary patterns. The Biblical literary conventions should also have determined the readers'/listeners' expectations vis-à-vis the texts as well as their way of understanding them.[46]

My suggestions in this paper concerning the genre problem of the Synoptic Gospels have certain consequences when it comes to using these texts as historical sources. This problem has many aspects, too, not least such as concern the underlying traditions, their types and origins. The genre problem is one of these aspects, and my suggestions above may, *inter alia*, have some consequences for the assessment of what the oldest traditions may tell us about the thinking of the earliest Church. The overall view, generally encountered in the handbooks together with the modifications thereof which I have suggested above, provides us with the following short answers to the questions on how to use the Gospels as historical sources. The Gospels are not to be equated to the chronicles or biographies by the historiographers. Instead, the features which seem to mark their generic type also emphasize that they are chiefly intended to function as bases for religious proclamation and teaching. Since the heydays of form-criticism, this is a widely spread opinion, but here it has acquired a particular slant. Insofar as there is history behind the texts, it is an interpreted and applied history, and this interpretation should be coloured by the same heritage as left its marks in the literary style. It is, for example, certain that Jesus appeared in Galilee, went to Jerusalem and was crucified there, but the narratives about these data represent interpreted history, in which it is not so easy to separate an interpreting layer from underlying levels; interpretation, preaching, and history form a unit.[47]

---

[46] Via 1975, and Lang 1977, 18ff., are of the opinion that Mark has shaped his Gospel as an analogy with a drama. In order to call this a similarity of genre, one must define "genre" with an wholly different approach from the one which I adopted, and, to my mind, in a manner which is hardly realistic.

Narrative Texts

The same holds true of the ways in which the Gospels present the teaching of Jesus. You cannot quote, say, John 8:58, "Before Abraham was born I am", and without reservations present it as a saying of Jesus. This may be an extreme example, but in principle the problem is the same with the Synoptics. The scholars who devote themselves to so-called history-of-tradition-analyses of New Testament material have suggested different criteria for the assessment of these questions. But, to a great extent, the questions are actually posed on the basis of considerations of the genre problem. At the same time, simple literary deliberations such as these may enable us to glimpse how people of the first Christian generation thought and felt concerning the main personage of the Gospels, and what he meant to them.

Bibliography

Achtemeier, P. J. 1970: "Toward the Isolation of Pre-Markan Miracle Catenae", in: *JBL* 89 (1970) 265-91.

Bieler, L. 1967: *ΘΕΙΟΣ ΑΝΗΡ. Das Bild der "göttlichen Menschen" in Spätantike und Frühchristentum*, new impr. Darmstadt: Wissenschaftliche Buchgesellschaft 1967 [originally: Vienna: Höfels 1935/36].

Billerbeck, P. [-Strack, H. L.] 1926: *Kommentar zum Neuen Testament aus Talmud und Midrasch III*, München: Beck 1926.

Brown, R. E. 1971: "Jesus and Elisha", in: *Perspective* 12 (1971) 85-104.

Bultmann, R. 1931: *Die Geschichte der synoptischen Tradition* (FRLANT 29), 2nd ed., Göttingen: Vandenhoeck & Ruprecht 1931.

Doty, W. G. 1972: "The Concept of Genre in Literary Analysis", in: L. C. McGaughy (ed.), *SBL Book of Seminar Papers 1972*, Missoula, MT: Scholars Press 1972, 413-48.

Filson, F. V. 1946: "The Septuagint and the New Testament", in: *BA* 9 (1946) 34-42.

Fowler, A. 1970-71: "The Life and Death of Literary Forms", in: *New Lit. Hist.* 2 (1970-71), 199-216.

Georgi, D. 1972: "The Records of Jesus in the Light of Ancient Accounts of Revered Men", in: L. C. McGaughy (ed.), *SBL Book of Seminar Papers 1972*, Missoula, MT: Scholars Press 1972, 527-42.

Gunkel, H. 1917: *Das Märchen im Alten Testament*, Tübingen: Mohr (Siebeck) 1917.

---

[47] Of course also historians as Thucydides and Polybios are interpreters, but their intention differs from that of the evangelists; the same holds true of the sociolinguistic function of their works. See, e.g., Montgomery 1965. For Polybios see, e.g., the contributions in Walbank etc. 1974.

Hägg, T. 1971: *Narrative Technique in Ancient Greek Romances. Studies of Chariton, Xenophon Ephesius, and Achilles Tatius* (SSIA 8), Stockholm: Åström 1971.

Hartman, L. 1963: *Testimonium linguae* (CNT 19), Lund: Gleerup/Copenhagen: Munksgaard 1963.

— 1975-76: "The Functions of Some So-Called Apocalyptic Time-Tables", *NTS* 20 (1975-76), 1-14. [No. 6 in this volume].

— 1978: "Till frågan om evangeliernas litterära genre", in: *AnASU* 21 (1978) 5-22 [= this essay].

Hengel, M. 1973: *Judentum und Hellenismus. Studien zu ihrer Begegnung unter besonderer Berücksichtigung Palästinas bis zur Mitte des 2. Jh.s v. Chr.* (WUNT 10), 2nd ed., Tübingen: Mohr (Siebeck) 1973.

Jauß, H. R. 1970-71: "Literary History as a Challenge to Literary Theory", in: *New Lit. Hist.* 2 (1970-71), 7-37.

Kertelge, K. 1970: *Die Wunder Jesu im Markusevangelium* (StANT 23), München: Kösel 1970.

Kleist, J. A. 1936: *The Gospel of St. Mark*, Milwaukee, WI: Bruce Publishing Company 1936.

Knierim, R. 1973: "Old Testament Form Criticism Reconsidered", in: *Interp.* 27 (1973) 435-67.

Koester, H. 1968/71: "One Jesus and Four Primitive Gospels", in: *HThR* 61 (1968), 203-47. [repr. in: J. M. Robinson/H. Koester 1971, 158-204].

Kümmel, W. G. 1973: *Einleitung in das Neue Testament*, 17th ed., Heidelberg: Quelle & Meyer 1973.

Lang, F. G. 1977: "Kompositionsanalyse des Markusevangeliums", in: *ZThK* 74 (1977) 1-24.

von Martitz, W. 1969: "υἱός im Griechentum", in: *ThWNT* 8, Stuttgart: Kohlhammer 1969, 335-40.

Montgomery, H. 1965: *Gedanke und Tat. Zur Erzählungstechnik bei Herodot, Thukydides, Xenophon und Arrian* (SSIA 8°, 6), Lund: Gleerup 1965.

Pesch, R. 1976: *Das Markusevangelium I*, Freiburg – Basel – Vienna: Herder 1976.

Petzke, G. 1970: *Die Traditionen über Apollonios von Thyana und das Neue Testament* (SCHNT 1), Leiden: Brill 1970.

Rahn, H. 1969: *Morphologie der antiken Literatur*, Darmstadt: Wissenschaftliche Buchgesellschaft 1969.

Robinson, J. M. 1965/71: "Kerygma and History in the New Testament", in: J. Ph. Hyatt (ed.), *The Bible in Modern Scholarship*, Nashville, TN: Abingdon Press 1965, 114-150 [repr. in: J. M. Robinson/H. Koester 1971, 20-70].

Robinson, J. M./Koester, H. 1971: *Trajectories through Early Christianity*, Philadelphia, PA: Fortress Press 1971.

Roloff, J. 1969: "Das Markusevangelium als Geschichtsdarstellung", in: *EvTh* 27 (1969) 73-93.

— 1970: *Das Kerygma und der irdische Jesus. Historische Motive in den Jesus-Erzählungen der Evangelien*, Göttingen: Vandenhoeck & Ruprecht 1970.

Rydbeck, L. 1967: *Fachprosa, vermeintliche Volkssprache und das Neue Testament* (AUU.SG), Uppsala: Almqvist & Wiksell 1967.

Schmidt, K. L. 1923: "Die Stellung der Evangelien in der allgemeinen Literaturgeschichte", in: H. Schmidt (ed.), *ΕΥΧΑΡΙΣΤΗΡΙΟΝ, Festschrift H. Gunkel II: Zur Religion und Literatur des Neuen Testaments* (FRLANT 19/2), Göttingen: Vandenhoeck & Ruprecht 1923, 50-134.

Schütz, R. 1922: "Die Bedeutung der Kolometrie für das Neue Testament", in: *ZNW* 21 (1922) 161-84.

Schulz, S. 1964: "Die Bedeutung des Markus für die Theologie des Urchristentums", in: *Studia Evangelica 2/1964* (TU 87), Berlin: Akademie-Verlag 1964, 135-45.

Schwartz, E. 1896: "'Απομνημόνευμα" in: *PRE 2*, Stuttgart: Metzler1896, 170-71.

Schweizer, E. 1967: *Das Evangelium nach Markus* (NTD 1), Göttingen: Vandenhoeck & Ruprecht 1967.

Söder, R. 1932: *Die apokryphen Apostelgeschichten und die romanhafte Literatur der Antike*, Stuttgart: Kohlhammer 1932 [repr. Darmstadt: Wissenschaftliche Buchgesellschaft 1969].

Tabachovitz, D. 1956: *Die Septuaginta und das Neue Testament* (SSIA 8°, 4), Lund: Gleerup 1956.

Theißen, G. 1971: *"Ergänzungsheft"* zu R. Bultmann, *Die Geschichte der synoptischen Tradition* (FRLANT 29), 4th ed., Göttingen: Vandenhoeck & Ruprecht 1971.

Urmson, J. O. 1967: "Austin, J. L.", in: *Encyclopedia of Philosophy 1*, New York: Mac Millan 1967, 211-15.

Via, D. O. 1975: *Kerygma and Comedy in the New Testament*, Philadelphia, PA: Fortress Press 1975.

Vielhauer, Ph. 1975: *Geschichte der urchristlichen Literatur. Einleitung in das Neue Testament, die Apokryphen und die Apostolischen Väter*, Berlin – New York: de Gruyter 1975.

Walbank, F. W. etc. 1974: *Polybe. Neuf exposés suivis de discussions* (Entretiens sur l'antiquité classique 20), Vandoevre-Geneva: Fondation Hardt 1974.

Weeden, T. J. 1968: "The Heresy that Necessitated Mark's Gospel", in: *ZNW* 59 (1968) 145-58.

Weinrich, H. 1971: *Literatur für Leser. Essays und Aufsätze zur Literaturwissenschaft,* Stuttgart etc.: Kohlhammer 1971.

Weisstein, U. 1968: *Einführung in die vergleichende Literaturwissenschaft,* Stuttgart etc.: Kohlhammer 1968.

Wellek, R./Warren, A. 1949: *Theory of Literature,* London: Jonathan Cape 1949.

Wifstrand, A. 1940: "Lukas och Septuaginta", *in: SvTK* 16 (1940) 243-62.

Supplement

See the Bibliography to Essay no. 2, below, and in addition:

Pörksen, U.:"Textsorten, Textsortenverschränkungen und Sprachattrappen", in: *Wirkendes Wort* 24 (1974) 219-39.

Gülich, E./Raible, W.: (eds.), *Textsorten, Differenzierungskriterien aus linguistischer Sicht* (Athenaion. Schriften Linguistik 5), 2nd ed., Frankfurt a. M.: Akademische Verlagsgesellschaft Athenaion 1975.

Karrer, W.: *Parodie, Travestie, Pastiche* (UTB 581), München: Fink 1977.

Fowler, A.: *Kinds of Literature. An Introduction to the Theory of Genres and Modes,* Oxford: Clarendon 1982.

Textsorten und literarische Gattungen. Dokumentation des Germanistentages in Hamburg vom 1. bis 4. April 1979, Berlin: Schmidt 1983.

Vorster, W. S.: "Kerygma/History and the Gospel Genre", in: *NTS* 29 (1983) 87-95.

—: "Der Ort der Gattung Evangelium in der Literaturgeschichte", in: *VF* 29 (1984) 2-25.

Gobyn, L.: *Textsorten. Ein Methodenvergleich, illustriert an einem Märchen* (VVAW.L 46, 111), Brussels: Academien voor Wetenschappen 1984.

Breytenbach, C.: *Nachfolge und Zukunftserwartung nach Markus. Eine methodenkritische Studie* (AThANT 71), Zürich: Theologischer Verlag 1984.

2. Das Markusevangelium, „für die lectio sollemnis im Gottesdienst abgefaßt"?

Es gibt gute Gründe dafür, einen Aufsatz mit dem obigen Titel Herrn Professor Martin Hengel zu widmen. Die gestellte Frage hat er selber mit „wahrscheinlich" beantwortet, und zwar in einem Aufsatz aus seiner Hand, aus dem die in der Überschrift zitierten Worte stammen[1]. Im folgenden werde ich sie mit einigen Beobachtungen zur Gattungsfrage des Markusevangeliums zu untermauern versuchen[2].

Die Frage nach der Gattung der Evangelien ist in den letzten Jahren sehr strapaziert worden[3]. Nachdem lange die Ansicht vorherrschte, die Evangelien seien als Gattung etwas ganz für sich, sind seit einiger Zeit mehrere Forscher der Meinung, die Evangelien seien eher als antike Bioi irgendeiner Art anzusehen (so, z.B., Stanton, Cancik, Burridge[4]), ja, der verehrte Jubilar hat sich auch in derselben Richtung geäußert, obwohl unter Vorbehalt, daß es beachtliche Unterschiede zwischen Biographie und Evangelium gibt[5]. Auf solche Unterschiede werden wir im Folgenden zurückkommen, indem ein Versuch unternommen wird, die Frage nach der Gattung dieser Texte unter Berücksichtigung einiger textlinguistischer Aspekte (jedoch in aller Bescheidenheit, denn das Gebiet ist für einen Nicht-Spezialisten sehr kompliziert!) zu behandeln.

1. Gattung

Erstens sollen einige kurze Vorbemerkungen zum Gattungsbegriff gegeben werden. Schon der Gebrauch des Wortes „Gattung" kann in Frage gestellt werden[6]; hier wird es jedoch beibehalten, vor allem aus Loyalität

---

[1] Hengel 1983, 256. S. auch ders. 1984, 34.

[2] Ich habe eine erste Skizze der Vorschläge dieses Beitrags in einem in 1978 veröffentlichten, schwedischen Artikel vorgelegt, „Till frågan om evangeliernas litterära genre" [Nr. 1 in dieser Aufsatzsammlung].

[3] Für eine Übersicht s. Dormeyer 1989, wo mit Justin begonnen wird. Burridge 1992, bietet im Kap. 1 einen Überblick über die Debatte während dieses Jahrhunderts.

[4] Stanton 1974, 116; Cancik 1984a, und ders. 1984b; Burridge 1992.

[5] Hengel 1984, 49, sowie ders. 1983, 223f.

[6] S. z.B. Werlich 1979, 116.

gegenüber dem exegetischen, besonders dem neutestamentlich-exegetischen, Sprachgebrauch.

Obschon gewisse Theoretiker „den Tod der Gattungen" proklamiert haben[7], ist von anderen mit Recht behauptet worden, daß „das Gerücht von ihrem Tode weit übertrieben ist"[8]. Jede sprachliche Kommunikation bedient sich ja nicht nur der Wörter sowie grammatikalisch beschreibbarer Regeln dafür, wie sie zu benutzen sind — alles von sprachlicher Konvention bedingt, sondern auch mehr umfassender und zugleich auf höheren Abstraktionsebenen zu findender Konventionen, die z.B. besagen, wie eine Anekdote oder ein Detektivroman abgefaßt zu werden pflegt. So können wir mit Eugenio Bolongaro Gattungen definieren als „nothing more and nothing less than organized sets of (communicative) conventions whose function is to establish a locus accessible to the parties involved in the communication, so that process of cognition can take place"[9].

Der Begriff „Abstraktionsebene" wurde soeben erwähnt. Auf einer solchen hohen Ebene unterscheidet Egon Werlich zwischen fünf verschiedenen „Texttypen", und zwar deskriptiven, narrativen, expositorischen, argumentativen und instruktiven, die „als idealtypische Normen für Textstrukturierung angenommen werden, die der erwachsene Sprecher als kognitiv determinierte Matrices textformender Elemente in der sprachlichen Kommunikation über Gegenstände und Sachverhalte generell verfügbar hat"[10].

Diese Texttypen konkretisieren sich gemäß Werlich nicht unmittelbar in einzelnen Texten, sondern *via* sogenannter „Textformen", die „als Aktualisierungen von Gruppen von Textkonstituenten zu verstehen [sind], die Sprecher einerseits in Übereinstimmung mit texttypischen Invarianten und andererseits gemäß bestimmten historisch ausgebildeten Konventionen für textliche Äußerungen in der Textproduktion auswählen"[11]. Die erwähnten Textformen werden dann als Textformvarianten[12] spezifiziert, indem zwischen subjektiver und objektiver Präsentation unterschieden wird. Man kann dann fortfahren, indem man auf noch niedrigeren Abstraktionsstufen mit Kompositionsmustern und Varianten rechnet.

Es handelt sich hier auf allen Ebenen um Phänomene auf der *langue*-Ebene, um Konventionen, die Verfasser und Empfänger bewußt oder

---

[7] Culler 1975.
[8] Bolongaro 1994, bes. 302f.
[9] Bolongaro 1994, 304.
[10] Werlich 1979, 44. Näheres zum Verhältnis zwischen den Differenzierungskriterien und den Abstraktionsebenen bei Hempfer 1973, 150-53.
[11] Werlich 1979, a.a.O.
[12] Werlich 1979, 70ff.

unbewußt kennen und benutzen. (Bisweilen verstoßen Verfasser dage-
gen, wie z.b. in der Parodie, aber auch so ist die Konvention wirksam.
) Aristoteles hat nur drei Gattungen (γένη) unterschieden, Drama, Epik
und Lyrik, was offensichtlich eine hohe Abstraktionsebene darstellt,
während andere Gelehrte der Antike *genera* auf niedrigeren Ebenen erörtert haben, und zwar unter Diskussion darüber, welchen Regeln für die
bezüglichen Gattungen zu folgen wären. Bei ihnen war also nicht von
Konventionen die Rede, sondern lediglich von Richtlinien[13].

Auf diesen verschiedenen Ebenen von literarischen Kommunikationskonventionen sind verschiedene partikuläre Faktoren oder Eigenschaften vorhanden, die dazu beitragen, die bezüglichen Texttypen,
Textformen, Textformvarianten (oder Gattungen!) usw. zu charakterisieren. Diese Faktoren können oft den unterschiedlichen, in der Textlinguistik definierten Aspekten oder Dimensionen zugeordnet werden, d.h.
einer syntaktischen, einer semantischen oder einer pragmatischen
Dimension, obgleich hier nicht von partikularen Texten (*paroles*), sondern vielmehr von Phänomenen im Sprachsystem (*langue*) die Rede ist[14].

Wenn wir im Folgenden unter den verschiedenen Faktoren, welche
Gattungen konstituieren, Beispiele solcher Faktoren anführen, ist es also
eigentlich recht gleichgültig, ob sie für eine gegebene Gattung (oder mit
Werlich: Textformvariante) oder für eine Unter-Gattung (Werlich: Kompositionsmuster) typisch sind. In jedem Fall dienen sie als Beispiele
dafür, wie Konventionen der einen oder anderen Art beim Schaffen eines
Textes sowie bei seinem Empfang am Werke sind.

Oben war schon mehrmals davon die Rede, daß Kommunikationskonventionen dieser Art sowohl für Verfasser als auch für Leser (oder
Hörer) gelten. Sowohl im Text als auch in der Situation, wo das Lesen
stattfindet, empfangen die Leser/Hörer Signale, die bei ihnen eine Lesererwartung erwecken, die während der Rezeption bestätigt, revidiert
oder getäuscht werden kann. Wenn z.B. im Sonntagsgottesdienst der
Pfarrer die Kanzel betritt, erwartet die Gemeinde eine Predigt; falls er
damit anfängt, einen Sportbericht zu geben, ist sie überrascht und fragt
sich vielleicht, ob dem Pfarrer etwas Seltsames passiert ist, oder ob dies
nicht vielmehr nur ein desperater Versuch ist, die Aufmerksamkeit der
Zuhörer zu erregen.

---

[13] Z.B. Lukian, *Wie man Geschichte schreiben soll.* S. ferner z.B. Hack 1916. Vgl. Gentili/
Cerri 1988.

[14] In seinem Aufsatz „The Problem of Apocalyptic Genre" ordnet Hellholm 1986 Gattungskonstituenten gemäß einer solchen Struktur. Die Sache kann schärfer und tiefer als es
hier geschieht analysiert werden, aber es ist in diesem Zusammenhang nicht nötig. S. die
Ausführungen in Hellholm 1991. Auf S. 137 bringt Hellholm, mit Bezug auf E. Coseriu, für
seine Diskussion vom Gattungsbegriff auch den Begriff „Norm" ein, der zwischen *parole*
und *langue* eingeordnet wird.

So stellt sich die Frage: als das Markusevangelium „erschien", hatte dann der Evangelist (und/oder die ihm vorangehende Tradition) gewissen Konventionen Folge geleistet, und, umgekehrt, als Leute seinen Text lasen — oder vorgetragen hörten —, gab es darin und in der umgebenden Situation Signale, die bei ihnen gewisse Erwartungen hervorriefen und sie zu einer gewissen Haltung dem Text gegenüber einluden?

Bevor wir uns an diese Fragen machen, werden wir aber uns einige Gruppen von Faktoren und Zügen ansehen, die solche Kommunikationskonventionen darstellen, welche eine Gattung konstituieren. Sie werden oft in der Literatur angeführt[15], aber im Folgenden mit Hinblick auf die Art der uns vorliegenden Aufgabe systematisiert.

Erstens sind *Züge auf der sprachlichen Oberfläche* des Textes zu beachten, z.B. Stil, Stimmungslage (satirisch, solenn usw.), ferner Phraseologie, Wortwahl, Darstellungsart (narrativ, argumentativ usw.), Anzahl einbezogener Personen, Größe, Umfang und Bau (rapsodisch, einheitlich usw.). So war z.B. das griechische Epos in einem bestimmten Stil gehalten, der auch den Gebrauch von gewissen Ausdrücken enthielt. In gewissen Fällen sind Züge dieser Art so gattungstypisch, daß sie durch ihr Vorkommen in einem Text diesen als der bezüglichen Gattung zugehörig anzeigen[16]. So wurde z.B. die Zahl denkbarer Gattungen durch den Umstand drastisch begrenzt , daß ein narrativer Text auf Hexametern und mit Verwendung homerischen Stils geschrieben war.

Zweitens sind *Konventionen für den Inhalt* von Belang, sowohl für das, was gesagt wird, als auch für die Art und Weise in der das Erzählte, das Argumentierte usw. strukturiert wird. Beides hat mit dem Werk als Ganzem zu tun, wie auch mit seinen Teilen. Hier geht es um Themen, Motive, Typen von Akteuren, um Fiktion – Nicht-Fiktion, Werte, Verflechtung von Teilthemen usw. sowie um Strukturverbindungen. So war z.B. für einen antiken Liebesroman der Thematyp relativ selbstverständlich, aber auch für das Gewebe des Geschehens gab es Konventionen, nämlich daß der Held und die Heldin voneinander geschieden wurden und dann weit umherfuhren, ehe sie sich wieder vereinen konnten. Diesem konventionellen Aufbau entsprach die funktionelle Struktur des Berichtes; die Scheidung der Liebenden schuf den spannungsschaffenden Anfang und trieb die Geschichte vorwärts[17]. Ein Typ von konventionellem Inhalt eines Teiltextes innerhalb eines Makrotextes war beispielsweise der der *narratio* einer Gerichtsplädierung – da sollte das Gesche-

---

[15] So ist es auch in Burridge 1992, 26-54 in großem Ausmaß der Fall. Außer den schon erwähnten Arbeiten von Hempfer und Werlich, s. Hellholms oben angeführte Arbeiten sowie die Literatur, auf welche in Hellholm 1991, 136 hingewiesen wird.

[16] Hempfer 1973, 148-50.

[17] Vgl. Hägg 1971, 150f., 173f., 214f., 324ff.

hen bei der im Rechtsfall umstrittenen Gelegenheit beschrieben werden. Eine typische Struktur eines Teiltextes findet sich z.b. in den öfters in den Philosophen-Viten vorkommenden *chreiai*, welche oft so gebaut waren: „gefragt von ... was ..., sagte er ...". (Andererseits spielen auch *chreiai* als Bausteine im Ganzen der *vitae* eine bestimmte Rolle.)

Die eben genannte Struktur des Ganzen hat nicht nur mit der typischen Abfolge der Teiltexte, mit je ihrem Inhalt, zu tun, sondern umfaßt auch die Funktion der Teiltexte gegenseitig und dem Ganzen gegenüber. Um wieder die *narratio* zu nennen, ist ihre Funktion, die Tatsachen vorzulegen, die der Anklage widersprechen, und für die kommende *argumentatio* einen Grund legen (um dadurch schließlich die Freisprechung des Angeklagten zu erreichen).

Drittens: wenn jemand einem etwas sagt, tut er es in der Regel um etwas damit zu sagen, d.h. für Texte besonderer Gattungen gilt es oft, daß sie einen besonderen *Typ von Botschaft* vermitteln, bzw. eine bestimmte Art von *Tendenz* oder *Zweck* haben. Man kann auch von der typischen Funktion einer Gruppe von Texten sprechen[18]. Zudem gab es ja auch in der Antike reine Unterhaltungsliteratur, z.B. der Roman; Unterhaltung ist aber auch ein Zweck. Eine für die Verteidigungsrede typische Botschaft war, daß der Angeklagte unschuldig war, bzw. daß er die mildest mögliche Strafe bekommen sollte, und zu den Konventionen einer normalen Geschichtsschreibung gehörte es, daß das Buch von einer bestimmten Tendenz geprägt war[19].

Viertens gehört zu den Kommunikationskonventionen einer Gattung *eine typische soziolinguistische Situation*. Dieser Faktor wird tatsächlich relativ selten bei Gattungsanalysen einbezogen; das gilt auch unter Bibelwissenschaftlern[20]. Der Begriff besagt in diesem Zusammenhang, daß Texte einer bestimmten Gattung normalerweise in gewissen typischen Situationen von bestimmten Leuten benutzt werden. Eine römische Grabrede (eine *laudatio funebris*) wurde z.B. auf dem Forum beim Staatsbegräbnis gehalten. Als sie aufgezeichnet wurde und später als Geschichtsquelle benutzt wurde, war dies eine sekundäre Anwendung, genauso, wie wenn sie als instruktives Beispiel in der Rhetorenschule diente.

Es kann beobachtet werden, daß wenn eine Gattung mit einer sehr spezifischen soziolinguistischen Situation verknüpft wird, dies in gewissen Fällen auch mit ihrer Funktion (im obigen Sinn von Botschaft und

---

[18] Das gilt auch, wenn man von typischen semantischen Funktionen der für verschiedene Gattungen typischen Botschaft oder Tendenz spricht (ein Bericht hat z.B. üblicherweise eine informative Funktion, eine Paränese eine präskriptive).

[19] Hahn 1991, bes. 388f., 394-404.

[20] S. jedoch Berger 1984, 1041f.

Zweck) fest verbunden ist. Wenn eine solche „feste" Situation verändert oder vertauscht wird, wird leicht die Botschaft- und Zweck-Funktion eine andere. Denken wir z.B. an die Briefe des Plinius an seine Frau. Der Zweck dieser Briefe wurde ganz anders als er sie – als Literatur – herausgab. Ein anderes, modernes Beispiel ist, wenn man „die Bibel als Literatur" liest, oder wenn z.B. ein Literatursoziologe in seiner eigenen beruflichen Perspektive Astrid Lindgrens Märchen von Pippi Langstrumpf studiert.

Diese Systematisierung von Gattungskonstituenten fällt zum grossen Teil mit der textlinguistischen Unterscheidung von syntaktischen, semantischen und pragmatischen Aspekten zusammen, wobei Gruppe drei und vier dem pragmatischem Aspekt entsprechen. Die Rollen der Konstituenten können aber auch aus einem syntagmatischen oder einem paradigmatischen Gesichtspunkt gesehen werden, wobei im zweiten Fall hauptsächlich das reine Vorkommen gewisser Konstituenten in einem Text beachtet wird, während im ersten die Relationen der Konstituenten sowohl untereinander wie auch im Ganzen ins Auge gefaßt werden, oder die Hierarchie der Konstituenten in Texten einer bestimmten Gattung dargestellt wird[21].

So können die für eine bestimmte Gattung infragekommenden Konstituenten mehr oder weniger streng konstitutiv sein. Auch relativ obligatorische Konstituenten brauchen eben nicht die bezügliche Gattung oder Untergattung — oder, in Werlich's Terminologie, die Textformvariante — anzuzeigen, sondern können einer höheren Stufe, z.B. der des Texttyps angehören[22]. Denken wir z.B. an ein Märchen. Es ist ein fiktiver Text, wie der Roman und das Drama. Das Märchen ist aber auch narrativ — wie der Roman und auch die Geschichtsschreibung, von denen aber die letzte nicht Fiktion darstellt. In einem Roman treten aber nicht dieselben Arten von Gestalten auf wie im Märchen, und die typischen Zuhörer und die Situation, in welcher diese sich das Märchen anhören, unterscheiden es vom Roman. Der Umstand, daß die Märchenleser in dersel-

---

[21] S. hierzu Hellholm 1991, 151-154, wo bedauert wird, daß bisher die Diskussion von der apokalyptischen Gattung so vorherrschend aus paradigmatisch angelegten Gesichtspunkten geführt worden ist. Dies dürfte auch für die Debatte vom Evangelium als Gattung gelten.

[22] S. Werlich 1979, 76f., wo von Hierarchiestufen der Textkonstituenten die Rede ist, „insofern als jede nachfolgende Stufe ... die Merkmale der vorhergehenden Stufen ... voraussetzt". Auch Hempfer 1973, 139-150, 189-191. Hellholm 1991 hat die theoretische Grundlage für eine Schichtung der Konstituenten für die jeweilige Gattung gelegt. Er unterscheidet dabei unter konstitutiven und entscheidenden Merkmalen (lat. differentiae specificae, welche in differentiae constitutivae und differentiae divisivae eingeteilt werden, wobei die letztgenannten den Ausschlag im gegebenen Fall geben). Letztlich hat schon Aristoteles diese Diskussion geführt.

ben soziolinguistischen Situation auch z.B. Liedern zuhören können, beeinträchtigt nicht den Schluß, daß es sich um ein Märchen handelt, denn die Lieder sind nicht narrative Prosa. Wir sehen also, daß so die Kombination von ein paar Konstituenten am Ende den Ausschlag geben. Hierauf kommen wir zurück.

2. Die antike Biographie

Seit etwa einem Jahrzehnt treten mehrere Forscher für die Ansicht ein, daß die Evangelien, bzw. die Synoptiker, oder spezifischer das Markusevangelium, der Gattung der antiken Biographie, dem Bios, zugehören[23]. R. A. Burridge hat dabei eine gründliche Arbeit geleistet, in der er einerseits zehn Beispiele aus dem antiken Material mustert, andererseits danach strebt, die Gattungsfragen text- und literatur-theoretisch bewußt zu bearbeiten[24].

Wir brauchen hier nicht der Geschichte des antiken Bios nachzugehen[25], auch nicht in Einzelheiten seine — eigentlich recht lose — Gattung zu beschreiben[26]. Da aber im Folgenden die These in Frage gestellt werden wird, u.zw. aufgrund einer unterschiedlichen Beurteilung der Gattungskonstituenten, sollen in aller Kürze die von R. A. Burridge herangezogenen Faktoren in die oben dargestellte Systematik eingeordnet werden[27].

Erstens, bezüglich der *textlichen Oberfläche:* am Anfang der Schrift wird normalerweise der Name der Hauptperson erwähnt, oft mit der Vokabel *bios* (lat. *vita*) verknüpft (133f., 160-162)[28]. Die darauf folgende Darstellung konzentriert sich dann auf diese einzige Hauptperson (134, 162f.). Die Darstellungsart (mode of representation) ist in der Regel narrativ und kann von Abschnitten von Dialogen oder Reden unterbrochen werden (138, 168). Der Bau (structure) ist chronologisch, aber in den Philosophenviten oft thematisch (139-141, 169-171). Der Gebrauch von

---

[23] Mit Burridge 1992, 219: „while they (d.h. die Synoptiker) may well form their own subgenre because of their shared content, the synoptic gospels belong within the overall genre of bioi". Auf S. 239 zieht Burridge denselben Schluß für das Johannesevangelium.

[24] Auch Fendler 1991 (35-80) stützt seine Diskussion auf literatur-theoretische Arbeiten, vor allem auf denen von Werlich 1979.

[25] Momigliano 1993; Cox 1983; Dihle 1987; Geiger 1985.

[26] Z.B. Dihle 1983. Auch Burridge 1992, 152f., 189f.

[27] In Klammern werden auf Seiten in Burridges Arbeit hingewiesen und auch auf gewisse von ihm verwendete Begriffe. Der Faktor „Sources" wird hier aus Gründen beiseitegelassen, die unten erläutert werden.

[28] Wenn Burridge dies so generalisiert, daß er die bloße Erwähnung des Namens am Anfang im Blick hat, müßte dies m.E. damit ergänzt werden, daß, wenn nicht der folgende Inhalt explizit als ein Bios charakterisiert wird, derartiges auf andere Weise ersichtlich wird.

Anekdoten, Geschichten und eingesprengtem Redestoff als Bausteinen (literary units) ist typisch. Der Ton der Darstellung ist respektvoll, öfters aber mit leichteren Stücken dazwischen (147f., 181f.). Die Bioi sind von mittlerer Länge (5 000 bis 25 000 Wörter)[29]. Das sprachliche Niveau (style) ist nicht immer hoch, und die Sprache etlicher Bioi ist relativ schlicht (147, 180f.)[30].

Zweitens, die *inhaltlichen Konstituenten.* Die Hauptperson wird durch Bericht ihrer Worte und Taten geschildert (143f., 175-177). Die Themen können dabei den ganzen Lebensverlauf abdecken (145-147, 178-180), oder das Hauptgewicht wird auf gewisse Dinge gelegt, die für den Helden typisch sind (allocation of space; 135-138, 162-167). Die zentrale Stellung der Hauptperson (scale; 141, 171f.) hat zur Folge, daß, vom Schicksal des Helden völlig abhängig, der Rahmen der Berichte weit oder eng wird (setting; 145, 177f.). Die Konzentration auf die Hauptperson, auf ihre Bedeutung und ihre Eigenschaften, hat in etlichen Fällen zur Folge, daß die Personschilderung einer Tendenz zur Stereotypisierung unterliegt (characterization; 148f., 182-184).

Drittens, Botschaft oder *Tendenz des Berichts.* R. A. Burridge findet hier eine Breite von „authorial intention and purpose" (149-152, 185-188): etliche Beispiele kommen dem Enkomion nahe, andere sind didaktisch, polemisch oder apologetisch, wieder andere sollen Information geben oder den Helden als exemplarisch in Tugend oder in politischer Haltung darstellen.

Viertens, die *soziolinguistische Situation* (in dem hier angenommenen Sinne). Diese Situation wird von R. A. Burridge in diesem Zusammenhang eigentlich nicht behandelt[31]. Statt dessen erläutert er kurz „the social setting" der Bioi, welches üblicherweise aus Gebildeten und aus Personen in Machtstellung bestand, obwohl er auch die Existenz von mehr populären, aber jetzt verlorengegangenen Viten annimmt. Erwähnt wird, daß Isokrats *Euagoras* als eine Bestattungs-Eulogie öffentlich vorgetragen wurde. Für Tacitus' *Agricola* wird als möglicher Rahmen

---

[29] Philo, *Vit. Mos.* jedoch 32 000. Hiermit vergleiche man Philostrat, *Vita Apolonii* mit 82 000 Wörtern.

[30] Von den von Burridge herangezogenen Texten befindet sich m.E. wohl eigentlich nur Cornelius Nepos' *Atticus* auf demselben Stilniveau wie das Markusevangelium. Gewiß ist der Stil in Lukians *Demonax* relativ einfach (so Cancik 1984, 121), aber trotzdem herrscht nicht die Parataxe in demselben Grade wie im Mk vor. Burridge scheint mir somit ein wenig zu eifrig zu sein, nachweisen zu wollen, daß Bioi auch in einer schlichten „Volkssprache" verfaßt werden konnten.

[31] Aber in der Zusammenfassung des übersichtlicheren Kapitels Genre criteria and Græco-Roman biography wird bemerkt: „a major purpose and function of bioi is in a context of didactic or philosophical polemic and conflict" (80). Leider wird diese Einsicht in der weiteren Gattungsdiskussion nicht verwendet.

ein Festmahl angegeben. Die (ein wenig vage!) Folgerung ist, daß für die Bioi mit einer Menge von verschiedenen sozialen Rahmen, auch auf populärer Stufe, zu rechnen ist (185)[32].

Um unsere Diskussion fortführen zu können, müssen wir die von R. A. Burridge nicht explizit gestellte Frage nach der typischen soziolinguistischen Situation der Bioi aufgreifen. Es ist jedoch hier nicht möglich, näher auf diesen Aspekt der Bioi einzugehen, und es muß leider hauptsächlich dabei bleiben, daß Einzelheiten aus der Sekundärliteratur entnommen werden.

Plinius d.J. nennt in *Ep.* VII.31.5 einen gewissen Pollio, der das Gedächtnis (*memoria*) einer Person so bewahrt und verbreitet hat, daß er eine Schrift von seinem Leben (*librum de vita eius*) herausgegeben hat[33]. Hier wird ein wesentlicher Zweck der Bioi ersichtlich, und zwar den Betreffenden zu ehren und seinen Ruhm zu verbreiten[34]. So kommt der Bios in die Nähe des Enkomion[35]. Vor allem wenn es sich um Personen wie Politiker und Philosophen handelte, entstand aus diesem Zweck auch die Aufgabe, die Verbreitung von politischen oder philosophischen Ideen zu fördern[36]. So hat auch der Philosophenbios einen Platz in der Philosophenschule für Polemik, Apologetik und Befestigung der eigenen Ideen gehabt[37]. Überhaupt wurden so Bioi u.a. von berühmten, tugendhaften, und weisen Männern ihres moralischen Gehalts wegen gelesen[38], sei es, daß sie oder ihre Taten als *exempla* dienten oder daß *chreiai* aus den Bioi als exemplarische Beispiele im Schulunterricht verwendet wurden[39].

Schon in dem obigen Überblick über die verschiedenen Zwecke der Bioi haben einige soziale Zusammenhänge und Situationen für den Gebrauch der Bioi durchgeschimmert: die Agora oder der Markt war

---

[32] Obwohl Burridge „use of sources" als einen Gattungszug heranzieht, wird dies hier außer acht gelassen, da dies keine Kommunikations-Konvention ist, sondern sich nur auf die Wirksamkeit des Verfassers bezieht. Kommunikations-Konvention wird es nur, falls, im Verkehr Verfasser – Leser, die Leser daran gewöhnt sind, Verweisen auf Quellen, Informationen usw. zu begegnen. Das wäre doch kaum als ein „external feature", sondern vielmehr als ein Topos oder ein Motiv anzusehen.

[33] S. auch *Ep.* IV.7.2: ein gewisser Regulus hat ein Buch über das Leben seines jungen, verstorbenen Sohnes (*librum de vita eius*) verfaßt, hat sein Vorlesen vor einem grossen Publikum von einem geschickten Vorleser besorgt, mehrere Kopien davon herstellen lassen und sie in Italia und in den Provinzen verbreitet.

[34] Stuart 1928, 56ff.; Baldwin 1979, 102; Berger 1984, 1043.

[35] Steidle 1963, 129-133; Berger 1984, 1236.

[36] Cox 1983, 16.

[37] Leo 1901, 317-321; Musurillo 1954, 243-246; Cox 1983, 135; Burridge 1992, 80; Berger 1984, 1043.

[38] Dihle 1970, 40-64; Gascou 1984, 433-436; L. C. A. Alexander 1993, 54; Baldwin 1979, 102; Leo 1901, 184-189.

solch ein Ort, wo öffentliche Kundmachungen, Diskussionen, Vorträge u.dgl. stattfanden[40]. Die Schule, vor allen Dingen die höheren Stufen, war auch offensichtlich ein natürliches Milieu dieser Literatur[41]. Dabei konnte eine Philosophenschule einen ziemlich engen und festen Kreis ausmachen, wo Bioi vorgetragen wurden, sowohl solche aus der eigenen Tradition als auch andere[42]. Natürlich haben auch Einzelpersonen, vor allem Gelehrte, *privatim* Bioi gelesen oder sich vorlesen lassen[43]. Möglicherweise wurden auch Bioi an festlichen Mahlzeiten oder Symposia vorgetragen, wo *clarorum virum laudes atque virtutes* vorgestellt werden konnten (doch vorzüglich Gedichte oder Stellen aus den Klassikern)[44].

Diese kurzgefaßte Darstellung von typischen Zwecken, bzw. Gebrauchssituationen der Bioi stellt eine erhebliche Breite dar, und hat keine Veränderungen oder Variationen ins Blickfeld genommen, die von zeitlichen, örtlichen, kulturgeschichtlichen oder formgeschichtlichen Faktoren abhängig sind.

3. Gehört das Markusevangelium der Bios-Gattung an?

Einige Umstände sprechen u.E. dafür, daß der Vorschlag von R. A. Burridge und anderen, das Markusevangelium — wie auch die drei übrigen kanonischen Evangelien — seien als antike Bioi anzusehen, in wesentlicher Hinsicht modifiziert werden sollte, und zwar in die Richtung daß das Markusevangelium in erster Linie zu einer Art narrativer Texte zu rechnen ist, die für gottesdienstlichen Gebrauch und für daran anknüpfenden Unterricht abgefaßt worden war. Um diese Haltung näher zu begründen, betrachten wir wieder die erwähnten Gattungskonstituenten, jetzt aber mit der in der Überschrift dieses Abschnitts gestellten Frage im Auge.

Oben wurde bemerkt, daß in den üblichen Gattungsdiskussionen die Gattungszüge öfters nur unter paradigmatischem Gesichtspunkt behandelt werden, während ein syntagmatisch angelegter Zugriff selten verwendet wird. Wir werden jetzt versuchen, beides zu tun, und fangen mit einer Erörterung der *paradigmatischen* Perspektive an.

---

[39] Hock 1986, 8 weist auf Diogenes Laertius und Athenaeus hin, die bezeugen, daß *chreiai* aus Bioi geholt werden konnten. — Clark 1954 gibt auf S. 177-212 eine Übersicht über den Elementarunterricht, wo sowohl *chreiai* als auch die Komposition von *encomia* ihren Platz hatten (194-198). Ferner L. C. A. Alexander 1993, 53; Leo 1901, 50; Fischel 1969; ders. 1968.

[40] Baldwin 1979, 105f.; Leo 1901, 103.

[41] L. C. A. Alexander 1993, 54 und die in Fußnote 37 angeführten Stellen.

[42] Clarke 1971, Kap. 3. bes. 86-99; Berger 1984, 1043.

[43] S. z.B. Quintilian, *Inst.* XII.11, 16-27.

[44] Cato, *Origines, fragm.* VII.13. Blümner 1911, 411 (mit Stellen aus der klass. Lit.); Lumpe 1966, 618 (mit Stellen aus der klass. Lit.); Pellizer 1990, 180; Baldwin 1979, 102.

Wir wenden uns zuerst der textlichen *Oberfläche* zu. Ich habe schon oben bemerkt, daß, wenn R. A. Burridge das bloße Nennen des Namens der Hauptperson am Anfang des Buches als ein Gattungskriterium annimmt, dies eine Vereinfachung ist: das Vorkommen des Namens Jesu in Mk 1:1 hat eine ganz andere Funktion, als wenn z.B. Philo am Anfang seiner Moses-Vita den Namen Mosis in einem Zusammenhang nennt, wo es klar ist, daß das folgende Werk ein Bios Mosis darstellen soll.

Auf der textlichen Oberfläche des Markusevangeliums gibt es aber auch einige andere bemerkenswerte Züge. Wenn jemand heutzutage eine Evangelienparodie schreiben würde, würde er sicherlich im Übermaß Ausdrücke wie „er antwortete und sprach", „und siehe", „es begab sich aber zu der Zeit", usw. verwenden. Wir begegnen solchen Wendungen in den Berichten der Septuaginta über Patriarchen, Propheten usw., sowie in jüdischen Texten, die an biblische Erzählungen anknüpfen oder sie ausbauen, z.B. in den narrativen Teilen der Zwölfpatriarchentestamente oder in *Vitae Adae et Evae*. Dieser „Bibelstil" ist für die Evangelien typisch. Gewiß unterscheiden sich die Evangelien voneinander auch in dieser Hinsicht, aber generell kann behauptet werden, daß wer so schreibt, einen Text schreibt, der dem Bereich „Texte mit biblischem Inhalt" angehört. Man sollte nicht einfach das Phänomen als eine markinische Art von „Judengriechisch" betrachten; davon zeugen sowohl das Sondergut des Matthäus- und des Lukasevangeliums, welches dieselben Eigentümlichkeiten aufweist[45], wie auch die Art und Weise des Lukas, seinen Stil mit neuen Biblizismen zu versehen[46]. Er folgt Markus' Spuren.

Es ist schwieriger zu entscheiden, inwieweit diese Stileigentümlichkeiten auch in den Traditionen, die von Markus verarbeitet wurden, vorhanden waren; da wir uns jetzt auf das Markusevangelium konzentrieren, lassen wir diese Frage beiseite[47].

Ferner sollte der parataktische Satzbau des Markusevangeliums beachtet werden. Entsprechendes finden wir unter den von R. A. Burridge herangezogenen Texten eigentlich nur im lateinischen (!) *Atticus* des Cornelius Nepos. In den Erzählungen der LXX ist dieser Satzbau aber gewöhnlich. Natürlich ist er vom unterliegenden Hebräischen abhängig. An und für sich ist jedoch solch ein Satzbau nicht als ein Semitismus zu beurteilen[48]. Zudem trägt dieser parataktische Stil dazu bei,

---

[45] S. Hartman 1963, 45-51.

[46] S. z.B. Fitzmyer 1981, 114-125.

[47] Pryke 1978, scheint den Stil auf das Konto des Evangelisten zu führen: „He operated in an area where the Christian faith had passed over from the Semitic to the Hellenistic World. The Septuagint was his Bible, and also his only book of style" (8; s. auch 151-176).

[48] S. Rydbeck 1995.

den Text in *kola* einzuteilen, was dem Vorleser erleichtert, ihn in Bedeu-
tungseinheiten vorzutragen, damit der Zuhörer ihn leichter versteht[49].

Auf der textlichen Oberfläche finden sich also einige Züge, die das
Markusevangelium deutlich von den Bioi unterscheiden *und* die
andererseits den Leser dazu einladen, es zum Bereich „Texte biblischen
Gehalts" zu rechnen.

Wir kommen so zu den Gattungsmerkmalen auf der *inhaltlichen*
Ebene. In der obigen Darlegung der vier Konstituentengruppen wurde
darauf hingewiesen, daß es hier nicht nur um inhaltliche Motive, sondern auch um die Struktur des Erzählten u.a.m. geht. Ein Punkt, wo die
Bioi und das Markusevangelium einander besonders ähneln, ist die
Struktur von aneinander gereihten kleineren Einheiten. Mit Recht sind
sie den *chreiai* gleichgestellt worden. Es ist oft auch darauf hingewiesen
worden, daß ähnliche Geschichten, Anekdoten u.a.m. auch von den Rab-
binen erzählt wurden, obschon sie nie zu längeren Darstellungen zusam-
mengestellt wurden[50]. Dies und die Tatsache, daß die *chreiai* in der
Schule in verschiedenen Weisen verwendet wurden, soll uns daran erinnern, daß dieselbe Form ganz verschiedene Funktionen in verschiedenen Literaturarten haben kann[51]. Offensichtlich verhält es sich mit den
chreiai genauso.

Wenn man das Markusevangelium in dieser Hinsicht mit den Bioi
vergleicht, muß man konstatieren, daß, trotz der oben erwähnten bibel-
sprachlichen Züge, es in diesem Punkt vielmehr den Bioi als den alttesta-
mentlichen Patriarchen- und Prophetenerzählungen ähnelt.

Bei Erörterung der inhaltlichen Züge sollte man ferner nicht nur das
Vorkommen oder Nichtvorkommen gewisser Motive und Themen in
verschiedenen Texten vergleichen, sondern auch beachten, welche Rolle
sie im ganzen sowie für den nächsten und weiteren Kontext spielen. So
kann die Summe solcher Strukturverbände zu Gattungskonstituenten
werden. Ohne ein näheres Studium ist es nicht möglich, festzustellen,
inwieweit solche gattungskonstitutive Inhaltsstrukturen in den Bioi vor-
liegen. Es gibt aber genug Untersuchungen zum Markusevangelium, die
darlegen, wie die Einzeltexte des Buches in solch einer Struktur zusam-
menwirken, daß es sinnvoll ist, z.B. mit Robert Gundry das Evangelium
als ein „Apology for the Cross" zu nennen. Gewiß könnte behauptet
werden, dieser Aspekt sei allzu spezifisch und gehöre zur *parole*-Ebene,
nicht zur *langue*-Ebene der Gattung; stattdessen, so könnte man fortfahren, sollte man sich damit begnügen, festzustellen, daß es sich um das
Leben eines verehrten Menschen handelt. Um dem Markusevangelium

---

[49] Kleist 1936. Der Jubilar hat in 1983, 256, unter Zustimmung, Kleist angeführt.
[50] Ph. S. Alexander 1984.
[51] S. Kee 1973, 415f.; Musurillo 1954, 243-246 (von Märtyrerakten).

gerecht zu werden, müßte man dann entweder behaupten, daß es ein untypischer Vertreter der Bios-Gattung sei, insofern seine Inhaltsstruktur auf den Tod und die Auferstehung der Hauptperson, *welche von bleibender Bedeutung sind,* ausgerichtet ist. Dabei wird der nähere Inhalt dieser Bedeutung in der vorhergehenden Geschichte erörtert, indem dort von dem Werk und der Verkündigung des jetzt Erhöhten berichtet wird. Oder das Evangelium sei kein Bios, sondern vertrete eine neue Gattung, die Züge von Bioi und biblischen Erzählungen enthält. Es ist typisch, daß der Bios Lukians des *Demonax* auf der Meta-Ebene so endet: „Von einer Menge von Dingen habe ich mich dieser wenigen erinnert, und aufgrund von ihnen ist es den Lesern möglich, sich davon eine Auffassung zu verschaffen, *was für ein Mann er war".* So etwas würde der inhaltlichen Struktur des Markusevangeliums nicht gerecht werden.

Schließlich wenden wir uns den Fragen nach *typischem Zweck* und *typischer Gebrauchssituation* zu. Wer verwendete die Bioi, bzw. das Markusevangelium für welche Zwecke in welchen Situationen? Erstens muß näher erhörtet werden, an welche „Leser" das Markusevangelium wahrscheinlich gerichtet wurde. H. Cancik hat behauptet, daß es für einen „hellenistischen und römischen Leser" als ein Bios hervortrat, aber für den mit dem Alten Testament Vertrauten auch als ein Text prophetischer Art[52]. Aber war nicht der Letztgenannte der hauptsächliche Adressat? Schon die ersten Zeilen des Evangeliums setzen wohl das oder etwas desgleichen voraus. Das dürfte sowohl für die zu vermutenden „wirklichen" Leser als auch für die vom Text „implizierten" oder für die „Modell-Leser" gelten[53]. So etwas von den Lesern/Zuhörern anzunehmen bedeutet indes nicht die Verneinung vom Besitz solcher kultureller und sozialer Voraussetzungen, die ihnen den Kontakt mit Bioi ermöglicht hätten[54]. *Das* wäre nicht der Grund dafür, daß sie mit dem Markusevangelium nicht in erster Linie Vorstellungen von einem Bios verknüpft hätten.

So weit, was die Leser betrifft. Was wären dann die Verwendungssituationen des Markusevangeliums, wenn es ein typischer Bios wäre? Wir haben gesehen, daß wie der Bios als literarisches Phänomen eine recht lose Gattung darstellte, dies auch für seine Verwendung gilt: die Konventionen waren in dieser Hinsicht sehr unpräzis. Aber wenn wir unter den vielen möglichen Gebrauchssituationen der Bioi eine für das Markusevangelium annehmen wollten, dürfte wohl die Schule und der Kreis der Philosophenjünger die nächste Analogie sein, wo die Taten und Worte des Meisters als Muster und Lebensanweisungen für das

---

[52] Cancik 1984, 96.
[53] Zu diesen Leser-Begriffen s. z.B. Müller 1994, 129-132.
[54] S. Burridge 1992, 251-154 und dort angeführte Literatur.

Leben studiert wurden. Und wenn die Lesererwartungen der Christen
der ersten Generationen dieser Art wären, dann müßten diese Erwartungen von der außertextlichen Situation geweckt worden sein, nicht von
den literarischen Eigenschaften des Textes. Wir haben uns oben in der
Erörterung der inhaltlichen Aspekte daran erinnert, daß die Hauptperson des Markusevangeliums nicht einfach als Ideal und Lehrer dargestellt worden ist[55]. Vielleicht hat das Bewußtsein dieses Unterschieds
einige Forscher dazu geführt, von einem „Kult" der Hauptperson gewisser Philosophen-Bioi zu reden[56] — dann käme man tatsächlich der Stim-
mung des Markusevangeliums näher. Aber solch eine Analogie dürfte
einfach falsch sein[57].

Es scheint also, daß einige Züge des Markusevangeliums zur Stütze
der Bios-Hypothese herangezogen werden können: vor allem die Anein-
anderreihung der *chreiai*, die Dominanz der Hauptperson und ihrer
Wirksamkeit, der Reise-Rahmen, die Deckung der wesentlichen Periode
im Leben der Hauptperson. Andererseits ist darauf hingewiesen worden, daß auf der Oberfläche der „Bibelstil" und die *kola*-Struktur beachtet werden müssen, und ferner, daß der Text sich nicht als ein Bios
darstellt, weder am Anfang noch am Ende. Was Zweck und Verwen-
dungssituation der Bioi anbelangt, so wissen wir davon etwas, sie sind
aber so verschiedenartig, daß man daraus keine Analogie-Schlüsse für
das Markus-evangelium ziehen kann. Von der Gebrauchssituation des
Markusevangeliums *wissen* wir andererseits eigentlich nichts.

Um festeren Boden unter den Füßen zu bekommen, werden wir jetzt
einerseits die bisher hauptsächlich paradigmatisch angelegte Erörterung
der Gattungskriterien mit einer *syntagmatischen* Annäherung komplettie-
ren, also die relative Bedeutung der genannten Züge auf verschiedenen
Abstraktionsebenen ins Auge fassen, andererseits versuchen, außertext-
liche Indikatoren für eine Antwort auf die in diesem Beitrag gestellte
Frage zu finden.

Oben wurde darauf hingewiesen, daß für verschiedene Gattungen
verschiedene Konstituenten von unterschiedlichem Gewicht sind, oder
vielmehr, daß auf einer höheren Abstraktionsebene gewisse Merkmale
trennend (divisiv) sind, welche dann auf niedrigeren Ebenen gewiß konstitutiv, aber nicht trennend sind. Das dürfte auch mit den von R. A. Burridge angezogenen Zügen der Fall sein. Ein Versuch, diese Merkmale der

---

[55] Obwohl Byrskog die Stellung Jesu als Lehrer im Matthäusevangelium sehr stark hervorhebt, sieht er dieses Evangelium nicht als einen (Philosophen-)Bios an (1994, 264f.).

[56] So Talbert 1977/78, 96-109. Ferner Berger 1984, 1043: „[die] Gemeinschaft von Schü-
lern, die den Stifter quasi-kultisch verehrt".

[57] So mit Recht Aune 1981, 40-42. Der Gedanke ist auch von Fendler 1991, 79, zurückge-
wiesen. – Wir sollen uns wohl auch nicht allzu schnell denken, daß eine Philosophenschule
normaliter nur den Bios eines einzigen Philosophen, d.h. des Stifters, las.

Bios-Gattung in die von E. Werlich beschriebene Hierarchie der Abstraktionsstufen einzuordnen, könnte wie folgt aussehen[58]. Im Hinblick auf unsere Diskussion werden dabei auch entsprechende Merkmale des Markusevangeliums berücksichtigt.

Textgruppe. Die Bioi sind im Prinzip nicht-fiktional, so auch das Markusevangelium. (Die Freigebigkeit sowohl der Bioi als auch des Evangeliums bezüglich von Phänomenen, die die Grenze der Alltagswelt überschreiten, hat hiermit nichts zu tun.)

Texttyp. Die Bioi sind narrativ und haben großenteils eine temporale oder chronologische Textstrukturierung (35). Beides trifft auch für das Markusevangelium zu.

Textform. Die Textform gestaltet sich erstens in der Sprecherperspektive. In den Bioi ist diese Perspektive überwiegend „objektiv", d.h. das Erzählte wird nicht als eigene Erlebnisse usw. des Verfassers, eventuell in erster Person, dargestellt (48)[59]. Ferner wählt der Sprecher thematisch relevante Faktoren (ebd.), indem er durch Episoden und Aussagen den Charakter der Hauptperson darstellt. Ein anderer Aspekt der Sprecherperspektive wird von Werlich „Fokus" genannt: für die Bioi ist der Fokus eindeutig ein „sich schließender", denn auch solche Bioi, die einen weltweiten Rahmen für ihren Bericht haben, sind auf eine Hauptperson deutlich fokusiert, die durchgehend allein das Ganze dominiert. Die Wahl einer vorherrschenden Tempusgruppe (51f.) stellt noch eine Sprecherperspektive dar: die Bioi erzählen vom Leben einer Person aus der Vergangenheit. Alle diese Textform-Merkmale der Bioi gelten auch für das Markusevangelium.

Eine anders geartete Schicht textformspezifischer Konstituenten wird durch die Wahl von Sprachvarianten etabliert (55). Eine Sprachvariante bezieht sich auf den Stil (59), und in den von ihm untersuchten Bioi findet R. A. Burridge eine große Vielfalt, wenn auch konstatiert werden muß, daß das einfache Stilniveau selten ist[60]. Zu den Sprachvarianten gehört auch das Kommunikationsmedium (61), im Falle der Bioi eine monologische, schriftlich abgefaßte Kommunikation von mittlerer Länge. Auch hier gelten dieselben Dinge für das Markusevangelium, doch mit der Ausnahme seines einfachen Stils. Auf dieser Abstraktionsebene stoßen wir also zum ersten Mal auf einen Unterschied zwischen dem Markusevangelium und dem typischen Bios.

Textformvariante. Unter die narrative Textform ist gemäß Werlich u.a. die Biographie einzuordnen (71). Züge der Bioi, die dieser Variante ent-

---

[58] Werlich 1979. In Klammern wird im Folgenden hierauf verwiesen.

[59] Fendler 1991, 79 betont denselben Zug. Die Anonymität des Verfassers verstärkt diesen Eindruck; sie kommt jedoch nicht in den Bioi vor (ebd. 78).

[60] Auch von Fendler 1991, 79, hervorgehoben.

sprechen, sind folgende: noch einmal die Tatsache, daß der Bericht eindeutig nur eine einzige Hauptperson hat, ferner, daß die Thematik in der
Regel Einzelheiten des Lebens des Helden darstellt und oft (aber nicht
immer) das Spektrum von seiner Geburt bis zu seinem Tod deckt. In den
meisten Fällen wird.ein Bios als ein solcher eindeutig dadurch charakterisiert, daß am Anfang auf einer Metaebene im Verhältnis zum übrigen
Text dieser als ein Bericht von der genannten Person angekündigt wird,
entweder durch eine Überschrift oder dadurch, daß der Verfasser den
Leser davon informiert, daß er jetzt den Bios der genannten Person zu
schreiben anfängt. Fürs Markusevangelium stimmt dies nur teilweise.
Wichtig scheint mir, daß die sich auf Metaebene befindende erste Zeile
des Markusevangeliums es nicht als ein Bios angibt; es gibt auch keine
anderen Signale auf Metaebene, die so etwas besagen. Im Gegensatz
wird der Text als „Evangelium" charakterisiert[61].

Kompositionsmuster. Unter diesem Begriff sammelt Werlich eine
Menge von Textform-Merkmalen, die die einschlägigen Texte ferner
typisieren (73f.). Hier werden z.B. Briefe von Geschichten oder Verträgen
unterschieden, insofern es um aus der Tradition gegebene Merkmale in
Aufbau und Anlage geht. Darunter finden sich auch solche Kompositionsmuster, die mit Konventionen oder Forderungen eines sozialen
Zusam-menhangs (z.B. einer Forschungsgemeinschaft) verbunden sind.
Unter den Zügen der Bioi könnte hier möglicherweise die schon bespro-
chene Struktur von aneinander gereihten *chreiai* u. dgl. herangezogen
werden, sowie ihre mittlere Länge. Dieselben Merkmale finden sich im
Markusevangelium. Aber in zweierlei Hinsicht weicht es ab, nämlich in
der *kola*-Struktur der Sätze und in der „Bibelsprache".

Unterhalb der Kompositionsmuster-Ebene schlägt Werlich eine Stufe
von *Kompositionsmustervarianten* vor, die epochengebunden oder spre-
chergebunden sein können (76f.), z.B. die verschiedenen Weisen, ein
Sonett zu konstruieren. Man könnte sich hier denken, Philostrats unty-
pisch lange *Vita Apollonii* als eine solche Variante anzusehen, sowie vielleicht das lukanische Evangelium im Vergleich mit dem des Markus.

Werlich faßt Texte als solche so ins Auge, daß er großenteils ihre prag-
matische Dimension und ihre soziolinguistische Situation beiseite läßt.
Aber trotzdem zeigt unsere Applikation von seiner Merkmalshierarchie,
daß Züge auf den Texttyp- und Textform-Ebenen die Bioi mit so vielen
anderen Gattungen vereinen, daß ein Vergleich mit den Evangelien kei-
nen Ausschlag geben kann. Um die von Hellholm benutzten Begriffe
aufzunehmen: sie sind konstitutiv aber nicht divisiv. Andererseits unterscheiden einige Züge auf den Textform- und Kompositionsmuster-Ebe-
nen das Markusevangelium klar von den Bioi. Zudem ist zu beachten,

---

[61] Vgl. Fowler 1991, 87.

daß diese Merkmale sich auf der textlichen Oberfläche befinden, und also, wie Hempfer hervorhebt, einen recht starken gattungsdifferenzierenden Effekt haben[62].

Falls wir uns das Markusevangelium als „für die lectio sollemnis im Gottesdienst abgefaßt" denken, könnte der „Bibelstil" darauf deuten, und die *kola*-Struktur der Sätze erleichtert den Gedanken. Die inhaltliche Struktur (mit typischen *chreia*-artigen Bausteinen) sollte nicht an und für sich und nicht unmittelbar bestimmte Lesererwartungen erwecken. Für die ersten Leser wurde die Gattung durch den Gebrauch deutlich gemacht und die textlichen Konstituenten paßten dazu. *Wir* aber müssen uns in die umgekehrte Richtung bewegen und mit den textlichen Indizien anfangen, um diese danach mit Analogieschlüssen und möglichen Hinweisen aus dem Leben und aus der Umwelt des Urchristentums auszubauen, um zu Wahrscheinlichkeitsurteilen zu gelangen.

Wir wissen ja nichts Sicheres von der Verwendung der Evangelien in den ersten christlichen Generationen. Die formgeschichtliche These, daß das Traditionsgut (im Prinzip) verschiedene Sitze im Leben hatte, ist von Beobachtungen der Formen und von Voraussetzungen von dem typischen Gebrauch abhängig. Das Markusevangelium sei, gemäß Bultmann, dann zustande gekommen, um eine Ergänzung und Veranschaulichung des Kerygmas zu sein[63]: „das Christuskerygma ist also Kultlegende und die Evangelien sind erweiterte Kultlegenden"[64]. Diese Behauptung ist wohl mehr dogmatisch als historisch fundiert, und hilft uns nicht, unsere historische Frage zu beantworten.

Der erste sichere Zeuge einer gottesdienstlichen Funktion der Evangelien ist bekanntlich Justin (*Apol.* I.67.3)[65]. Ich möchte aber vorschlagen, daß Kol 3:16 uns ein Indiz dafür gibt, daß ein Text wie das Markusevangelium seinen Ort im Gottesdienst und in dem direkt oder indirekt daran anknüpfenden Unterricht hatte[66].

Kol 3:16 gehört der Paränese Kol 3:6-4:1 an. Die überlastete Satzkonstruktion ist nicht völlig durchsichtig, aber in diesem Zusammenhang ist das wenig bedeutsam. Es ist erwiesen worden, daß mehrere der Ermahnungen in dem Kontext Variationen der Gebote des Dekalogs sind, die auf die hellenistisch-römische Diasporasituation visieren[67].

---

[62] Hempfer 1973, 148-150.

[63] Bultmann 1931, 396.

[64] Bultmann, ebd.

[65] M. Goulder hat in mehreren Werken die These eindrucksvoll verfochten, die Synoptiker seien je für sich einem liturgischen Jahreszyklus angepaßt, der sich einem (von ihm rekonstruierten) jüdischen Lesezyklus anschließe. S. z.B. Goulder 1978. Leider fehlt es wohl an zureichendem historischen Boden unter der Konstruktion.

[66] S. zum Folgenden Hartman 1987, 241.

[67] Gnilka 1980, 185.

Statt „Du sollst nicht falsches Zeugnis reden wider deinen Nächsten" steht z.B. „Belügt einander nicht" (3:19). Bei näherem Hinsehen wird auch ersichtlich, daß dem Gebot, seine Eltern zu ehren, die Haustafel entspricht. So ist es auch wahrscheinlich, daß das Sabbatsgebot in 3:16 eine Entsprechung hat[68].

Daß der Vers sich auf den christlichen Gottesdienst bezieht, wird allgemein anerkannt[69]. Falls aber der Vers von einer neuen Anwendung des Sabbatsgebotes handelt, ist es besonders sinnvoll, nach eventuellen Analogien im jüdischen Gottesdienst zu suchen. Die Züge des Gottesdienstes, die in Kol 3:16 angedeutet werden, erinnern an das — möglicherweise idealisierte — Bild, das Philo von dem Gottesdienst der Therapeuten gibt, in dem die Verlesung der Schrift von Auslegung, Belehrung und Gesängen aller Art gefolgt wurde[70]. Von ähnlichen Bestandteilen des Sabbatsgottesdienstes der „gewöhnlichen" Juden hören wir in anderen Stellen bei Philo[71]. Gewiß hat er, wie auch Josephus, eine Tendenz, das Lehren zu betonen — „was anders ist unsere Gebetsstätte (προσευκτήρια) als Lehrstätte (διδασκαλεῖα) ..."[72]; derselbe Akzent findet sich jedoch auch in der Theodotus-Inschrift in Jerusalem, gemäß welcher eine Synagoge eingerichtet worden ist „zur Verlesung des Gesetzes und zum Unterricht in den Geboten"[73].

Die gottesdienstlichen Gebräuche, von denen Kol 3:16 zu zeugen scheint, haben also im Judentum verschiedene Analogien, sowohl im Synagogengottesdienst wie auch in dem direkt oder indirekt damit verbundenen Unterricht[74].

Mit Bezug auf den im Neuen Testament nur hier vorkommenden Ausdruck *logos Christou* verweisen die Kommentare auf Kol 1:5f., wo der Verf. von der Hoffnung spricht, von der die Adressaten vorher „im Wort der Wahrheit des Evangeliums" gehört haben, sowie an 1:25, wo „Paulus" in seinem Dienst gemäß der *oikonomia* Gottes „das Wort Gottes" „auf euch hin" erfüllen soll. In ihrer Auslegung der Stelle umschreiben die Kommentatoren den Ausdruck als „Verkündigung und Auslegung des Wortes" (Lohse), als „Predigt" (Gnilka), oder als „das lebendige Geschehen der Verkündigung" (Schweizer).

---

[68] Hartman 1987, 240-242.

[69] Lohse 1968, 216f.; Schweizer 1976, 156; Gnilka 1980, 199.

[70] Philo, *Vita contempl.* 28-32.

[71] Philo, *Vita Mos.* 2.216; *Spec. leg.* 2.62-64; *Quod omn.* 80-82. Auch *Opif.* 128.

[72] Das Zitat aus *Vita Mos.* 2.216; s. ferner Jos., *C. Ap.* 2.175 (= Eus., *Praep. ev.* 8.8.11). Hengel 1971b, 162, macht darauf aufmerksam, daß Josephus als Pharisäer den Unterricht betont.

[73] S. Schürer 1979, 424-427; Safrai 1976, 927-933; Perrot 1988, bes. 154-159.

[74] Schürer 1986, 160-176, und Fußnote 73 oben.

Der Ausdruck vom „Wohnen" des Wortes Christi kann uns vielleicht weiter führen. Die Kommentatoren pflegen darauf hinzuweisen, daß er am nächsten an Sir 24:8 erinnert, wo vom Wohnen der Weisheit in Israel die Rede ist. Im Kontext geht hervor, daß „dies alles vom Buch des Bundes des Höchsten gilt, dem Gesetz, das uns Moses auferlegt hat" (24:23). Hinter diesem Ausdruck liegt eigentlich die Art und Weise, von der Anwesenheit Gottes zu reden: er „wohnt" unter den Seinigen oder in ihrem Tempel, so daß er aus der Nähe ihre Gebete hören und zu ihrer Hilfe „kommen" kann. Diese konkrete Redeweise kann dann so spiritualisiert werden, daß von der Nähe der Herrlichkeit Gottes (Ex 24:16 usw.) oder des Namens Gottes (Dt 12:11; Jer 7:12 usw.) gesprochen wird[75]. So scheint der Verfasser des Kolosserbriefes an eine machtvolle Nähe des erhöhten Siegers (Kol 3:15!), Christus, in der Gemeinde zu denken. Diese Nähe wird hier besonders mit ihrem Gottesdienst verknüpft. Die Sirach-Stelle kann aber die Annahme stützen, daß das in der Gemeinde wohnende Wort Christi auch textliche Gestalt gehabt hat, und ohne eine Evangelienschrift (so etwas verneint Schweizer ausdrücklich) vorauszusetzen, scheint es doch natürlich, anzunehmen, daß der Verkündigung und gegenseitigen Belehrung und Ermahnung eine Form von Evangelientradition unterlag. Auch von anderen geistlichen Führern waren ja Traditionen zugänglich, u.a. in Form von Apophthegmen und tradierten Aussagen. Hier ist es auch am Platz daran zu erinnern, daß es sehr wahrscheinlich vor den Evangelien, die wir jetzt besitzen, frühere Sammlungen gegeben hat[76].

Verlesung beinhaltet zugleich Belehrung und Ermahnung, eine Belehrung, die an und für sich auch außerhalb des eigentlichen Gottesdienstes, als eine Art Verlängerung davon, stattfinden konnte. Es gibt im Neuen Testament einige Spuren von solch einer Belehrung (um nicht den Sitz im Leben allerlei katechetischen und paränetischen Materials zu nennen)[77].

So würde ich also vorschlagen, daß Kol 3:16 von einer soziolinguistischen Situation zeugt, in der, wenn sie abgefaßt worden waren, die Evangelien einen natürlichen Ort fanden, und zwar einen, der nur teilweise an den der Bioi erinnert[78].

Mit solch einer soziolinguistischen Situation des Markusevangeliums passen die Züge der Konstituentengruppen zusammen, die das Markusevangelium von den Bioi unterscheiden, und zwar auf der textlichen

---

[75] Wenn im TM Lv 26:11 Gottes Wohnung (מִשְׁכָּנִי) in Israel genannt wird, wird dies in LXX mit διαθήκη wiedergegeben und in den Targumen mit Gottes Schekinah oder Wort (מימרי).

[76] S. Kuhn 1971, 231ff.

[77] Lk 1:4; Apg 13:1; Röm 12:7; 1 Kor 4:6; 12:28f., Gal 6:6; Heb 13:7, 17.

Oberfläche, die Bibelsprache und die *kola*-Struktur, und ferner, auf der inhaltlichen Ebene, die auf Jesu Heilstat ausgerichtete Gesamtstruktur, welche die Bedeutung der Teiltexte bestimmt. Auch die Komposition des Evangeliums paßt zu einer gottesdienstlichen Verlesung, insofern in einer natürlichen Weise die kürzeren Abschnitte herausgeholt werden können[79].

So hat unsere Gattungsdiskussion folgendes ergeben: das Markusevangelium hat gewiß wesentliche Züge mit den Bioi gemeinsam. Aber bedeutsame Konstituenten unterscheiden es so sehr von den Bioi, sowohl auf der textlichen Oberfläche als auch betreffs der inhaltlichen Struktur und der soziolinguistischen Funktion und Situation, daß es irreführend ist, es einfach als einen Bios darzustellen. Falls man es als „eine Sonderform der Biographie"[80] oder als eine „neugeschaffene biographische Untergattung" charakterisieren will[81], muß beachtet werden, daß die bioi-artigen Gattungskonstituenten es nicht zulassen, daß man aus dieser gattungsmäßigen Ähnlichkeit Schlüsse für die Interpretation zieht. Das Markusevangelium stellt eine relativ neue Gattung dar, die – da ja Gattungen normalerweise nicht *ex nihilo* entstehen – von den traditionellen, erzählenden Schriftlektionen des Judentums inspiriert worden ist und zudem auch Züge enthält, die sich u.a. auch in den Bioi finden.

4. Einige hermeneutische Folgen

Der Schluß, die Evangelien gehören zur Gattung der griechisch-römischen Bioi, veranlaßt R. A. Burridge, hermeneutische Folgerungen daraus zu ziehen.

Dies ist etwas an und für sich völlig Richtiges: Gattungszugehörigkeit eines Textes prägt sowohl die Erwartungen des Lesers als auch sein Verstehen. So behauptet R. A. Burridge, daß Jesu Person und Leben im Zentrum des Interesses der Evangelien stehen („Jesus – the key to the gospels"); dieses Thema ist solchen Themen übergeordnet wie „the reality of Christian experience, the Kingdom of Heaven, or the revelation of God in history and other proposed subjects", welche mehrere Exegeten

---

[78] Anzunehmen, daß das Markusevangelium in dem Gottesdienst verlesen wurde, heißt aber nicht, daß die Jesustradition und später das Evangelium schlechthin solch eine Stellung eingenommen hatten, daß es der Torah gleichgestellt wurde oder die „Schrift" ersetzte. Die Annahme bedeutet auch nicht, daß es als „kanonisch" betrachtet wurde, und ebensowenig wird damit ein Kalendarium oder ein festgestelltes Ritual vorausgesetzt.

[79] Fendler 1991, 59.

[80] So Fendler 1991, 79. Vgl. Dormeyer 1993, 220-222: „Das Markusevangelium als erzählende Idealbiographie".

[81] So Dormeyer 1989, 189.

für das wirkliche Anliegen der Evangelisten erklärt haben, während ihnen der historische Jesus von geringerer Bedeutung wäre[82].

Die Frage, ob das Markusevangelium vielmehr Geschichtschreibung als kerygmatische Verkündigung oder umgekehrt darstellt, wird von den Kommentaren regelmäßig aufgenommen. So sei es z.B. „indirekt Predigt, direkt Geschichtserzählung – nicht umgekehrt"[83], ferner wird es als „Bericht als Verkündigung, im Dienst der Verkündigung" charakterisiert[84]. Oder: Markus will „proclaim the significance of Jesus for the community of his days ... we do not think ... that he had no interest in history"[85].

Hiermit vergleiche man z.B. W. Marxsen: „das Werk ist als Verkündigung zu lesen, nicht aber als 'Bericht von Jesus'"[86]. Aber auch R. A. Burridge meint, daß, während „the primary concern" der Evangelien als Bioi „the person of Jesus" ist, „they include 'the reality of Christian experience' (Anspielung an N. Perrin), or the Kingdom of Heaven, or the salvation of God in history"[87].

Wenn aber das Markusevangelium primär ein Text für gottesdienstliche Verlesung war, dann wirft dies ein ganz besonderes Licht auf den Text. Im Gottesdienst begegnen Gott und Mensch einander — dieser Gedanke ist in der Welt der Religionen allgemein. Diese Begegnung bedeutet u.a., daß göttliche Taten der Vergangenheit im Kultus vergegenwärtigt und auf die Kultusteilnehmer und ihre Situation bezogen werden. Im jüdischen Sabbatsgottesdienst geschah dies durch die Schriftlesungen und durch die darauf (eventuell) folgende Auslegung[88]. So wurde auch durch die Verlesung des Evangeliums und in der damit verbundenen Belehrung und Ermahnung sowie — warum nicht, wie in Kol 3:16 — in Gesängen das Vergangene vergegenwärtigt und für das aktuelle Leben fruchtbar gemacht. So spielte das Evangelium eine wesentliche Rolle für die Identität der Zuhörer; sein Inhalt legte dafür ein Fundament, und sie wurde in der Vergegenwärtigung davon bestätigt und bekräftigt. (Die Bioi haben *normaliter* keine solche sozusagen existentiell fundamentale Funktion gehabt.)

In diesem Licht stellt sich wieder die Frage von der Bedeutung der historischen Person Jesu. Die Vertreter der Bios-These meinen, daß die Gattungszugehörigkeit der (synoptischen) Evangelien eine solche

---

[82] Burridge 1992, 256, unter Verweis auf N. Perrin.

[83] Pesch 1976, 51.

[84] Gnilka 1978, 24.

[85] Hooker 1991, 4. S. auch Hengel 1971a, 323f., und Fendler 1991, 191-194.

[86] Marxsen 1959, 87.

[87] Burridge 1992, 256.

[88] Safrai 1976, 932: „es ist zweifelhaft, ob am jeden Sabbat in jeder Synagoge gepredigt wurde".

Bedeutung beweist. Wir haben oben die Stichhaltigkeit eines solchen Schlusses bezweifelt, sowohl betreffs der Möglichkeit von der Verwendung der Bioi auf eine Verwendung des Evangeliums, der dem der Philosophen-Viten ähneln würde, zu schließen, als auch was überhaupt die Bestimmung der Evangelien als Bioi anbelangt.

Hier sollte man die historische Frage nach dem historischen Jesus von der urchristlich-ideengeschichtlichen, bzw. der theologischen unterscheiden. Ideengeschichtlich (also bezüglich der Ideengeschichte des Urchristentums) sollte man sich also m.E. hüten, aus einer angeblichen Bios-Ähnlichkeit des Markusevangeliums Schlüsse zu ziehen. Daß für den Evangelisten sowie für seine Gemeinde die Person Jesu, des einmal in Palästina Wirkenden, von zentraler Bedeutung war, sollte aus anderen Gründen wahrscheinlich sein — um es z.B. mit C. H. Dodd, zu sagen: die Urgemeinde scheint besser tradiert als verstanden zu haben. Aber trotzdem liegt der Ton nicht auf dem Bios des Mannes Jesus, sondern wie es dem gottesdienstlichen Zusammenhang geziemt, auf der existentiellen Bedeutung seiner Person und seines Werkes.

Die historische Frage nach dem historischen Jesus ist teilweise mit der Gattungsfrage verflochten. Sowohl für die Bioi als auch fürs Evangelium gilt nämlich, daß die Gattung faktisch eine Art Historiographie, d.h. nicht fiktiven Berichtens, ist. Andererseits müssen in beiden Fällen die historischen Fragen immer mit den gewöhnlichen kritischen Methoden verarbeitet werden. Zu den Schwierigkeiten gehört im Fall der Bioi, daß wir uns „in der Zone zwischen Wahrheit und Fiktion" befinden, „die für den beruflichen Historiker so verwirrend ist"[89]. Vor dieselbe Arbeitsweise und dieselbe Schwierigkeit stellen uns die Evangelien[90]. Ja, wenn die soziolinguistische Hauptfunktion des Evangeliums im Gottesdienst und in daran anknüpfender Belehrung und Ermahnung zu finden ist, können die Voraussetzungen eines historischen Suchens noch schwieriger sein, insofern die im Kult verwendete Sprache weniger kühl informativ-analytisch als metaphorisch und impressionistisch ist; sie überschreitet leicht die Grenzen der Alltagssprache[91].

So stellt sich auch die theologisch-hermeneutische Frage nach der Bedeutung von der Person Jesu. Es dürfte ratsam sein, diese theologische Frage nicht die Erörterung der zwei anderen Fragen, d.h. der urchristlich-ideengeschichtlichen und der historischen, beeinflussen zu lassen. Umgekehrt scheint es mir nicht theologisch verantwortungsvoll,

---

[89] Momigliano 1993, 46.

[90] Berger 1984, 1239.

[91] Vielleicht sind solche, religionsphänomenologisch begründeten Einsichten hinter Bultmanns Behauptung zu suchen, das Markusevangelium sei als eine Kultlegende zu verstehen.

die theologische Frage ohne Rücksicht auf die Ergebnisse der Arbeit mit den beiden anderen anzugreifen. Hier ist jedoch nicht der Ort dafür, diese Probleme näher zu erörtern. Die bisherigen Andeutungen müssen genügen. Hiermit kommen wir zum Schluß. Hoffentlich ist es uns nicht nur gelungen, die Antwort „wahrscheinlich" des verehrten Jubilars auf die in der Überschrift gestellte Frage erhärtet, sondern auch die Antwort ein wenig ausgebaut zu haben, indem wir damit Erwägungen zur Gattungsbestimmung des Markusevangeliums verbunden haben: es ist für eine gottesdienstliche Verlesung abgefaßt worden, die auch mit Unterricht verbunden war. Diese soziolinguistische Funktion lädt dazu ein, es als einen Exponenten einer Gattung zu betrachten, die nicht am wenigsten von älteren im Gottesdienst gebrauchten Texten inspiriert worden ist. Eine solche Sicht scheint auch Folgen zu haben, sowohl für die geschichtliche als auch für die hermeneutisch-theologische Arbeit am Evangelium.

Bibliographie

Alexander, L. C. A. 1993: „Acts and Ancient Intellectual Biography", in: B. W. Winter/A. D. Clarke (Hrsg.), *The Book of Acts in the First Century Setting I*, Grand Rapids, MI: Eerdmans/Carlisle: Paternoster 1993, 31-63.

Alexander, Ph. S. 1984: „Rabbinic Biography and the Biography of Jesus: A Survey of the Evidence", in: C. M. Tuckett (Hrsg.), *Synoptic Studies: The Ampleforth Conferences of 1982 and 1983* (JSNTS.S 7), Sheffield: JSOT Press 1984, 19-50.

Aune, D. E. 1981: „The Problem of the Genre of the Gospels: A Critique of C. H. Talbert's What is a Gospel," in: R. T. Frame/D. Wenham (Hrsg.), *Gospel Perspectives II*, Sheffield: Sheffield University Press 1981, 9-60.

Baldwin, B. 1979: „Biography at Rome", in: C. Deroux (Hrsg.), *Studies in Latin Literature and Roman History I* (Coll Lat 164), Brüssel: Latomus 1979, 100-118.

Berger, Kl. 1984: „Hellenistische Gattungen im Neuen Testament", in: *ANRW* II.25.II, Berlin–New York: de Gruyter 1984, 1031-1432.

Blümner, H. 1911: *Die römischen Privataltertümer* (HAW IV.2.II), München: Beck 1911.

Bolongaro, E. 1992/94: „From Literariness to Genre: Establishing the Foundations for a Theory of Literary Genres", in: *Genre* 25 (1992, gedr. 1994) 277-313.

Bultmann, R. 1931: *Die Geschichte der synoptischen Tradition* (FRLANT 29), 2. Aufl., Göttingen: Vandenhoeck & Ruprecht 1931.

Burridge, R. A. 1992: *What are the Gospels? A Comparison with Græco-Roman Biography* (MSSNTS 70), Cambridge: Cambridge University Press 1992.

48 *Narrative Texts*

Byrskog, S. 1994: *Jesus the Only Teacher. Didactic Authority and Transmission in Ancient Israel, Ancient Judaism and the Matthean Community* (CB.NT 24), Stockholm: Almqvist & Wiksell International 1994.

Cancik, H. 1984a: „Die Gattung Evangelium. Markus im Rahmen der antiken Historiographie", in: ders. (Hrsg.), *Markus-Philologie* (WUNT 33), Tübingen: Mohr (Siebeck) 1984, 85-113.

— 1984b: „Bios und Logos. Formgeschichtliche Untersuchungen zu Lukians 'Leben des Demonax'", in: ders. (Hrsg.), *Markus-Philologie* (WUNT 33), Tübingen: Mohr (Siebeck) 1984, 131-163.

Clark, D. E. 1954: *Rhetoric in Greco-Roman Education*, New York: Columbia University Press 1954.

Clarke, M. L. 1971: *Higher Education in the Ancient World*, London: Routledge & Kegan Paul 1971.

Cox, P. 1983: *Biography in Late Antiquity: A Quest for the Holy Man*, Berkeley–Los Angeles–London: University of California Press 1983.

Culler, J. 1975: „Toward a Theory of Non-Genre Literature", in: R. Federman (Hrsg.), *Surfiction, Fiction Now ... and Tomorrow*, Chicago, IL: Swallow 1975, 255-262.

Dihle, A. 1970: *Studien zur griechischen Biographie* (AAWG.PH III, 37), 2. Aufl., Göttingen: Vandenhoeck & Ruprecht 1970.

— 1983: „Die Evangelien und die griechische Biographie", in P. Stuhlmacher (Hrsg.), *Das Evangelium und die Evangelien. Vorträge vom Tübinger Symposium 1982* (WUNT 28), Tübingen: Mohr (Siebeck) 1983, 383-411.

— 1987: *Die Entstehung der historischen Biographie* (SHAW.PH 1986:3), Heidelberg: Winter 1987.

Dormeyer, D. 1989: *Evangelium als literarische und theologische Gattung* (EdF 263), Darmstadt: Wissenschaftliche Buchgesellschaft 1989.

— 1993: *Das Neue Testament im Rahmen der antiken Literaturgeschichte. Eine Einführung* (Die Altertumswissenschaft), Darmstadt: Wissenschaftliche Buchgesellschaft 1993.

Fendler, F. 1991: *Studien zum Markusevangelium. Zur Gattung, Chronologie, Messiasgeheimnistheorie und Überlieferung des zweiten Evangeliums* (GThA 49), Göttingen: Vandenhoeck & Ruprecht 1991.

Fischel, H. 1968: „Studies in Cynicism and the Ancient Near East: the Transformation of a Chria", in: J. Neusner (Hrsg.), *Religions in Antiquity*, Leiden: Brill 1968, 372-411.

— 1969: „Story and History: Observations on Græco-Roman Rhetoric and Pharisaism", in: D. Sinor (Hrsg.), *American Oriental Society, Middle West Branch — Semicentenial Volume* (Asian Stud. Res. Inst., Orient. Ser. 3), Bloomington IN: Indiana University Press for the International Affairs Center 1969, 59-88.

Fitzmyer, J. A. 1981: *The Gospel According to Luke (I-IX)* (AncB 28), Garden City, NY: Doubleday 1981.

Fowler, R. M. 1991: *Let the Reader Understand. Reader-Response Criticism and the Gospel of Mark*, Minneapolis, MN: Fortress 1991.

Gascou, J. 1984: *Suéton historien* (BEFAR 253), Rom: École française de Rome 1984.

Geiger, J. 1985: *Cornelius Nepos and Ancient Political Biography* (Historia, Einzelschr. 47), Stuttgart: Steiner 1985.

Gentili, B./Cerri, G. 1988: *History and Biography in Ancient Thought* (London Studies in Classical Philology 20), Amsterdam: Gieben 1988, 98-103.

Gnilka, J. 1978: *Das Evangelium nach Markus I* (EKK II:1), Einsiedeln–Köln: Benziger/Neukirchen-Vluyn: Neukirchener Verlag 1978.

— 1980: *Der Kolosserbrief* (HThK 10:1), Freiburg–Basel–Wien: Herder 1980.

Goulder, M. 1978: *The Evangelists' Calendar. A Lectionary Explanation of the Development of Scripture*, London: SPCK 1978.

Hack, K. 1916: „The Doctrine of Literary Forms", in: *Harvard Studies in Classical Philology* 27 (1916) 1-15.

Hahn, I. 1991: „Klassengebundenheit, Tendenz und Anspruch auf Objektivität in der antiken Geschichtsschreibung," in: J. M. Alonso-Núñez (Hrsg.), *Geschichtsbild und Geschichtsgedenken im Altertum* (WdF 631), Darmstadt: Wissenschaftliche Buchgesellschaft 1991, 363-405.

Hartman, L. 1963: *Testimonium linguae* (CNT 19), Lund: Gleerup/Copenhagen: Munksgaard 1963.

— 1978: „Till frågan om evangeliernas litterära genre", in: *AnASU* 21 (1978) 5-22 [Nr. 1 in dieser Aufsatzsammlung].

— 1987: „Code and Context. A Few Reflections on the Parenesis of Col 3:6—4:1", in: G. Hawthorne/O. Betz (Hrsg.), *Tradition and Interpretation in the New Testament*, Grand Rapids, MI: Eerdmans/Tübingen: Mohr (Siebeck) 1987, 237-247.

Hellholm, D. 1986: „The Problem of Apocalyptic Genre and the Apocalypse of John", in: A. Y. Collins (Hrsg.), *Early Christian Apocalypticism. Genre and Social Setting* (Semeia 36), Atlanta, GA: Scholars Press 1986, 13-64.

— 1991: „Methodological Reflections on the Problem of Definition of Generic Texts", in: J. J. Collins/J. H. Charlesworth (Hrsg.), *Mysteries and Revelations. Apocalyptic Studies since the Uppsala Colloquium* (JSPE.S 9), Sheffield: JSOP Press 1991, 135-163.

Hempfer, Kl. W. 1973: *Gattungstheorie. Information und Synthese* (UTB 133), München: W. Fink 1973.

Hengel, M. 1971a: „Kerygma oder Geschichte", *in:* TThQ 151 (1971) 323-336.

— 1971b: „Proseuche und Synagoge. Jüdische Gemeinde, Gotteshaus und Gottesdienst in der Diaspora und in Palästina", in: G. Jeremias/H.-W. Kuhn/H. Stegemann (Hrsg.), *Tradition und Glaube* (FS K. G. Kuhn), Göttingen: Vandenhoeck & Ruprecht 1971, 157-184.

— 1983: „Probleme des Markusevangeliums," in: P. Stuhlmacher (Hrsg.), *Das Evangelium und die Evangelien. Vorträge vom Tübinger Symposium 1982* (WUNT 28), Tübingen: Mohr (Siebeck) 1983, 221-265.

— 1984: *Die Evangelienüberschriften* (SHAW.PH 1984:3), Heidelberg: Winter 1984.

Hock, R. F./O'Neil, E. N. 1986: *The Chreia in Ancient Rhetoric. Vol. I. The Progymnasmata* (Texts and Translations 27; Graeco-Roman Series 9), Atlanta, GA: Scholars Press 1986.

Hooker, M. 1991: *The Gospel according to Saint Mark* (Black's NT Commentaries), London: Black 1991.

Hägg, T. 1971: *Narrative Technique in Ancient Greek Romances. Studies of Chariton, Xenophon Ephesius, and Achilles Tatius* (SSIA 8), Stockholm: Åström 1971.

Kee, H. C. 1973: „Aretalogy and Gospel", in: *JBL* 92 (1973) 402-422.

Kleist, J. A. 1936: *The Gospel of Saint Mark*, Milwaukee, WI: Bruce Publishing Co. 1936.

Kuhn, H.-W. 1971: *Ältere Sammlungen im Markusevangelium* (StUNT 8), Göttingen: Vandenhoeck & Ruprecht 1971.

Leo, F. 1901/65: *Die griechisch-römische Biographie nach ihrer literarischen Form*, Leipzig: Teubner 1901 [Nachdruck, Hildesheim: Ohlms 1965].

Lohse, E. 1968: *Die Briefe an die Kolosser und an Philemon* (KEK 9:2), Göttingen: Vandenhoeck & Ruprecht 1968.

Lumpe, A. 1966: „Essen", in: *RAC* 6, Stuttgard: Hiersemann 1966, 612-635.

Marxsen, W. 1959: *Der Evangelist Markus. Studien zur Redaktionsgeschichte des Evangeliums* (FRLANT 67), 2. Aufl. Göttingen: Vandenhoeck & Ruprecht 1959.

Momigliano, A. 1993: *The Development of Greek Biography. Expanded ed.*, Cambridge, MA: Harvard University Press 1993.

Musurillo, H. A. 1954: *Acts of the Pagan Martyrs (Acta Alexandrinorum)*, Oxford: Clarendon 1954.

Müller, P. 1994: *"Verstehst du auch, was du liest?". Lesen und Verstehen im Neuen Testament*, Darmstadt: Wissenschaftliche Buchgesellschaft 1994.

Pellizer, E. 1990: „Outlines of a Morphography of Sympotic Entertainment" , in: O. Murray (Hrsg.), *Sympotica. A Symposium on the Symposion*, Oxford: Oxford University Press 1990, 177-184.

Perrot, Ch. 1988: „The Reading of the Bible in the Ancient Synagogue", in: *Mikra* (CRI II:1), Assen: van Gorcum/Philadelphia, PA: Fortress 1988, 137-159.

Pesch, R. 1976: *Das Markusevangelium I* (HThK II:1), Freiburg–Basel–Wien: Herder 1976.

Pryke, E. J. 1978: *Redactional Style in the Marcan Gospel. A Study of Syntax and Vocabulary as Guides to Redaction in Mark* (MSSNTS 33), Cambridge: Cambridge University Press 1978.

Rydbeck, L. 1995: „ΕΥΣΕΒΕΙΑΝ ΕΔΕΙΞΕΝ ΤΟΙΣ ΑΝΘΡΩΠΟΙΣ. The Significance of the Bilingual Asoka Inscription for New Testament Philology and for Research into the Notion of Hellenism", in: T. Fornberg/D. Hellholm (Hrsg.), *Texts and Contexts. Biblical Texts in Their Textual and Situational Contexts. Essays in Honor of Lars Hartman*, Oslo–Copenhagen–Stockholm–Boston: Scandinavian University Press 1995, 591-596.

Safrai, S., 1976: „The Synagogue", in: *The Jewish People in the First Century II* (CRI I:2), Assen: van Gorcum/Philadelphia, PA: Fortress 1976, 908-944.

Schweizer, E. 1976: *Der Brief an die Kolosser* (EKK XII), Zürich–Einsiedeln–Köln: Benziger/Neukirchen-Vluyn: Neukirchener 1976.

Schürer, E. 1979: *The history of the Jewish People in the age of Jesus Christ II* (rev. and ed. by G. Vermes, F. Millar, M. Black), Edinburgh: T. & T. Clark 1979.

— 1986: *The history of the Jewish People in the age of Jesus Christ III:1* (rev. and ed. by G. Vermes, F. Millar, M. Goodman), Edinburgh: T. & T. Clark 1986.

Stanton, G. 1974: *Jesus of Nazareth in New Testament Preaching* (MSSNTS 27), Cambridge: Cambridge University Press 1974.

Steidle, W. 1963: *Sueton und die antike Biographie* (Zetemata 1), 2. Aufl., München: Beck 1963.

Stuart, D. R. 1928: *Epochs of Greek and Roman Biography*, Berkeley, CA: University of California Press 1928.

Talbert, C. H. 1977/78: *What is a Gospel? The Genre of the Canonical Gospels*, Philadelphia, PA: Fortress 1977 (London: SPCK 1978).

Werlich, E. 1979: *Typologie der Texte. Entwurf eines textlinguistischen Modells zur Grundlegung einer Textgrammatik* (UTB 450), 2. Aufl., Heidelberg: Quelle & Meyer 1979.

3. Reading Luke 17:20-37

1. Introductory

The exegetical world is well provided with investigations of the eschato-logical-apocalyptic material in Luke, including 17:20-37. As a rule their authors pose redaction-critical questions to determine the evangelist's purpose as documented in his manner of using his sources and in the redactional passages.[1] I by no means deny the legitimacy and usefulness of such redaction-critical investigations, but nevertheless believe that we should learn from the warnings issued by some literary critics (W. K. Wimsatt and M. C. Beardsley), when they proclaim "the intentional fallacy".[2] Looking into the mind of an author or redactor is beset with difficulties. If, on the other hand, we regard the text as a collection of signals whereby something is communicated to the reader, our situation may be somewhat less complicated. We concentrate on the text, which is undeniably more palpable than its author and look for its communication to the reader. This means spending less energy on finding out about the prehistory of the text and of its elements.

In the following pages I intend to discuss Luke 17:20-37 from such a reader's perspective. At the beginning I leave aside the possible distinctions between authorial reader, implied reader, actual reader, etc., and content myself with simply defining "the reader" as a plausible, normal reader/listener to Luke-Acts in the church where Luke's Gospel was first used.[3] Under 10 below, I shall, however, complicate the concept somewhat. A major interest of mine will be the problem of the semantic function of the "apocalyptic" motifs. This means that over against a whole text I put the questions which otherwise mostly concern clauses.

Does, e.g., the clause "the session begins" convey information? Or is it a way of telling a habitual latecomer, "hurry up, otherwise you will be late for the meeting"? Or is it a cry out of desperation from a nervous

---

[1] Except for the commentaries see Rigaux 1970; Schnackenburg 1971; Zmijewski 1972; Geiger 1976. Often these studies contain some discussion with Conzelmann 1954, and later editions. Bovon 1978/88, is an excellent report on, and discussion of, the discussions.

[2] Wimsatt/Beardsley 1944/54.

[3] See footnote 27, below.

participant, meaning something like, "oh dear, how shall I do it?". Or, finally, is it the words of the chairman, by which he officially proclaims the opening of the session? Thus we can differentiate between four possible semantic functions of the clause, an informative, an exhortative, an expressive and a performative. Does this "apocalyptic" passage of Luke 17 have mainly an informative function, foretelling future events, or does it function in another way, at least for the most part?[4] When I finally favour the second alternative, the result is not very provocative or revolutionary,[5] but based on a reading of the text which differs from the ordinary redaction-critical approach.

2. The Structure of 17:20-37

The reader has no knowledge of Mark, Q or the Lucan *Sondergut* to influence his relation of the elements of the text to each other. Instead markers in the text distinguish the smaller units from each other and group them into larger blocks. Thus, factors in the text itself organize it for the reader, e.g., notices of localisation, of time, and of (new) actors/speakers, introduction of topics or situations, etc.[6] I am convinced that markers of this type on the surface of the text normally play a more important role than purely semantic relations.[7] Organisation of the textual surface also means organisation of the contents.

Luke 17:20-37 naturally falls into two parts, 20-21 and 22-37.[8] Luke 17:20-21 introduces what appears to be the topic to be treated in what follows: the Pharisees ask a question about the coming of the Kingdom of God, to which Jesus gives an answer. In 22-37 the Pharisees have disappeared as conversation partners, and the disciples play that role instead.[9] The topic is now the day(s) of the Son of Man. Verses 22-37 give

---

[4] I applied this distinction in Hartman 1975-76 [No. 6 in this volume].

[5] Often commentaries underline the paraenetic interest of the composition; see, e.g., Zmijewski 1972, 537-39; Fitzmyer 1985, ad loc.

[6] Fundamental studies of the phenomenon have been performed by E. Gülich and W. Raible. Hellholm 1980 and Johanson 1987, have taken them up and applied them to early Christian material.

[7] Such relations are more decisively taken into account, e.g., when Talbert (1989, 164) sees an ABCD/A'B'C'D' structure in 17:11-19:44.

[8] The commentaries differ in their assessment of how the two parts belong together. They are held together by, e.g., Schnackenburg 1971, 221f.; Ernst 1977; Schneider 1977; Schweizer 1982; Wiefel 1988; and Talbert 1989, 357: Jesus' answer in 20f. is applied and developed in 22-25. They are held apart by, among others, Fitzmyer 1985 and Marshall 1978.

[9] A similar procedure in terms of restricting the audience can be observed, e.g. in 12:13-22: in 12:13 *a man in the crowd* asks Jesus to help him in his inheritance affairs, in 12:15 Jesus tells "*them*": "beware of covetousness", and in 12:22 Jesus says to *his disciples*: "do not be anxious about your life ...".

instruction on that topic. First, in 22-23, Jesus predicts a future critical situation in which the audience is warned against heeding people saying "lo there, lo here". In 24-35 follow the reasons (γάρ) for this warning. After three comparisons of the coming day of the Son of Man with the lightning and with the days of Noah and Lot, respectively (24-30), 31-35 add further admonitions concerning "that day" and "that night".[10] V. 37, finally, adds a saying, introduced by an intervening question from the disciples, "where?".

3. The Relation Between 20-21 and 22-37

Above I assumed that 20-21 and 22-37 constitute a single text, although the audiences differ to some extent and the first part introduces the theme of the Kingdom of God and the second deals with the days of the Son of Man.[11] But there are features which hold the two passages together. Thus concerning both the Kingdom and the Son of Man people appear saying "lo there, lo here", but wrongly so, in the former case because the Kingdom is ἐντὸς ὑμῶν, in the latter because, when the day comes, there will be no doubt. Furthermore, the παρατήρησις in the sense of calculation (20) is contrary to the three comparisons (24-30) with the lightning and with the unexpected catastrophes in the days of Noah and Lot, respectively, and also to the instruction in 31-35, which tells of *inter alia* the man on the roof whom the sudden crisis does not allow to enter his house.[12]

When the text seems to establish a rather close relationship between the day(s) of the Son of Man and God's Kingdom, this is consistent with what is otherwise found in Luke. If we assume that "the days of the Son of Man" stands for the Parousia, then a similar coupling between the Parousia and the Kingdom of God is to be seen in 9:3-27, where the saying on the Son of Man's shame over renegades at his Parousia (9:26) is immediately followed by the promise that some of those present will not die before they have seen God's Kingdom (9:27). In 21:31 too the future Kingdom is closely connected to the Parousia.

Without entering upon a discussion of how Luke deals with the concept of the Kingdom of God, it can be stated with some certainty that

---

[10] V. 36 in the traditional text is to be regarded as secondary.

[11] Schnackenburg 1971, 222, states that Luke does not differentiate. According to Perrin (1976, 57-60), Luke 17:22-37 interprets Jesus' reference to the coming of the Kingdom as a reference to the coming of the Son of Man, who could be more easily understood in a "stenosymbolic" manner than the "tensive symbol" of the Kingdom of God.

[12] But the contrast between παρατήρησις and ἐντὸς ὑμῶν has a different significance from that between the generations of the Flood and Sodom living their everyday life, and the sudden catastrophe.

according to Luke God reigns in the present time of the reader. God also made His reign especially effective in the work of Jesus (e.g. 4:43; 11:20) and in Jesus' and the disciples' preaching (4:43; 8:1; 9:2; Acts 28:31 etc.): thereby people in some sense "entered" the Kingdom and became the subjects of God's reign. But, as the Book of Daniel can both think of the present reign of God (2:20-21, 47; 3:33; 5:21) and look forward to its glorious establishment (2:44; 7:14), so Luke and Acts also expect a future irresistible establishment of God's Kingdom.

4. The Characters and the Reader

There are three groups of characters in the passage:

(a) The main character, viz. Jesus, who is also the Son of Man. He is the hero, the one who knows the answers to the questions asked. He is the addressee's Lord (37), and the coming one.

(b) The disciples in the narrative situation, and in the future situation; on their side are Noah and Lot, furthermore those who do not turn back (31), those who risk their lives (33), and those who will be "taken away" (34-35). All these are people with whom the reader can easily identify himself.

(c) The "others", or the opponents, viz. the Pharisees, the people who say "lo there, lo here", those who were surprised by the catastrophes in Noah's and Lot's days, furthermore the ones who turn back and are like Lot's wife, the ones who want to spare their lives, and those who are "left".

Of these characters, we now consider the disciples, the Pharisees, and the "lo there"-people, in order to return later on, to the others.

Seen from the reader's point of view, the Pharisees are, firstly, the Pharisees of the narrated past (be they justly depicted or not); there they do not realize that the signs of the Kingdom should be rightly understood "within" themselves, i.e. in their minds;[13] instead, they stand for a sort of *Naherwartung* interest, which is also represented by other people in Jesus' environment according to Luke, like the "some" who expect that the Kingdom is near when Jesus approaches Jerusalem (19:11), as well as by the two disciples on the road to Emmaus (24:21; cf. also Acts 1:6).

Furthermore, however, the Pharisees of the text may also stand for an attitude in the reader's situation, viz. a failure to realize that God makes his reign effective in the reader's own time, in the Christian community, as he once did in Jesus' and his disciples' days.

---

[13] This understanding is close to Riesenfeld's interpretation of the troublesome preposition (1982).

The "lo there" people belong, both in 21 and 23, to the future. In both cases the future should be understood as the present of the reader or at least as his virtual present. They claim that the eschaton is already there and do not realize that also the future Kingdom is bound to Jesus, viz. to his powerful Parousia. This conviction is, or should be, typical of Jesus' disciples as the text depicts them.

Thus these reflections on the roles of some of the characters in the discourse indicate how Luke, instead of saying "the Kingdom will not come according to man's calculation but suddenly" rather used his traditions in such a way that the text tells the reader: as God's finger was active among men in Jesus' days and all did not realize it, so in his own time the same thing holds true; in addition this situation will develop into a future crisis which means decisive demands. These demands are treated in the instruction in 22-37.

5. The Three Comparisons (24-30)

After the introductory setting of the problem through the Pharisees' question and Jesus' answer, 22-23 sketches the future situation of the disciples, i.e. of the readers, when they will "long for one of the days of the Son of the Man" and the "lo there" people will appear. The warning not to pay heed to them is explained (γάρ) by three comparisons. What do they tell the reader concerning "that day"?[14] The comparison with the lightning obviously says that when the Son of Man comes, there will be no doubt. This is to be held against the "lo there" people, and against the reader's temptation to replace the watchful hope with something more "objective". The comparisons with Noah's and Lot's days add that, to the majority, the day will come as an unexpected catastrophe, when the Son of Man "is revealed".

Noah's and Lot's days are compared with the days of the Son of Man, and with the day of his revelation, respectively, for which the readers are presupposed to long (22). That for which they yearn is hardly the destruction of those others, but their own "redemption" (cf. 21:28). Thus, the three comparisons also confront the reader with the question of how to behave in order not to be overtaken unawares. Noah stands for righteousness (Gen 6:9), and Lot may be understood in a similar manner

---

[14] As the text is structured, 24-30 develops the reasons why the disciples should ignore people saying "lo there, lo here". One may want to delimit this development to the lightning simile and to assume that with v. 26 ("and as it happened in Noah's days ...") the text starts wandering new paths. There are, however, signals that keep the whole of 22-37 together. Thus the motif of the day(s) of the Son of Man — for which the "you" are said to long in a future situation according to 22-23 — returns in all three comparisons, and actually the whole of 24-37 is determined by this future situation.

(Wis 10:6-9; cf. 2 Pet 2:7). So the comparisons should have an exhortative function over against the reader.

To the first comparison is added something of a parenthesis, "but before (i.e., before the appearance of the Son of Man) he must suffer much and be rejected by this generation" (25). To the reader he had not yet appeared like the lightning, and his suffering had occurred long ago. Was the effect of this statement that the reader was informed that in Jesus' days there were people who held Messianic ideas, represented also in 19:11 and 24:21, not to mention 17:20 (cf. also Acts 1:6)? I.e., ideas which did not include that the Messiah had to suffer "before" "entering his glory" (24:26). Notwithstanding, this dogmatic necessity was strongly brought home to the reader of Luke's two books: Jesus' suffering was a divine "must", belonging to the divine counsel; any idea of a glorified Messiah or of a Son of Man coming in glory presupposed that he had first suffered and died (9:44; 18:31-33; 24:6-7; Acts 2:23-31; 3:18; 13:27-29).

6. The Three Admonitions

The last of the three comparisons in 24-30 ends in a reference to "the day when the Son of Man is revealed". Luke 17:31-33 presents three admonitions concerning how it will be precisely "on that day". Of the three, the first two appear as concrete examples, one concerning a man on his roof and the other mentioning a man in the field: the former "must not" (third person imperative) enter his house, the latter "must not" return (also third person imperative). Both admonitions (or maybe only the latter) are in some way illustrated by a reference to Lot's wife: she should be remembered (second person imperative). The third admonition is held in a general key (ὃς ἐάν). The three admonitions are actually very tightly held together: "he who is on the roof ... shall not go down, *and* (καί) he in the field shall *likewise* (ὁμοίως) not turn back". Hereto is added asyndetically "remember Lot's wife ...", on which follows, also asyndetically: "anyone who seeks to win his life ...". On the other hand, the verses give a somewhat uneven impression; the clause on Lot's wife breaks the flow, and one may be uncertain how to relate it both to what precedes and to the following saying on saving and losing one's life.

When we now ask ourselves which pictorial value to assume for the admonitions not to enter the house or to return (or turn back) (31), and how to relate this to the third admonition on winning and losing one's life, we start with the admonition which is directed directly to the audience, i.e., both to the narrative audience and to the one in the reading situation, viz. "remember Lot's wife".

According to Gen 19:26, Lot's wife ἐπέβλεψεν εἰς τὰ ὀπίσω, which is suggestive (but not more!) of 31 (the one in the field shall not ἐπιστρέφειν εἰς τὰ ὀπίσω). Some commentators suggest that the one who enters his house and the one who returns home do so because of attachment to earthly property.[15] Such an understanding may have some support in the wording of the text: the first man has his σκεύη in his house and he enters in order to ἆραι αὐτά and the second returns ὁμοίως. Then one has to assume that this was the sin of Lot's wife. This interpretation need not, however, be the most natural.[16] For the reader who "remembered" Lot's wife would not only recall her turning εἰς τὰ ὀπίσω but also that in the story of Genesis the angels told Lot: σῴζων σῷζε τὴν σεαυτοῦ ψυχήν. Μὴ περιβλέψῃς εἰς τὰ ὀπίσω μηδὲ στῇς.... That is, the reader would realize that she disobeyed the command to the family and was not saved.[17] In other words, the Lot story focuses on the same motif as the third, general admonition, viz. on saving one's life,[18] Then it is a reasonable conclusion that the imagery of the two exemplary admonitions should be understood in the light of the Lot story, in which some were saved but not Lot's wife, and in the light of the generalizing saying on saving and losing one's life. This is at stake "on that day".

If somebody holds to the interpretation that Lot's wife must be remembered because she wanted to fetch the belongings from her house, then this should colour the understanding of the saying on winning and losing one's life, i.e., one loses one's life through clinging to earthly goods. If, however, we let the Genesis context of the statement on Lot's wife together with the saving-losing saying determine the understanding of the two former admonitions, the accent becomes somewhat different. Then the fault of the man who enters the house and of him who turns around (or: returns home) is a hesitation which becomes fatal to their lives. A possible, coherent understanding of the three admonitions would then be that what is at stake is an obedient, unhesitating resolu-

---

[15] E.g., Creed 1930/57; Marshall 1978; Schweizer 1982 etc. Talbert 1989 speaks of "worldly interests", and Ernst 1977 of "Bindungen an irdischen Besitz".

[16] σκεῦος, σκεύη is, in addition, somewhat imprecise as signifying property, meaning "things" etc. But in Gen 31:7 it stands for the household belongings Jacob brought when leaving Laban.

[17] The Genesis story does not explain why she was punished, but Wisdom (10:7) makes her an example of an unfaithful, or incredulous, or disobedient mind (ἀπιστούσης ψυχῆς), which *may* refer to what was implied by the Genesis story. Other explanations were given by the Rabbis or Josephus (see [Strack–]Billerbeck 1924/59, 237; Josephus' *Antiquities* 1, 203), but we cannot take it for granted that any one of these explanations was the reason why Luke's reader should remember Lot's wife.

[18] Geiger 1976, 125.

tion, even if one's life appears to be endangered, because this is a life-giving resolution. I prefer this latter understanding.

These admonitions can be understood in two ways by the Lucan reader. The exemplary admonitions are said to apply to how to act "on that day". A natural understanding of the instructions might then refer to some action to be taken on that very day, i.e., then one should act obediently and with resolution, even risking one's life. One may, however, be doubtful what the advice to perform such action might mean at the Parousia. Commentators sometimes refer to the flight motif in Mark 13:14-20: one shall flee to the mountains when seeing "the abomination of desolation";[19] note, however, that in Luke we read instead of a flight to the mountains when Jerusalem is besieged (21:20-21). The scope may, however, also be less precise in terms of time: the instruction concerns a way of resolute action, already in the present, but having "that day" in mind, which will occur as unexpectedly as the sinners were overtaken by the Flood and the rain of sulphur and fire. Earlier in the Gospel the reader has met a similar exhortation to show resolution: "no one who puts his hand to the plough and looks back (εἰς τὰ ὀπίσω) is fit for the Kingdom of God" (9:62). Someone may feel that this interpretation rather reflects a will to make a knotty text more comprehensible by a modern mind than a natural understanding of Luke. But I suggest that the wider literary context in chapter 18 favours this understanding. Luke 9:23 and 21:34-36 also demand an attitude which corresponds to this choice.[20]

7. The Indirect Admonitions ("In That Night")

Whereas that which is said concerning "that day" in 31-33 is openly admonitory, the saying concerning "that night" seems, on the surface, to be only foretelling: in the two pairs, one is to be "taken away", the other to be "left". But we are still under the spell of the three comparisons, and thus the reader easily realizes that the fates are similar to those told in the Noah and Lot stories: some are left, some taken away. In addition, their activities are of the same everyday life type.

It is reasonable to assume that the cases adduced tell the reader something, and the commentaries suggest that this "something" is the division among men[21] or the suddenness of the judgment.[22] But to the reader both possibilities should have the same effect: he should ensure

---

[19] E.g., Ernst 1977: "von Lk allegorisch umgedeutet"; Marshall 1978: "precipitate flight", but metaphorically meant.

[20] Actually this understanding of mine is very similar to that of Léon-Dufour 1981.

[21] Marshall 1978; Schneider 1977; Wiefel 1988.

[22] Kremer 1988.

that he is one of those taken away. His affinity to this group is not the result of a lottery on that day, but — as in the cases of Noah and Lot — depends on his being righteous, i.e., a concern for the present time.

8. Verse 37, "Where?"

To anybody who does not read the text in a synopsis the saying about the vultures in 37, gathering to the body, is not automatically associated with the coming of the Son of Man in 24 which will be as clearly observable as the lightning. The disciples of the text ask in terms reminiscent of 23, where people say "lo there" to those who long for one of the days of the Son of Man. Are the disciples just depicted as stupid[23] so that they ask for the place of the coming of the Son of Man / the judgment / the King-dom of God? Or do they ask whither those taken away are brought?[24] However the question is to be understood, it receives a restraining answer: there is no need to know anything about this in the present — and when the day comes, there will be no need for foreknowledge. I.e., the saying's semantic function is non-informative, in the sense that it refuses to give information on the topic introduced.

9. The Kingdom-of-God Attitude in the Following Context

The Kingdom of God or related themes are in the centre of interest from 17:20 and through 18:31. This means that in the immediate context the reader encounters some further aspects of the Kingdom of God, present and coming. Thus 17:20-37 is followed by the parable about the widow and the unjust judge (18:1-8). It is introduced by a meta-level sentence which tells the reader what kind of text is coming up (a parable), and what is its moral: one should persevere in prayer. The sentence forms a certain boundary to the preceding text, but does not really mark that which follows as a new episode, since there is no new action, no new place, no new constellation of characters, no new time. This soft dividing line is made even less divisive when the finale in 18:8 asks: "but will the Son of Man find τὴν πίστιν on earth when he comes?". Regarded within the theme indicated on the meta-level in 18:1 it is not too far-fetched to assume that the faith sought is one expressed in faithful and steadfast prayer in the time when the disciple longs for the days of the Son of Man.[25]

The meaning of the next passage, 18:9-14, is also indicated by the author: the words of Christ are directed "against self-confident people

---

[23] Fitzmyer 1985.

[24] Zmijewski 1972, 513-17.

[25] Thus, e.g., Fitzmyer 1985; Kremer 1988; and similarly Schneider 1977.

who despise" the humble sinners who, like the tax-collector, ask God for mercy, and will be "exalted" (ὑψωθήσεται). The preceding texts give a very special connotation to this exaltation, meaning, e.g., being one of them who are taken away.

The following 18:15-17 deals with a similar topic: the Kingdom of God belongs to such as are as little children. The same Kingdom also appears in 18:18-27: the topic is introduced by the question of an ἄρχων who wants to inherit eternal life and is promised a treasure in heaven if he sells and gives away what he has and follows Jesus. His failure produces the comment: how hard it is for those who have riches to enter the Kingdom of God. In v. 26 this entrance is mentioned as being saved (σωθῆναι), which brings to mind the features in 17:26-35.

Lastly 18:28-30 is directed to the disciples again, those who have left their own to follow Jesus "for the sake of the Kingdom of God": they will be rewarded in the present and "in the coming age will have eternal life".

Thus, in 18:1-30 the reader learns more about the attitude which is needed for the Kingdom: faithful and steadfast prayer, humility, childish simplicity and trust, non-attachment to riches, following Jesus. Some of the accents of this attitude are typically Lucan.[26] The close relationship between chapter 18 and 17:20-37 indicates that although the Lucan reader should not doubt that there will be a final crisis when the Kingdom "comes", the main semantic function also of 17:26-37 is not informative, i.e. its purpose is not to give a calendar of the coming crisis, but to exhort the reader to lead a life worthy of the Son of Man, having such a future in mind.

10. The Reader as Envisaged By the Text

Hitherto I have chosen to speak of the "reader" in a rather unsophisticated manner. Now, however, in order to press a little further, I shall specify the concept in a way which we find with some theorists of literature, when they discern the "implied" reader.[27] I dare to simplify what the technical term signifies and speak of "the reader as envisaged by the text" instead. Any text somehow presupposes a reader, who is hidden behind and between the lines. Often he is to be conceived as the addressee of the author's use of "you", or there are characters in the story with whom he easily identifies himself. E.g., the "you" of 17:22-23, or the disciples who have followed Jesus, 18:28-29.

---

[26] Schrage 1982, 146-54.

[27] For the concept, introduced by Iser, see, e.g., Selden 1985, 112-14; Lategan 1984, esp. 10-12; and Petersen 1984.

A quick glance through Luke, paying special regard to the eschatological perspective of the reader thus implied, gives the following picture: he is thought to have received some Christian instruction, which Luke shall confirm and complement (1:1-4). In him is fulfilled what John the Baptist said: he has a share in the Spirit and expects to be gathered into the barn of the coming one (3:16-17). Unlike "the others" he has knowledge of the secrets of the Kingdom (8:10), and he belongs to the little flock to whom the Father has promised to give the Kingdom (12:32). He knows that he shall not worry but first seek God's Kingdom (12:31), he shall not fear to confess the Son of Man (9:26; 12:8) in order to be recognized by him at his Parousia. He belongs to the generation who will see God's Kingdom (9:27; 21:33) and expects to be among the people from east, west, north and south who will gather in the Kingdom (13:29). In this world, he lives in the time of the Gentiles (21:24), and the fall of Jerusalem, foretold by Jesus (21:20-24), belongs to his past, as do (probably) the persecutions of 21:12-19, which were said to take place "before" the wars, catastrophes and omens of 21:10-11 (which presumably are still to come). Our reader looks forward to the cosmic signs of 21:25-27 which will indicate the approaching redemption (21:28), the nearness of God's Kingdom (21:31). Given this situation, the reader is told to be watchful of himself and beware of worldliness, in order to be able to "stand" before the Son of Man, when "that day" suddenly "comes upon you" (21:34-36).

In the reader's environment people may have worried about the time of the consummation (17:20-21). The majority, however, do not share his own hope for the coming of the Son of Man and for the full realization of God's Kingdom. A few people may point to phenomena which indicate its nearness or presence, but these are false claims (17:23). Instead the reader, as he is shaped in Luke's text, has to be prepared and see to it that, when the day comes, he will belong to those who are saved and receive life (17:26-35).

It should be remembered that this implied reader should not without reservations be identified with the real, historical readers. He is a construct solely out of the text, but he may have a few or many features in common with the actual readers in Luke's community and/or with the ones Luke envisaged.

Thus, 20-37 confirms this reader's hope of the revelation of the Son of Man, for which he longs; but the verses also promise: you will not be passed by, i.e. when the great occasion comes, you will have no doubts about what is happening. The same reader is finally admonished: do not worry about time and place — no foreknowledge is given; but always live with this perspective before your eyes. Some positive advice on various aspects of such a life is given in 18:1-30.

11. *Type of Text*

The question of which type of text 17:20-37 represents has consequences for the key in which it should be understood. On the surface it appears as an instruction, introduced by a controversy story and finished by a simple question-answer-composition. But there are several dark or slippery spots in the text. Thus the relationship between the Kingdom of God and the revelation of the Son of Man is not made clear. There is an undefined relationship between the present Kingdom within[28] the Pharisees and the future perspective of 22-37. Furthermore, what is the relationship between (one of) the days of the Son of Man (22,26) and "the day when the Son of Man is revealed" (30), or "that day" (31)? What is the significance of not entering the house or turning back and not caring to save one's life "on that day" (31-33)? Is it, in addition, related to the pictures of Noah and Lot? Does it only seemingly refer to the future and instead demand a certain attitude in the present? Furthermore, what sort of scenery, if any, is implied behind the being taken away in 34-35? And, again, what about the puzzling "before" of 25? The chiaroscuro impression is enhanced by 37, asking a question "when?" with a very uncertain reference; whatever the reference is, the answer is far from straightforward. I need not reiterate our present approach: the Lucan reader — be he the implied or the "ideal", or just any decent reader of Luke we may imagine in an wholly unsophisticated way — could not explain these problems away by taking into consideration that the author-redactor had mixed different traditions.

Not only should we take into account the puzzling details of the contents mentioned in the previous paragraph, including its slippery temporal references. The contents are also moulded in what modern scholars have called mythic language. The concept of the Kingdom of God belongs there, so does the idea of the "revelation" of the Son of Man. Being "taken away" and "left" in "that night" also belong to this sort of language and intimates a scenery like that of 1 Thess 4:17.

It might be a just appreciation of the Parousia imagery in Luke to state, on the basis of Acts 1:11, that to Luke and his reader the Parousia was as much *and as little* a concrete event as the Ascension of Jesus. The idea that the mythic language of 17:20-37 has worked in the same impressionist way as other such "apocalyptic" terminology is supported by the observations above of the lack of precision, of the oddities and puzzling features in our text, which simply do not allow the text to be understood as naked, sober information concerning a future event.[29]

---

[28] For the suggested meanings of the preposition see, e.g., Fitzmyer 1985, 1161 and Riesenfeld 1982.

12. The Main Semantic Function

So we are, lastly, brought back to some conclusions about the semantic function of the text. The discussion above has indicated the falsity of the impression that the text mainly gives information on the future. Already the introductory dialogue means a warning. So does also the description of the situation of eschatological longing, foretold in 22-23. The second and third comparisons (26-30) appeared not only to say that "the day" will come unexpectedly, but also that the addressees should prepare themselves by a just life. The discussion of 31-33 led me to assume that the risking of one's life as well as the resolute attitude are demanded in the present, although with respect to "that day". Furthermore, the implicit significance of the two examples from the family at night (34-35) is that the addressee should see to it that he be not "left". Lastly, the answer to "where?" in 37 is directly anti-informative.

We can conclude, then, that the "apocalyptic" piece of 17:20-37 has a mainly admonitory semantic function, a function which is strengthened by what is said in the passages which follow in 18:1-30. They impose demands on those who look forward to the coming of the Son of Man, or to entering the Kingdom, or to inheriting the eternal life, or to being saved, or to be taken away — all of them seem to have meant more or less the same thing to the reader!

Thus it has appeared that the "eschatologische Belehrung"[30] of Luke 17:20-37 has the same principal semantic function as so much other "apocalyptic" material. It has also proved that at the same time it does so in a manner which is typically Lucan, in terms of both eschatology and ethics.

Bibliography

Billerbeck, P. [–Strack, H. L.] 1924/59: *Kommentar zum Neuen Testament aus Talmud und Midrasch*, Band II, München: Beck 1924 [repr. 1959].

Bovon, F. 1978/88: *Luc le théologien. Vingt-cinq ans de recherches (1950-1975)* (Le monde de la Bible), Neuchâtel: Delachaux & Niestlé 1978 [2nd ed. 1988].

Conzelmann, H. 1954: *Die Mitte der Zeit* (BHTh 17), Tübingen: Mohr (Siebeck) 1954 (and later editions).

Creed, J. M. 1930/57:*The Gospel According to Luke*, London: Macmillan (1930), 1957.

Ernst, J. 1977: *Das Evangelium nach Lukas* (RNT), Regensburg: Pustet 1977.

---

[29] This was a matter of heart in Perrin 1976.

[30] Klostermann 1929/75, 175.

Fitzmyer, J. A. 1981:*The Gospel According to Luke (I-IX)* (AncB 28), Garden City, NY: Doubleday 1981.

— 1985: *The Gospel According to Luke (X-XXIV)* (AncB 28A), Garden City, NY: Doubleday 1985.

Geiger, R. 1976: *Die lukanischen Endzeitreden. Studien zur Eschatologie des Lukas-Evangeliums* (EHS 23/16), Frankfurt am Main – Bern: Lang 1976.

Hartman, L. 1975-76: "The Function of Some So-Called Apocalyptic Time-Tables", in: *NTS* 22 (1975-76) 1-14 [No.6 in this volume].

Hellholm, D. 1980: *Das Visionenbuch des Hermas als Apokalypse I* (CB.NT 13/1), Lund: Gleerup 1980.

Johanson, B. C. 1987: *To All the Brethren. A Text-Linguistic and Rhetorical Approach to I Thessalonians* (CB.NT 16), Stockholm: Almqvist & Wiksell 1987.

Klostermann, E. 1929/75: *Das Lukasevangelium* (HNT 5), 2nd ed., Tübingen: Mohr (Siebeck) 1929 (= 3rd ed. 1975).

Kremer, J. 1988: *Lukasevangelium* (NEB 3), Würzburg: Echter 1988.

Lategan, B. 1984: "Current Issues in the Hermeneutical Debate", in: *Neotestamentica* 18 (1984) 1-17.

Léon-Dufour, X. 1981: "Luc 17:33", in: *RSR* 69 (1981) 101-12.

Marshall, I. H. 1978: *The Gospel of Luke* (NIGTC), Exeter: Paternoster 1978.

Perrin, N. 1976: *Jesus and the Language of the Kingdom: Symbol and Metaphor in New Testament Interpretation*, London: SCM 1976.

Petersen, N. R. 1984: "The Reader in the Gospel", in: *Neotestamentica* 18 (1984) 38-51.

Riesenfeld, H. 1982: "Gudsriket – här eller där, mitt ibland människor eller inom dem? Till Luk 17:20-21", in: *SEÅ* 47 (1982) 93-101 [French transl.: "Le règne de Dieu, parmi vous ou en vous? (Luc 17,20-21)", in: *RB* 98 (1991) 190-98].

Rigaux, B. 1970: "La petite apocalypse de Luc XVII, 22-37", in: J. Coppens (ed.),*Ecclesia a Spiritu Sancto edocta. Hommage à Mgr G. Philips* (BEThL, 27), Gembloux: Duculot 1970, 107-38.

Schnackenburg, R. 1971: "Der eschatologische Abschnitt Lukas 17:20-37", in: idem (ed.), *Schriften zum Neuen Testament*, München: Kösel 1971, 220-43 [Earlier in: *Mélanges Bibliques B. Rigaux*, Gembloux: Duculot 1970, 213-34].

Schneider, G. 1977: *Das Evangelium nach Lukas* (ÖTBK 3), Gütersloh: Mohn/Würzburg: Echter 1977.

Schrage, W. 1982: *Ethik des Neuen Testaments* (GNT 4), Göttingen: Vandenhoeck & Ruprecht 1982.

Schweizer, E. 1982: *Das Evangelium nach Lukas* (NTD 3), Göttingen, Vandenhoeck & Ruprecht 1982.

Selden, R. 1985: A *Reader s Guide to Contemporary Literary Theory*, Brighton: Harvester 1985.

Talbert, C. H. 1989: *Reading Luke: a Literary and Theological Commentary on the Third Gospel*, New York: Crossroad 1989.

Wiefel, W. 1988: *Das Evangelium nach Lukas* (ThHK 3), Berlin: Evangelische Verlagsanstalt 1988.

Wimsatt, W. K., Jr./M. C. Beardsley 1946/54: "The Intentional Fallacy", in: *Sewanee Review* 54 (1946) 468-88 [repr. in: W. K. Wimsatt, *The Verbal Icon*, Lexington, KY: University of Kentucky Press 1954, 3-18].

Zmijewski, J. 1972: *Die Eschatologiereden des Lukas-Evangeliums. Eine traditions- und redaktions-geschichtliche Untersuchung zu Lk 21,5-36 und Lk 17,20-37* (BBB, 40), Bonn: Hanstein 1972.

Supplement

Leburlier, J.: "*Entos hymôn*. Le sens 'au milieu de vous' est-il possible?", in: *Bib.* 73 (1992) 259-62.

Nolland, J.: *Luke 9:21-18:34* (WBC 35B), Dallas, TX: Word 1993.

4. An Attempt at a Text-Centered
Exegesis of John 21

1. Some Introductory Considerations

In this paper I will try to understand John 21 as part of the fourth gospel, assuming that, whatever the history of tradition of the chapter may be like, the redactor has published John 1-21 as a text that he considered made sense.[1] To a certain extent my approach is indebted to text-linguistics and similar methods, but I am no specialist in those fields. So, what follows has next to no similarities to the highly technical studies the specialists can produce.

As most texts, John was a means of (one-way)[2] communication between author and addressees. This presupposes that author and addressees had enough linguistic and other cultural material in common so that the latter understood the message.[3] To these common factors also belongs (a knowledge of) the situation of the addressees. The linguistic heritage contained, inter alia, a common feeling of how, e.g., particles and conjunctions organize a text or of how introductions, framing notices, repetitions, etc., help to structure a narrative or an argument.

I will approach John 21 with a series of questions that I have used in seminars on the Fourth Gospel where the students are expected to arrive at an historical understanding of the texts as they stand. Anyone may recognize the extent to which the questions are inspired by text-linguistics, structuralism etc. They are these: How is the text linked to its literary context? How is it built, from a literary perspective? Is there a climax or turning point? Does the author give any comments on or explanations of his text? What of principal and subordinate characters, heroes, opponents? Their relationships to each other? How are pronouncements

---

[1] A concentration on that aspect is also found in Thyen 1977, and Ruckstuhl 1977. As compared to these contributions I pay more attention to the linguistic aspects of the text, to other passages within John, and to the communication perspective.

[2] See Berger 1977, 92.

[3] Of course one has to reckon with different degrees of understanding with different people. But that shall not bother us now, nor the fact that one can plunge into deep discussions of what "understanding" is.

related to each other and to the narrative of which they form a part? Is anything brought out through contrasts or repetition (of the same or related expressions)? Do the answers to these questions indicate that one or several themes or topics or motifs are more important than others? How are they related to each other? What do they mean? What is the relationship between the text and its situation?

The theorist may notice that most of these questions concern the "syntactic" and the "semantic" aspects of the text. The "pragmatic" aspect (regarding the text in its situational context) is dealt with in the last question).[4]

2. The Literary Context

The first thing to note concerning the context is that our chapter ends the book, which means that it is the passage which can give a perspective to, comment on or contain echoes from any passage of the rest of the book. It is the author's last word to his readers and can be very suitable as a means to bring out his intentions.[5]

The μετὰ ταῦτα and the πάλιν of 21:1 bind the following story to those of 20:19-23 and 20:24-29. In 21:14 the preceding verses are said to have reported the third appearance of the resurrected to his disciples.[6] This, of course, makes 20:30f. sound strange. The reference to "this book" and to the purpose for writing may make the reader believe that he is facing the last lines of the work, but 21:1ff. must make him change his mind and rather understand 20: 30f. as commenting on the appearance to Thomas, and, especially, on the saying concerning not-seeing and yet believing (v. 29).[7]

The resurrection narratives of chapter 20, to which 21:1ff. is added, all convey messages that go beyond a mere "he is resurrected" and develop the implications thereof for Christians of a later generation.[8] Vehicles for those messages are narrative details that are commented on by the evangelist (v. 9) or by Jesus sayings (v. 17a, 22), and, not least, weighty pronouncements by Jesus (17b, 21ff., 29) or others (Thomas, v. 28). This should make the reader expect that the following narrative also has something like a symbolic meaning for a later generation and that Jesus' sayings bear on the situation of the Church.

---

[4] For these three aspects of a text see Morris 1938/71.

[5] See, e.g., Dressler 1973, 62.

[6] The appearance of 20:11-18 to Mary Magdalene is not included, she not being a disciple.

[7] Thyen 1977, 260f.

[8] E.g., Barrett 1978, 567; Schnackenburg 1976, 354; Lindars 1972, 598.

3. Literary Organization

3.1 The author comments on what he tells his readers or characterises it in 21:1 (ἐφανέρωσεν ... οὕτως), 14 (τοῦτο ... τρίτον ἐφανερώθη), 19 (τοῦτο ... εἶπεν σημαίνων), 23 (οὐκ εἶπεν ... ἀλλ᾽), 24f. (οὗτός ἐστιν ... ὁ γράψας ταῦτα ... ἔστιν δὲ καὶ ἄλλα πολλά). I call these "comments" meta-narrative statements.

3.2. The first two meta-narrative statements delimit the narrative of 1-14, which is structured in this way:

1. Introduction (to 2-14, but also to 15-23): topic, main characters, place
2-13. Story

2-3.	Actors (Peter and 6 disciples), situation (general and specific: fishing — no catch)
4-13.	Event (new start with δέ, time, re-mentioned actor)
4-8.	Fish-catch, Jesus ashore, disciples at sea
4.	Jesus introduced as unknown main character
5-6a.	Dialogue (Jesus-question [οὖν], disciple-answer, Jesus-order [δέ] and -promise)
6b.	Performance of Jesus-order (οὖν), fulfilment of promise
7-8.	Consequences (οὖν)
7a.	BD (the beloved disciple) recognises Jesus
7b.	Consequence of 7a (οὖν): Peter acts
8.	The other (δέ) disciples act
9-13.	Meal, Jesus and disciples ashore
9.	Situation
10-11.	Jesus-order and its performance (οὖν)
12-13.	The actual meal
12a.	Jesus-order
12b.	Disciples' reaction (δέ)
13.	Jesus-action

14. Conclusion, characterisation of the story.

3.3. V. 15 (ὅτε οὖν ἠρίστησαν) marks the end of the meal of 12f. and introduces the dialogue of 15-23. Nothing is said of any change of place or of any movements, except possibly in 20: Peter turns around and sees the BD "following". V. 19 contains the third meta-narrative comment, and v. 20 introduces the BD in a rather broad fashion as the new topic of the dialogue. So the dialogue falls into two parts, 15-19 and 20-23 (23 being the next meta-narrative comment), and we get the following:

15-23. Dialogue (Jesus and Peter)
    15 - 19. On Peter's future
    15-17.   Peter as shepherd (3 Jesus-questions + 3 Peter-answers + 3 Jesus-orders)
    18- 19. Peter as follower
    18.   Amen-saying of Jesus
    19a.   Comment (δέ) on 18 by the author
    19b.   Jesus-order
    20-23.   On BD's future
    20.   BD introduced
    21-22.   Dialogue (οὖν; Peter-question + Jesus-answer)
    23.   Comment on 22 by the author (a resulting [οὖν] misunderstanding and correction [δέ] of it)

3.4. 21:24f. is the ending of the book. It is connected to the preceding passage through the οὗτος ... ὁ μαθητής. The demonstrative pronouns of the expressions ὁ μαρτυρῶν περὶ τούτων and ὁ γράψας ταῦτα probably refer to the whole book, which is characterized as the true μαρτυρία of the BD. The ending introduces the author in two — or three — ways: the BD is said to be ὁ γράψας, and the "I" behind the οἶμαι of v. 25 should be the writer too. The third instance would be the "we" who know that the testimony of the BD is true (v. 24; cf. 1:14).

3.5. The transitions between the units are rather smooth. The stage is the same, but the focus passes calmly from one event or center of interest to another.

In the narrative there is a movement, in that the disciples move from the sea to join Jesus on the shore. At the meal the δεῦτε is met by Jesus' coming. We may speak of a similar movement in the dialogue, in that Peter's following Jesus means passing from this world to where he is.

3.6. Throughout the text the Jesus-sayings play an important role: those of 6a, 10, and 12a trigger significant phases in the narrative, viz. the catch, Peter's hauling it ashore, and the meal. This suggests to me that the message of the narrative is to be sought mainly in its narrative elements. In the dialogue, on the other hand, everything else is subordinate to the Jesus-pronouncements. Thus Peter's answers to the three questions only lead to Jesus' order to him, and the author's comments in v. 19a and 23 accentuate the weight of what Jesus says according to vv. 18 and 22. Finally, Peter's question in 20b with its broad introduction in 20a is placed there to prepare the ground for the Jesus-saying of v. 22.

4. Isotopies

There are some recurring concepts and motifs (let us label them isotopies) in chapter 21. The main line of the narrative (3-13) concerns the catch of fish: it goes from the introduction in v. 3 through the story as far as the notice that the net was not torn (11b). It includes the contrasts between, on the one hand, the disciples' purpose to fish and their failure, and, on the other, between this failure and the big catch taken after Jesus' order.

Another line of thought concerns food. It maybe begins already in v. 5 with the double possibilities of προσφάγιον — *Zukost* or fish? and continues via v. 9 (fish and bread) on to v. 12f. (the ἄριστον, also v. 15). Through both parts of the narrative runs the motif of recognising and not recognizing Jesus: from v. 4b, via v. 7 (*bis*) through v. 12.

The dialogue contains the following isotopies: that of shepherding, that of following, that of love (v. 15-17, 20; also v. 7), and that of death (18f., 23).

It might be worthy of notice that the isotopies mentioned so far are delimited to either the narrative or the dialogue. On a somewhat abstracter level, however, there are two motifs that run through the whole chapter, viz. the leadership of Peter and the BD's intimacy with the Lord.

5. The Characters and Their Relationships

5.1. Jesus is the authority both behind what is done in the narrative and in his pronouncements in the dialogue. The movements of the disciples bring them closer to Jesus: from the sea to the shore and to the meal there. The dialogue concerning Peter's future brings out his relationship of love and his following him, which (implicitly, though) brings him to where Jesus is.

5.2. Peter's relationships to Jesus are these: he is informed of his identity and then leaves the others, maybe to approach Jesus on his own; alone he performs Jesus' order directed to the group in v. 11. He is Jesus' partner in the dialogue, and against the background of his love for him he receives the responsibility for Jesus' flock and the admonition to "follow" him. In the second phase of the dialogue Peter's relation to Jesus is modified by the position given to the BD: Peter's question in v. 21 is turned aside, and the way of presenting the BD in v. 20 places the BD in a closer relationship to Jesus.

Peter is also presented in relation to the other disciples: he takes the lead in v. 3 and acts independently of the others in v. 7f. In v. 10f. he alone carries out Jesus' order to the group, and, finally, in v. 15, he is asked whether he loves Jesus "more than these do", the latter verisimilarly being the other disciples.

5.3. The BD is presented in relation to Peter. He informs Peter in v. 7 and Peter's question in v. 21 concerns him. The way in which he is presented puts him in a secret intimacy with Jesus: he is the beloved one, he recognises Jesus, and is the one who lay next to his breast at the supper. He acts on his own in the text when "following" in v. 20. Finally, he is also related to the "brethren" of v. 23, i.e. his fellow-Christians, who have had wrong ideas concerning his "remaining", and, as well, to the "we" behind the text, viz. as the one they regard as its ultimate origin and guarantee.

6. The Information Flow

6.1. V. 14 is something of a dividing line in the chapter. In a sense it puts an end to the narrative of the third appearance to the disciples, announced in v. 1. But the dialogue of v. 15ff. makes the reader realize that, in another sense, the appearance narrative goes on, viz. by leaving the seven disciples (at least mainly — cf. "more than these", v. 15) out of sight and focusing on, first, Peter, and then on the BD.

Furthermore, we found, under 4, that the explicit isotopies were largely delimited to either the narrative or the dialogue, whereas two implicit themes, Peter's leadership and the BD's favoured position, went through both halves of the chapter. Thus, the miraculous fish-catch and the meal involve all of the seven disciples, who can be *ausgeblendet* when the author concentrates on two of them in v. 15ff.

6.2. The chapter contains some oddities and extra details.[9] Thus v. 5f. may suggest that the catch will provide the fish for a meal, if, namely, one pays some attention to the –φαγ– component of the προσφάγιον. Does Jesus ask "you have not anything to eat, have you?" or: "you have not got any fish, have you?" Both translations are viable, but the vagueness might very well be intentional and can be compared to other such instances in John.[10] But when the reader has passed vv. 9 and 13, he has

---

[9] Of course many of these oddities can be genetically explained by a traditio-historical analysis, but it is hardly fair to assume that the reader assessed the text under such presuppositions.

[10] Thyen 1977, 263. Cf. Cullmann 1948.

the feeling that the 153 fishes are not for food,[11] whatever reason they are hauled ashore for.

Other oddities: Peter goes into the sea after having put on his garment[12] — why the latter information and what does he do in the water? It is not mentioned that he swims ashore to Jesus, although that is a natural assumption (cf. οἱ δὲ ἄλλοι ... ἦλθον). The next thing he is reported to do is in v. 11: ἀνέβη. Does he remain in the water until that point in the story,[13] or is he ashore already and "gets up" onto the bank[14] or into the boat?[15] There is some discrepancy between Jesus' order to (a) the group (b) to bring (c) some of the catch, and that which happens: (a) Peter (b) hauls ashore (c) the whole net. Finally, there is a slight tension between the invitation in v. 12, δεῦτε, and the notice that Jesus "comes" giving the bread and fish.

Details that seem to be a bit "extra" are the mention of the coal-fire in v. 9, the number of fish (v. 11), the notice of the untorn net (v. 11), and the notice in v. 12b that none of the disciples dared to ask for Jesus' identity, knowing that he was the Lord. In the dialogue the information that the BD "follows" (v. 20) is a little peculiar.

6.3. It seems reasonable to conclude from these notices of the information flow of the narrative that the oddities and extras create a dream-like atmosphere[16] that invites the reader to consider some hidden meanings under the straightforward story. As he has come across similar phenomena before in the gospel, he would not be surprised at finding such in the last chapter.

7. Some Observations Prior to an Attempt at an Exegesis

Before using the analytical results above for an exegesis it might be worthwhile to remind ourselves of some points that have transpired in the foregoing deliberations and that may be of a more general impact.

Thus, chapter 21, as the ending of the gospel, can be a rounding off of much of what has been said in the preceding text. Its mode of presentation and its connection to the preceding resurrection narratives make the reader expect the text to have symbolic overtones and to envisage the sit-

---

[11] But Rissi 1979, 81, is of the opinion that they are. Cf., on the other hand, Derrett 1980, 132. Further, below, note 39.

[12] Brown 1966-71, *ad loc.*, has an ingenious suggestion for translation, "tucked in his outer garment".

[13] Thus Zahn 1921, *ad loc.* and Loisy 1921, *ad loc.*

[14] Bultmann 1941, *ad loc.*

[15] Barrett 1978, *ad loc.*; Brown 1966-71, *ad loc.*

[16] Cf. Haenchen 1980, 595.

uation of the Church. This means that the narrative on Jesus' appearance
in 21:1-23 should be regarded as a text through which the author told his
readers something more, not spelled out. It is not a parable or a *mashal*,
but it is as full of symbolism as those types of literature.[17]

One might ask oneself whether the story (vv. 2-14) and the dialogue
(vv. 15-23) are related to each other in the same way as other stories and
dialogues/speeches in John are, like, e.g., those of chapter 6 on the feed-
ing of the 5000 and the following deliberations on the bread of life.[18] Our
observations on the explicit isotopies indicate that the relationship
between this story and the following discourse is looser than their counterparts in, e.g., chapter 6, in which the central isotopy of bread is thorough-going.[19] Accordingly, the story should convey a message on its
own in terms of its particular isotopies. On the other hand, the implicit
isotopies unite story and discourse in such a way that it might be justified to assume that, on another abstraction level, the latter part of the text
develops details from the first one, i.e., a situation that is somewhat anal-
ogous to that in, e.g., chapter 6.

It seems that, in the narrative, most of the message is conveyed by
narrative details, triggered by the Jesus-sayings, whereas in the dialogue
everything is focused on the pronouncements of Jesus. The roles of Peter
and the BD are themes that run through the whole passage, whereas the
topics of catching fish and of having a meal, which involve the seven disciples, are limited to vv. 1-14.

Do the earlier considerations indicate any hierarchy of the themes?
The construction of the text intimates that the theme of the BD's reliabil-
ity is of crucial importance. The rebuttal to the inquiry of his otherwise
dominant co-disciple and the meta-narrative notes at the end support
such a view. This may also have something to do with the situational
context (cf. below under 9.). But the authority of the BD also backs up
that which is said of Peter's leadership, viz., the second of the two thorough-going, implicit isotopies. The fact that the narrative is so well held
together by vv. 1 and 14 is a sign that it must not be taken as merely a
point of departure for the dialogue. Rather, when seen as the continuation of chapter 20, chapter 21 deals with essential aspects of the life of the
Church under the auspices of the authority of (the traditions from) the
BD.

---

[17] On this and/or other Johannine texts as having a symbolic meaning, see Olsson 1974,
114, 256f. and passim; Shaw 1975, 311; Schneiders 1976; Haenchen 1980, 595f.; Ruckstuhl
1977, 351.

[18] Cf. Barrett 1978, 583; Haenchen 1980, 597.

[19] Cf. Schnackenburg 1976, 407.

8. Exegetical Suggestions

The preceding deliberations may form some sort of basis for an exegesis. They may help to suggest how to choose between the different interpretations exegetes have given to the whole and to its details. I will start with the two larger themes, viz. the roles of Peter and of the BD, and thereby also bring in material from the earlier parts of John.[20] Then, in a similar manner, I will comment on the story of the fish-catch and of the meal (8.2.). In both cases the themes will be dealt with in two steps, the first presenting interpretations that I find relatively well ascertained, the second bringing up looser suggestions (8.1.3 and 8.2.2, respectively).

8.1. Peter and the Beloved Disciple

8.1.1. The BD is obviously presented as the reliable warranter behind the whole gospel.[21] He is no leader like Peter, and there is no antagonism between the two.[22] But he has a deeper and a more direct relationship to the Lord, being loved by him and having insights that strengthen his authority as a mediator of the divine revelation in Jesus. This understanding takes care of both v. 7 and v. 20, as well as of the dismissal of Peter's question in v. 22. Apparently the BD is dead after a long life, but it seems that although he is dead, he "remains" in some sense, viz. as the valid witness whose testimony is "written down" in John.[23] The shifting between ὁ γράψας, "we", and "I" in v. 24 intimates to the reader that there is an underlying group or a school, which pushes the authority of the BD (their previous head, presumably), even if he actually has not wielded the pen.

These features become a follow-up of some passages in the preceding text.[24] At Jesus' cross the BD receives some distinction when he is designated to replace Jesus as son of his mother (19:26f), and evidently he is the one who "sees" Jesus' death and can witness to it (19:35). The other times he explicitly appears in John, he does so with Peter: apart from our text this is so in 13:22f. (the supper, cf. 21:20) and 20:2ff. (at the tomb). In these passages Peter is, somehow, in the lead, but the BD is closer to the mystery of Christ, he is the mediator of true knowledge.[25]

---

[20] I leave out much comparative, elucidating material, not because it is not relevant, but for the sake of brevity. A broader investigation, even following the lines I work after, would have to bring such material in, belonging as it does to the languageconditions of the communication between author and readers.

[21] Especially worked out by Thyen 1977.

[22] Barrett 1978, 577; Thyen 1977, 266; Ruckstuhl 1977, 356ff.; Haenchen 1980, 599f.

[23] Of course as seen from the point of view of the text, not historically.

[24] They are discussed at some length in Thyen 1977, 274ff.

This gives a reverential importance to the gospel text: the addressees believe "through their (i.e. the disciples') word", but the word — testimony — of the BD is the most reliable one and is of "remaining" importance. His role becomes very much the same as that of the Paraclete: "from mine he shall take and tell you" (16:14), "he shall teach you everything and remind you of everything I have told you" (14:26). Indeed, as the Paraclete and his testimony fulfil Jesus' promise "I shall not leave you alone, I come to you" (14:17f., 15:26), the witness of the BD (19:35, 21:22, 24) might be said to have the same function. So also the Paraclete was to be with the disciples "for ever" (14:16), i.e. also after the death of the BD. One might even assume that this "coming" of Jesus through the "remaining" testimony of the BD receives an even greater importance in the light of the expectations for the (delayed) parousia behind 21:22f.

8.1.2. From v. 3 and on, Peter is presented as the leader, a role into which the triple Jesus-sayings (15-17) solemnly[26] install him. There is no rivalry between him and the BD;[27] on the contrary the pronouncements of v. 15-17 belong to the ταῦτα (v. 24), "written" by the trustworthy BD. The flock belongs to Jesus, and Peter replaces Jesus as its shepherd. It becomes natural to regard Peter's hauling the net ashore in v. 11 as intimating the same responsibility,[28] and he receives it on Jesus' order. The net is not torn — the Church is one, and it is verisimilar that the number of 153 somehow signifies the universality of the Church.[29]

The reader of the gospel has heard of Jesus' flock in 10:7ff., the one for which Jesus lays down his life and takes it back again (10:17f.). That has come true when we arrive in 21:15ff. The sheep from "this fold" together with others shall form "one flock" under him (10:16 — cf. 21:11, as well as 17:21).

The connections between chapter 21 and chapter 13 are often pointed out, and, of course, the author makes one explicit linkage himself in

---

[25] Thyen 1977 also discusses 1:14, 1:35-41, and 18:15f. On p. 285 he points out the serious possibility that Mary stands for the believing community, for which the BD has a responsibility. See also Olsson 1974, 111ff.

[26] Note the three-fold repetition, the solemn address, the *variatio sermonis*.

[27] See, e.g., Barrett 1978, *ad loc.*; Ruckstuhl 1977, 358ff.; Thyen 1977, 292. Cf. Brown 1979, 82f.

[28] Similarly Ruckstuhl 1977, 343. Some combine Peter's and the disciples' (v. 6) "hauling" with the Father's "drawing" people to the Son (6:44) or with how Jesus "draws" all men to himself according to 12:32; see, e.g., Brown 1966-71, Ruckstuhl 1977 (with some hesitance), Barrett 1978.

[29] E.g., Barrett 1978, Brown 1966-71, Schnackenburg 1976, Thyen 1977, Ruckstuhl 1977. Rissi 1979 goes in a different direction interpreting this detail in the light of his eucharistic understanding of the passage (153 being a triangular number of 17, made up by 5 (breads) and 12 (baskets); cf. Barrett 1978: 7 and 10 being numbers of completeness and perfection). Cf. also Romeo 1978; McEleney 1977.

21:20. The three questions probably correspond to the three denials fore-told in 13:36ff., where Peter is also told that he will not be able to 'follow' Jesus, i.e., in death, until "later". That "later" following is explained in 21:19f. On the other hand, when Peter "followed" Jesus into the court-yard of the high priest (18:15), the denials were the result.

Peter's love becomes the condition of his commission.[30] Earlier in John the one who loves Jesus is he who keeps his commandments (14:15, 21, 23); he will be loved by the Father and by Jesus who is going to reveal himself to him (14:21); indeed, the Father and the Son will come to him and dwell with him (14:23). In so far as the passage envisages not only Peter and his role (which belong to the past), but also the present time of the readers, the three-fold confession of love is not simply a repentance ordeal,[31] but should indicate something of the author's view of the con-ditions for Church leadership.

Peter's referring to Jesus' knowing that he loved him repeats previous statements of Jesus' knowing everything (13:2f., 16:30, 18:4), but may also be some sort of counterpart to Jesus' foreknowledge of Peter's denial. It is the same kind of divine knowing that inspires Thomas' con-fession in 20:28.

The dialogue brings Peter's shepherd role and his martyrdom together. 12:25f. contain the invitation for Jesus' 'servant' to 'follow' him. In doing so he saves his life by hating it. In 15:13 it is stated that the one who has the greatest love, lays down his life for his friends, and in 13:37 Peter identifies his own "following" Jesus with laying down his life for him. Finally, according to 10:11, the good shepherd lays down his life for the sheep. This background in the preceding gospel may explain why the amen-saying of v. 18 is joined so directly to the dialogue on love and commission.[32] As in the passages quoted the supreme example of love is Jesus, so Peter's following Jesus also means a glorifying of God like Jesus' own passion.

Lastly, we should not forget that the "following" meant going where Jesus was. This is so in the crucial text 13:36 ("where I go … you will fol-low later") as well as in 12;26 and 14:2ff.

8.1.3. Some of the suggestions under 8.1.1. and 2 may already have seemed a bit fanciful. The following ones concern details and fit into the understanding suggested so far, but are more tentative.

---

[30] Bultmann 1941 and Haenchen 1980 think that the "more than these" is to be related, not to any information given in John, but to Mark 14:29 or Matt 26:33, which the author is supposed to know of. But what about the readers? Cf. below, under 8.1.3.

[31] Thyen 1977, 264.

[32] Cf. Ruckstuhl 1977, 352f.

Peter's action according to v. 7 has been interpreted in several ways: if we assume that he puts on his garment and jumps into the sea in order to meet with Jesus as quickly as possible, then the latter motif can be taken together with the "more than these" of Jesus' first question.[33] His putting the garment on may remind of the paradise story and indicate shame,[34] *or* it may be a token of veneration facing the encounter with the Lord,[35] *or* it may be (in addition?) a point of departure for the foretelling of the girding of martyrdom of the elderly Peter in v. 18.[36] One could even imagine an interpretation according to which the jumping into the water prefigures the death of Peter. With some hesitation I would favour an understanding that goes parallel to the contents of vv. 15-17: on the narrative level his dressing may be due to veneration, but it also points to his being girded against his will in martyrdom; on the narrative level his getting into the water may be due to his eagerness to reach the Lord, but it also stands for his being brought to death, a death out of a love greater than that of others.[37]

In 10:9 there is a somewhat obscure statement about the shepherd who enters the fold through Jesus—the door: is Peter's instalment in 21:15ff. his entering the fold through Jesus?

8.2. The Fish-Catch and the Meal

8.2.1. The main features of the narrative concern the whole group of disciples: *they* fish, *they* go by boat to the shore, *they* know, but dare not ask, *they* are fed. We have already understood Peter's hauling the fish ashore as an expression of his pastoral task, and it is rather common that commentators are of the opinion that the disciples' fishing enterprise stands for their task as fishers of men (to use the phrase from the synoptics).[38] They succeed in it only after Jesus' order, as it is said in 15:5 "without me you can do nothing" (cf. also 15:16, 20, 27). Accordingly, the caught fish are not for food.[39]

As a matter of fact the appreciative reader may read the story in the perspective of 17:18ff.: there — as in 20:21, the first appearance to the disciples — the Son has sent the disciples as the Father has sent him; through their word people will believe in the Son, and he prays that they be one — cf. the net, not torn; furthermore, he prays that they shall be

---

[33] Ruckstuhl 1977, 353.

[34] Thyen 1977, 265, referring to Agourides.

[35] E.g., Barrett 1978.

[36] E.g., Haenchen 1980, 598.

[37] Also, e.g., Schnackenburg 1976, 414, and Ruckstuhl 1977, 353, connect Peter's action in v. 7 with his loving Jesus "more than these do".

[38] Haenchen 1980; Barrett 1978, Brown 1966-71.

[39] Hoskyns/Davey 1947, 554; Haenchen 1980, 596. cf. above, note 11.

with him where he is. This would suggest that the taking ashore of the catch represents the "in order that they be where I am".

The meal episode has some echoes from chapter 6. Chapters 6 and 21 are the only places where the Lake of Tiberias is mentioned in John, and the wording of 21:13 reminds of 6:11. It is probable that, as the episode of the catch of fish has a symbolic meaning, so has the meal. Then the interpretations of the meal in John 6 present themselves: the Son of Man will give the food that endures for eternal life (6:27), Jesus is the bread of life, and the one who comes to him shall not be hungry (35), Jesus shall not throw him out (37), and it is the Father's will that the one who sees and believes in the Son shall have eternal life and be raised by him on the last day (39-40, 47) "the bread that I will give is my flesh given for the life of the world" (51).

Passages like these suggest that the meal on the shore symbolises the gift of eternal life, available after Jesus' death—departure to the Father. The continued community between Jesus and his disciples can be regarded as an element of this gift of life.[40]

One may ask whether the reader should think of eternal life as a gift available already in the present or as something belonging to an afterlife (cf. 21:22, which represents a "traditional" eschatology), but in the light of the "both-and" in the gospel as a whole, it seems unwise to make such a distinction for our passage, although it should be expected that the present time aspect is salient. As to the possible eucharistic overtones, see below.

8.2.2. The notice that the disciples did not dare to ask "who are you", knowing that it was the Lord (v. 12), is rather mystifying. Several commentators suggest that it points to the idea of recognising the Lord's presence in the Eucharist[41] (cf. Luke 24:31). Or does it reflect "the awe that the disciples have for the risen Jesus", and does it so hint "at the mystery of his transformed appearance"?[42]

Perhaps one should first notice that ἐξετάζειν is more than "pose a question": rather it means "inquire", "cross-examine". Then the verb used could be taken as indicating a kind of examination that reminds of the one Thomas wanted to perform according to 20:25. On the narrative level, the notice might then concern a knowledge that, although it might want further assurance, inspires so much awe that one does not dare to require that confirmation. On a symbolic level, then, the message might remind of that contained in Jesus' answer to Thomas' confession, "my

---

[40] Schnackenburg 1978, 428; Ruckstuhl 1977, 348; Corell 1950, 248f.

[41] Schnackenburg 1978, 427f. (also citing Schwanck); Haenchen 1980, 596f.; Brown 1966-71, 1100 (hesitant).

[42] Brown 1966-71, 1098; cf. Bultmann 1941, 549.

Lord and my God", viz. "blessed is he who believes without seeing".
The addressees were "to have life through his name" as πιστεύοντες
(20:31), only as πιστεύοντες. The step between the concepts of knowledge
and faith is a short one in John, and, as matter of fact, our passage may
be regarded as typical of how knowledge equals faith.[43] (Cf. by the way,
8:24, 28; 13:19, believing/knowing that ἐγώ εἰμι).

9. Reactions from the Readers

Let us assume that the text was written to be understood by a Christian
community towards the end of the first century. The weighty Jesus pronouncements in the preceding two narratives were naturally read as
bearing on their situation: to them Jesus' messengers had come, they had
received the remission of their sins (20:21ff.), and they were to believe
without seeing (20:29). Thus, at the end of this paper, it is proper that we
try to focus the situational aspect of chapter 21, and to do so, again
assessing the two parts of the dialogue and the narrative.

9.1. The authority of the BD is claimed as that of one who had closer
insights than anybody else among the disciples or the later Christians.
The stress on the veracity (v. 24) of his testimony indicates that the
author felt a need to emphasize it, be it to counter docetism or other tendencies to divisions (cf. v. 11). The BD's authority is not weakened by his
death —it remains,[44] and the community is dependent on it.

The same community knows of Peter, who has died as a martyr some
time ago after serving as a supreme pastor of Christ's flock. Not least in
the light of chapter 10 there is every possibility that they thought that
they belonged to the flock of 21:15f., and to the catch of fish in the untorn
net of v. 11. It is hardly to be assumed that in the readers' mind vv. 15-19
only concerned Peter. But that does not tell us in which sense others (or
another?!) were envisaged. Yet the stress on the BD's remaining in some
sense, in contrast to Peter's fate may indicate that the reader's situation
did not presuppose a continued Petrine principate. On the other hand, it
seems that the picture of Peter in chapter 21 might also serve as a kind of
pastor's mirror. (That the community had some kind of ministry I find
probable,[45] and I think our passage with its bearing on the present supports such an opinion.) The ministry has not only the task of "fishing
men", keeping the unity of the Church, but it is also conditioned by love

---

[43] Bultmann 1941, 435; Barrett 1978, 82: "The verb πιστεύειν is used almost synony-
mously with γινώσκειν". Bultmann 1933, 711-13.

[44] This is a dominant theme in Thyen 1977.

[45] Brown 1979, 87, contra Schweizer 1961, 127.

for the Lord and willingness to follow him. The Epistles (1 John 3:17ff.; 2 John 6f.; 3 John 6ff.) hint at situations in which similar exhortations were given (at a somewhat later time?), and precisely given because the situation demanded it.[46]

9.2. As it is natural to assume that the readers could count themselves as members of the one and only flock of Jesus, gathered from many "folds",[47] they should regard themselves as belonging to the fish caught by Jesus' messengers on his order and brought into a worldwide Church. However, as in many other texts in John, the disciples also may represent the addressees.[48] Then the hauling ashore of the fish and the meal may stand for roughly the same thing: already in the present time the Christians had a real communion with their Lord, already they had eternal life in him, but they also looked forward to his coming, and to being brought to the μοναί with the Father (14:1ff.). Given the eucharistic overtones of chapter 6 (most explicit in 6:53ff.), it seems a fair guess that the readers heard such overtones also in 21:13:[49] their eucharist became a particular, realized eschatology — a coming of Jesus (21:13), a sharing of the eternal life given through his sacrificial death, a being where he is.

An understanding of this sort also makes it possible to see the disciples — the readers as a group under a certain pressure. Peter's martyrdom is, then, not only something in the past, but something similar could become a present reality. However, there was not only a hostile, Gentile world. There were also the Jews (cf. 20:19, in the first of the three appearance stories). Over against both sides they believed in a risen Lord, whom they could not see. Nor could they demonstrate or check on his being the living, divine Lord, even if incited so to do (cf., e.g., 8:24f; 10:24ff.). To Christians in such a situation, the text may have something to say, when it reports that even the disciples had "known", but had not dared to check on the accuracy of their knowledge. (I do concede that this understanding is rather speculative, but the "Jews" are there, and the belief, as well as the debates, at least as memories of such in the past).[50]

---

[46] Cf. Brown 1979, 93ff.

[47] As I can see no indications that the unity in 21:11 is a unity to be hoped for in the future, and since chapter 21 has the potential to shed light on the whole preceding gospel, as I have argued above, I find it less probable that the unity in 10:16 and 17:20f. is something the Johannine Christians hoped for in the future. This is supported by J. L. Martyn 1977, 171f., and Brown 1979, 90.

[48] Cf. Ruckstuhl 1977, 343.

[49] Perceived by several commentators, e.g., Barrett 1978; Brown 1966-71; Bultmann 1941; Haenchen 1980; Schnackenburg 1976; Thyen 1977, 264; Ruckstuhl 1977, 347.

[50] Brown 1979, 66ff.

10. Looking Back

Looking back on my paper, I would ask myself some questions that I guess also present themselves to many a reader. Is there, after all, any profit in approaching a text in this way? Do we learn anything new of the text, really? Or does one not recognize most of the suggested interpretations from before?

I would like to answer my own questions, first, by saying that it would be a shame if people had not understood John 21 until now, and, to a large extent, come to conclusions that are similar to mine. That has, not least, to do with the fact that the textual features that I have tried to build my understanding on are understood and used intuitively by any normal reader. By focusing these features before our eyes we can discuss their impact and so get some help to choose between several suggested understandings and, possibly, to press a bit further.

A further question: are not several of the interpretations presented above a bit too speculative and even sliding over into a repugnant allegorical method of reading? My feeble answer to this accusation is: the text itself clearly presents itself in such a way that it invites us to at least some symbolic understanding. The problem, then, is only how far one should go in that respect.

Finally, when looking back, I realize that there still are several details in the text that I have not discussed, but which could have merited my attention.[51]

Bibliography

Barrett, C. K. 1978: *The Gospel according to St. John*, 2nd ed., London: S.P.C.K. 1978.

Berger, Kl. 1977: *Exegese des Neuen Testaments* (UTB 658), Heidelberg: Quelle & Meyer 1977.

Brown, R. E. 1966-71: *The Gospel according to John* (AncB), Garden City: Doubleday 1966-1971.

— 1979: *The Community of the Beloved Disciple*, New York: Paulist 1979.

Bultmann, R. 1933: "γινώσκω κτλ.", in: *ThWNT* 1 (1933) 688-719.

— 1941: *Das Evangelium des Johannes* (KEK 2), Göttingen: Vandenhoeck & Ruprecht 1941.

---

[51] E.g., the expression ἐφανέρωσεν (v. 1; cf. 1:31; 2:11; 7:4), the *seven* disciples (v. 2), the mentioning of Cana (v. 2), the right side of the boat (v. 6), the distance to the shore (v. 8; cf. Ruckstuhl 1977, 349), the sea and the shore (cf. Ruckstuhl 1977, ibid.), the coal-fire (v. 9; cf., e.g., Haenchen 1980, 586, 598), the partitive ἀπό (v. 10), the BD's following (v. 20).

Corell, A. 1950: *Consummatum est*, Stockholm: Diakonistyrelsen 1950 [Engl. transl. London: SCPK 1958; New York: Macmillan 1959].

Cullmann, O. 1948: "Der johanneische Gebrauch doppeldeutiger Ausdrücke als Schlüssel zum Verständnis des vierten Evangeliums", in: *ThZ* 4 (1948) 360-72.

Derrett, J. D. M. 1980: "ἦσαν·γὰρ ἁλιεῖς (Mk I.16). Jesus' Fishermen and the Parable of the Net", in: *NT* 22 (1980) 108-37.

Dressler, W. *Einführung in die Textlinguistik* (Konzepte der Sprach- und Literaturwissenschaft 13), 2nd ed., Tübingen: Niemeyer 1973.

Haenchen, E. 1980: *Das Johannesevangelium*, Tübingen: Mohr (Siebeck) 1980 [Engl. transl. *John 1: A Commentary on the Gospel of John. Chapters 1-6* and *John 2: A Commentary on the Gospel of John. Chapters 7-21* (Hermeneia), Philadelphia: Fortress 1984].

Hoskyns, E. C./Davey, F. N. 1947: *The Fourth Gospel*, 2nd ed., London: Faber 1947.

Lindars, B. 1972: *The Gospel of John* (NCeB), London: Oliphants1972.

Loisy, A. 1921: *Le quatrième Evangile*, 2nd ed., Paris: Picard & Fils 1921.

Martyn, J. L. 1977: "Glimpses into the History of the Johannine Community", in: M. de Jonge (ed.), *L'Evangile de Jean* (BEThL 44), Gembloux: Duculot/Louvain: University Press 1977, 149-75.

McEleney, N. J. 1977: "153 Great Fishes (John 21,11) — Gematrical Atbash", in:*Bib.* 58 (1977) 411-17.

Morris, Ch. W. 1938/71: "Foundations of the Theory of Signs", in: idem, *Writings on the General Theory of Signs*, The Hague: Mouton 1971, 17-71 [first published in 1938].

Olsson, B. 1974: *Structure and Meaning in the Fourth Gospel* (CB.NT 6), Lund: Gleerup 1974.

Rissi, M. 1979: "Voll grosser Fische, hundertdreiundfünfzig, Joh. 21, 1-14", in:*ThZ* 35 (1979) 73-89.

Romeo, J. A. 1978: "Gematria and John 21:11 — The Children of God", in: *JBL* 97 (1978) 263-64.

Ruckstuhl, E. 1977: "Zur Aussage und Botschaft von Johannes 21", in: R. Schnackenburg/J. Ernst/J Wanke (eds.), *Die Kirche des Anfangs. FS H. Schürmann* (EThSt 38), Leipzig: Benno 1977, 339-62.

Schnackenburg, R. 1976: *Das Johannesevangelium III* (HThK IV:3), 2nd ed., Freiburg – Basel – Vienna: Herder 1976 [Engl. transl.: *The Gospel According to St. John, Vol. III: Commentary on Chapters 13-21*, New York: Crossroad 1982].

Schneiders, S. M. 1976: "Geschichte und Symbolik im Johannesevangelium", in: *EuA* 52 (1976) 30-35.

Schweizer, E. 1961: *Church Order in the New Testament*, London: SCM 1961.

Shaw, A. 1975: "Image and Symbol in Joh 21", in: *ET* 86 (1975) 311.

Thyen, H. 1977: "Entwicklungen innerhalb der johanneischen Theologie und Kirche im Spiegel von Joh. 21 und den Lieblingsjüngertexten des Evangeliums", in: M. de Jonge (ed.), *L'Evangile de Jean* (BEThL 44), Gembloux: Duculot/Louvain: University Press 1977, 255-99.

Zahn, Th. 1921: *Das Evangelium des Johannes*, 5-6. ed., Leipzig – Erlangen: Deichert 1921.

Supplement

Bartholomew, G. L.: "Feed My Lambs: John 21:15-19 as Oral Gospel", in: *Semeia* 39 (1987) 69-96.

Beasley-Murray, G. R.: *John* (WBC 36), Waco, TX: Word 1987.

Trudinger, P.: "John 21 Revisited Once Again", in: *DR* 106 (1988) 145-48.

Gee, D. H.: "Why Did Peter Spring into the Sea? (John 21:7)", in: *JThS* 40 (1989) 481-89.

Hengel, M.: *The Johannine Question*, London: SCM/Philadelphia, PA: Trinity 1989.

Kieffer, R.: *Le monde symbolique de Saint Jean* (LeDiv 137), Paris: Cerf 1989.

Owen, O. T.: "One Hundred and Fifty-Three Fishes", in: *ET* 100 (1989) 52-54.

Ross, J. M.: "One Hundred and Fifty-Three Fishes", in: *ET* 100 (1989) 375.

Brown, R. E.: "The Resurrection in John 21 — Missionary and Pastoral Directions for the Church", in: *Worship* 64 (1990) 433-45.

Neirynck, F.: "John 21", in: *NTS* 36 (1990) 321-36.

Pitta, A.: "*Ichthys* ed *opsarion* in Gv 21,1-14: semplice variazione lessicale o differenza con valore simbolico?", in: *Bib.* 71 (1990) 348-64.

Trudinger, P.: "The 153 Fishes: a Response and a Further Suggestion", in: *ET* 102 (1990) 11-12.

Napole, G. M.: "Pedro y el discipulo amado en Juan 21,1-25", in: *RevBib* 52 (1990) 153-77.

Sabugal, S.: "Las resurreción de Jesús en el cuarto evangelio (Jn 20,1-29; 21,1-14)", in: *Sal* 53 (1991) 649-67.

Segovia, F. F.: "The Final Farewell of Jesus: A Reading of John 20:30-21:25", in: *Semeia* 53 (1991) 167-90.

Schenk, W.: "Interne Strukturierungen im Schluss-Segment Johannes 21: Συγγραφή + σατυρικόν/ἐπίλογος", in: *NTS* 38(1992) 507-30.

Hengel, M.: *Die johanneische Frage. Ein Lösungsversuch mit einem Beitrag zur Apokalypse von J. Frey* (WUNT 67), Tübingen: Mohr (Siebeck) 1993.

Thyen, H.: "Noch einmal Johannes 21 und 'der Jünger den Jesus liebte'", in: T. Fornberg/D. Hellholm, (eds.), *Text and Contexts. Biblical Texts in Their Textual and Situational Contexts. Essays in Honor of Lars Hartman,* Oslo – Copenhagen – Stockholm – Boston: Scandianvian Univ. Press 1995, 147-89.

5. Survey of the Problem
of Apocalyptic Genre

1. Introductory Remarks

As I have understood the task laid before me in this communication, I am to point to some *general* problems that we come across when entering a discussion of genre in apocalyptic. The assessment of apocalyptic genre in specific religions and traditions will then be undertaken by other members of this colloquium.

1.1. Usually "apocalyptic" and "apocalypticism" concern things within the phenomenology of religion and the sociology of religion. But I will concentrate on some problems that have to do with the fact that genre is a literary phenomenon. Therefore, that which I give in terms of a *Forschungsbericht* is rather selective and, furthermore, is determined by my way of assessing the genre problem.

1.2. That there is a genre problem in apocalyptic is certain. G. von Rad stated: "in literary respect apocalyptic does not represent a specific 'genre'. On the contrary, it is, in terms of form criticism, a *mixtum compositum* ...".[1] On the other hand, there are many scholars in the field, who are quite prepared to discuss and present definitions of apocalyptic, not only as a religious phenomenon, but also as something moulded in a specific literary genre.[2]

1.3. Apparently, such a diversity of opinions is possible only because terms such as "apocalyptic" and "genre" are being used in different ways. Therefore, for my purpose, it is necessary that we first reflect on the genre concept. My next step will be to suggest what seems to me a justifiable description of "genre". Then, I will confront this description with some recent discussions of apocalyptic genre, and, lastly, make a few suggestions for future research in the area.

---

[1] von Rad 1975, 331. Cf. Collins 1979a, 3; Brashler 1977, 83.
[2] See, *e.g.*, Collins and Brashler, *loc. cit.*

2. *The Concept of Genre*

Commenting first on the concept of genre, I must say that I lack both time and competence to enter upon a presentation of how scholars in the fields of literary criticism and linguistics have wrestled with the questions as to whether genres exist, and if so, in which sense, and what one then should mean by the term.[3] Nonetheless, I will not conceal the fact that I have learnt a good deal from what has been going on in these areas.

2.1. I mentioned that there exists a certain confusion in terminology. That is true, not least among Biblical scholars. Thus, German authors in the fields often use *Gattung* when they speak of smaller literary units such as psalms of individual lament, miracle stories or proverbs. But they can also speak of the *Form* of such texts and mean the same thing. On the other hand, they can discuss, *e.g.*, the *Gattung* of the gospel as well as its *Form* and again in this case mean the same thing with the two terms.[4] English-speaking authors tend to use the word "genre" about whole works such as gospels, collections of oracles, or epic works, whereas "form" is used to designate smaller textual units. In addition, however, "form", both in English and in German, can be used concerning both, let us say, "specific form" and "general form". By "specific form" I mean the specific shape of a given text, and by "general form" structure and other characteristics that occur in several similar literary pieces and that manifest themselves in the shape of the texts.[5] In the following I will use the term "genre" in the general English sense just mentioned.

2.2. Before entering upon genre in detail, let us briefly consider a classical piece of European literature that may prove illustrative of the problem before us, viz. *Gulliver's Travels* by Jonathan Swift. On the surface, the book appears as a travel-book, not least by its matter-of-fact style. But this primary impression is soon dissolved by the contents of the story, with the result that the youngest readers take it rather as a children's story. A reader who has come a little more of age recognizes that

---

[3] A useful survey is Doty 1972. Cf. also the discussion in Knierim 1973. A thorough investigation of principles and theories brought forward in literary criticism and linguistics is Hempfer 1973. — At this point I should also mention that I have learnt very much for this paper from my discussions with Mr. David Hellholm whose Uppsala dissertation (1980) goes deeply into these matters confronting form criticism, linguistics and philosophy.

[4] It seems that NT scholars and their OT colleagues differ in their usage: see, *e.g.*, Rendtorff 1956 and Conzelmann 1956, two dictionary articles under the same headline – the former uses *Gattung* of, *e.g.*, hymns and proverbs, whereas the latter refers to *die Gattung des "Evangeliums"* in contrast to *die "kleinen Formen" in den Evangelien*.

[5] Cf. Doty 1972, 434.

such a genre classification also does not fit, for he senses how much ironic criticism of mankind's follies is contained in the story. And, as we know, this is not enough, for the work also consists of a slightly disguised political polemic in an allegorical form. As a matter of fact, Swift himself said that the book was written "to vex the world rather than divert it".[6]

2.2.1. Regarded in the genre perspective Swift's *Gulliver's Travels* may give occasion to the following reflections. The work displays features of different kinds of literature, so that a precise genre classification of it seems impossible. It is certain, though, that the text is ironic and allegoric, although interpreters may doubt how far the irony and allegory go. Now it seems obvious that to a large extent the irony and its message depend on the fact that different features, typical of different genres, have been used in an irregular manner. One does not usually write a travel-book to scourge man's weaknesses, nor does one as a rule write stories to jeer at politicians. But when such and similar things are done, the effects can be stronger, because the readers recognize the odd usage of the genre features, consciously or unconsciously. Of course, in order that something should be felt as irregular, something regular must exist. If this regularity is dissolved, the possibilities of irony, parody, satire, etc., diminish, as far as they depend on this feeling of irregularity. For when addressees somehow distinguish between different kinds of literature, they also tend to associate them with specific situations, contents and functions. In other words, the recognition of a genre creates a certain "reader's expectation" (*Lesererwartung*)[7] which determines the understanding and the reception of the addressee. Further, there is often a connection between genre and sociolinguistic situation and function. But, in order that both regular and irregular uses of genres may "work" with the reader, he must have learnt them; his "*Lesererwartung*" has to have been trained.

2.2.2. Thus, it seems to me, the example of *Gulliver's Travels* points to some essential aspects of genre and also indicates why one should bother about genre at all, *viz.* that it serves the understanding of a text. Or, in N. Frye's words on genre criticism: "its purpose is to clarify, not to classify".[8]

2.3. What, then, is a genre? I leave aside how Plato and Aristotle have already differentiated between lyric, epic and drama, and also how one

---

[6] Quintana 1975, 858. Much has been written on Swift's literary technique: see, *e.g.*, Price 1953, esp. 95ff.; Bullitt 1953; Quintana 1967; Leavis 1968.

[7] See, *e.g.*, Weinrich 1971, 30f., 140.

[8] N. Frye as cited with agreement by Todorov 1974, 962. Hempfer 1973, 105ff., 160f., stresses the hermeneutic implications of genre studies.

has thought of genres as established-rule-systems, which should be followed by authors.[9] Instead I think of vaguer but yet distinguishable literary conventions which characterize so many works in a given cultural context that one can speak of some type of literature.[10] Such a convention is shared by reader and author: the author accepts it, more or less faithfully, and shapes his text in adherence to it; the reader's expectations and attitude when approaching the text are coloured by it, and it affects his understanding of the text. This is to say that discussing genre means discussing something that has to do with communication.[11]

2.3.1. The expression "a given cultural context", used in the preceding paragraph, may appear to be rather vague. It becomes a little more precise, when we also take into account that genre is a structure that functions within a communication between author and readers. When or where the cultural context is so different from the original one of a given text that its genre does not function as genre in at least a similar way any more, then one has passed the limit for the cultural context that provides the literary conventions that determine genre, its use and understanding. This means placing oneself on a certain level of abstraction: if one abstracts further, one gets a wider genre concept and also has to reckon with wider cultural contexts for the genre, implying less precise historically given cultural conventions behind text-making *and* text-understanding. One should, then, in my view, allow the communication aspect to determine how far one goes in abstraction.

2.3.2. A genre convention can manifest itself in various characteristics of a text, and one may discuss to what extent it necessarily must expose this or that feature or quality on the literary surface in order to be referred to a certain genre. But also elements that are not directly visible in the text belong to a genre convention, elements that have to do with its place in the life of the community in which it appears and to which it is directed — we Biblical scholars speak of the *Sitz im Leben* of a text.

3. Constitutive Elements of a Genre

After these rather general deliberations I now venture to enter upon a more specific discussion. I will present to you some groups of phenomena, which, I believe, to a greater or lesser extent, combine to constitute a genre. All of these phenomena — or constituents, as I shall call them —

---

[9] So, *e.g.*, with Cicero and the Neo-classicism; see, *e.g.*, Weisstein 1968, 143f.; Hempfer 1973, 41ff., 57f., etc.

[10] Cf. the presentation by Hempfer 1973, § 3.3.6.

[11] Hempfer 1973, 89ff., 98ff., etc.

are dealt with more or less at length in works by literary critics, but I have systematised them in a way I have not come across elsewhere.[12]

3.1. The first group of constituents concerns the linguistic[13] characteristics of a text and regards its style, vocabulary and phraseology, *e.g.*, turns of phrase like "once upon a time", "they lived happily ever-after", etc. of the children's story; or the "we"-style of certain scholarly works; or the meter, the epithets, etc. of the classical epic.

3.2. My second group has to do with the contents of a text, with what may be called its propositional level. Here, on the one hand, we have to consider characteristics of a work as a whole, on the other, characteristics of parts of it. In the work as a whole one has to take into account the structure of the presentation, the plot, the main themes, and the topic. Some examples would include: (1) the characteristic construction of a detective story, from the discovery of the body, *via* the introduction of more or less hidden clues and of false tracks, and on to the finale, in which the hero presents the solution; (2) the plot patterns of folk tales, be they the ones Propp investigated or others; (3) the manner of writing history in Antiquity: the general narrative sequence, the knitting of the episodes to each other, the insertions of descriptions of places and people, of speeches, etc.; (4) the topic of the romances in Antiquity, *viz.* some sort of love story; and, perhaps, (5) the manner of writing apocalypses: the introduction of a divine revelation in one or another way, the revelation itself, consisting of a series of visions or travels and/or dialogues with a revealer, and a conclusion which often stresses the importance of the revelation.

3.2.1. In sections of the text one has to consider characteristics of a similar kind: the structure of smaller episodes or of other smaller units, motifs, ways of organizing and presenting the material in shorter stories or other literary pieces. Examples of these characteristics include: (1) the repetition with slight variations in the tales, where, say, at a certain stage, three brothers have to fulfil a task, and the first two do not succeed, but the third one does; (2) the motif found in ancient Greek romances, where both the hero and the heroine travel widely after being separated;[14] and (3) for the apocalypses, the appearance of a heavenly messenger, an *angelus interpres*, who interprets, *e.g.*, a vision.

---

[12] I restrict myself to referring my reader to the works referred to in n. 3 above, and to the vast literature that is discussed in them. The following discussion of some groups of constituents is a slightly elaborated version of a section in an earlier article, Hartman 1978 (No. 1 in this volume).

[13] "Linguistic" in the meaning of "*sprachlich*", not "*sprachwissenschaftlich*".

[14] Cf. Söder 1932; Hägg 1971.

3.2.2. I suggested above that, in terms of the text as a whole, this group of genre constituents takes into account the structure of the presentation. This was not only meant to cover what one may call the sequence of the elements of a text, like the one in a detective story or in a speech by a rhetor. I want to point out, too, that this "structure" should also be regarded as including the functional relations between the elements.[15] In the example of the ancient romance one should, accordingly, not only notice the motif of travelling, but also how it functions in relationship to the story as a whole and to other elements in it. That is, one has to consider how it is caused by the separation that gets the story rolling, how it connects the episodes, and, above all, how it creates a suspense that is not eliminated until the amorous couple is happily reunited.[16] And, as to the apocalypses, one should *e.g.*, not only observe the appearance of the motif of a heavenly journey but also pay heed to its function within the whole: how it becomes a means to join heaven and earth, so that divine secrets can be brought to human beings; further, how it anchors the authority of the message of the revelation in the divine Being Itself.

3.3. The phenomena dealt with so far exist in a text whether it functions in a communication or not. I now come to some constituents that to a greater or lesser extent bring an addressee into the picture.

3.3.1. First, then, I will examine the characteristics of what could be termed the "illocution" of the text,[17] *i.e.*, what its author wants to say with that which he says. We could also speak of this constituent as the message, or the type of message conveyed by the text. Also in this case one should look both at the smaller units of the work and at the work as a whole. To give an example, let us think of a scholarly paper: a typical message of the passages which refute other scholarly opinions is that things must be the way the author argues. Such refutations form parts of the lecture as a whole, and their messages contribute to the message of the whole. This, in its turn, is of the type that sheds light on or solves one or several scholarly problems. If, instead, somebody at a dinner table uses the literary form of a paper to express his thanks to the hostess for a delightful meal, it might be entertaining, but the "paper" has acquired a non-typical message. In the case of apocalypses, a typical message is one of comfort and exhortation to steadfastness.

In this context of illocution it may often prove useful to distinguish between different semantic functions. This holds true for the "message" both of the text as a whole and of its minor units. As the function of indi-

---

[15] See the discussion in Hempfer 1973, 138ff., 190.

[16] Cf. Hägg 1971, 150f., 173f., 214f., 324ff., etc., and the literature discussed 340f.

[17] The term is, of course, inspired by J. L. Austin. Cf. Urmson 1967, 213.

vidual clauses may be informative, prescriptive, expressive or performative,[18] so texts and parts of texts can have similar semantic functions. Accordingly, also the fact that a text belongs to a certain genre means that it may have a specific semantic function.

3.3.2. As stated above, also this group of genre constituents concerns the text as a communication. I am here thinking of the usage of a text, which corresponds to a certain audience. The audience has a certain expectation which is coloured by things belonging to the constituent groups I have brought forward already. To give an example, let us return to the scholarly paper. It belongs to the cultural convention shared by the lecturer and his audience that the paper has a typical sociolinguistic function.[19] If somebody gives the shape of a lecture to an after dinner speech, the situation is wrong, the audience may be non-typical, and certainly this audience has no expectations for an academic paper. But if enough of the motifs and of the theme points to the real topic of the speech and to its real illocution, it might be a success. A presupposition is, however, that the audience recognizes the unusual shape and understands to appreciate the pleasantry. As to the apocalyptic genre, we do not know of how apocalypses were used in Jewish and Early Christian circles, but, at any rate, there are rather clear indications that the Revelation of John was written to be read at the divine service.

Thus, in general one tends to combine a given genre to a typical sociolinguistic function. But already the assumed example of burlesque[20] in the preceding paragraph, and, above all, the quantity of other material should remind us that we have to beware of assuming a one-to-one relationship between genre and sociolinguistic function.[21]

3.4. The groups of genre constituents I have presented in the paragraphs above are not altogether sharply delimited from each other. For example, one should remember that it is next to impossible to draw a clear-cut borderline between form (both "general" and "specific") and contents. Furthermore, even though one may list some genre constituents in this way, one should not expect to find all the characteristics of a given genre in all instances of it. And, reversely, not all the types of characteristics that *can* constitute genres need necessarily be represented in an individual genre. It is, for example, only for some genres that one has to count on a specific style and phraseology.

---

[18] Here I use the word "performative" in a narrow sense. It may also have a wider meaning: see, *e.g.*, Hempfer 1973, 161ff. – Cf. Hartman 1975-76 (No. 6 in this volume).

[19] Already in ancient rhetoric one was aware of the different functions of rhetoric *genera*: see Lausberg 1960, §61.

[20] I use the term as suggested by Abrams 1971, *ad voc.*

[21] See, *e.g.*, Güttgemanns 1971, 140ff.; Doty 1972, 424; Hempfer 1973, 186ff.; Knierim 1973.

We may ask whether some of these constituents are more important than others for demarcating a genre. I have a feeling that, if a text displays a certain set up of stylistic and phraseological features that normally characterize a certain genre, they are relatively decisive indicators.[22] But then they must also go together with other constituents. *I.e.*, the text should have a particular content on the propositional level and represent a specific structure of a particular kind of plot, or a distinct set up of motifs in a definite hierarchy (§3.2.). Furthermore, it is likely to have a particular kind of sociolinguistic function (§3.3.2.). The kind of illocution for some genres should be next to obligatory (§3.3.1.), but then it ought also to go together with certain features such as themes and motifs in a specific structure (§3.2.) and, as a rule, with a specific use, a sociolinguistic function (§3.3.2.).

4. Recent Contributions to the Discussion of Apocalyptic Genre

Against the background of the foregoing deliberations I now proceed to a brief presentation of a few recent contributions to the discussion of the problem of apocalyptic genre. All of these concentrate on the Jewish and Christian material.

4.1. Thus, Ph. Vielhauer dealt with "the literary characteristics" of apocalypses in his *Geschichte der urchristlichen Literatur.*[23] Under this heading he listed the following *"Stilelemente"*: pseudonymity, account of vision, pictorial language (*Bildersprache*), interpretation, systematisation (especially through numbering), and furthermore, combinations of smaller forms such as surveys of history in future form, descriptions of the other world, visions of the divine Throne, paraenesis, and prayers. Apparently these phenomena can be referred to my first two groups of constituents (§3.1. and §3.2.). In discussing them Vielhauer also makes a few observations on the literary function and interrelation of some of these elements. He also touches upon certain things that I gathered into my latter groups of genre constituents, *viz.* those concerning illocution and sociolinguistic function (§3.3.1. and §3.3.2.). Thus, the surveys of history are said to aim at creating confidence in the reader who is confronted by the eschatological predictions in the text. The visions of the Throne are meant to clarify the *Unnahbarkeit* of God and prove that the competence of the visionary goes back to Him. Furthermore, the descrip-

---

[22] See also Hempfer 1973, 148f. The present writer has suggested some consequences of these observations for the assessment of the gospels in Hartman 1978 [No. 1 in this volume].

[23] Vielhauer 1975, 487ff. He also dealt with the matter in Vielhauer 1964. There he discussed *"die literarischen Merkmale"* at somewhat greater length but with less specification as compared to the later work.

tions of future and transcendent secrets are meant to determine the present life of the readers by binding them to God and His will. Although these observations of an experienced *Formgeschichtler* are not presented as the results of detailed literary analyses, it seems to me that they represent some essential insights into how different factors co-operate within a genre.

4.2. In the Supplement to the *Interpreter's Dictionary of the Bible* (1976) Paul D. Hanson has made a contribution to the discussion of apocalyptic genre. Taking as his point of departure the Book of Revelation, he presents some typical genre features not only of this book, but also of some Jewish texts. The result is not unlike Vielhauer's, though perhaps with somewhat less attention paid to the literary function of the phenomena. The setting of the genre, says Hanson, was a time of tribulation and persecution, and its principal function was to reveal the future, thereby comforting the oppressed and encouraging them to faithfulness.

4.3. To my knowledge the most thorough-going recent attempts to render further precision to the discussion before us are those brought forward within a workgroup on apocalypse within the SBL Genres Project. I am most obliged to professor J. J. Collins for having provided me with a copy of a paper from his hand which seems to sum up the achievements of this group so far.[24]

4.3.1. In his article, J. J. Collins establishes a master-paradigm by listing recurring features in all the works which are either called apocalypses or regarded as such by modern authors. This paradigm is divided into two main sections, dealing with the framework of the revelation and its contents, respectively. The framework concerns the manner of the revelation, and here Collins lists the medium: is it a visionary or auditory revelation, is it an otherworldly journey or something like a heavenly book? Further, the framework confronts us with the otherworldly mediator, as well as with the human recipient, his pseudonymity, his disposition and reaction.

4.3.2. As to the contents Collins first observes a temporal axis: one finds matters dealing with the beginning of history or prehistory, and, further, reviews of history and revelations of eschatological crises like persecutions and/or other upheavals. Here we also encounter statements on the eschatological judgment and salvation. In gnostic apocalypses, salvation through knowledge is a distinct feature. On the spatial axis Collins refers to revelations concerning otherworldly regions or beings. He further notes that paraenesis through the mediator is relatively rare, being prominent only in a few Christian and gnostic apoca-

---

[24] Collins 1979a. He applies his analytical method on Jewish texts in the same volume: Collins 1979b.

lypses. Finally, he lists a couple of concluding elements, in which the recipient is told what to do next, and the action of the text is somehow brought to an end.

4.3.3. Prof. Collins comments on this list reminding us that these elements do not necessarily constitute an entire independent work, and, reversely, that apocalypses may include subsidiary literary forms which are independent of the genre, *e.g.*, prayers. Of course all elements do not appear in all apocalypses, and furthermore not all of them are equally important. But some are constant: thus there is always a narrative framework including an otherworldly mediator and a human recipient, and the contents always concern both a future eschatological salvation and present otherworldly realities.

4.3.4. Collins then arrives at a definition of the genre: "'Apocalypse' is a genre of revelatory literature with a narrative framework, in which a revelation is mediated by an otherworldly being to a human recipient, disclosing a transcendent reality which is both temporal, in so far as it envisages eschatological salvation, and spatial, in so far as it involves another, supernatural world."

4.3.5. If I may compare Collins' exposition with my own grouping of genre constituents above, it appears that the elements that he lists in the master-paradigm all belong to my second group, the one which contained the propositional constituents (§3.2.). This also holds true of the phenomena that are covered by his definition of apocalyptic genre. In dealing with this second group of mine I stressed that one should not only consider plot, themes, and motifs, but also take into account the hierarchic structure and literary interrelations of those elements. It seems that Collins is of a similar opinion; for, in his paper, he finishes a short discussion of the inner coherence of the genre by saying: "an adequate discussion of these matters can only be achieved through the detailed analysis of individual apocalypses and the examination of the precise ways in which the various elements of the paradigm function" (p. 12).[25] I am so convinced that he is right in this statement that I am afraid that his following attempts to establish a typology of the genre risk being a classification with too little respect for the literary functions and interrelations of the elements.[26] (The suggested typology involves a distinction between two main types of apocalypses, those which have an otherworldly journey and those which have not. These two are both divided further into those which have, and which do not have a historical review, respectively.)

---

[25] I suspect that "function" here covers both the literary function within the text and the function with regard to the readers, including the sociolinguistic one.

4.3.6. Finally, as to my latter groups of constituents, viz. those concerning illocution and sociolinguistic function (§3.3.1. and §3.3.2.), we may note that Collins and the SBL workgroup are aware of the fact that one "must eventually address the history and social function of the genre" (p. 4). However, in discussing the inner coherence of the genre, Collins touches briefly on what I have called illocution and sociolinguistic function. He suggests that the emphasis on transcendence in the texts has to do with a sense of alienation in the milieu of the readers.

5. Communication and Genre

As the work of the SBL group, including that of prof. Collins, seems to be the most advanced so far in the area, I refrain from discussing other contributions of this kind.[27] It seems to me, though, that the time has come to deepen the analysis and to take into account as exactly as possible the hierarchic structure and literary function of the propositional elements,[28] the illocution of the texts, and their sociolinguistic functions.

5.1. One example of how one can work with profit in the direction just mentioned is an article by K. Koch on the first vision of 4 Ezra.[29] He works on form-critical and text-linguistic lines and arrives at results in these areas that seem convincing, based as they are on a thorough analysis of the text as it stands. Taking a firm hold of the text as a text[30] he puts himself into a certain opposition to traditional approaches according to which the text becomes something like a box containing specimens of apocalyptic ideas, of apocalyptic phenomenology.

5.2. Others have also stressed the need for distinguishing between apocalypses and apocalyptic as a religious phenomenon.[31] Thus, Viel-

---

[26] Hempfer 1973, 190, states: at genre criticism "ist einem taxonomisch-klassifizierenden Vorgehen, das Texte allein aufgrund des Vorhandenseins oder Fehlens bestimmter Eigenschaften (Elemente) einer bestimmten 'Gattung' zuordnet, ein im eigentlichen Sinne 'strukturierendes' vorzuziehen, das spezifische Relationen zwischen diesen Elementen erstellt, die für den jeweiligen Texttyp bezeichnender sind als die einfache Kumulation isolierter Elemente". (See also 138f.) – In several studies E. Gülich and W. Raible (*e.g.* 1975; 1977; cf. also 1977a) have suggested methods for distinguishing *Teiltexte* within narrative texts and for determining their relationships to each other as well as their function within the text as a whole. In Hellholm 1980 the author analyses the Shepherd of Hermas using their methods. The present writer has tried to apply them to the beginning and ending of the Book of Revelation in Hartman 1980 (No. 7 in this volume).

[27] Brashler 1977. He refers also to the unpublished work by Parrott 1970, and to Collins 1977; Perkins 1977; Dexinger 1977, esp. 9ff.

[28] It is only fair to mention that in Collins 1977 Prof. Collins discusses the literary function of some elements in Rev.

[29] Koch 1978. See also Hellholm 1980.

[30] Cf. also the approach in Breech 1973.

[31] *E.g.*, Ringgren 1957.

hauer and the SBL group also keep apocalyptic genre and apocalypticism apart.[32] This justified distinction can prepare us to be aware of some further aspects which are implied by the genre questions. I will touch upon them briefly.

5.2.1. Thus, apocalypticism as a religious phenomenon can be considered synchronically: one exposes its *Vorstellungswelt* and observes motifs and themes belonging to different times, religions, and cultures.[33] We need not now enter upon a discussion on how far apocalypticism as a religious phenomenon can be assessed as something which refers to common human experiences and ways of thinking and feeling,[34] neither need we try to answer the question as to whether the motifs go back to some kind of religious *universale*, common to all mankind. But it is exactly this question of the relationship between the general and the specific that is relevant, I think, to anyone who reflects on apocalyptic genre.

5.2.2. As I have understood genre, it should be discussed especially under the category of communication. The genre belongs to a cultural set up which author and reader have in common. In the terminology of de Saussure, the genre of apocalypse is part of a *langue*, the linguistic competence of a cultural and linguistic milieu. The individual apocalypse is then a *parole*, a manifestation of this general *langue*. With regard to the groups of genre constituents I have adopted, all of them of course apply both to the *langue* and to the *parole*. Thus, one learns to understand an apocalypse as one learns to understand other phenomena in one's culture, not least the language.[35]

5.2.3. As intimated at the beginning of this paper, this way of looking at things means that I understand apocalyptic genre as being something narrower than, say, narrative as genre. Such a narrower concept of genre then corresponds with a narrower scope in terms of a historically given, cultural context, which contains the conventions that include the genre, its use and understanding.[36]

5.2.4. The way of regarding genre I have intimated in the last paragraphs has some consequences. First, an understanding on the side of the readers that is more or, sometimes, less perfect is to be expected.[37] Second, the literary convention of a genre is fluid, it changes and devel-

---

[32] Also Stone 1976, 439, and Hanson 1976. Both also distinguish between apocalyptic eschatology in terms of religious ideas and apocalypticism as a sociological phenomenon. As to the latter, see also Raphaël 1977.

[33] See, *e.g.*, Ringgren 1957; Widengren 1969, chap. 16. Also Raphaël 1977.

[34] Cf. Sickenberger 1950, 505.

[35] Hempfer here brings in aspects from Piaget (1973, 122f. *et passim*).

[36] See my discussion above §2.3.

[37] *E.g.*, Hempfer 1973, 127. Cf. Hartman 1975-76 (No. 6 in this volume). As my reader may notice, I do not reckon with "ideal readers" in Chomsky's manner.

ops, and admits varied and new usages.[38] Third, although there is normally a certain tendency to connect a given genre to a particular illocution and sociolinguistic function, one should not assume that such a connection is obligatory.[39] Fourth, human beings seem to have a common tendency to ask the questions of why, whence and whither and to give some of the answers to these questions the form of an apocalypse. Thereby one often uses mythical language[40] which contains motifs and themes that appear in quite different times, places and cultures. Nevertheless, on the abstraction level I have assumed, the *langue* comprising an apocalyptic literary genre should be regarded as limited to specific contexts that are relatively coherent culturally. That is, one can bring the Nordic Voluspa into the discussion of the religious phenomenon of apocalypticism, but not, at least not directly, into the deliberations concerning the literary genre of apocalypse in Jewish, Christian and gnostic circles of late Antiquity. Fifth, one must be aware of the possibility that apocalyptic, or perhaps eschatological motifs and themes, are dealt with in other literary genres. This is, in fact, true, when such motifs appear, *e.g.*, in a halachic discussion in the Mishnah (*m. Sota ix*), or, I have been told, in Egypt, where apocalypses are rare, if at all existent, but where apocalyptic (in the sense of eschatology) is well represented.[41]

6. Desiderations for Future Investigations

Finally, I venture to finish this survey with some desiderations for the future investigation of the literary genre of apocalypse.

6.1. Thus, I think that we should take serious account of what is going on in the areas of literary criticism and linguistics. Accordingly, we should advance to detailed studies of individual texts. Thereby we need not necessarily work with exactly the groupings of genre constituents I have presented above, but, nevertheless, continue from mainly listing themes and motifs on to analyses of the hierarchic structure of the elements, unfolding in this way their functions on the propositional level. This should be distinguished from the quest for the illocutionary and sociolinguistic functions of the parts and of the whole, even though, of course, such investigations depend heavily on the results of the former ones. Furthermore, one should pay attention to the communication aspects, *i.e.*, consciously connect the literary analysis with the fact that

---

[38] See Hempfer 1973, 98f., 192-220; Fowler 1970-71.

[39] Cf. above §3.3.2.

[40] Cf. Delcor 1977.

[41] Cf. now the contributions by J. Assmann, J. Bergman and J. Gwyn Griffiths in: Hellholm (ed.) 1983/89.

the genre problem is part of the larger one concerning understanding and interpretation of human expressions in social interplay.

6.2. In this way our work may bring us into a deeper understanding of what the authors of apocalypses wanted to say to which kind of readers in what kind of situation. But in the long run it may also turn out to be even more interesting, as we may recognize that their problems are reminiscent of ours.

Bibliography

Abrams, M. H. 1971: *A Glossary of Literary Terms*, 3rd ed., New York etc.: Holt, Rinehart and Winston 1971.

Brashler, J. 1977: *The Coptic Apocalypse of Peter. A Genre Analysis and Interpretation* (PhD diss., Claremont, CA 1977).

Breech, E. 1973: "Theses Fragments I have Shored Against my Ruins: The Form and Function of 4 Ezra", in: *JBL* 92 (1973) 267-74.

Bullitt, J. M. 1953: *Jonathan Swift and the Anatomy of Satire. A Study of Satiric Technique*, Cambridge, MA.: Harvard University Press 1953.

Collins, J. J. 1977: "Pseudonymity, Historical Reviews and the Genre of the Revelation of John", in: *CBQ* 39 (1977) 329-43.

— (ed.) 1979: *Apocalypse: The Morphology of a Genre (Semeia* 14), Missoula, MT: Scholars Press 1979.

— 1979a: "Introduction: Towards the Morphology of a Genre", in: Collins (ed.) 1979, 1-20. [Previously published in the *SBL Seminar Papers* 1977.]

— 1979b: "The Jewish Apocalypses", in: Collins (ed.) 1979, 21-59.

Conzelmann, H. 1956: "Formen und Gattungen II. NT", in: *EKL* I (1956) 1310-15.

Cross, F. M. Jr./Lemke, W. E./Miller, P. D. Jr. (eds.) 1976:*Magnalia Dei. The Mighty Acts of God. FS G. E. Wright*, Garden City, N.Y.: Doubleday 1976.

Delcor, M. 1977: "Mythologie et apocalyptique", in: Association catholique française pour l'étude de la Bible (ed.): *Apocalypses et théologie de l'espérance* (LeDiv 95), Paris: Cerf 1977, 143-77.

Dexinger, F. 1977: *Henochs Zehnwochenapokalypse und offene Probleme der Apokalyptikforschung* (StPB 29), Leiden: Brill 1977.

van Dijk, T. A./Petöfi, J. S. (eds.) 1977: *Grammars and Descriptions* (Studies in Text Theory and Text Analysis) (RTT 1), Berlin–New York: de Gruyter 1977.

Doty, W. G. 1972: "The Concept of Genre in Literary Analysis", in: McGaughy (ed.) 1972, 413-48.

Fowler, A. 1970-71: "The Life and Death of Literary Forms", in: *NLH* 2 (1970-71) 199-216.

Gülich, E./Raible, W. 1975: "Textsorten-Probleme", in: Moser (ed.) 1975, 144-97.

— 1977: "Überlegungen zu einer makrostrukturellen Textanalyse: J. Thurber, The Lover and His Lass", in: van Dijk/Petöfi (eds.) 1977, 132-75.

— 1977a: *Linguistische Textmodelle. Grundlagen und Möglichkeiten* (UTB 130), Munich: Fink 1977.

Güttgemanns, E. 1971: *Offene Fragen zur Formgeschichte des Evangeliums* (BEvTh 14), 2nd ed., München: Kaiser 1971.

Hägg, T. 1971: *Narrative Technique in Ancient Greek Romances. Studies of Chariton, Xenophon Ephesius, and Achilles Tatius* (Skrifter utgivna av Svenska institutet i Athen, 8°, VIII), Stockholm: Almqvist & Wiksell 1971.

Hanson, P. D. 1976: "Apocalypse, Genre", and "Apocalypticism", in: *IDBSup* (1976) 27-34.

Hartman, L. 1975/76: "The Function of Some So-Called Apocalyptic Time-Tables", in: *NTS* 20 (1975/76) 1-14 [No. 6 in this volume].

— 1978: "Till frågan om evangeliernas litterära genre", in: *AnASU* 21 (1978) 5-22 [Engl. transl. in this volume no. 1].

— 1980: "Form and Message. A Preliminary Discussion of 'Partial Texts' in Rev 1-3 and 22:6ff.", in: Lambrecht (ed.) 1980, 129-49 [No. 7 in this volume].

Hellholm, D. 1980: *Das Visionenbuch des Hermas als Apokalypse. Formgeschichtliche und texttheoretische Studien zu einer literarischen Gattung.* 1. Methodologische Vorüberlegungen und makrostrukturelle Textanalyse (CB.NT 13:1), Lund: Gleerup 1980.

— (ed.) 1983/89: *Apocalypticism in the Mediterranean World and the Near East. Proceedings of the International Colloquium on Apocalypticism Uppsala, August 12 – 17, 1979*, Tübingen: Mohr (Siebeck) 1983 [2nd ed. enlarged by Supplementary Bibliography 1989].

Hempfer, K. W. 1973: *Gartungstheorie. Information und Synthese* (UTB 133), Munich: Fink 1973.

Hennecke, E./Schneemelcher, W. (eds.) 1964: *Neutestamentliche Apokryphen in deutscher Übersetzung. Band 2*, 3rd. ed., Tübingen: Mohr (Siebeck) 1964.

Jeffares, A. N. (ed.) 1968: *Swift. Modern Judgements*, London: Macmillan 1968.

Knierim, R. 1973: "Old Testament Form Criticism Reconsidered", in: *Interpretation* 27 (1973) 435-67.

Koch, K. 1978: "Esras erste Vision. Weltzeiten und Weg des Höchsten", in: *BZ* 22 (1978) 46-75.

Lambrecht, J. (ed.) 1980: *L'Apocalypse johannique et l'Apocalyptique dans le Nouveau Testament* (BEThL 53), Gembloux-Louvain: Duculot-University Press 1980.

Lausberg, H. 1960: *Handbuch der literarischen Rhetorik. Eine Grundlegung der Literaturwissenschaft I-II*, München: Hueber 1960.

Leavis, F. R. 1968: "The Irony of Swift", in: Jeffares (ed.) 1968, 121-34.

McGaughy, L. C. (ed.) 1972: *SBL ... Book of Seminar Papers ... 1972*, Missoula, MT: Scholars Press 1972.

McHugh, R./Edwards, Ph. (eds.) 1967: *Jonathan Swift 1667-1967*, Dublin: Dolmen Press 1967.

Moser, H. (ed.) 1975: *Linguistische Probleme der Texlanalyse* (Jahrbuch des Instituts für deutsche Sprache 1973. Sprache der Gegenwart. Schriften des Instituts für deutsche Sprache in Mannheim 35), Düsseldorf: Schwann 1975.

Parrott, D. 1970: A *Missionary Wisdom Gattung*: Identification, Sitz im Leben, History and Connection with the New Testament (PhD diss., Berkeley, CA 1970).

Perkins, Ph. 1977: "Apocalypse of Adam: The Genre and Function of a Gnostic Apocalypse", in: *CBQ* 39 (1977) 382-95.

Philonenko, M./Simon, M. (eds.) 1977: *L'Apocalyptique* (EHiRel 3), Paris: Librairie Orientaliste Paul Geuthner 1977.

Price, M. 1953: *Swift's Rhetorical Art*. A Study in Structure and Meaning, New Haven, CT: Yale University Press 1953.

Quintana, R. 1967: "Gulliver's Travels: The Satiric Intent and Execution", in: McHugh et al. (eds.) 1967, 78-93.

— 1975: "Swift, Jonathan", in: *Encyclopaedia Britannica Macropaedia* 17 (1975) 856-59.

von Rad, G. 1975: *Theologie des Alten Testaments* II, 6th ed., Munich: Kaiser 1975.

Raphaël, F. 1977: "Esquisse d'une typologie de l'apocalypse", in: Philonenko/Simon (eds.) 1977, 11-38.

Rendtorff, R. 1956: "Formen und Gattungen I. AT", in: *EKL* 1 (1956) 1303-10.

Ringgren, H. 1957: "Apokalyptik", in: *RGG*[3] 1 (1957) 463-66.

Sickenberger, J. 1950: "Apokalyptik", in: *RAC* I (1950) 504-10.

Söder, R. 1932: *Die apokryphen Apostelgeschichten und die romanhafte Literatur der Antike*, Stuttgart: 1932 [repr. Darmstadt: Wissenschaftliche Buchgesellschaft 1969].

Stone, M. E. 1976: "Lists of Revealed Things in the Apocalyptic Literature", in: Cross et alii (eds.) 1976, 414-52.

Todorov, T. 1974: "Literary Genres", in: *CTL* 12 (1974) 957-62.

Urmson, J. O. 1967: "Austin, J. L.", in: *EncPh* 1 (1967) 211-15.

Vielhauer, Ph. 1964: "Apokalypsen und Verwandtes. Einleitung", in: Hennecke/Schneemelcher (eds.) 1964, 407-27.

— 1975: *Geschichte der urchristlichen Literatur. Einleitung in das Neue Testament, die Apokryphen und die Apostolischen Väter* (dGL), Berlin/New York: de Gruyter 1975.

Weinrich, H. 1971: *Literatur für Leser. Essays und Aufsätze zur Literaturwissenschaft,* Stuttgart etc.: Kohlhammer 1971.

Weisstein, U. 1968: *Einführung in die vergleichende Literaturwissenschaft,* Stuttgart etc.: Kohlhammer 1968.

Widengren, G. 1969: *Religionsphänomenologie,* Berlin – New York: de Gruyter 1969.

Supplement

Aune, D. E.: "The Apocalypse of John and the Problem of Genre", in: A. Y. Collins (ed.), *Early Christian Apocalypticism. Genre and Social Setting* (*Semeia* 36 [Decatur, GA: Scholars Press 1986]), 65-96.

Hellholm, D.: "The Problem of Apocalyptic Genre and the Apocalypse of John", in: *Early Christian Apocalypticism. Genre and Social Setting* (*Semeia* 36 [Decatur, GA: Scholars Press 1986]), 13-64.

Vorster, W. S.: "'Genre' and the Revelation of John. A Study in text, context and intertext", in: *Neotest.* 22 (1988) 103-23.

Collins, J. J.: "Genre, Ideology and Social Movements in Jewish Apocalypticism", in: J. J. Collins/J. H. Charlesworth (eds.), *Mysteries and Revelations. Apocalyptic Studies since the Uppsala Colloquium* (JSPE.S 9), Sheffield: JSOT Press 1991, 11-32.

Hellholm, D.: "Methohological Reflections on the Problem of Definition of Generic Texts", in: J. J. Collins/J. H. Charlesworth (eds.), *Mysteries and Revelations. Apocalyptic Studies since the Uppsala Colloquium* (JSPE.S 9), Sheffield: JSOT Press 1991, 135-63.

Vielhauer, Ph./Strecker, G.: "Apocalypses and Related Subjects. Introduction", in: E. Hennecke/W. Schneemelcher (eds.), *New Testament Apocrypha,* English trans. ed. by. R. McL. Wilson, Vol. 2, Cambridge: Clarke & Co / Louisvillle, KY: Westminster/John Knox Press 1992, 542-68.

6. The Functions of Some So-Called Apocalyptic Timetables[1]

1. Introductory

There seems to exist a relatively common opinion about the apocalyptic circles in Judaism, which Dr Russell in his book on Jewish apocalyptic expresses in these words: "In answer to the prophets' cry 'How long, o Lord, how long?', the apocalyptists gave the year, the day and the hour".[2] And in his classical study, *Die Eschatologie der jüdischen Gemeinde*, P. Volz stated: "*Die zahlenmäßige Berechnung des Weltendes ist vor allem das charakteristische Geschäft des Apokalyptikers.*"[3]

When we look for the support which authors bring forward to substantiate statements like these, we notice that the direct evidence is rather scarce. By direct evidence I mean texts which present something like "the year, the day and the hour" — using Dr Russell's words. Actually, these passages are so few that I should suppose rather that different kinds of indirect evidence cause scholars to defend opinions like those I have just quoted. By indirect evidence I mean especially: *(a)* texts which periodize history until the end in such a way that an informed reader should be able to spot his place in the developing drama; *(b)* sayings like the famous one by R. Jose b. Ḥalaphtah, which excludes the end-calculator from the age to come (*Derek Erez* 10); *(c)* texts which enumerate signs of the end, such as catastrophes, persecutions, and general sinfulness; *(d)* discussions of questions like "When will the Messiah come?"; *(e)* texts which may be interpreted as reflecting a frustrated expectation of the end; *(f)* incidents like the ones Josephus relates of prophets who brought the crowd with them out into the desert to encounter salvation.

I shall attempt now to find out what function some of the texts have which are adduced as proofs of the interest of the apocalyptists in calculations of the end. I call them "timetables". My method of discussion implies a widening and a narrowing of our possible object of investigation. It implies a widening in so far as I do not deal only with texts which

---

[1] Paper delivered at the SNTS Congress in August 1974 at Sigtuna, Sweden.

[2] Russell 1964, 1.

[3] Volz 1934, 141.

give a precise date of the end — actually such a thing applies only to Daniel. But I shall discuss also a few texts which deal with the date of the end in a more general manner, including a couple of presentations of history. On the other hand, I narrow down the scope so as to stay with certain Jewish *apocalyptic texts*.[4] That is to say that I want to keep the apocalyptic texts apart from several of the indirect evidences I mentioned, such as the popular prophets, or rabbinic traditions which calculate the time of the end or condemn such calculations.

Further, by asking for the function of these "timetables" I introduce something we learn from some philosophers of language, namely the realization that sentences may have different functions.[5] Thus a sentence like "the Lord is coming" may have a purely informative, theoretical function, just telling somebody a fact concerning a certain lord. But, depending on the context, the same sentence can also have one or several practical functions, e.g. an expressive one, expressing, for instance, joy, consolation, pain, surprise or sorrow. Or, it may have a prescriptive function, meaning something like: "the Lord is coming — so see that you are ready to receive him". It seems to me that it may prove useful to apply a similar set of distinctions also to configurations of sentences, namely, in our case, to whole texts of an apocalyptic timetable type. I shall try to answer the question of the function, or functions, of a given text with the help of its context and the general line of thought; in a couple of cases I shall also discuss how the text was understood by early readers.

2. The Book of Daniel

(1) The only text which really answers the question "How long?" by giving the year and the date is Daniel. There, as is well known, the prophecy of Jeremiah about the 70 years is reinterpreted in chapter 9 to mean 70 heptads of years. After two periods of seven and sixty-two weeks respectively, the seventieth week is the time of the author in which desolation, war and abomination prevail. In chapter 12 the calendar of the end is further specified, and the date of the end is given. First, it is said to occur after a time, times and a half, which corresponds to the same three years and a half which have appeared before in Daniel. Then the text becomes even more precise, and the end is said to appear after 1,290 days, and after 1,335 days. Generally scholars assume that the author or a redactor

---

[4] I use the words "apocalyptic", "apocalypse", etc. as suggested by Ringgren 1957.

[5] To ask, in an analysis of a sentence, for its semantic function is a commonplace in today's philosophy of language; see, e.g. Alston 1964, chap. 2; Ferré 1961, 54ff. But it seems that this kind of assessment has not yet been extended to whole texts. This question has been raised, however in the field of linguistics: see, e.g. the discussion of W. O. Hendricks in idem 1973, where also other recent contributions to the subject are quoted.

has by these figures successively revised or corrected the earlier date of 1,150 days in 8:12f.[6] I shall adopt this view in this paper.[7]

What function had these statements of the date of the end in Daniel? A commentator like O. Plöger answers in this manner: "The book of Daniel does not only want to nourish fidelity in times of trouble and tribulation. It wants also to indicate how one can receive a satisfying answer, based on Israel's confession, to the question: what will God do at the end of the days? They who have agreed to this answer are supported by the book in the tribulations which are caused by the worldly power as well as in the attacks of those who refuse the eschatological confession. Towards such a consolation and encouragement are directed especially the deliberations concerning the burning question of the date of the end, which, as it were, seizes God by the arm ...".[8]

Thus it seems that Professor Plöger would assign some kind of practical function to the Danielic timetables, talking of consolation and encouragement rather than of theoretical information. What support does the text itself offer to such an interpretation? Obviously it would not be fair to say that the figures which date the end are only symbolically meant. This is so, even if I be excused for a careless usage of the word "symbolic". The very fact that the author — or the redactor — felt that he had to revise the figures indicates that they meant something more than, say, "the end will come and, in addition, quite soon". If their meaning were something of that sort, then it should not matter too much whether the writer told his readers that the end would come 1,150, 1,290 or 1,335 days after a given occasion. On the other hand it seems remarkable that the reviser did not erase the outdated figures. Thus the given information seems to be embarrassingly inconsistent, and this may be a hint that, although the figures did denote months and days, none the less their context gave them a function that was not solely informative.

We turn now to the somewhat less precise figures of the seventy heptads in chapter 9. The author's chronology is not too exact, either when he deals with the long period of the 62 heptads, which may be excusable, or when he comes to his own time. Rather, the number for the time of desolation, 3 1/2, is a round number denoting a certain time, not too short.[9] Explicitly the figure of the 70 heptads is based on Jeremiah's prophecy. But implicitly, by the vocabulary, other texts are brought in,

---

[6] See Gunkel 1895, 269; Charles 1929, *ad loc.*; Plöger 1965, *ad loc.*; Delcor 1971, *ad loc.*

[7] I do so very much with the same feeling of reluctance as that of J. Barr, according to his commentary from 1962, *ad loc.*

[8] Plöger 1965, 177f. Similar assessments are common in the commentaries, see e.g. the commentary by Porteous 1962 on 8:14, and further Eißfeldt 1964, 716f., and Dexinger 1969, 74ff.

especially 2 Chr 36:21, Lev 25-26 and Jer 25:10f. Together they give a specific ring to the number of seventy, which Professor Grelot has demonstrated.[10] They denote ten periods of jubilees which lead up to the Great
Sabbath with the great remission of the slaves. So the way these figures
are presented makes them interpret the situation of the author and of his
first readers or listeners. They were living shortly before the great remission which God has promised.

Further, the context in Daniel indicates that the author interprets the
desolation he is living under as the desolation which Jeremiah (25:11)
and Leviticus (26:34) proclaim as a punishment of a nation which has
broken the covenant. But both texts continue in a positive tone, Leviticus
by saying: "If they confess their iniquity and the iniquity of their fathers
... then I will remember my covenant with Jacob...". The passage in Dan
9 which precedes the words of the seventy weeks fulfils this *protasis*,
being a confession of sins.[11] The *apodosis*, that God remembers the covenant, is represented by the 70 weeks which finish the transgression,
bring in everlasting righteousness and seal vision and prophecy. In Jer
25, on the other hand, the proclamation of desolation is combined with a
promise that after the 70 years of desolation the enemy and their princes
will themselves be the object of desolation; this is also taken up in Dan
9:27.[12]

Thus our author finds that the desolation he experiences is the one
which was proclaimed in Leviticus and Jeremiah, and which there was
combined with promises of vindication. He seems to be convinced that
this vindication is not far away, and he expresses that by his intimations
of the great jubilee. So the heptads become more than a calendar to an
understanding reader — not least the passage declaring to him that his
suffering had a place in a history that was not forgotten by God. It
encourages him by intimating that the situation would lead to the glory
of the faithful and to the shame of the apostates. So his time was a time
of crisis. That is the knowledge the author wanted to convey, a knowl-

---

[9] [Strack-]Billerbeck 1928, 760f. Cf. Porteous 1962 on 12:5ff. The figure appears as the
time of Antichrist in Rev 11:2f., 12:14. *Pirqe R. El.* 48 assumes the same duration of Pha-
raoh's edict against the Israelite children.

[10] Grelot 1969. See also Bentzen 1952, 73. Cf., in addition, how the jubilees are used for
the purpose of dating in 6Q12 and how Lev 30:11 receives an eschatological interpretation
in 11QMelch.

[11] This speaks against the relatively widespread opinion among commentators that that
passage of Daniel is secondary. See e.g. Charles 1929, Bentzen 1952, and Porteous 1962, *ad
loc.*, and cf. Plöger 1965, *ad loc.*, and Jones 1968.

[12] There are more texts in the background of Dan 9:24ff., not least those dealing with the
Day of Yahweh — see von der Osten-Sacken 1969a, 39ff.

edge which I suspect was more important to him than any idea that there was a certain number of leaves left on the end-time wall calendar.

(2) I want to return now to the end of Daniel which contains the different precise figures of days left till the end, and ask how this passage may have been understood by contemporary readers.[13] We can be reasonably sure that these figures stood there, once the book of Daniel got something like a wider public. That can form the point of departure for a series of considerations. It is quite probable that Daniel was first studied by an 'in-group'.[14] Maybe, with Daniel 12, they expected the end to arrive at least within the 1,335 days, maybe not — we do not know. But if they did, what happened after the deadline had been passed? We do not know. Canon Charles assumed that the readers became so disappointed that the Book of Daniel fell into disrepute for a century or more.[15] But on that point I think we can correct the learned Canon Charles, for there is good evidence that Daniel was in high esteem even some few years after the assumed deadline, the proof being some texts from *1 Enoch* and the Qumran library.[16] That is to say: whoever published Daniel, whoever started a procedure of copying it for private or public usage, it seems questionable whether he expected the end to appear in some few weeks. And if he did, it did not take long until the measured time had run out. What did the readers do? Or to term it otherwise: which function did the first discernible readers and interpreters give to the Danielic timetable in chapter 12?

One of the earliest texts which uses Daniel is the first column of the Qumran War Scroll, for which I accept the dating by Dr von der Osten-Sacken.[17] The language of this passage is coloured by an interpretation of the last part of Dan 11 and of the beginning of Daniel 12. It presupposes that one understands the evil king of Daniel 11 as meaning Belial and his armies, and that the Danielic prophecy is regarded as a text on the last things. Of the figures at the end of Daniel 12 there is no certain trace in the War Scroll column. So we cannot know what the Qumran

---

[13]Possibly the *Traditionsgeschichte* of the passage could be explained by a hypothesis that a Maccabean redactor has applied the eschatological imagery to events of history. It remains a hypothesis, however, and in addition quite a speculative one. Cf. Schedl 1964.

[14]See e.g. Plöger 1962, 16ff.; Delcor 1971, 15ff. Cf. Lebram 1970, 522ff.

[15]Charles 1913/63, 189.

[16]See *1 Enoch* 90:13-19 (cf. Hartman 1966, 81ff.) which forms part of the text which Charles himself dated to a time before 161 BC (1913, 170). Of the Qumran texts I will discuss 1QM1 below. As to the date of this latter I follow von der Osten-Sacken 1969b, 42ff., 88, where he argues for a date very close to that of Daniel. Cf. Yadin 1962, 244ff. Mertens 1969/ [71], was not available to me.

[17]See the preceding note.

author actually made of the 1,290 days, etc. but what we do know is that he did not make anything of them in this text, and, in addition, we know how he used their context. He saw it as a prophecy on the last things, which he views in a chiaroscuro, on a level beyond or above that of ordinary history.[18] That this is so — and that the text does not envisage a real battle with real spears — is suggested also by the other motifs which are interwoven with the Danielic ones, namely from OT traditions on the day of Yahweh and on the holy war.[19]

Per se, it is possible that the author could have associated the Daniel texts with the calamities under Antiochus.[20] But instead he uses the Danielic interpretation of the time of Antiochus as a kind of transparency, through which he projects his eschatological picture. The numbers do not enter his mind — the closest we get to them is when he mentions the times of the sons of darkness *versus* God's time, and when he says that there will be three 'lots'[21] of attacks in which the sons of light are victorious, three in which the sons of darkness prevail, and one, the seventh, when God himself defeats Belial and his army.[22] On the whole, the passage shows an eschatological dualistic understanding of the sharp contrasts between Israel and the nations and an intensive supra-historic understanding of the situation.[23]

The same manner of interpreting the end of Daniel eschatologically occurs in the Florilegium 4Q174. There we find a direct quotation of Dan 12:9f., namely of the immediate context of the verses that give the dates of the end (12:7, 11f.). The quotation is used to illustrate the *pesher* of Ps 2:1, on the princes of the world who rise against the Lord and His anointed. This is said to refer to the elected ones at the end of the days, as Daniel prophesies that there will be a time of testing, during which "let the wicked do wickedly and let the righteous make themselves white". Thus the Danielic text is understood to say something important of the *eschaton*, the figures in it play no role at all, and indirectly the commentator makes the quotation of Daniel admonish to steadfastness in righteousness.

---

[18] von der Osten-Sacken 1969b, 30ff. Cf. Bruce 1959, 62ff.; idem 1969, 233f.

[19] von der Osten-Sacken 1969b, 34ff. Cf. Becker 1964, 75ff.

[20] At least the Nahum *pesher* demonstrates that a later Qumran writer knew of traditions on Antiochus.

[21] On the expression, see von der Osten-Sacken 1969b, 78ff.

[22] This might have some connection with the "time, times and a half" or with the number of weeks in Dan 10:24 — see von der Osten Sacken 1969b, 33. Possibly one could assume that the expressions "the times of the darkness" (מועדי חושך) and "God's time" (מעד אל) in 1QM1:8 were derived from Dan 12:7 (למועד מועדים וחצי).

[23] Cf. von der Osten-Sacken 1969b, 84ff.

A couple of centuries after Daniel was written, Josephus discusses the book. He puts Daniel into a place of its own among the prophets, for, he says, Daniel in his prophecies did not only convey what was going to happen, but he also told the time at which it would occur (*Ant* 10.267). This gift of Daniel Josephus exhibits by referring to the vision of chapter 8 of the ram and the goat, and he ends up by saying that in the same way Daniel wrote of the Roman Empire. In other words, Josephus hardly saw the book of Daniel and its timetables in the same misty chiaroscuro as did the Qumran commentator. He had nothing against regarding God as active in history, but not in terms of extraordinary divine interventions. Oracles, portents, etc. he had room for; but when it came to expecting concrete extraordinary actions of divine salvation in the present, he was reluctant.[24] Thus he reported that it was mostly an ambiguous oracle that incited the Jews to the war (*Bell* 6.312f.). It is possible, but hardly demonstrable in a binding manner, that the oracle in question was the 70-weeks prophecy of Daniel.[25] Many of the wise men went astray in their interpretation of it, says Josephus, although it signified, in his own opinion, Vespasian's sovereignty.

This seems instructive to me. The apocalyptic language in the Danielic timetables was open in such a way that different people understood it in different ways. Thus we have met with three such ways of understanding: (a) the one in the War Scroll, with less concretion, moving in a chiaroscuro in its eschatology, using quite general expressions of times of darkness and the time of God, disregarding the figures of the date and betraying an intensive supra-historic understanding of the situation; (b) Josephus' non-eschatological understanding, seeing in principle historical rulers and dates predicted, although a special gift was needed for a correct understanding; (c) the understanding which according to Josephus was held by "many of the wise men", namely an understanding very much like Josephus' own, but applying it to an expected divine extraordinary intervention in worldly history.

We could try to describe these three types of understanding in this way: the Qumran understanding gives to the Danielic text an expressive, religious function; Josephus a theoretical, informative one, with a certain religious flavour; and the "wise men" seem to provide it with a function that we might also term a theoretical, informative one, which, as it were, objectifies the content of the prophecy.

Somebody may object that this last understanding is exactly the typically apocalyptic one, the one behind the strange numbers at the end of Daniel, behind other apocalyptic timetables, as well as behind different

---

[24] Cf. Delling 1958; Lindner 1972 and cf. Michel 1969.
[25] Hahn 1963, 167ff.; Bruce 1965.

modern kinds of religious or eschatological horoscopes. Of course, I do not deny the existence of the two last-mentioned ways of understanding, but I doubt that that is the main function the authors of the Jewish apocalyptic texts gave to their timetables, or that the Qumran commentator understood them so.

3. The Assumption of Moses, The Apocalyps of Abraham

(1) We turn now to another timetable, namely one that gives a date of the end, but less precisely than seems to have been the case in Daniel, namely the *Assumption of Moses.*

In speaking of timetables in *As. Mos.,* I refer to two things. On the one hand I think of the presentation by Moses of Israel's history from the entrance into Canaan until the consummation, on the other I have in view the date which is given in this context in 10:12: there will be 250 times from Moses to the Lord's coming.

In order to feel the function of this timetable, we have to have a brief look at the main theme of this apocalypse and at the structure of its contents. Thus a principal theme of *As. Mos.* is the conditions of the covenant between God and His people. This of course, is a central idea in the Deuteronomy passages on which the *As. Mos.* heavily depends. The people must not transgress the commandments, and when they do, or rather, when some of them do, the Gentiles will perform the punishment of divine vengeance, which however strikes the whole people including the faithful ones. If, however, these keep faithful to the covenant, God will avenge them when His kingdom appears.[26]

As we have the text now, it is rather problematic to recognize the different epochs in history which lead up to the author's time.[27] But his choice of events and the way of presentation are apparently determined by the main theme, namely that of transgression, punishment, and obligation to fidelity. There is little doubt that in chapter 7 he deals with his contemporary rulers, to whom no sins or blasphemies are alien. But, according to chapter 8, vengeance will come upon them under the reign of "the king of the kings of the earth", who is painted in colours from the Danielic picture of Antiochus IV. These persecutions receive a comment in chapter 9, where the enigmatic Taxo gives a speech calling the persecutions a cruel and shameful vengeance on the people and a punishment without mercy (9:2). But he and his sons will rather die than transgress the commandments of God, he says, and the reason for such a stubborn faithfulness is, he says, "then our blood shall be avenged before the

---

[26]See Licht 1961; Nickelsburg, Jr. 1972, 29ff.

[27]Licht, *op. cit.,* Nickelsburg, *op. cit.,* 43ff.

Lord".[28] Such an avenging is immediately described in the theophany of chapter 10: Michael shall avenge the faithful of their adversaries, and God shall appear with indignation and wrath for His sons and punish the nations.[29] Thereafter the apocalypse returns to its framework, namely Moses' farewell to Joshua, and in the last chapter the main theme recurs. I quote the very last lines: "they that perform and carry out the commandments of God shall flourish and be prospered, but sinners and they who neglect His commandments shall lack the good things before mentioned, and they shall be punished by the nations with many torments. Yet it is not possible that He should wholly destroy and forsake them. For God will go forth, who has foreseen all things from the beginning, and His covenant is established by the oath ...." The rest of the book is destroyed.

What function does the timetable have, i.e. the presentation of Jewish history until the author's days and on into the consummation? Already my brief account of the context indicates that it is not primarily a theoretical-informative one in the sense that it forms a calendar at the disposal of the informed reader, nor is it a chronicle of the future from which a privileged reader may get enlightenment. But it assures the man of faith that he is not out of God's sight, that the evil of his own time is foreseen, that God will annihilate the present injustice, and that He will do so in the consummation of the times, which is near. We may notice however that the information on the author's present is very general, and so also is the picture of the king of the kings of the world. There are no traces of or basis for a calculation of the date of the end. But the way in which the description of the last evil time is kept together with the appearance of God's vengeance and His Kingdom, results in a kind of *Naherwartung*. This *Naherwartung* does not however seem to be obsessed by the expectation of a calculated date for the end, but rather it is a *Naherwartung* in the form of a strong eschatological hope. Let us remember also that this *Naherwartung* did not prevent the author from writing and publishing his booklet.

Now, neither this *Naherwartung* nor the other assurances just mentioned are to be termed theoretical information. Rather they go together with the statement of Taxo on the necessity of keeping the commandments, even when this has death as a consequence. Their aim is to comfort and to encourage, and thus the timetable and its elements have as their main function an expressive and a prescriptive one.

---

[28] The wording is probably inspired by Deut 32:43.
[29] For an analysis of the OT motifs and of their role in this passage, see Hartman 1966, 126ff.

There is also something like a date of the end in this text. For after the theophany scene Moses says: "now must you Joshua, son of Nun, keep these words and this book. For there shall be from my death and assumption to His coming 250 times" (10:11f.). As far as I can see this notice says: the message here given is valid not for Joshua's generation · but for the one of the real author and his readers.[30] The figure may mean 250 jubilees,[31] but even so it is mystifying. Personally, I suspect that this mystification has a function together with the other general, and non-precise, allusions to the time before the consummation. One could call it a kind of test of faith. The reader is summoned to believe that the message of the apocalypse bears on him and his time, both in terms of hope and of ethics, but he has no history book of the future, of which he can turn over the leaves and see, month after month, how it tallies with the developing events.

(2) The next timetable is from the *Apocalypse of Abraham*. The text as a whole is an elaboration of Genesis 15. This chapter deals with the making of a covenant between God and Abraham and with the sacrifice of Abraham, at which he falls asleep and receives a revelation of Israel's slavery in Egypt during 400 years and of its return to Canaan in the fourth generation. According to the Apocalypse Abraham is brought up to heaven and is allowed to see a picture of the whole history. The people in the picture stand half of them on the right side and half of them on the left, the ones to the right being the Jews. What is taken up from history is the fall of man, the murder by Cain followed by a list of vices, and then a mention of the Temple and of idolatry there. At last the picture sways, and the Gentiles on its left side burn the Temple and plunder. Abraham asks how long that which he has seen will last. Obviously the question is caused by the basic text in Genesis 15, and the answer is also taken from it: on account of a multitude of His people God will be provoked for four generations, and these four generations will also bring the retribution for their deeds (chapter 28). In the fourth generation of 100 years and one world-hour the Gentiles will be struck by misfortune. This world-hour is defined as 12 hours — or maybe we have to amend it to 12 years — during which the ungodly age will last. Then comes the judgement of the nations through ten plagues, followed by the coming age.

In this case also we notice how vague and round the figures are. There are no clear starting points from which to count them, either. The slavery in Egypt and its duration according to Genesis 15 are translated into the sad situation of the author's own time. Thus it is natural that the final

---

[30] Cf. Dan 10:4, 9 and see, e.g., Delcor 1971, *ad loc.*
[31] See, e.g., Clemen 1904, *ad loc.*; Charles 1913, *ad loc.*; Russell 1964, 208, 226.

plagues of the Gentiles are ten in number, just as were the ones which struck the Egyptians. As far as I can see, the text gives next to nothing to hold on to, when it comes to calculating the end.

What function then has the timetable, namely the vision of history with the numbers included? I think it is advisable that we consider that these are embedded in a presentation where certain distinct lines of thought are essential. One is the problem of evil, not least the evil which the author sees in the hostile Gentiles and in the apostates among his fellow-Jews. Thus the Gentiles on the left side of the picture are joined to Azazel, and the fall of man is reported in order to explain why Azazel has so much power.[32] This evil power is especially exerted by Azazel's Gentile companions in the last ungodly age. As a kind of counterpoint to this theme we hear of righteousness. Obviously the author and his readers identify themselves with Abraham's seed, or rather with those whom the text calls "the righteous men of your seed" (chapter 29) and "those who have chosen to do (God's) will and have openly kept (his) commandments" (chapter 31). The vision of history gives a kind of explanation why they are oppressed by the evil powers, and the figures assure them that this situation will have an end, just as their ancestors were once released from Egypt. If we should term the message of this timetable a theoretical-informative one, its theory is not a calculation of the end, but rather an attempt to solve the moral and religious problem posed by the situation of the faithful.

At this point we have dealt with most of the Jewish apocalypses we know of which give anything like figures which calculate the date of the end. There are a great many texts which contain such calculations, but they are not apocalypses, but belong mostly to the rabbinic traditions.[33]

4. The Ten-Weeks Apocalypse

Lastly, I will discuss a timetable which has no figures for the date of the end, but which represents the genre of periodized history.[34] I refer to the ten-weeks apocalypse of *1 Enoch*. If we assume, as one generally does, that this pocket-apocalypse is a fragment incorporated into the present *1 Enoch*, then we have no guidance from the context when asking for the function of this timetable. The text itself, however, gives us some hints as to its main interest. The introduction states: "Concerning the children of

---

[32]See Rubenstein 1957.

[33]Cf. the material gathered in Volz 1934, 141ff.; [Strack-]Billerbeck 1928b, 977-1015; Hahn 1963.

[34]The phenomenon of a schematization of history, of course, has parallels in several religions outside Judaism: see, e.g., Widengren 1969, 459ff.; see also the discussion in Hengel 1969, 348ff. For a survey of the Jewish material see Russell 1964, 224ff.

righteousness and concerning the elect of the world and concerning the plant of righteousness I will speak these things". Then the theme of righteousness and its opposite is carried through. The righteousness of the first week is changed into the wickedness of Noah's times. Abraham starts a renewed period of righteousness at the end of the third week, a period continued through the fourth week with the lawgiving on Sinai until the building of the Temple in the fifth. Then begins a decline in the sixth week, in which the Temple is burnt and the people dispersed. This evil time continues in the seventh week, but at its close the righteous community of the author introduces a new righteousness, which receives wider room through the following three weeks of meta-history. They contain a righteous judgement of the sinners in the eighth, and then a judgement on the nations in the ninth, so that all mankind shall look to the path of righteousness. Finally, in the tenth week after the judgement of the angels, a new heaven shall appear, and then there shall be many weeks for ever, and all shall be in goodness and righteousness.

The apocalypse is symmetrically constructed.[35] The erection of the Temple is in the centre, the three weeks of meta-history correspond to the three weeks before Abraham, Abraham's place in the scheme answers exactly to that of the righteous community, and the falling and rising curve of righteousness forms a regular zigzag pattern. Obviously the author and his group identify themselves with Abraham: he is introduced in this way: "a man shall be elected as the plant of righteous judgement and thereafter he shall become the plant of righteousness for ever". The entrance of the community is reported in this manner: "the elect righteous of the eternal plant of righteousness shall be elected".

When I try to discover the message of these lines, it occurs to me that they largely deal with the identity of the author and his group. This question of identity has several aspects which are covered by different answers in the text: in that they occupy a place in history which corresponds to that of Abraham, they are Abraham's true inheritors, righteous like him and God's elect like him. The details of symmetry and regularity in the scheme of history tell them that the history in which they are involved makes sense and follows God's plans according to the heavenly tablets. They live in a time of transition, for the group is said to appear at the close of the seventh week with all its apostate deeds and thus not long before the three weeks of righteousness and judgement. This way of giving identity to the group suggests that the text has a practical function in terms of comfort and encouragement rather than a theoretical one

---

[35] J. Licht is to be credited for this and several other observations in this and the following paragraph: see his article 1965.

which would give precise answers to the "what and when" concerning the future.

As we now have the text of *1 Enoch*, the apocalypse of weeks is part of a larger text which is the result of a redactor's work.[36] It is easier to surmise which function the redactor gave to this timetable. He has cut it into two and placed the part concerning the three last weeks in chapter 91, and the part concerning the first seven weeks he has put later in chapter 93. In 91 Enoch begins his farewell speech to his sons in this way: "I exhort you ...: love uprightness and walk therein ...". The reason for such an exhortation is, says the text, that unrighteousness will be punished in the Flood and once and for all in the end time. Then the righteous shall arise from their sleep (91:10) and the roots of unrighteousness shall be cut off (91:11). After that the redactor inserts the last third of the apocalypse, starting with the eighth week, that of righteousness with a just judgement of the sinners. The reader is placed in the time before the end when wickedness increases, but no connections to any specific political or religious events can be discovered. The whole passage is carried by the exhortation to a righteous life, and it seems to me that the eschatological introduction mentioning the punishment of evil and the reward of righteousness is subservient to this exhortation.

The first seven weeks, from the one of the righteous Enoch up till the one in which the elect group appears, were placed in chapter 93. They are introduced by 92, which gives the eschatological perspective which the apocalypse lost when the last three weeks were removed. Thus in 92 Enoch says: "let not your spirit be in trouble on account of the times, for the Holy and great one has appointed days for all things. The righteous one shall arise from sleep ... he shall walk in eternal light ... and sin shall perish in darkness for ever" (92:2-5). Then comes the section from the apocalypse of weeks. The last words concerning the seventh week say that the elect are instructed concerning all God's creation, and that line is followed by a lengthy exclamation of how great and wonderful God's creation is. Chapter 94 then goes on to say: "Now I say to you, my sons, love righteousness and walk therein".

About the anxiety on account of the times the redactor has two things to say: first, God will certainly reward righteousness and let sin perish; secondly, God has history in His hand, as is certified by the introduction of the seven-weeks apocalypse. The following exhortation to a righteous life casts a special shadow over the apocalypse. Deprived of its eschatological weeks, it ends with the righteous group appearing; and so the

---

[36] The fact that the present organization of the text seems to give a certain meaning causes me to suggest a redactor's work behind it, instead of assuming a displacement of sheets (cf. e.g. Eißfeldt 1964, 837).

apocalypse directs its reader to the duty of leading a righteous life. Thus the redactor has given a relatively stronger practical-exhortative function to the two parts of the apocalypse of weeks.

5. 4 Ezra, 2 Apocalypse of Baruch

I cannot discuss any more 'timetables' now, but I shall only mention that other scholars have arrived at similar results in more detailed investigations. Thus, for instance, Dr Harnisch found that the 'timetables' of 4 Ezra and 2 *Apoc. Bar.* tell the reader that he is close to the *eschaton* — which is a challenge to him — but there are no attempts to give a date for the end.[37] And Dr Breech has demonstrated how the literary structure of 4 Ezra shows that the book has an aim of consolation.[38]

6. Conclusions

In conclusion, I think that the few examples of different timetables I have laid before you could be said to have different functions. In Daniel the "timetables" seem to have had a certain informative theoretical function concerning the date of the end, but it seems to me that that function was coupled with others in such a way that these latter practical functions could prevail with some readers. In the other, later texts I have discussed, the theoretical time-informing function is very weak, if it exists at all.[39] Instead, I think, their main function is practical, whether that practical function be expressive or exhortative or something else. By this I do not deny that these or other timetable texts could have been differently understood in antiquity. The language of the apocalypses is also in these texts semantically so open that a person could interpret them in a literalistic manner.[40] But I think we have to differentiate. It can hardly be fair to pour into one single bottle Jewish and Christian apocalypses from a period of 300 years; Josephus' reports on popular prophets leading the crowd astray; rabbinic sayings which forbid calculations of the end; the many rabbinic statements on the duration of the world, on the date of Messiah's advent or of the end, etc.: to mix all these ingredients and others, call the brew "apocalypticism" and have individual texts taste of this

---

[37] Harnisch 1969, 320 and passim. Also Strobel 1967, 85ff.

[38] Breech 1973.

[39] This is not to say that some kind of 'calculating' activity could not, in some instances, be surmised behind the texts, e.g., in the case of the 'ten weeks' apocalypse — cf. [Strack-] Billerbeck 1928b, 986ff.; Thorndike 1961. But that does not mean that the upshot of such a process, perhaps even a lengthy one, had a theoretical-informative function in the situation of communication.

[40] Cf. the reports on Christian prophets who brought their followers with them into the desert, Hippol., *In Dan.* 4.18-19, Tert., *Adv. Marc.* 3.24.

"apocalypticism".[41] To me, it is by no means given that, for example, the prophets Josephus tells us about are to be equated with the sophisticated authors of *As. Mos.* or of 4 Ezra. Maybe there was not a wide gap between them (and the gap did not necessarily depend on the degree of sophistication — we remember the wise men in Josephus' account); but none the less there seem to have been differences which I think we have to respect.

Thus I hope I am not too much mistaken when I contend that when the literary convention of different kinds of apocalyptic timetables was developed in Jewish apocalyptical literature, it had not primarily a theoretical, informative, and calculating function, but rather some practical one. To put it another way: the timetables were aimed less at the brain than at the heart and hands.[42]

Bibliography

Alston, W. P. 1964: *Philosophy of Language*, London etc.: Prentice Hall 1964.

Barr, J. 1962: "Daniel", in: M. Black/H. H. Rowley (eds.), *Peake's Commentary on the Bible*, London etc.: Nelson 1962, 591-602.

Becker, J. 1964: *Das Heil Gottes. Heils- und Sündenbegriffe in den Qumrantexten und im Neuen Testament* (StUNT 3), Göttingen: Vandenhoeck & Ruprecht 1964.

Bentzen, Aa. 1952: *Daniel* (HAT 19), 2nd ed., Tübingen: Mohr (Siebeck) 1952.

Billerbeck, P.[-Strack, H.] 1928a: *Kommentar zum Neuen Testament aus Talmud und Midrasch, III: Die Briefe des Neuen Testaments und die Offenbarung Johannis,* München: Beck 1928.

— 1928b: *Kommentar zum Neuen Testament aus Talmud und Midrasch, IV:2: Exkurse zu einzelnen Stellen des Neuen Testaments,* München: Beck 1928.

Breech, E. 1973: "These Fragments I have Shored Against my Ruins: the Form and Function of 4 Ezra", in: *JBL* 92 (1973) 267-74.

Bruce, F. F. 1959: *Biblical Exegesis in the Qumran Texts* (Exegetica 3:1), The Hague: van Keulen 1959.

— 1965: "Josephus and Daniel", in: *ASTI* 4 (1965) 148-62.

— 1969: "The Book of Daniel and the Qumran Community", in: E. E. Ellis/M.Wilcox (eds.), *Neotestamentica et Semitica. Studies in Honour of M. Black,* Edinburgh: T. & T. Clark 1969, 221-35.

---

[41]Cf. the discussion of Koch 1970, 86 et passim, which rightly presents itself as *eine Streitschrift.*

[42]Cf. the stimulating studies by Wilder 1930, and idem 1971. Cf. also Perrin 1974.

122

Narrative Texts

Charles, R. H. 1913/63: *Eschatology. The Doctrine of the Future Life in Israel, Judaism and Christianity*, London: A. Q. C. Black 1913 [repr. New York: Schocken 1963].

— 1913: *Apocrypha and Pseudepigrapha of the Old Testament, Vol. II*, Oxford: Clarendon 1913.

— 1929: *A Critical and Exegetical Commentary on Daniel*, Oxford: Clarendon 1929.

Clemen, C. 1904: *Die Himmelfahrt des Mose* (KlT 10), Bonn: Marcus & Weber 1904.

Delcor, M. 1971: *Le Livre de Daniel* (SB), Paris: Gabalda 1971.

Delling, G. 1958: "Josephus und das Wunderbare", in: *NT* 2 (1958) 291-309.

Dexinger, F. 1969: *Das Buch Daniel und seine Probleme* (SBS 33), Stuttgart: Katholisches Bibelwerk 1969.

Eißfeldt, O. 1964: *Einleitung in das Alte Testament*, 3rd ed., Tübingen: Mohr (Siebeck) 1964.

Ferré, F. 1961: *Language, Logic and God*, New York – Evanston – London: Harper & Row 1961.

Grelot, P. 1969: "Soixante-dix semaines d'années", in: *Bib.* 50 (1969) 169-86.

Gunkel, H. 1895: *Schöpfung und Chaos in Urzeit und Endzeit*, Göttingen: Vandenhoeck & Ruprecht 1895.

Hahn, I. 1963: "Josephus und die Eschatologie von Qumrān", in: H. Bardtke (ed.), *Qumrān-Probleme*. Vorträge des Leipziger Symposiums über Qumrān-Probleme vom 9. bis 14. Oktober 1961 (SSA 42), Berlin: Akademie-Verlag 1963, 167-91.

Harnisch, W. 1969: *Verhängnis und Verheißung der Geschichte. Untersuchungen zum Zeit- und Geschichtsverständnis im 4. Buch Esra und in der syr. Baruch-apokalypse* (FRLANT 97), Göttingen: Vandenhoeck & Ruprecht 1969.

Hartman, L. 1966: *Prophecy Interpreted. The Formation of Some Jewish Apocalyptic Texts and on the Eschatological Discourse Mark 13 Par.* (CB.NT 1), Lund: Gleerup 1966.

Hendricks, W. O. 1973: "On the Notion 'Beyond the Sentence'", in: idem, *Essays on Semiolinguistics and Verbal Art*, The Hague – Paris: Mouton 1973, 11-47.

Hengel, M. 1969: *Judentum und Hellenismus*, Tübingen: Mohr (Siebeck) 1969.

Jones, B. N. 1968: "The Prayer in Dan. ix", in: *VT* 18 (1968) 488-93.

Koch, K. 1970: *Ratlos vor der Apokalyptik. Eine Streitschrift über ein vernachlässigtes Gebiet der Bibelwissenschaft und die schädlichen Auswirkungen auf Theologie und Philosophie*, Gütersloh: Gerd Mohn 1970.

Lebram, J. C. H. 1970: "Apokalyptik und Hellenismus im Buche Daniel", in: *VT* 20 (1970) 503-24.

Licht, J. 1961: "Taxo, or the Apocalyptic Doctrine of Vengeance", in: *JJS* 12 (1961) 95-103.

— 1965: "Time and Eschatology in Apocalyptic Literature and in Qumran", in: *JJS* 16 (1965) 117-82.

Lindner, H. 1972: *Die Geschichtsauffassung des Flavius Josephus in Bellum Judaicum* (AGJU 12), Leiden: Brill 1972.

Mertens, A. 1969/[71]: *Das Buch Daniel im Lichte der Texte vom Toten Meer* (Diss. Mainz, 1969) [now published: (SBM 12), Würzburg: Echter 1971].

Michel, D. 1969: "Studien zu Josephus apokalyptische Heilsaussagen im Bericht des Josephus (B.J. 6, 290f. 293-95); ihre Umdeutung durch Josephus", in: E. E. Ellis/M.Wilcox (eds.), *Neotestamentica et Semitica. Studies in Honour of M. Black*, Edinburgh: T. & T. Clark 1969, 240-44.

Nickelsburg, Jr., G. W. E. 1972: *Resurrection, Immortality and Eternal Life in Intertestamental Judaism* (HThS 26), Cambridge, MA: Harvard University Press/London: SCM 1972.

von der Osten-Sacken, P. 1969a: *Die Apokalyptik in ihrem Verhältnis zu Prophetie und Weisheit* (TEH 157), München: Kaiser 1969.

— 1969b: *Gott und Belial* (StUNT 6), Göttingen: Vandenhoeck & Ruprecht 1969.

Perrin, N. 1974: "Eschatology and Hermeneutics", in: *JBL* 93 (1974) 1-14.

Plöger, O. 1962: *Theokratie und Eschatologie* (WMANT 2), 2nd ed., Neukirchen-Vluyn: Neukirchener Verlag 1962.

— 1965: *Das Buch Daniel* (KAT 18), Gütersloh: Gerd Mohn 1965.

Porteous, N. W. 1962: *Das Danielbuch* (ATD 23), Göttingen: Vandenhoeck & Ruprecht 1962.

Ringgren, H. 1957: "Apokalyptik, 1, II", in: *RGG*, Vol. X, 3rd ed., Tübingen: Mohr (Siebeck) 1957, 463-66.

Rubenstein, A. 1957: "A Problematic Passage in the Apocalypse of Abraham", in: *JJS* 8 (1957) 45-50.

Russell, D. S. 1964: *The Method and Message of Jewish Apocalyptic 200 BC – AD 100*, London: SCM Press 1964.

Schedl, C. 1964: "Mystische Arithmetik oder geschichtliche Zahlen? Daniel 8,14; 12,1l-13", in: *BZ* 8 (1964) 101-05.

Strobel, A. 1967: *Kerygma und Apokalyptik. Ein religionsgeschichtlicher und theologischer Beitrag zur Christusfrage*, Göttingen: Vandenhoeck & Ruprecht 1967.

Thorndike, J. P. 1961: "The Apocalypse of Weeks and the Qumran Sect", in: *RdQ* 3 (1961) 163-84.

Volz, P. 1934: *Die Eschatologie der jüdischen Gemeinde*, Tübingen: Mohr (Siebeck) 1934 [Reprinted: Hildesheim: Olms 1966].

Widengren, G. 1969: *Religionsphänomenologie* (GLB), Berlin: de Gruyter 1969.

Wilder, A. 1930: "The Nature of Jewish Eschatology", in: *JBL* 50 (1930) 201-06.

— 1971: "The Rhetoric of Ancient and Modern Apocalyptic", in: *Interp.* 25 (1971), 436-53.

Yadin, Y. 1962: *The Scroll of the War of the Sons of Light against the Sons of Darkness*, Oxford: Oxford University Press 1962.

Supplement

Collins, J. J.: *The Apocalyptic Imagination. An introduction to the Jewish Matrix of Christianity*, New York, NY: Crossroad 1984.

Collins, A. Y.: *Crisis and Catharsis: The Power of the Apocalypse*, Philadelphia, PN: Westminster 1984.

Schüssler Fiorenza, E.: *The Book of Revelation — Justice and Judgment*, Philadelphia, PN: Fortress 1985.

Aune, D. E.: "The Apocalypse of John and the Problem of Genre", in: A. Y. Collins (ed.), *Early Christian Apocalypticism. Genre and Social Setting* (*Semeia* 36 [Decatur, GA: Scholars Press 1986]), 65-96.

Boring, M. E.: "The Theology of the Book of Revelation: 'The Lord our God the Almighty Reigns'", in: *Interp.* 40 (1986) 257-69.

Du Rand, J. A.: "A Socio-psychological View of the Effect of the Language (parole) of the Apocalypse of John", in: *Neotest.* 24 (1990) 351-65.

Giesen, H.: "Symbole und mythische Aussagen in der Johannes-Apokalypse und ihre theologische Bedeutung", in: K. Kertelge (ed.), *Metaphorik und Mythos im Neuen Testament* (QD 126), Freiburg – Basel – Vienna: Herder 1990, 255-77.

Giblin, C. H.: *The Book of Revelation. The Open Book of Prophecy* (Good News Studies 34), Collegeville, MN.: Liturgical Press 1991.

7. Form and Message

A Preliminary Discussion of "Partial Texts" in Revelation 1-3 and 22:6ff.

1. Introduction

It is a complicated procedure to try to understand a text of antiquity that stems from a cultural situation different from ours.[1] In this paper I will discuss some particular aspects of one phase in that procedure with regard to some texts in the Book of Revelation, viz. those of the formcritical analysis. My discussion is not a traditional form-critical one, however, because my approach to some extent is inspired by certain methods of analysis which have been elaborated by scholars in linguistics and literary criticism. One typical feature of these methods is that they stress the fact that the text is the main instrument in a communication from the author to his reader.

To regard Revelation as an instrument of communication means that we assess the present text of the book. Such an approach does not invalidate, e.g., attempts to reconstruct the prehistory of the text, looking for sources,[2] or studies of the history of different motifs, tracing them back, for example, to the *Keret*-texts,[3] or works concerning the redaction process or the history of traditions.[4] But it gives one reason to ask how far such studies inform us of what the texts communicated. Let us, e.g., assume that in Rev 1:5 the writer has changed an original aorist tense of a traditional baptismal confession into a present, so that we now read ἀγαπῶντι.[5] Such a change may very well tell us something about the writer's ideas. But when we regard the text as a communication, this change, as a change, becomes significant only in so far as we find it rea-

---

[1] I use the word "understand" in a common-sense manner.

[2] See. e.g., the commentaries by Bousset 1896; Charles 1920a and b; Massyngberde Ford 1975.

[3] E.g., Bousset 1896; Boll 1914/67; Lohmeyer 1926; Müller 1963.

[4] For the passages we are going to discuss see esp. Schüssler Fiorenza 1972, and Hahn 1972.

[5] Schüssler Fiorenza 1972, who refers to von der Osten-Sacken 1967, 256.

sonable to assume that the traditional formula belonged to the common background of both author and reader. If so, this background formed part of the referential frame which determined and conditioned the communication.

This communication perspective also has a bearing on form criticism, particularly in so far as the latter is to serve the understanding of a text. Classical NT form criticism concentrated on the prehistory of the individual forms and traditions, mainly with respect to the gospels, but also with respect to the epistles. This is something different from studying the forms within an existing text. This is already true for the gospels,[6] and even more so for other texts which do not represent traditions to the same extent as the gospels. To study the forms within a text should mean that one tries to evaluate how passages that are shaped according to more or less established literary patterns are related to each other and interplay in a text's conveyance of its message.

Text-linguistics may prove helpful for the analysis of the relationships between the different passages of a text. Not least, E. Gülich and W. Raible have, with a communication perspective in mind, analysed how elements of narrative texts are organized.[7] They speak of *Teiltexte* of different degrees which co-operate within the whole of the text and which have an organization that can be seen from different "*gliedernde*" signs on the textual surface. While a simple "he said" can be regarded as such a *Teiltext*, so also can the dialogue in which the "he said" is embodied, although it would be one of a higher degree.[8] The passages on which biblical scholars are used to putting different "form" labels can easily be regarded as such *Teiltexte*, and this is where traditional form-criticism and text-linguistics of this kind can meet.

In the following I will try to adapt and apply some observations of Gülich and Raible to certain chapters of Revelation. I will use the English "partial text" for *Teiltext*, and, furthermore, restrict myself to dealing with "*Teiltexte*" that correspond to "paragraphs". Most of these paragraphs represent "forms" in the traditional form-critical sense of the word. It should be borne in mind, however, that my discussion can be only preliminary and tentative. One reason is that I do not take into account the structure of Revelation as a whole, although it is to be expected that one can ultimately form an opinion about the function of the partial texts only after one has reached a grasp of the whole.[9]

---

[6] Güttgemanns 1971, 186ff.

[7] Gülich/Raible 1975; iidem 1977a.

[8] E.g., Gülich/Raible 1977b, 53ff., 92ff.

[9] There are several ways of explaining the structure of Revelation; see, e.g., the suggestion and discussion of other contributions in Schüssler Fiorenza 1977.

(Another reason for stressing the tentativeness of the following suggestions is that their author can, at the most, be regarded as an amateur in the area of text-linguistics.)

The most important devices for demarcating a passage as a unit, a paragraph, are signals on the text's surface which organize the text (*Gliederungsmerkmale*).[10] But this organisation of a text can also be dependant upon or even mainly controlled by text-external conventions, e.g., literary "form"-conventions, which make it natural for a reader to delimit a partial text in a certain way.[11]

The *Gliederungsmerkmale* just mentioned not only separate partial texts, but they may also indicate in which hierarchical relationship they stand to each other, and how they interplay within the whole.[12]

Literary conventions outside of the text, of the kind just mentioned, may also contribute to the reader's structuring of the units. Here the genre concept enters the picture. One essential aspect of it is that, within a text that represents a genre, there is a two-way interplay between the whole and the partial texts. The parts interact and are organized hierarchically, thus constituting the whole. But this whole determines, as representing a genre, the parts, their intertextual functions, their function vis-à-vis the reader, their role in the communication of the message.[13]

Gülich and Raible present the following hierarchy of organizing signals (*Gliederungsmerkmale*):[14]

1. Meta-narrative (or meta-communicative) clauses, which delimit the narrative as a whole, dealing with communication on lower levels.
2. Substitution on a meta-level, i.e., reference to a text or a part of it as a communication through nouns like "story", "tale", etc.
3. Episode demarcators (*Episodenmerkmale*), i.e., signals concerning time, change of time, localization and re-localization.
4. Changes in the constellation of main actors.
5. Renominalization, i.e., the phenomenon that a main actor is reintroduced with a noun or his proper name. This signal often goes together with no. 4.
6. Adverbs and conjunctions which relate clauses or partial texts to each other.
7. Other signals that can have a text-organizing function in some languages are the changes between certain tenses like the *imparfait* and *passé simple* in French, and, furthermore, substitution on a level of abstraction. The latter

---

[10] See Gülich/Raible 1977b, 54.

[11] See Gülich/Raible 1977a, 151.

[12] Gülich/Raible 1977b, 42ff., 54f.

[13] E.g., Hempfer 1973, 92ff.

[14] Gülich 1976, esp. 242f. A somewhat broader presentation in Gülich/Raible 1977a, 140ff.

should be distinguished from 2 above, in that here "das Substituens einen grösseren Bedeutungsumfang hat als das Substituendum".[15]

We now turn to our texts. In dealing with each passage I will ask three groups of questions: (1) How is the passage delimited from its context? What "form" has it, i.e., does it follow any established literary convention, and how is it shaped? (2) What literary function does it have, and how does it interplay with the context? Here, as well as under (1) above, we will have to take into consideration not only Revelation but also material that presumably belongs to or bears witness to the referential background of author and reader. (3) Do the observations under (1) and (2) have any relevance for the message of the text?

2. Revelation 1-3

Rev 1:1-2. (1) The two verses are delimited from v. 3 by having different subjects. The "form" of the passage is that of a *titulus*.[16] As such it should give the title of the book, mention something about its content and inform about the author. In this case, however, it tells the reader about the writer and about the origin of that which he has written. John, the writer, is introduced in the third person. This way of introducing the divine messenger is similar to that in which Enoch is presented in 1 Enoch and, e.g., Jeremiah and Amos in their books in the OT.[17] The text is not unlike the beginning of, e.g., *1 Enoch*:

> The words of blessing of Enoch, with which he blessed the righteous elect who will be present on the day of tribulation to remove all the enemies, and the righteous will be delivered. He took up his parable and said — Enoch a righteous man whose eyes were opened by God, saw the vision of the Holy One in the heavens....

That is, the *titulus* of Revelation is rather normal in style and content.[18]

(2) Obviously these clauses are meta-communicative. They stand, so to speak, beyond the following text, introducing it and characterizing it.[19] The introductory lines quoted from 1 Enoch have a similar function.

(3) In dealing with the whole book and following traditional patterns in so doing, vv. 1-2 provide the reader with some basic information and give him a certain expectation and attitude as he approaches that which

---

[15] Gülich/Raible 1977a, 142.

[16] Kraft 1974, *ad loc.*

[17] Cf. also *3 Apoc. Bar.* 1:1f.: "A narrative and revelation of Baruch, concerning the ineffable things which he saw by command of God. Bless, Oh Lord". See also *Apc. Abr.*, title, and *Apc. Mos.* 1:1.

[18] That the author is not pseudonymous as in other apocalypses hardly matters — see Collins 1977.

[19] Gülich/Raible 1977a, 140f.

follows. The manner of revelation is intimated: ὅσα εἶδεν. Not least does the title render a most heavy authority to what follows by its chain of transmission: from God to Christ, to his servants.[20] This is then specified: the links closest to the reader are God's angel and John, whose testimony is thus God's words.

Rev 1:3. (1) As mentioned above, v. 3 stands apart from vv. 1-2 by having a different subject. The same is true in its relation to vv. 4ff. Its form is that of the macarism, and it is the first of seven macarisms in Revelation.[21] Even if they are right who think that a redactor has inserted the macarism of 1:3 in order to arrive at the number of seven, this can hardly justify a judgment like "aus diesem Grund ist die vorliegende Seligpreisung nichtssagend".[22] As compared to the other six, this macarism is peculiar in that it not only blesses the addressees (or rather a third person who apparently should be a representative of the addressees), but also the person who fulfils the cultic function of reading the text at the Christian service.[23] Mark 13:14 par. is a parallel as an exhortation to the reader to pay attention.

The grammatical construction of the macarism[24] is somewhat odd in its joining a singular and a plural subject under a singular μακάριος. Furthermore, it represents a longer variant of a macarism, i.e., it has an appended statement of the reason for the macarism, as in Matt 5:3: "blessed are the ones who are poor in spirit, *for* theirs is the kingdom of heaven". A macarism that is quite similar to the one in our text, but in a shorter form, is Luke 11:28: "blessed are the ones who hear the word of God and guard it".[25]

(2) Vv. 1-2 were characterized as meta-communicative clauses. Also the macarism of v. 3 certainly stands on a meta-level as compared to the following text. If vv. 1-2 take into account the text of Revelation, one may say that v. 3 also does so, but in addition, and above all, it does so with regard to the actual communicative act in which the text is made to work, i.e. the reading in the community.

---

[20] In the light of Rev 2:20; 7:3, and 19:2 "the servants" should denote not only the prophets. See the commentary. by Lohmeyer 1926, Lohse 1971, Kraft 1974 and cf. the ones by Bousset 1896 and Hadorn 1928, *ad loc.*

[21] Also Rev 14:13; 16:15; 19,9; 20,6; 22:7, 14.

[22] Kraft 1974, ad loc.

[23] This rare mentioning of the reader may go together with the fact that the author is not pseudonymous; in, e.g., *1 Enoch* or *Apc. Esdr.* the real author certainly has contemporary readers in mind as receivers and users of his text, but wearing the mask of, let us say, Enoch, he must use a more indirect style, stating as in *1 Enoch* that the blessing of the patriarch is "not for this generation but for a remote one" (1:2).

[24] For the form criticism of macarisms see Dupont 1969, 274ff.; Kähler 1974.

[25] In Rev 14:13 an explaining clause is added, and something similar is also found in 22:14, although there in the form of a ἵνα-clause.

With the wording "the words of the prophecy" the macarism takes up the expressions in vv. 1-2 that refer to the coming text ("revelation", "show", "signified", "witnessed God's words and the testimony of Jesus Christ") and specifies them: what follows is a prophecy.

A direct mentioning of the reader like the one in v. 3 is peculiar. But an *indirect* reference to the reader concerning the importance of the book is not uncommon in apocalyptic texts, although as a rule, the phenomenon occurs at the end of the text, as also in Rev 22:7, 18f. One should, however, remember that both at the beginning of a text and at its end one finds oneself on a border where it may be natural to survey the text as a whole. So the instruction that Gabriel gives Daniel in Daniel 9 is introduced by this exhortation: "understand the matter and consider the vision" (9:23). Cf. also a few lines from the ending of *Apc. Esdr.*: (Ezra prays:) "give all who copy this book and keep it and remember my name and celebrate my memory, give them blessing from heaven" (7:9).[26]

There are, however, texts which in other ways take the reader into account and which do so at the beginning, pointing to the importance of what follows. Such is the case in *1 Enoch* 37:2ff., were Enoch says:

> *This is the beginning of the words of wisdom which I lifted up my voice to speak and say to those who dwell on earth: Hear, men of old time, and see, you that come after, the words of the Holy One which I will speak before the Lord of Spirits. It were better to declare them only to the men of old time, but even from those that come after we will not withhold the beginning of wisdom. Till the present day such wisdom has never been given by the Lord of Spirits as I have received according to my insight, according to the good pleasure of the Lord of Spirits by whom the lot of eternal life has been given to me.*[27]

Thus, it seems to me, the function of Rev 1:3 is similar to that of other expressions at the beginning and at the end of similar texts, viz., to underline the importance of the text.

Maybe a certain light can be shed on the appearance of precisely a macarism at this place, if one takes into account the fact that macarism and blessing are closely related and almost interchangeable.[28] The macarism at this place may have a parallel in the benediction which, in the synagogue service, preceded the Scripture reading.[29] A similar practice may have left its traces in the first lines of *3 Apoc. Bar.* 1:1: εὐλόγησον δεσπότα.[30]

---

[26] See also *1 Enoch* 104:11ff.; *3 Apoc. Bar.* 17:4; *2 Apoc. Bar.* 86; *Apoc. Sedr.* 16:6, and cf. *Ep. Arist.* §311; *4 Ezra* 14:46f. For rabbinic parallels see Daube 1956, 424ff.

[27] See also *1 Enoch* 92:1; *4 Macc* 1:1; Luke 1:3.

[28] See e.g., Lefèvre 1957; Lipinski 1968, esp. 321f.

[29] See [Strack–]Billerbeck 1928, 159, 168. Presumably this custom has a continuation in the blessing of the deacon before his reading the gospel in the Mass.

In sum, as an utterance about the subsequent text and about the explicitly mentioned reader and his listeners, v. 3 renders further content to the readers' expectation. Though without exact parallels in terms of place and contents, it has the same function as other passages at the beginning or the ending of texts which are meant to impress their importance on the reader.

(3) Far from being "nichtssagend" this macarism draws the reader into the text itself, and thus also confronts him personally with the authority that, according to vv. 1f., is the origin of the revelation. In traditional usage a macarism tended to promise divine grace or salvation to the one who fulfilled the conditions given.[31] Here such gifts are bound to the "keeping" of the following prophecy.[32] All this renders an awful weight to a book so introduced.

Rev 1:4-5b. (1) These lines are separated from the preceding verses through the shift of person and the adoption of a fixed form, that of an epistolary address. The well established convention that a letter should begin in this way works as a strong demarcator that draws a clear borderline between vv. 3 and 4. No adverbs or conjunctions knit the address to vv. 1-3, nor are there any pronouns or articles that connect it to what precedes, although ὁ μάρτυς brings τὴν μαρτυρίαν Ἰησοῦ Χριστοῦ to mind. As normal, the address includes the mention of the writer, the addressee, and a salutation. The salutation is expanded in a manner found in the Pauline letter form.

The passage contains several triads: the salutation is given from the Holy Trinity, God has a threefold name, and Christ receives three attributes. Both the divine name and Christ's attributes are somewhat singled out by being kept in the nominative in spite of the governing ἀπό.

(2) and (3). With v. 4 we enter a new level of communication. The writer appears on the stage in first person, addressing his addressees. His name is explicitly mentioned. The fact that this name is the same as the one of the "servant" of v. 1 indicates to the reader that he is now going to receive the testimony of the word of God with which this servant was commissioned (v. 2). The epistolary address has the effect of making the rest of Revelation appear as a letter until its final greeting in 22:21.

The letter was an established form of Christian communication.[33] We come across it also in Jewish apocalypticism, where, in the *subscriptio* of the Chester Beatty manuscript, the last part of *1 Enoch* (91ff.) is called the

---

[30] Cf. also *Apoc. Esdr.* 1:1.

[31] E.g., Kraft 1974, *ad loc.*

[32] Cf. also *1 Enoch* 99:10.

[33] As generally in Antiquity see. e.g., Rahn 1969, 157ff.

Epistle of Enoch. Furthermore, *2 Apoc. Bar.* ends with the Epistle of
Baruch (78-86), which also is transmitted separately in the ms tradition.[34]

Seen against its context the address introduces the "word of God"
announced in vv. 1-3. John writes God's words to the receivers. I.e., the
form serves the aim to bridge the distance between God and man.

Rev 1:5c-6. (1) Without any connections with vv. 4-5b on the surface of
the text, vv. 5c-6 are a unit by themselves, being a doxology to Christ,
which is terminated, as normal, by an "amen". It is noteworthy that the
doxology is directed to Christ, and that it, as such, is rather developed in
that it expands on his work. In other early Christian literature there are
some Christ-doxologies in the later epistles (e.g., 1 Pet 4:11; 2 Tim 4:18),[35]
but they are of the shorter type: "to him be the glory for ever and ever,
amen". A longer form is represented by the one to God in 1 Tim 1:17: "to
the king of the ages, the immortal, invisible, only God — to him be
honour and glory for ever and ever, amen".[36] Actually Revelation is the
only writing in the NT in which one directs expanded doxologies to
Christ. Furthermore, no examples of it are to be found in the Apostolic
Fathers.

This doxology appears at the place where the Pauline letter form usually has a thanksgiving. But the difference is relatively small between our
doxology and some examples from the Pauline tradition. Thus, the
eulogy of 2 Cor 1:3ff. praises God's mercy and comfort, and the one of
Eph 1:3ff. blesses God for the realization of his eternal salvific counsel.
And in Gal 1:5 the address finishes in this way: "... our God and Father,
to whom be the glory for ever and ever, amen". I.e., in Galatians there is
a doxology and no thanksgiving.[37]

Outside the Christian tradition, although in its milieu, the Epistle of
Baruch (*2 Apoc. Bar.* 78ff.) begins in a way that may remind of our text.
After the salutation the text goes on: "I bear in mind (ʿhyd), my brethren,
the love of him who created us from old and never hated us, but above
all educated us".

The material in the address (1:4-5b) may be traditional to some
extent.[38] Some of these traditions may have had an original *Sitz im Leben*
at baptism.[39] But it is by no means given that this original *Sitz im Leben*

---

[34] To the Epistle as separately transmitted see Bogaert 1969, Vol. I, 67, 72f.; Vol. II, 140f.
[35] Also Heb 13:21; 2 Pet 3:18; 1 *Clem.* 20:12; 50:7.
[36] Also Eph 3:21; cf. 2 *Clem.* 20:5.
[37] Gal 1:5 is discussed in connection with Rev 1:5f. by Schüssler Fiorenza 1972, 172f. The
lack of the thanksgiving is usually explained as due to Paul's attack against his adversaries
in this letter. Cf. also Betz 1974-75.
[38] See Schüssler Fiorenza 1972, 198ff.
[39] See Schüssler Fiorenza 1972, 203ff.

meant anything in terms of what the wording communicated when the material had been recast into its present context.

(2) The convention established by the Pauline epistolary form makes a doxology at this place natural. The three ἡμᾶς refer to the writer and to his addressees in the preceding address. There might have existed a literary fashion that a praise of God at the outset of a letter should have some bearing on the theme of the *corpus* of the letter.[40] Such a relationship is evident, e.g., in the example from the Epistle of Baruch cited above, and something similar could possibly be expected also in Revelation.

(3) A couple of problems which bear on the message of the doxology and its relations to a wider context have appeared: on the one hand the question of how far an original *Sitz* of the recast traditions colours their meaning in the present text, on the other, how far a convention existed that a praise in an epistolary introduction puts forward things to be dealt with later on. If the latter can be affirmed, this doxology, together with the preceding address, has a steering effect on the understanding of the following pages.

Rev 1:7. (1) V. 7 could be termed a prophetic saying. It is separated from v. 6 through ἀμήν. As a rule commentators take v. 7 together with v. 8, but, as a matter of fact, the two verses are separated by ναί, ἀμήν and by the rather abrupt introduction of v. 8. The speaker is still the letter-writing John, although the saying is a conflation of OT passages and represents a traditional early Christian interpretation of the OT. It concerns an unmentioned third person who "comes with the skies". No doubt the subject is the same as that of the preceding doxology, Jesus Christ.

(2) In asking for the function of this verse in its context, we may start by quoting Lohse's statement on it (although he takes it together with v. 8): "ohne Übergang werden an den Eingangsgruss die Verse 7 und 8 angeschlossen, um den Inhalt des Buches anzukündigen".[41] W. Bousset and E. Schüssler Fiorenza call the two verses the "motto" of the book.[42] Leaving aside for the moment the function of v. 8, it is natural to ask whether such a suggestion can be substantiated for v. 7 by some kind of genre analysis. I cannot provide anything of this sort here, but I will adduce a couple of other texts in which we come across a manner of structuring the beginning of a book so that it contains a passage which may have a "motto"-like function.[43]

Thus, the first chapters of the Book of Zechariah contain the following: (a) an introduction in conventional style: in such and such a year the word of Yahweh came to so and so, saying…, (b) a call to conversion, (c)

---

[40] See Caragounis 1977, 50ff.; O'Brien 1977, 263.

[41] Lohse 1971, *ad loc.*

[42] Bousset 1896, *ad loc.*, Schüssler Fiorenza 1977, 358, referring to her 1972, 180-98.

visions. Here the sayings under (b) may have a place that recalls the "motto" of Rev 1:7. The beginning of the fifth book in 1 *Enoch* can also be mentioned. 1 *Enoch* 92:1 is a short prescript, then 92:2-5 says: "let not your spirit be troubled... for the Holy and Great One has appointed days for all things. And the righteous one shall arise from sleep...". Then the Ten Weeks Apocalypse is introduced: Enoch has been shown everything in a heavenly vision and has read the heavenly tablets.

It seems to me that both the passage in Zech 1 and the one from 1 *Enoch* 92 have a function that is reminiscent of the one Rev 1:7 may have[44], viz., they give an important hint at where the accents of the following should be found. As with Revelation, essential features of 1 *Enoch* 92:2ff. return at the end of the book (104:1ff.). One may discuss whether "motto" is the best term to describe its function; at any rate it seems plausible to regard the verses as a kind of solemn entering into the *corpus* of the writing which gives an indicator as to where important accents in what follows are to be found.

(3) If my deliberations concerning the "motto"-function are correct, they should have some consequences for the understanding of the whole work. But then one should have to find a balance in comparison to vv. 4-6, for which I suggested that they could reflect certain aspects of the book.

Rev 1:8. (1) V. 8 is a self-predication by God himself, introduced in the quotation formula by the same divine attributes as in the epistolary address in v. 4. It has the theme of "coming" in common with v. 7.

In his commentary to the Gospel of John,[45] R. Bultmann has differentiated four different forms of ἐγώ εἰμι formulas, viz. (a) *die Präsentationsformel*, answering the (explicit or implicit) question "who are you?". In the answer the speaker introduces himself. (b) Die *Qualifikationsformel*, answering the question "what are you?" by stating "I am this or that" or "I am the sort of man who". (c) Die *Identifikationsformel*, "in which the speaker identifies himself with another person or thing". (d) Die *Rekognitionsformel*, in which, in contradistinction to the previous cases, the *ego* is the predicate. It answers the question "who is the one expected, asked for, talked about?".

---

[43] Berger 1977, 29. understands the sayings as "Gerichtsankündigungen" which he thinks have a fixed place in the beginning of compatible writings, such as 1 *Enoch* 1:3-9; Mic 1:3; Nah 1:2; Zeph 1:2ff.; Amos 1:2. Although I would tend to agree with his general approach of explaining the arrangement by the "Form", I am not so convinced that his interpretation is correct. Also the texts adduced can very well be understood in the way I suggest as to Revelation.

[44] For a source analysis of 1 *Enoch* 92, see Dexinger 1977, 102ff.

[45] Bultmann 1941, 167f.

A problem is how to balance the type of content of the predication and its context. This is evident, e.g., from the fact that Bultmann refers to Rev 1:17 ("I am the first and the last") as a *Präsentationsformel*, but to Isa 44:6 ("I am the first and the last") as a *Qualifikationsformel*. It seems that, although it is not worked out, the context is given the upper hand in Bultmann's distinctions, and rightly so. In Rev 1:17 the context presents an epiphany that raises an implicit question answered by the formula. But Isa 44:6 is introduced by a quotation formula: "Thus says Yahweh…", and the preceding context contains divine promises of a salvation to be brought about by Yahweh. So Isa 44:6 "qualifies" the God who speaks through his prophet in the context.

What, then, about the context of Rev 1:8? It hardly gives cause for any kind of implicit question "who are you?" as in 1:17. So we are left with the second and third types, as it is evident that 1:8 is no *Rekognitionsformel*. I think that v. 8 is best labelled a qualification formula. "Alpha and omega" is evidently pictorial language and does not identify the Almighty with two letters, nor is he identified with that which the imagery denotes, viz., the beginning and the end.

(2) and (3) To call 1:8 a *Qualifikationsformel* is already saying something of its possible function in the context. He who gives himself this "qualification" is the one from whom the greeting in v. 4 is given, "who is, who was, and who comes". He is also the God who, according to 1:1, "gave the revelation to show that which will happen soon", and the God behind "the word of God" of which John was a witness (v. 2).

It seems difficult to establish the existence of a convention which could make in particular a divine self-predication natural at this place. Yet its position is so salient — together with v. 7 inserted between the doxology and the clearly demarcated new start in 1:9. The only literary convention we possibly have for our guidance is the one of the *Qualifikationsformel*. The self-predications of Isa, the contents of which are similar to ours (Isa 44:6; 48:12), seem both to underline the divine authority behind the prophecies in the context. Although it begins as a *"Präsentationsformel"* the self-predication at the beginning of the apocalyptic part of *Apoc. Abr.* (chap. 9) may help us a bit further:

> *A voice came to me speaking twice: "Abraham, Abraham". And I said: "Here am I". And he said: "Behold, it is I: fear not, for I am before the worlds, and a mighty God who has created the light of the world. I am a shield over you; and I am your helper. Go, take me a young heifer… And in this sacrifice I will lay before you the ages (to come), and make known to you what is reserved…*[46]

---

[46] English translation by Box.

At the outset of the apocalyptic part of *Apoc. Abr.*, this self-presentation of God indicates the authority behind the coming revelation, but there is also a clear connection between the contents of the predication and those of the apocalypse.

All in all, the foregoing deliberations may suggest the following as to the function of 1:8: it states the authority of "the words of prophecy" here introduced, an authority that holds the history, the secrets of which will be revealed. Furthermore, this all-mighty God is also, somehow, the authority behind the "coming" of v. 7. Thus the self-predication is also coupled to the "motto" of v. 7.

We have now dealt with the eight verses that commentators commonly designate as the introduction of Revelation. Is there any "hierarchy" among these partial texts? Obviously vv. 1-3 are the first partial text of the first degree, dealing on a meta-level with the letter, 1:4-22:21. This letter is, then, the second partial text of the same degree. Vv. 1-3 are, in their turn, divided into two partial texts, the *titulus* and the macarism, but they still, so to speak, hold sway over the rest of the introduction. The letter so introduced is divided into an introduction (1:4-8), a body (1:9-22:20), and a final greeting (22:21). The introduction, in its turn, is organized by the address, the doxology, and the two sayings of v. 7 and 8, respectively. It may be graphically displayed as follows:

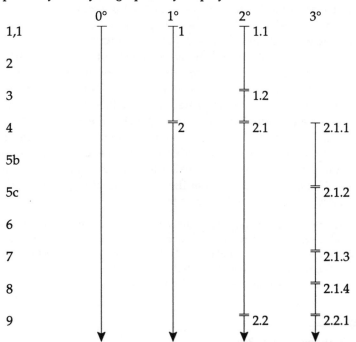

Rev 1:9-20. (1) The beginning of the passage represents several indicators that we are at a borderline in the text. Thus, to follow Gülich's and Raible's list above, we encounter episode-demarcators, i.e., information concerning time and place at the beginning of a narrative (Patmos, the day of the Lord), a change in the constellation of main actors (the voice, the one like a son of man), a re-nominalization (of John), and a transition to the narrative aorist tense. In addition, a further detail is of some importance, namely, that in the passage the first step in a transition from this world to another is taken — the ego "was in the spirit". These signals indicate the beginning of the main part of the letter begun in 1:4, or, if we want to use the term, the "inner story" (*die Binnenerzählung*)[47] of the work.

After 1:20 follow the seven messages, which are dictated within the framework of the vision of 1:9-20 and kept apart from it only through their closed form.

1:9-20 is a vision narrative[48] and can be described thus: (a) the visionary, place, time[49] and circumstances (vv. 9-10a), (b) ecstasy, (c) an audition, containing an order to write (vv. 10b-11), (d) the otherwordly being appears (vv. 12-16), (e) the visionary is afraid and is reassured (vv. 17a), (f) a self-presentation of the otherwordly being (vv. 17b-18), (g) a commission (v. 19), (h) an interpretation of a part of the vision (v. 20). It is noticeable that the passage combines an audition and a vision, and that it ends with an interpretation.[50] The general structure of the text is fairly similar, for example, to that of Daniel 10 and Ezekiel 1f. The form gives it two peaks, one being the commission to write, repeated twice, the other being the interpretation in v. 20.

(2) and (3) The vision is often labelled a call-vision and as such compared, for example, to those in Jeremiah 1, Isaiah 6 or Ezekiel 1f.,[51] Regarded in its context, the passage tells us about John's commission, which is presupposed behind the reference to John as revelation mediator in 1:1f. and behind his address to the seven churches in 1:4. So far the designation call-vision is justified. But the vision also contains an imagery that is a μυστήριον to be interpreted, and, moreover, one that apparently has to do with the commission to write to the churches. The

---

[47] Cf. Gülich/Raible 1975, 170f.

[48] Lindblom 1968, 220ff.: the text is a "Schilderung einer echten Vision" (220).

[49] The dating of the scene to the "Day of the Lord" may possibly be compared to the rather frequent feature in similar introductions, viz., some kind of worship; see e.g., Dan 9; 10:2ff.; 1 Enoch 12:3; 4 Ezra 5:20ff.; *Herm. Vis.* I,1,3.

[50] The verse has disturbed Kraft, who regards it as a redactional addition. Lindblom 1968, 222, does not think that the verse belongs to the "genuine vision" but to the "following reflection".

[51] E.g., Lohse 1971, *ad loc.*; Kraft 1974, *ad loc.*; Beasley-Murray 1974, *ad loc.*

description of the "one like a son of man" gives specific aspects to the authority behind that which follows. Its importance is stressed by the fact that features from the vision reappear in the seven messages of chaps. 2-3. The visions in, e.g., 4 Ezra have a similar authorizing function, and the heavenly journeys in *1 Enoch* 1:2 (cf. *1 Enoch* 12ff.), *T. Levi* 2ff. etc. are but variants with the same function.

It is certain that 1:9-20 introduces the seven messages of chaps. 2-3. Nevertheless it is clear that the demarcators on the literary surface strengthen the impression one gets that the order to write (v. 11) also refers to the writing of the whole book (cf. 1:4; 22:16). I will return to this question after having dealt with chaps. 2-3.

Rev 2-3. (1) As already stated, the seven messages are dictated within the vision of 1:9ff. The common identification of them as "letters" hardly meets the facts. Instead one should call them "prophetic messages".[52] Professor Hahn has analysed their construction form-historically and suggested that they represent a literary form used by early Christian prophets.[53] The messages are composed of four main parts, viz., (a) the messenger formula (*die Botenformel*), (b) the οἶδα-part, which is the most elaborate and the one that shows the most variants, (c) the call to hear (*der Weckruf*), and (d) the saying concerning the one who overcomes (*der Überwinderspruch*). Of these (a) is well rooted in OT prophecy, (c) belongs to a wider Christian tradition, and (d) is largely inspired by Jewish apocalyptic. As to (b), the οἶδα-part, Hahn says that one may find several *Vorstufen* to the individual elements but that there are no analogies to their combination. Instead he thinks that, both in terms of contents and form, the οἶδα-parts represent early Christian prophecy.[54]

Hahn's analyses seem to be to the point, but as there are no analogies to the οἶδα-parts outside of the Revelation, his contention as to the *Sitz* must remain a conjecture, and so must his suggestion concerning the form of the whole messages.

A few details in the vocabulary could be worthy of notice, since they tie the messages so closely to prophecy. The γράψον that introduces every message need not be understood as "write this letter to...". Rather we should paraphrase (sic!) it: "in the book you are writing to the seven churches write concerning...". It seems to me that the author is bound by the fact that he is commissioned with a written message, not a spoken one. Thus he cannot write, e.g., as in Ezek 20:30: "say to (the house of Israel): this says (the Lord Yahweh)...". For him it must be: "write to...: this says...".

---

[52] Cf. Lohmeyer 1926, 40, and Kraft 1974, *ad loc.*
[53] Hahn 1972.
[54] Hahn 1972, 376f.

Moreover, the οἶδα that introduces the central passages of these messages reflects the rather common expression in OT prophecies, according to which God "knows" the situation of those to whom the prophecy is directed.[55] One should also adduce 1 Cor 14:24f., according to which the prophecy reveals the secrets of the heart, accuses and judges.

Thus, even if Hahn's contentions about the form of the messages and its *Sitz* must remain conjectural, enough details in the form of the elements indicate that they should be understood as prophetic messages.

(2) As to the relationships to the context, we may first consider how the vision together with the seven messages is related to 4:1ff. It seems that in 4:1 a new partial text of the same degree as 1:9ff. begins. For there we encounter what Gülich and Raible call a relative episode demarcator (*relatives Episodenmerkmal*), viz., μετὰ ταῦτα, a change of place, a new main actor, and a renominalization (the voice).[56] The voice's promise that the writer will be shown ἃ δεῖ γενέσθαι μετὰ ταῦτα takes up 1:1 and the commission of 1:19: "write what you have seen and what is and ἃ μέλλει γενέσθαι μετὰ ταῦτα". Commentators have understood this commission as a short summary of the contents of Revelation:[57] the seven messages could correspond to "what is", and with chap. 4 the revelation of what is coming would begin. Others have thought that the messages contain enough of threats and promises for the future to satisfy the commission.[58]

Even though it is natural to think first that the seven messages are the fulfilling of the γράψον of 1:11 and 19, 4:1 widens its application. Further, it might be sound not to draw too sharp a line between present and future tenses in texts of this kind. For that which happens between the vision of 1:9ff. with its seven messages and the vision in chap. 4 is not only that the author is promised to see "what will happen hereafter" but also, and at least as important, that a further and more decisive step is taken in the transition from this world to another: in this case when the ego "was in the spirit" (4:2, cf. 1:10), he was ordered to ascend to heaven after having seen a heavenly door opened. This means that there is a more definite transition from Patmos to heaven. The writer will be shown things from the hidden, divine point of view.

What, then, can be the role of the seven messages in the composition? Without having been able to study the problem profoundly I dare propose the following answer. The seven messages have a double func-

---

[55] E.g., Jer 48:30; Hos 5:3; Amos 5:12; also 2 Kgs 8:12. Cf. *1 Enoch* 98:6.

[56] Gülich/Raible 1977a, 144ff., 152f.; Gülich 176, 242ff.

[57] So, e.g., Bousset 1896, *ad loc.*; Lohmeyer 1926, *ad loc.*; Hadorn 1928, *ad loc.*; Lohse 1971, *ad loc.*; Wikenhauser 1959, *ad loc.*; Beasley-Murray 1974, *ad loc.*

[58] Schüssler Fiorenza 1977, 362.

tion:[59] on the one hand they engage the readers/listeners, so that they become directly and explicitly involved in the prophecy; their own and their neighbours' virtues and vices are mustered. On the other hand, the messages correspond to a common phenomenon in revelatory literature, viz., that the divine revelation usually responds to problems and situations presented before or brought forward during the visions.

Thus *1 Enoch* 1-36 begins with a theophany which contains an accusation speech in 1-5, followed by an interpretation of Gen 6-9 that evidently takes the present time and its problems into view; e.g., the things which the fallen angels taught men are largely such as are easily associated with Hellenistic culture (*1 Enoch* 8). Enoch's vision of the divine throne follows in 14. In *2 Apoc. Bar.* there is a similar heightening of the degree of revelation in 22:1, in that the heavens are opened. Before this we have encountered a broad presentation of the problem at stake, viz., the destruction of Jerusalem.

(3) If my suggestions under (1) and (2) above hold water, they mean that Rev 2-3 should be regarded as prophetic messages that point to the real situation of the addressees, on which, from chap. 4 and on, they will have further light shed from a higher, divine perspective.

3. Revelation 22:6-21

It is a commonplace among authors dealing with Revelation that there is some kind of relationship between the beginning and the end of the book.[60] One usually explains it as the result of a redactor's work, which, moreover, is a bit awkward. It might, however, be of some interest to read the passage while asking the same questions as those with which we have approached the first chapters. It is, however, considerably more difficult to come to grips with these concluding passages. The reason for the confusion may of course, historically seen, be due to the redaction. But taking the text as a piece of communication, it is reasonable to ask how it may have worked as such in its present shape. The somewhat confused impression experienced by the reader may, then, lead him to feel that the author oscillates between different roles in his communication. As the classical prophets he may be regarded as the mediator of a divine message, as a spokesman for his fellowmen, and, furthermore, as one of those who receive the divine message.[61]

---

[59] Berger 1977, 181, thinks they function as farewell exhortations before the heavenly journey. It seems to me that the texts I adduce deliver better explanations.

[60] See, e.g., Schüssler Fiorenza 1977, who finds a chiastic structure of Revelation, in which, i.a. 1:1-8 and 1:9-3:22 correspond to 22:10-22:21 and 19:11-22:9, respectively.

[61] See, e.g., Rendtorff 1959, esp. 810ff.; von Rad 1968, 30ff.

In 1:1-8 we observed the steps leading into the main body of the letter, the "inner story" of the book. We will now see how we leave this story.

Rev 22:6f. is typical of the difficulties mentioned above. (1) The two verses are separated from the preceding context by the introductory "and he said", which signals a new start over against the preceding description of paradise. In 22:8 there is an even clearer demarcation line. Within the verses so brought together we can recognize one saying by a third person introduced by "he said" (v. 6), one saying in the first person sing., without any introduction but added to v. 6 by a καί (v. 7a), and one macarism on "the one who keeps the words of the prophecy of this book" (v. 7b).

The context suggests that the speaker of v. 6 is the angel[62] who is on the stage from 21:9 (cf. 21:9f.; 22:1, 6). In the first-person saying in v. 7a we recognise the "motto" of 1:7, held there in the third person, Christ being the subject. The macarism of v. 7b reminds of the one in 1:3, and the one who utters it is the "I" of v. 7a *or*, possibly, the angel of v. 6.

Confronted with this unevenness between v. 6 and v. 7a the understanding that seems most natural is that the angel is thought to convey God's or Christ's words to such an extent that he can do so without using an explicit introductory formula — the preceding ἀπέστειλεν has to be enough. One may compare Gen 31:11ff., where Jacob says, "the angel of God said to me: 'Jacob...'. I answered: 'Here I am', and he said: '... I am the God who appeared to you...'".

(2) Seen in its context vv. 6f. are the concluding phase of the passage which began in 21:9, where the presentation of the angel signals the introduction of a new main actor. The angel "shows" the visionary the heavenly Jerusalem (21:10), "shows" him the river of life (22:1), and ends up by "saying" 22:6f. Thus, the two verses are a partial text on the same level as 21:10ff. and 22:1ff. forming together with them a partial text that represents the last "demonstration" of the book. But, on the other hand, the words of the angel refer to the preceding text as a totality by labelling it οὗτοι οἱ λόγοι[63] and evaluating it. In a sense the saying may be on a meta-level in relation to the whole book, as is the macarism of v. 7b. If, however, οὗτοι οἱ λόγοι refers only to the heavenly scroll of 5:1,[64] then the macarism widens the outlook to the whole prophetic work of John. As compared to the meta-clauses of 1:1ff. these clauses (or at least the macarism) are parts of the communication they deal with.

---

[62] E.g., Rissi 1972, 84.

[63] The expression appears earlier in 19:9 and 21:5, but this time its denotation is obviously wider than in those instances.

[64] Bornkamm 1963, esp. 205.

At any rate, the verses are a marker that we are approaching the end of the book. One may compare with the following "Substitution auf Metaebene" that E. Gülich gives as an example from M. de Navarre: "Voylà, mes dames, une histoire veritable qui doibt bien augmenter le cueur à garder ceste belle vertu de chasteté".[65] The phrase puts an end to the story, looks back on it, contains an address to the audience of the "utter story", and evaluates the "inner story".

It is not uncommon that in Jewish apocalypses the authors end their books by referring to the publication and to the importance of the contents in view of the eschaton. Daniel 12 is one example, and in *1 Enoch* 104 the righteous are summoned to be hopeful (104:2, 4), not to fear but to keep away from all the wickedness of the sinners (cf. Rev 22:11) — then they will become the companions of the host of heaven (104:6 Eth.). In 104:11ff. references are made to the book itself: "my (i.e., Enoch's) books will be given to the righteous and the wise for joy and righteousness and much wisdom ... then shall all the righteous who have learnt from them all the paths of righteousness be recompensed" (Eth.).

It seems to me that the author of Revelation follows a similar literary convention in ending his book by evaluating its contents and stressing its importance for the reader in view of the eschaton.

(3) Our discussion of 22:6f. has pointed to the function the verses have as an evaluation of the revelation which now is ending. The citation of the "motto" as a direct divine saying becomes a reminder from the source of the revelation about the perspective in which the multicoloured visions, etc., should be understood. The same source is made responsible for the promise to the faithful observer of the prophecy.

Rev 22:8-11. (1) A borderline is created by the "renominalization" ("I, John") in v. 8 (cf. 1:4, 9). The scene has some features of an epiphany: a human being before a divine being is struck by awe and is then reassured, after which he receives a commission.

(2) There are several details that mark the passage as one which prepares for the ending of the book: the seer refers to his visions and auditions and to that which the angel has shown him. That means that a new string is being tied around the text-package, but by John, and, strictly speaking, only concerning the previous text from 1:9 where the first vision began. The angel's reference to the book in v. 9 should be of the same meta-type as in v. 7. This is the last time that the angel and John are on the stage.

The first saying of the angel makes the visionary *and* his addressees the companions of the angel, i.e., the addressees who keep the words of the book that they are presented with. The second saying of the angel (v.

---

[65] Gülich 1976, 245.

10f.) receives a stronger paraenetic accent in the perspective of the approaching crisis.

The exhortation as well as the commission to publish the book remind of Daniel 12, but also the example from *1 Enoch* 104 cited above is a parallel.[66]

(3) On his way out from the world of visions the author ties the readers/listeners more securely to the mysteries he has revealed. They are the presumed companions of the revealing angel, the message they have received has a divine authority and is meant to be kept by them till the salvation is theirs.

Rev 22:12-16. (1) The verses represent some sayings of Jesus. They take up the "motto" again, now with an added promise of reward (v. 12). Next follows a self-predication that is a variation of the one in 1:8, although here the "I" is Jesus (v. 13). V. 14 is a macarism (cf. Dan 12:12) upon the ones "who have cleansed their robes" — they will enter the city. V. 15 puts the "dogs", etc., in contrast — they will remain outside. It is not until v. 16 that it becomes clear that Jesus is the speaker from v. 12 and on. This late-coming information of the identity of the "I " draws the line between vv. 11 and 12ff. through a change of the main actor. The ἐγὼ Ἰησοῦς also means a renominalization. The self-predication seems to be of the same type as the one in 1:8, i.e., a qualification formula.

(2) and (3). If we count three links between God and the reader, the book not included, viz., Christ, the angel and John, the angel leaves by v. 11, and so does John in as far as his "seeing" (cf. 1:2; 22:8) is concerned. Christ, the speaker of vv. 12-16, remains. Of course one could have wished to be informed of *how* Jesus speaks, let us say, through a vision or an audition. Such things are, however, left behind by vv. 8-11. One might combine this phenomenon with the fact that the book is introduced as ἀποκάλυψις Ἰησοῦ Χριστοῦ. Jesus appears, as an author may do when the "action" or the "inner story" of his work has come to an end, and now addresses his readers himself.

The place of these Jesus-sayings, which, by the way, contain a good proportion of traditional material,[67] reminds of the ending of Daniel. There the *angelus interpres* gives his order on sealing the book in v. 4 (cf. Rev 22:10). Then in vv. 5-13 we encounter additional sayings and promises.

So 22:12ff. indicate one further step out of the book: the introduction presented the book as a revelation of Jesus sent to the churches (1:1, 4).

---

[66] Cf. also the ending of 4 Ezra (14:42ff.), according to which the books are written down under divine inspiration, after which twenty-four of them are published to be read by worthy and unworthy and seventy kept to be delivered to the wise.

[67] See Kraft 1974, *ad loc.*

Now this revealer looks back on his revelation (ταῦτα, v. 16) which his angel has witnessed to the churches. He adds a self-predication that somehow should be combined with the contents of the testimony. That is to say, it should be of some significance that the one who sent his messenger with "this" presents himself as exactly one who is described with two originally OT Messianic motifs, viz., the root of David and the morning star. Maybe the attributes qualify the origin of the revelation as the one who comprises the salvation history and "in whom the dawn of the new age of righteousness and peace has already broken".[68]

Rev 22:17 raises intricate questions in terms of communication. Who says that "the spirit says"? And to whom? I cannot answer these questions here, but it may be helpful to remind ourselves of the different roles of a prophet intimated above: God's messenger, man's spokesman, himself one of the addressed.[69] Here it seems fair to assume that the public setting (cf. 1:3) of the book is brought into the book itself, presumably in a reflection of the *Maranatha* cry. The shift from the Jesus-voice (ἐγώ ...) to that of the spirit and the bride (λέγουσιν) may be compatible to the different prophetic roles just suggested. The ὁ ἀκούων, then, is also the one who listens to the book.

This way of drawing the audience into a more active role in the communication at the end of a book has certain parallels in other apocalypses. In the ending of *1 Enoch*, touched upon already, the righteous are addressed and summoned to pray: "in your cry, cry for judgment" (*1 Enoch* 104:3), and *3 Apoc. Bar.* ends thus: "you brethren, who have obtained such a revelation, glorify God also yourselves" (17:4).

Rev 22:18-19. A stressed shift of person introduces this paragraph. Commonly it is regarded as John's words, although it is quite possible to ascribe them to Jesus.[70] Its function is to ascertain the authority of the book in its entirety.[71] It goes back to Deut 4:2 and has a counterpart, e.g., in *1 Enoch* 104:10ff.

Rev 22:20 is singled out as introducing ὁ μαρτυρῶν as a speaker. If Christ is the first person behind μαρτυρῶ in v. 18, then ὁ μαρτυρῶν, which clearly is Christ, takes up v. 18 again. The verse takes into account the cultic use of the book in a way reminding of v. 17. Furthermore, v. 20a contains a third citation of the "motto" at the ending of the book, but now with a stronger reference to the communication situation: it is not only the "motto" of the communication contained in the recited text, but also a direct address through the mouth of the prophet to the audience,

[68] Beasley-Murray 1974, *ad loc.*
[69] Cf. *Did.* 13:3 "... they (i.e., the prophets) are your high priests".
[70] As is done by Moe 1965, *ad loc.*
[71] Beasley-Murray 1974, *ad loc.* Cf. Bousset 1896, *ad loc.*

whose answer is voiced by the same prophet in v. 20b: "yes, come O Lord Jesus".

Rev 22:21, finally, is the end of the letter, begun in 1:4. The salutation is similar to that of several early Christian letters (1 Cor 15:24; 2 Cor 13:13; Gal 6:10; Phil 4:23, etc.).

Looking back at the partial texts of chapter 22 that we have discussed, we may ask ourselves whether it is possible to surmise any kind of hierarchy similar to the one I suggested for the introduction.

Our deliberations have shown that the partial texts of the last chapter lack the relatively distinct demarcators found at the beginning. A very tentative suggestion is, however, the following: it seems that 22:6f. is the last partial text within 21:9-22:7, which is the last series of visions and demonstrations, begun in 1:9. Simultaneously this concluding partial text prepares for the ending of the book and gives a first evaluation. 22:8-11 is the last of the narrative partial texts, the first of which is 1:9ff. 22:12-20 may be taken as two concluding groups of sayings of Jesus, the "author" of the ἀποκάλυψις (1:1), each followed by a kind of reaction. The passage could then be regarded as the third partial text within the letter begun in 1:4 (the first being 1:4-8 and the second the narrative part 1:9-22:11). Rev 22:21 is then the fourth partial text of the letter, its final benediction.

So much for these remarks on partial texts in the beginning and concluding parts of Revelation. They certainly are anything but firm and decisive, but maybe they have demonstrated that text-linguistics may be helpful when biblical scholars want to use form criticism for their task to try to understand the communication of biblical texts. If this is so, it could be worthwhile to pursue a study of this kind through the whole of Revelation, and, not least, to do it with more depth and accuracy than has been possible in this contribution.

Bibliography

Beasley-Murray, G. R. 1974: *The Book of Revelation* (NCB), London: Marshall, Morgan & Scott 1974.

Berger, Kl. 1977: *Exegese des Neuen Testaments* (UTB 658), Heidelberg: Quelle & Meyer 1977.

Betz, H. D. 1974-75: "The Literary Composition and Function of Paul's Letter to the Galatians", in: *NTS* 21 (1974-75) 353-79.

Billerbeck, P. [–Strack, H. L.] 1928: *Kommentar zum Neuen Testament aus Talmud und Midrasch IV/1*, München: Beck 1928.

Bogaert, P.-M. 1969: *Apocalypse de Baruch* I-II (SC 144/145), Paris: Cerf 1969.

Boll, F. 1914/67: *Aus der Offenbarung Johannis* (ΣΤΟΙΧΕΙΑ 1), Leipzig – Berlin: Teubner 1914 [= reprint Amsterdam: Hakkert 1967].

Bornkamm, G. 1963: "Die Komposition der apokalyptischen Visionen in der Offenbarung Johannis", in: idem, *Studien zu Antike und Urchristentum* (BEvTh 28), 2nd ed., München: Kaiser 1963, 204-22.

Bousset, W. 1896: *Die Offenbarung Johannis* (KEK 16), 5th ed., Göttingen: Vandenhoeck & Ruprecht 1896.

Bultmann, R. 1941: *Das Evangelium des Johannes* (KEK II), Göttingen: Vandenhoeck & Ruprecht 1941.

Caragounis, C. C. 1977: *The Ephesian Mysterion* (CB.NT 8), Lund: Gleerup 1977.

Charles, R. H. 1920a: *The Revelation of St. John*, Vol. I (ICC), Edinburgh: T. & T. Clark 1920.

— 1920b: *The Revelation of St. John*, Vol. II (ICC), Edinburgh: T. & T. Clark 1920.

Collins, J. J. 1977: "Pseudonymity, Historical Reviews and the Genre of the Revelation of John", in: *CBQ* 39 (1977) 329-43.

Daube, D. 1956: *The New Testament and Rabbinic Judaism*, London: Athlone 1956.

Dexinger, F. 1977: *Henochs Zehnwochenapokalypse und offene Probleme der Apokalyptikforschung* (StPB), Leiden: Brill 1977.

Dupont, J. 1969: *Les béatitudes* I (ÉB), Paris: Gabalda 1969.

Gülich, E. 1976: "Ansätze zu einer kommunikationsorientierten Erzähltextanalyse (am Beispiel mündlicher und schriftlicher Erzähltexte)", in: W. Haubrichs (ed.). *Erzählforschung 1* (Zeitschrift für Literaturwissenschaft und Linguistik [LiLi], Beiheft 4), Göttingen: Vandenhoeck & Ruprecht 1976, 224-57.

Gülich, E./Raible, W. 1975: "Textsorten-Probleme", in: H. Moser (ed.), *Linguistische Probleme der Textanalyse* (Institut für deutsche Sprache. Jahrbuch 1973; Schriften 35), Düsseldorf: Schwann 1975, 144-97.

— 1977a: "Überlegungen zu einer makrostrukturellen Textanalyse: J. Thurber, The Lover and His Lass", in T. A. van Dijk/J. S. Petöfi (eds.), *Grammars and Descriptions (Studies in Text Theory and Text Analysis)* (RTT 1), Berlin – New York: de Gruyter 1977, 132-75.

— 1977b: *Linguistische Textmodelle* (UTB 130), München: Fink 1977.

Güttgemanns, E. 1971: *Offene Fragen zur Formgeschichte des Evangeliums* (BEvTh 54), 2nd ed., München: Kaiser 1971.

Hadorn, W. 1928: Die Offenbarung des Johannes (ThHK 18), Leipzig: Deichertsche Verlagsbuchhandlung 1928.

Hahn, F. 1972: "Die Sendschreiben in der Johannesapokalypse. Ein Beitrag zur Bestimmung prophetischer Redeformen", in: G. Jeremias/H.-W. Kuhn/H. Stegemann (eds.), *Tradition und Glaube. FS K. G. Kuhn*, Göttingen: Vandenhoeck & Ruprecht 1972, 357-94.

Hempfer, K. W. 1973: *Gattungstheorie* (UTB 113), München: Fink 1973.

Kähler, G. Chr. 1974: *Studien zur Form- und Traditionsgeschichte der biblischen Makarismen* (typed diss., Jena), Jena 1974 (abstract in: *ThLZ* 101 [1976] 77-80).

Kraft, H. 1974: *Die Offenbarung des Johannes* (HNT 16a), Tübingen: Mohr (Siebeck) 1974.

Lefèvre, A. 1957: "Malédiction et bénédiction", in: *DBS* 5 (1957) 746-51.

Lindblom, J. 1968: *Gesichte und Offenbarungen. Vorstellungen von göttlichen Weisungen und übernatürlichen Erscheinungen im ältesten Christentum* (SHVL 65), Lund: Gleerup 1968.

Lipinski, É. 1968: "Macarismes et psaumes de congratulation", in: *RB* 75 (1968) 321-67.

Lohmeyer, E. 1926: *Die Offenbarung des Johannes* (HNT 16a), Tübingen: Mohr (Siebeck) 1926.

Lohse, E. 1971: *Die Offenbarung des Johannes* (NTD 11), 3rd ed., Göttingen: Vandenhoeck & Ruprecht 1971.

Massyngberde Ford, J. 1975: *Revelation* (AncB 38), Garden City, NY: Doubleday 1975.

Moe, O. 1965: *Johannes uppenbarelse* (Tolkning av Nya testamentet XI), Stockholm: Diakonistyrelsen 1965.

Müller, H.-P. 1963: "Die himmlische Ratsversammlung. Motivgeschichtliches zu Apc 5:1-5", in: *ZNW* 54 (1963) 254-67.

O'Brien, P. T. 1977: *Introductory Thanksgivings in the Letters of Paul* (NT.S 49), Leiden: Brill 1977.

von der Osten-Sacken, P. 1967: "'Christologie, Taufe, Homologie' — Ein Beitrag zu Apc. Joh 1,5f.", in: *ZNW* 58 (1967) 255-66.

von Rad, G. 1968: *The Message of the Prophets*, London: SCM 1968.

Rahn, H. 1969: *Morphologie der antiken Literatur*, Darmstadt: Wissenschaftliche Buchgesellschaft 1969.

Rendtorff, R. 1959: "προφήτης", in: *ThWNT* 6 (1959) 796-813.

Rissi, M. 1972: *The Future of the World. An exegetical Study of Revelation 19.11-22.15* (SBT; 2nd Ser. 23), London: SCM 1972.

Schüssler Fiorenza, E. 1972: *Priester für Gott* (NTA 7), Münster: Aschendorff 1972.

— 1977: "Composition and Structure of the Revelation of John", in *CBQ* 39 (1977) 344-66.

Wikenhauser, A. 1959: *Die Offenbarung des Johannes* (RNT 9), 3rd ed., Regensburg: Pustet 1959.

Supplement

Lambrecht, J.: "A Structuration of Revelation 4,1 - 22,5", in: J. Lambrecht (ed.), *L'Apocalypse johannique et l'apocalyptique dans le Nouveau Testament* (BEThL 53), Paris – Gembloux: Duculot / Leuven: Leuven University Press 1980, 77-104.

Vanni, U.: *La struttura letteraria dell' Apocalisse*. (Aloi. 8a), 2nd ed., Brescia: Morcelliana 1980.

Prigent, P.: *L'Apocalypse de Saint Jean* (CNT(N) 14), Louvain – Paris: Delachaux & Niestlé 1981.

Popkes, W.: "Die Funktion der Sendschreiben in der Johannes-Apokalypse. Zugleich ein Beitrag zur Spätgeschichte der neutestamentlichen Gleichnisse", in: *ZNW* 74 (1983) 90-107.

Müller, U. B.: *Die Offenbarung des Johannes* (ÖTBK 19) Gütersloh: Mohn/ Würzburg: Echter 1984.

Roloff, J.: *Die Offenbarung des Johannes* (ZBK 18), Zürich: Theologischer Verlag 1984.

Schüssler Fiorenza, E.: *The Book of Revelation — Justice and Judgment*, Philadelphia, PA: Fortress 1985.

Hellholm, D.: "The Problem of Apocalyptic Genre and the Apocalypse of John", in: A. Y. Collins (ed.), *Early Christian Apocalypticism. Genre and Social Setting (Semeia* 36 [Decatur, GA: Scholars Press 1986]), 13-64.

Hemer, C. J.: *The Letters to the Seven Churches of Asia in Their Local Setting* (JSNT.S 11), Sheffield: Sheffield Academic Press 1986.

Karrer, M.: *Die Johannesoffenbarung als Brief. Studien zu ihrem literarischen, historischen und theologischen Ort* (FRLANT 140), Göttingen: Vandenhoeck & Ruprecht 1986.

Deutsch, C.: "Transformation of Symbols: The New Jerusalem in Rv 21:1-22:5", in: *ZNW* 78 (1987) 106-26.

Contreras Molina, F.: "Las cartas a las siete iglesias", in: *EstB* 46 (1988) 141-72.

Kirby, J. T.: "The Rhetorical Situations of Revelation 1-3", in: *NTS* 34 (1988) 197-207.

Aune, D. E.: "The Form and Function of the Proclamations to the Seven Churches (Revelation 2-3)", in: *NTS* 36 (1990) 182-204.

Hellholm, D.: "The Visions He Saw or: To Encode the Future in Writing. An Analysis of the Prologue of John's Apocalyptic Letter", in: Th. W. Jennings, Jr. (ed.),

Text and Logos. The Humanistic Interpretation of the New Testament. FS H. W. Boers (Scholars Press Homage Series), Atlanta, GA: Scholars Press 1990, 109-46.

Schüssler Fiorenza, E.: *Revelation, Vision of a Just World* (Proclamation Commentaries), Minneapolis, MN: Fortress 1991.

Scobie, C. H. H.: "Local References in the Letters to the Seven Churches", in: *NTS* 39 (1993) 606-24.

8. "Teste Sibylla"

Construction and Message
in the Fourth Book of the Sibylline Oracles[1]

Scholars often use texts as "material" for their investigations of subjects within the fields of history. Thus, Professor Borgen, to whom this article is dedicated, has made a name for himself through his studies of texts by Philo, in order not only to enlarge our knowledge on this philosopher's thinking but also to inform the scholarly world about ideas held in wider circles of non-Palestinian Greek-speaking Jews at the beginning of our era.

Notwithstanding, a risk lurks in textual work of this kind, viz. that the texts are reduced to receptacles of ideas, motifs or conceptions. When a scholar tries to reconstruct the author's thinking as reflected in these texts, he may combine items from several such receptacles. The risk does not consist in consideration of the ideas contained in the texts, nor in the attempts to reconstruct the ideologies underlying them. But reduction of the texts into pots of conceptions may lead to a disregard for the fact that these conceptions function both within the literal contexts in which they are contained and vis-à-vis the reader; the latter function is achieved *via* the text-internal one. In consequence of such misuse, in my opinion, not least many so-called apocalyptic texts have been seriously misinterpreted — I have in mind chiefly those of the early Judaism.[2] In this paper, I shall attempt to demonstrate the possibility of discerning the main purpose of an "apocalyptic"[3] text, merely by reading it carefully in seeking the two functions I just mentioned. The text chosen, *Sibylline Oracles IV*, will be our "witness".[4]

---

[1] English transl. of Hartman 1987.

[2] I have dealt with this issue several times; see particularly Hartman 1975-76 [No. 6 in this volume]; idem 1979, esp. chapter 5, and idem 1983.

[3] I do not use "apocalyptic" here as referring to a genre, but as an adjective concerning the type of contents. But note that the term is vague. It is mostly used with reference to eschatological contents of a particular kind, but there are apocalypses which do not have such contents.

The fourth book of the so-called Sibylline Oracles belongs to the Jewish portions of this otherwise mostly Christian collection (books 3-5 in particular have a Jewish origin). The book was written around 80 C.E., but its geographical origin is a matter of dispute.[5]

In order to make it easier to follow my deliberations below, I shall translate selected parts of the hexameter into a somewhat rough prose.[6] For every passage I shall ask how the motifs work within the context, and what the author is doing vis-à-vis his reader. The reader of these pages who is interested in the theory of interpretation, will realize that my approach is coloured by a text-linguistic focus on communication. I shall not, however, use its complicated, technical terminology.

> 1   *Listen, you people of boastful Asia and Europe,*
>   *to the perfect truths which, through my wide-sounding mouth,*
>   *I shall prophesy from our Great One.[7]*

This is the beginning of an introduction which continues until v. 23. It deals with the following text and is thus on a meta-level in relation thereto. In this position it is, on the one hand, an appeal to the audience, and on the other, characterizes that which is to follow. The attributes with which the audience is addressed indicate that the speaker has serious objections to their conduct. Moreover, information is given as to which kind of message the listener will encounter: it is a prophecy, i.e. its contents are serious and come from the divine world through a human medium. The author also claims that this prophecy is true *per se*.

> 4   *I am not an oracle-monger of the false Phoibos, whom vain*
>   *men called a god and, falsely, a seer,*
>   *but of the Great God, whom hands of men have not made*
>   *like the speechless idols of hewn stone,*
>   *for he has no image,[8] no stone set up in a temple,*
>   *dumb and toothless, a painful shame to humans.*

---

[4] The Latin expression of the headline is of course inspired by the first strophe of the *Dies irae* of the Requiem Mass.

[5] Because of the baptism, mentioned in v. 165, several scholars suggest that the book has its origin in Syria or in the Jordan valley. Others prefer Asia Minor, yet others Egypt. See further J. J. Collins' introduction to his translation of book 4 in Collins 1983, 381f. It seems to me, however, that his argument against regarding Egypt as the place of origin is weak; he advances the temple criticism of vv. 5-12 and 27-30 as support. Most of its strength is dissolved if we read εἰκόν instead of οἶκον in v. 8.

[6] The numbering of the verses follow, as does the translation, the edition of the Greek text by Kurfess 1951.

[7] Or with a conjecture (which is unnecessary in my opinion): "from our temple".

[8] Or, with other mss., "no house".

10 But he cannot be seen from earth, nor be measured
    with human eyes, he is not shaped by mortal hand;
    seeing all at once, he is himself seen by none;
    his are the dark night, the day and the sun,
    the stars and the moon and the fish-filled sea,

15 and the earth and rivers and the mouth[9] of the ever-flowing
        springs,
    things created for life, the rains also, which engender the fruit
        of the soil,
    and the trees and the vine and also the olive.
    This one drove his whip in my mind
    in order that everything present and everything that once
        will be

20 from the first generation until the coming of the tenth —
    this I was to narrate accurately. For he will prove everything
        (to be true)
    by accomplishing it. So, listen, you people, to the Sibyl in
        everything,
    when she pours forth true speech from her holy mouth.

These lines too are a text about the following text. It consists of two main sections: vv. 4-17 first explain who the sender really is, so indicating the authority of the coming message. It can be divided into some minor parts: in vv. 4-5 the traditional view that the Sibyl was Apollo's prophet-ess is rejected; instead (v. 6 onward; note the "not – but" of vv. 4 and 6), the origin is with "the Great God"; he is firstly characterized in negations as compared with the idols — we easily recognize the echoes of tradi-tional Jewish polemic: he is un-created and invisible (vv. 6-11); thereafter he is presented in positive terms: he is the creator of the universe who holds everything in his hand (vv. 12-17).

In the second section (vv. 18-23) the presentation of the Great God serves the message: it is this powerful god who compels the Sibyl — the author's mouthpiece — to speak. ("This one" of v. 18 covers the descrip-tion in vv. 4-17 and confirms that it is a unit.) Vv. 19-20 briefly tell the readers/listeners the content of the coming message, viz. the future as regarded from the point of view of the primeval Sibyl, covering the his-tory through the tenth, i.e. the last, "generation". They will soon realize that "generation" could rather be rendered "age". The authority of the prophecy — and of its origin — will be demonstrated by its coming true (vv. 21b-22). The fact that the real author is at work shortly after most of the "prophesied" events have occurred, i.e. after the eruption of Vesu-vius in 79 C.E. (vv. 130ff.), enables him to undergird the validity of his

---

[9] Or, with other mss., "beverage".

message concerning what to expect thereafter. With a new appeal and a further hint that the prophecy is true (v. 22-23), the introduction comes to an end.

Thus, the introductory lines are not primarily a polemic against polytheism (as suggested by Professor Collins' headline in the Charlesworth edition), but rather emphasize the authority of the coming message and intimate its contents.

With v. 24 the corpus of the text begins:

> *Happy will be those men on earth*
>
> 25 *who love the Great God, saying a blessing*
> *before eating and drinking, trusting in piety.*[10]
> *They reject all temples which they see,*
> *and the altars, vain statues of deaf stones,*
> *stained with blood from living creatures and with sacrifices*
>
> 30 *of four-footed animals. They will regard the great glory of the*
>   *only god,*
> *not committing reckless murder or making money*
> *with stolen goods — all most horrible deeds —*
>
> 33 *nor have shameful desires for another's bed.*
>
> 35 *Their pious life and manners other men will*
> *never imitate — they strive for shame.*
> *They sneer at them with mockery and laughter*
> *and childishly accuse them falsely without sense*
> *of the reckless and evil deeds they themselves commit,*
>
> 40 *for unfaithful is the whole human race. But when once*
> *comes the judgment of the world and of the mortals, which*
>   *God himself*
> *will hold, judging impious and pious,*
>
> 43 *then*[11] *he will send the impious down into the dark, into fire.*
>
> 45 *But the pious will stay on the fruitful earth*
> *and God will give them spirit and life and grace.*
> *But all this will be fulfilled in the tenth generation.*

One may wonder what is the function of this introductory part of the textual body. The author has informed his readers/listeners that he will tell them what will come to pass through ten generations (v. 20); why does he not begin by so doing but devote this passage to morality? If, for

---

[10] Or, "in faithful piety".

[11] The καί before τότε may appear somewhat harsh. But the author expresses himself in the same way in vv. 43, 87, and 159.

a while, we refrain from asking about the author's intention and seek instead the probable effect of what he is doing in these lines, we may surmise an answer. Thus, the morality he predicts belongs to a future which is only partly a future to the first readers/listeners, for they easily perceive that the morality which will one day prevail, according to the Sibyl, closely resembles that of their own days. The righteous way of life so described apparently complies with Jewish rules; it will stand out as impeccable and receive its recompense in the judgment which will be held in the tenth generation. The readers will soon understand that they belong to this tenth generation, and, furthermore, that they live in its final phase. So, two features in this passage on ethics apply to them: the Sibyl's blessing of the righteous should be comforting, and, reversely, her proclamation of the terrible destiny which awaits the wicked, should warn them against falling away. Thus, the readers are told that they live in a time of crisis, and they are indirectly admonished to stay faithful in order to receive the blessed reward of the pious and to avoid the dreadful fate which may otherwise befall them.

The construction of the passage is evident. In v. 24 the people who are blessed are easily identified as Jews: they love God (cf. Deut 6:5) and demonstrate this by saying the *berakhah* before meals (v. 25-26), In vv. 27-33, the author enlarges on how these Jews show their love of God: they obey the commandments on monotheism (vv. 27-30), on stealing (vv. 31-32), and on adultery (v. 33). In contrast, their wicked slanderers are depicted in vv. 35-40a. With v. 40b the eye is lifted to the future: the future tense becomes future also from the point of view of the readers, and we glimpse the ultimate reason behind the blessing of the righteous, viz. the last judgment and its consequences (vv. 40b-47). The change to this outlook to the future is made through the turn of phrase "but when …, then" (ἀλλ' ὅταν … καὶ τότε; vv. 40b, 43), which we shall encounter at several other similar transitions. Again, the author proceeds through contrasts, opposing the fate of the wicked (v. 43) to that of the righteous (δυσσεβέας μέν … εὐσεβέες δέ; vv. 43-46).

The readers have now learnt that the events which will come to pass during ten generations have a goal in the tenth, and, furthermore, that then only those who have led a godly life, viz. one which is somehow Jewish can be considered happy; they can also surmise what sort of bliss awaits these persons. Those who recognized their own way of life in that praised by the Sibyl, and who had also experienced the derision described — and such experiences were common among Diaspora Jews — should feel encouraged by this message.

In the context of the literary composition as a whole, vv. 24-47 provide the readers with a clue to the book. It does not simply concern "everything which will one day occur", as was intimated in v. 19. Instead, the final stage, "all these things" (v. 47) of the tenth generation constitute what really matters in the coming presentation, because then the impious will be condemned and the pious rewarded; the impious and the pious are precisely those described in vv. 24-40 who belong to the days of the readers. So it also turns out that in these Sibylline prophecies the topic piety – impiety is crucial in the final phase of the tenth generation, when this enters what we would term its eschatological phase. There the topic constantly returns,[12] indeed in each of the periods which — as we shall see — are delimited by the "but when ...".

> 48   But now I shall tell what will happen from the first generation.
>   First, the Assyrians will rule over all mortals,
>
> 50   having the world in their power for six generations
>   from the time when, because of the wrath of the heavenly god
>   with the cities themselves and with all men,
>   the sea covered the earth when the Flood burst forth.
>   When the Medes have destroyed them, they will boast on
>   their thrones.
>
> 55   To them but two generations are given ...
>
> 65   The power of the Persians will be the greatest of the whole world;
>   to them is given a single generation of prosperous rule.
>   All evil will occur which men pray to be spared:
>   wars and murders and discord and exile ...
>
> 76   But from Asia a great king will come, raising his great spear ...
>
> 83   Hellas will have strife; raging against each other
>   they will overthrow many cities ...

Here nine generations pass in rapid succession, from the Flood onwards. Verse 48 introduces the review to the readers (on a meta-level) and tells them what will come. The phases too are defined: six (v. 59) + two (v. 55) + one generation (v. 66), and the readers can recognize some details from the history with which they may be familiar, e.g., Xerxes (v. 76) and the Peloponnesian Wars (vv. 83ff.).

Since the readers have recognized at least some events which have hitherto been prophesied, the authority and trustworthiness of the Sibyl and of her god are thereby confirmed — as we remember, they were emphasized in the very beginning of the book. Inasmuch as the passage on ethics in vv. 24-47 ended in an anticipation of the tenth generation, the

---

[12] Of course other terms belong in the word field, but let me just select the words from the root –σεβ–: εὐσεβ– in vv. 26, 35, 42, 45 in this introduction; then in vv. 117, 136, 152, 156, 170, 187, 190; ἀσεβ– or δυσσεβ– in vv. 42, 43, 112, 167, 171, 184.

section concerning the first nine generations comes to resemble a parenthesis, the contents of which tend to confer the authority in the way just
mentioned.

86 *But when the human race comes to the tenth generation,*
then the Persians must submit to yokes of slavery and terror.
But the Macedonians will boast of scepters ...

102 *Nor will the strength of the Macedonians remain, but from*
the West
a great Italian war will rise, under which the world
will serve the Italians, bearing the yoke of slavery.

105 *And you, miserable Corinth, will one day see yourself captured ...*

115 *Also to Solyma the evil storm of war will come*
from Italy, and it will assault the great Temple of God ...

119 *And then a great king will flee from Italy like a runaway slave ...*

125 *To Syria from Rome will come a chief, who in fire*
will burn the Temple of Solyma and then kill many
and devastate the great land of the Jews with its broad highways ...

The transition to this phase is marked by a renewed "but when ... then"
(ἀλλ᾽ ὅταν ... καὶ τότε; vv. 86f.), and by the explicit mention of the tenth
generation. We are now at the beginning of the generation which we
have been told will be the last, the decisive. The reader is still able to
identify the events predicted. First, we hear of the two great powers
which are characteristic of the generation, viz. the "Macedonians" (vv.
87-102a) and the "Italians" (vv. 102b-128). The lines selected from the text
contain examples of the predicted deeds of the Romans, viz. the capture
of Corinth in 146 B.C.E. (v. 105), the fall of Jerusalem (vv. 115ff. and
125ff.), and the flight of Nero (v. 119). The notice of the latter is inserted
into the prophecy on Jerusalem, which, to some extent corresponds to
history: the Jewish revolt began in 66 C.E., Jerusalem was stormed by
Titus in 70, and Nero fled from Rome in 68 (and committed suicide later
in the same year, although there were rumours that he was not dead but
would return — cf. vv. 137ff.).

130 *But when, erupting from a cleft in the land of Italy,*
a firebrand reaches to the broad heaven ...

135 *know then the wrath of the heavenly God,*
because they will destroy the innocent tribe of the pious.
Then the struggle of a rising war will come to the West
and the fugitive from Rome will raise the great spear,
crossing the Euphrates with many thousands.

140 *Wretched Antioch ...*

142 *Woe betide you, miserable Cyprus, the broad wave of the sea*
       will cover you ...

145 *Great wealth will come to Asia; riches which once Rome*
       herself stole and stored in her house of many possessions;
       and then she will pay back twice as much and more
       to Asia, and then there will be a surfeit from the war.
       And the cities of the Carians, along the waters of the Maeander,

150 *all with beautiful towers, a bitter famine will destroy,*
       when the Maeander hides its dark water.

On the textual surface these lines are delimited by "but when ... then" (ἀλλ' ὁπόταν ... τότε) at the beginning of v. 130 and in v. 135. The similar construction in v. 152 (ἀλλ' ὅταν) marks the beginning of a new phase in the series of events contained in the prophecy. Here the construction holds vv. 130-136 together: "when" (v. 130) the volcanic eruption takes place, "then" (v. 135) this shall be taken as a sign that God is angry because of the assaults on the pious (note that now the topic of piety etc. returns!), When these lines pick up that what was said in vv. 37f. on aggression, and in vv. 41f. on God's judgment, this tells the reader that the new phase which now starts, is the beginning of the end. The whole message becomes more intrusive when the readers realize that this is the last historical event reported which they can clearly identify. (Probably the eruption did not lie far back in time when the text reached its first audience.) The gravity of the situation is emphasized by the "theological" interpretation: God's wrath should be glimpsed therein; no similar comment is made on any previous event apart from the Flood, vv. 51ff.[13]

The second part of this section, vv. 137-151, is introduced by "then" (τότε, meaning "at that time" or "after that"). We still hear of concrete mundane events, but they occur under the shadow of God's wrath which now prevails. But the wars and disasters now prophesied are such as the writer expects to ensue, and to some extent his expectations seem to be coloured by his Jewish traditions, which could attribute such phenomena to the tribulations of the last days.[14] The scene is Syria and Asia Minor under a Roman Empire which appears to be tottering. The latter point of view also holds true of vv. 145-148 which seem to expect the Asian communities to take vengeance on Rome.

---

[13] There may be a vague hint at God's punishing wrath in v. 117 which says that the Temple is destroyed because people put their trust in folly.

[14] Thus we also recognize them from New Testament texts which have a similar outlook: wars (v. 137) — cf., e.g., Mark 13:7f., natural disasters (vv. 142ff.) — cf., e.g., Mark 13:8, famine (vv. 149ff.) — cf., e.g., Mark 13:8.

Thus, the section has the following construction. Under the shadow of God's wrath wars are first predicted (vv. 137-139); thereafter follow two woes (vv. 140f.[15] and 143f.) and two further predictions of disasters (vv.145-148 and 149-151), the first of which, however, is fatal mainly for Rome.

> 152 *But when piety disappears from men,*
>   *faith and righteousness are hidden in the world ...*
>
> 156 *And nobody takes account of the pious, but also them*
>   *will all the wholly puerile destroy in foolishness,*
>   *rejoicing in outrage and with their hands ready for bloodshed,*
>   *then know that God is no longer mild*
>
> 160 *but gnashes his teeth in anger and destroys*
>   *all humankind in a great fire.*
>   *Oh, wretched mortals, change these things and do not lead*
>   *the Great God to all sorts of wrath, but put away*
>   *sword and groaning, murder and outrage,*
>
> 165 *wash the whole body in perennial rivers*
>   *and stretch out your hands to heaven and ask*
>   *for forgiveness for your former deeds and cure*
>   *your bitter impiety with praise. And God will grant conversion*[16]
>   *and not destroy. He will still his anger again, if you all*
>
> 170 *practise honourable piety of heart.*
>   *But if you do not obey me, you evil-minded, but love*
>   *impiety and receive all these things with evil ears,*
>   *there will come a fire over the whole world and a mighty sign*
>   *with sword and trumpet with the rising of the sun.*
>
> 175 *The whole world will hear a cry and a mighty noise.*
>   *He will set the whole earth on fire and destroy the whole*
>   *human race*
>   *and all cities and rivers, as well as the sea.*
>   *He will burn everything and it will become smoking dust.*

A renewed "but when ... then" (ἀλλ᾽ ὅταν ... καὶ τότε, vv. 152 and 159) marks the beginning of a new phase, the topic of which is presented in the first line: this deals with impiety in the last days and its consequences. Impiety – piety were envisaged in vv. 24-47 and taken up again in v. 136 onwards; now they are drawn into the centre of interest[17] and, in addition, with a theological framework — when people see the moral

---

[15] If v. 142 is taken into the text — which Kurfess 1951 does not — it becomes somewhat more muddled.

[16] Or: "God will repent".

[17] The root –σεβ– is found in vv. 152, 156, 167, 170, 171, and then in vv. 184, 187, 190.

misery they shall "know" that God is angry and threatens to burn the whole world. This holds vv. 152-161 together. V. 159 sounds like an echo from v. 135, but here the motif of God's wrath is more developed and the mindful readers will recall the anticipatory section, vv. 40-47, where the impious were threatened with darkness and fire. Thus, it is made clear to the audience that this end is near when, and because, immorality increases. But they must remember too that this end is also intended to lead to a blessed life on the part of the righteous (v. 45f.).

Vv. 162-178 are closely linked with the preceding passage by the "this" (τάδε) of v. 162, for it refers to the wrath-evoking immorality described in vv. 152-161. It is defined as a section by the use of the second person plural, directed to the "mortals" and introduced by the particle ᾶ. This address reveals the author's principal interest, because before, he employed a more general mode of speech, presenting the crisis; in this crisis he now directly addresses the impious in his audience, exhorting them to "change" (v. 162): they must repent and be baptized. The imperatives of vv. 162-168a constitute, as it were, a protasis to an apodosis made up of the positive assurances of vv. 168b-170: do this — and God will .... Then he resorts to a negative note, now in an explicit protasis – apodosis-construction: if the impious do not act as he urges them, then the great conflagration will ensue (vv. 171-178). The second person plural address is retained. "All these things" (τάδε πάντα) of v. 172 refers to the whole of the preceding text, but particularly to the warnings and accusations therein; this indicates once more the aim of this text, viz. that the wicked in the audience should repent.

One could say that the writer presents the Sibyl as speaking to a non-Jewish audience with a message which is similar to that of John the Baptist. He preached about the approaching judgment using such imagery as the axe laid to the root of the tree, a baptism in fire, and the cleansing of a threshing floor and the burning of the chaff. According to the Sibyl the conflagration of all is at hand. Both John and the Sibyl proclaim the necessity of conversion in such a situation, and point to a baptism linked up with a confession of sins. Moreover, as already stated, here is the heart of the text, and there are signs in the text itself that this is so.

179 *But when everything has already become dust and ashes*
   and God quenches the unspeakable fire as he kindled it,
   God himself will again give shape to man's bones and ashes
   and raise up the mortals as they were before.
   And then there will be a judgment, in which God himself
      dispenses justice
   and judges the world again. And all who in impiety

185 *sinned, them will again a mould of earth cover*
    and the broad Tartarus and the dreadful nooks of Gehenna.
    But all who are pious will live again on earth,

189 *when the Immortal gives life and imperishable riches.*[18]

190 *Then all the pious will thank him,*[19]
    when they see the pleasant light of the delightful sun.
    Oh, most blessed the man who then will be on earth!

For the last time a new phase of the tenth generation is marked by a "but when ..." (ἀλλ᾽ ὅταν). The preceding text implied that the great conflagration could be avoided if people would obey the Sibyl and repent. But nevertheless, the author apparently assumes that the conflagration will take place. Maybe if a few converted, these could instead rejoice with the saved, for in them is obviously the author's interest. So the pious readers need not be unduly distressed by the terrible fate of the world, because in some kernel passages the book says that to them the conflagration is only a transition to a new and better world which will be theirs. The piety topic returns also here in the culmination of the book, which was actually expected from vv. 45f. in the introduction.

In this section we hear of the steps on to the new age. Although God is the agent behind the preceding conflagration,[20] he is here emphatically presented as the actor, just as in the anticipatory vv. 40-47. First, he performs the resurrection of the body (vv. 179-182), then he acts as judge. This judgment is the theme of vv. 183-184a (cf. vv. 41f.), to which is added a description of the fates of the pious and the impious, divided into two parts, each beginning with "and all who are" (ὅσσοι δ᾽; vv. 184b-186, 187-191, respectively). The fate of the wicked is the tomb and Gehenna (cf. v. 43), whereas the pious can look forward to bliss on a new earth (in praise of God? — the text is uncertain). When the happy fate of the pious is mentioned at the end and, moreover, is emphasized through the final macarism, this makes being and remaining pious a goal really worth striving for. This concluding macarism corresponds to the macarism at the beginning of the corpus in v. 24. There, as well as here, the reason is that the pious are pious and are therefore to be rewarded.

In my understanding, this way of speaking of the bliss which awaits the pious has a double effect. On the one hand, vis-à-vis the impious it emphasizes the positive consequences which a conversion would have,

---

[18] Geffcken 1902, 102 takes this verse as no. 188, deletes it, and chooses, with several mss., to render as v. 189 a reading which is a repetition of v. 46.

[19] The mss. offer many variant readings. Collins 1983, 389 chooses one saying: "they will see themselves".

[20] Thus v. 161, but in vv. 173-178 he is not mentioned.

on the other, it encourages those who already recognize themselves as pious, to remain steadfast, despite persecutions and adversities (which can be surmised at some places in the text[21]). That the piety topic plays such an important role in every stage of the "interesting" section dealing with the tenth generation, points in the same direction.

In a survey I shall now summarize how the text appears to be structured.

1.   1-23 introduction *on* the book.
   1.1.   1-3 summons to attention.
   1.2.   4-17 presentation of the authority behind the text.
      1.2.1.   4-5 who is not the authority.
      1.2.2.   6-17 who is the authority.
         1.2.2.1.   6-11 his negative attributes.
         1.2.2.2.   12-17 his positive attributes.
   1.3.   18-22a the commission; how given, contents.
   1.4.   22b-23 summons to attention.
2.   24-192 the body of the message.
   2.1.   24-47 introductory macarism of the heroes and description of them (3rd pers.).
      2.1.1.   24-40a the heroes as living in the time of the readers.
         2.1.1.1.   24-33 the identity of the heroes.
         2.1.1.2.   34-40 the opponents of the heroes.
      2.1.2.   40b-47 the heroes in the future (as related to the readers' time) (ἀλλ' ὅταν ... καὶ τότε).
   2.2.   48-192 the promised message (νῦν δ'; meta-clause on what follows).
      2.2.1.   48-85 preparatory portion (generation 1-9; confirming authority).
      2.2.2.   86-192 the promised, topical portion (generation 10).
         2.2.2.1.   86-129 prophecies on the first part (relatively un-interpreted and neutral; ἀλλ' ὅταν ... καὶ τότε).
         2.2.2.2.   130-192 prophecies on the eschatological part.
            2.2.2.2.1.   130-151 part on mundane things but with a transcendent perspective (*i.a.*, "pains"; ἀλλ' ὁπόταν ... τότε).
               2.2.2.2.1.1.   130-136 point of departure: introductory historical event (Vesuvius; ὁπόταν).
               2.2.2.2.1.2.   137-151 predictions of expected events (wars, disasters; τότε).

---

[21] Vv. 35ff., 136, 156ff.

2.2.2.2.2.   152-178 "moral" part with a transcendent, eschatological perspective (ἀλλ᾽ ὅταν ... καὶ τότε).

  2.2.2.2.2.1.   152-161 prediction of a phase of immorality, causing God's wrath.

    2.2.2.2.2.1.1.   point of departure: immorality (ὅταν).

    2.2.2.2.2.1.2.   consequence: God's wrath (καὶ τότε).

  2.2.2.2.2.2.   162-178 admonitions (2nd pers. plur.; ἃ).

    2.2.2.2.2.2.1.   162-170 admonitions to repentance, and promises in case of obedience.

    2.2.2.2.2.2.2.   171-178 threats ("if not – [then]).

  2.2.2.2.3.   179-192 final eschatological part (ἀλλ᾽ ὅταν ... καὶ τότε).

    2.2.2.2.3.1.   179-182 prediction of situation of departure (resurrection; ὅταν).

    2.2.2.2.3.2.   183-191 prediction of the decisive event (distinguishing heroes from opponents through judgment; τότε).

      2.2.2.2.3.2.1.   183-184a setting the theme (judgment).

      2.2.2.2.3.2.2.   184b-186 prediction of the fate of the opponents (ὅσσοι μέν).

      2.2.2.2.3.2.3.   187-191 prediction of the fate of the heroes (ὅσσοι δ᾽).

    2.2.2.2.3.3.   192 macarism on the heroes (ὦ μακάριστος).

The above chart may prompt somebody to ask the present writer: "do you think that the author planned this composition in such an organized and systematic manner?" My answer is "yes and no". Of course he knows what he is doing when he structures the contents of his text according to a pattern of ten generations. It was also an established practice, *inter alia*, in Jewish apocalypticism, to lay a foundation of trustworthiness under one's message. Moreover, it is a normal rhetorical device for a speaker to introduce his message in such a way that the audience becomes interested in it and is also informed of some essential features of its contents. Moreover it is normal in human language to use fixed, repeated turns of phrase to structure a text and to mark phases in the development of its contents.

Furthermore, to create tensions within a text through contrasts is a common rhetorical device, and we all know how to hold a text together and to create structures in it by using summarizing and deictic pronouns and adverbs. Thus, most of the factors which organize our text are more or less conventional. For consequence it becomes well nigh meaningless to ask whether the author of the fourth book of the Sibylline Oracles used them consciously or unconsciously. Undeniably they are there, and, to my mind at least, they make sense.

To a reader who does not share the conventions behind texts like the Fourth Book of the *Sibylline Oracles*, such a myopic reading as the above may be helpful when it comes to understanding them. At least it is my contention that this has come true in our case. The analysis has shown how the text has two aims: on the one hand, it seeks to proclaim the need for conversion and baptism for those whom the author calls impious. That which he says of the pious shall emphasize this message. On the other hand, the text should encourage those already pious to be steadfast. The message has an eschatological perspective, but its point is not to present the diary of the future; rather, such an outlook gives a meaning to the present time and its demands on the pious.

Bibliography

Collins, J. J. 1983: "The Sibylline Oracles, Book 4. Introduction and Translation", in: J. H. Charlesworth (ed.), *The Old Testament Pseudepigrapha, Vol. 1: Apocalyptic Literature and Testaments,* Garden City, NY: Doubleday & Co 1983, 381-89.

Geffcken, J. 1902/67: *Die Oracula Sibyllina,* Leipzig: Hinrichs 1902 [= reprint: Leipzig: Zentral-Antiquariat der DDR 1967].

Hartman, L. 1975-76: "The Function of Some So-called Apocalyptic Time-Tables", in: *NTS* 22 (1975-76) 1-14 [No. 6 in this volume].

— 1979: *Asking for a Meaning. A Study of 1 Enoch 1-5* (CB.NT 12), Lund: Gleerup 1979.

— 1983: "Zur Hermeneutik neutestamentlicher eschatologischer Texte", in: H.-J. Zobel (ed.), *Hermeneutik eschatologischer biblischer Texte,* Greifswald: Ernst-Moritz-Arndt-Univ. 1983, 30-48.

— 1987: "Vad säger Sibyllan? Byggnad och budskap i de sibyllinska oraklens fjärde bok", in: P. W. Boeckman/R. E. Kristiansen (eds.), *Context. Essays in Honour of P. Borgen* ("Relieff" 24), Trondheim: Tapir 1987, 61-74 [This is the English transl. of that essay].

Kurfess, A.-M. 1951: *Sibyllinische Weissagungen,* Berlin: Heimeran 1951.

II.

Argumentative Texts

Pauline and Deuteropauline Letters

9. On Reading Others' Letters

"My mother taught me that reading others' letters isn't nice." Those, or something like them, were the words of Krister Stendahl when he once tried to open the eyes of his audience to some of the hermeneutical problems which pertain to the fact that Christians read Paul's letters as if they were addressed to themselves rather than to their original recipients.[1] The following reflections deal with these problems, and they are meant as a humble tribute to my first teacher in New Testament exegesis. I begin by recalling a few facts that are intriguing once one puts them together. This will lead me to the suggestion that, when he wrote his letters, Paul had a wider usage in mind than we usually assume. Against such a background I shall discuss, in a rather unsophisticated way, some conditions that may apply to a rereading of the Pauline letters and some possible consequences for so-called historical exegesis.

First, then, a few well-known facts concerning Paul's letters. The old differentiation between "letter" and "epistle"[2] is still often referred to in NT introductions, although their authors assure us that the Pauline letters are real letters, not artificial ones (i.e., epistles).[3] On the other hand, the same introductions usually tell us that Paul's are not to be equated with private letters. Certainly several details can be compared to what one finds in private letters,[4] such as epistolary address, introductory thanksgiving, etc. But their length alone makes them appear to be something else, not to mention their contents. In these respects one may regard them, instead, as some sort of treatise. In some cases, notably 2 Corinthians and Philippians, their length, together with other peculiarities, has led to suggestions that they are, in fact, an editorial conflation of several letters.[5]

A further fact about the Pauline letters has not yet really been integrated into the handbooks, namely, that an increasing number of studies

---

[1] Stendahl 1976, 6.

[2] Deißmann 1923, 193-213.

[3] Kümmel 1975, 249; Wikenhauser and Schmid 1973, 385; Vielhauer 1975, 53; Schenke/ Fischer 1978a, 27.

[4] E.g., Doty 1973.

[5] Schmithals 1964; Gnilka 1968, 5-11. For 2 Corinthians see, e.g., Kümmel 1975, 289.

point to the role that rhetoric played in their composition, style, and argumentation.[6] That is, they represent types of argument and construction that one would not expect to encounter in occasional private letters.

The fact that texts characterized by such length, content, and style have been written down is in itself noteworthy. In the age of computers and word processors, one easily forgets that conceiving and writing a text like Galatians or Romans was a long and wearisome procedure.[7]

The rhetorical features could fit with some considerations raised in the scholarly discussion of the literary form of Paul's letters. It was a rather common idea in antiquity that a letter replaced or represented its author.[8] In our case the letters represented the presence of the apostle, the missionary. Letter-writing was almost a necessity for a man like Paul, who was burdened with extensive obligation and responsibility.[9] Letter-writing offered him further possibilities for fulfilling his missionary duties. Thus several NT introductions invite one to regard Paul's letters as apostolic ministerial writings.[10]

In dealing with Paul's apostolic zeal, we should also remember Paul's tendency to develop a broad theological argument, even when he is dealing with a comparatively small or trivial matter.[11]

It may be too much to say that the above-mentioned facts present us with a riddle. But there is a tension between the occasional character of the letters — their addressing a quite specific situation — on the one hand, and these facts on the other. I suggest that this tension is resolved if we assume that Paul intended his letters to be read and reread in the communities to which they were addressed, and in others as well. He probably also kept copies of his letters.[12] Those letters which may be the result of compilation also fit into such a picture; the edition may have been made by Paul himself, or even by his "school",[13] though on his behalf. We need not posit a later generation of devotees to find someone who held in high esteem Paul's apostleship and his acting as an apostle. Paul himself did so. It was not a post-Pauline generation that got the

---

[6] One of the pioneers has been Hans Dieter Betz; see idem 1974-75, and 1979, 14-25. See also Berger 1974, 224-28, and Standaert 1983. Cf. White 1984, 1733.

[7] Roller 1933, 8-14.

[8] Funk 1967; Thraede 1970, 146-50.

[9] Schenke/Fischer 1978a, 31.

[10] Kümmel 1975, 249; Wikenhauser/Schmid 1973, 385; Vielhauer 1975, 62. Cf. Berger 1974.

[11] Dahl 1967.

[12] It seemed a matter of course to Hermann von Soden; see idem 1913, VII (cf. Roller 1933, 260); see further Henshaw 1963, 208.

[13] For the idea of a Pauline "school", see Conzelmann 1965-66, 233; Lohse 1971, 181. Hans Martin Schenke dates the collection and editing activity of the "school" to a time after Paul's death (idem 1974-75, 508-14).

bright idea that a teacher's letters deserved to be reread and even to be more widely known. This idea and practice existed in the contemporary world among both Jews and Gentiles.[14] Moreover, Paul's letters are not private letters (like Cicero's to his family), but are apostolic messages.

The suggestion of the preceding paragraph can be supported by certain characteristics of the letter to the Colossians, depending on how one dates the letter. In an article in 1966, E. P. Sanders demonstrated that Colossians is literally dependent on the seven undisputed Pauline letters, and in a unique manner at that.[15] His results indicate that the author of Colossians was not Paul and that he knew and was well versed in several, if not all, of the letters recognized as genuine.

The person who wrote (or dictated) Colossians did not go through a collection of Pauline letters, seeking good Pauline expressions in order to be able to sound like the apostle.[16] Although familiar with Paul's texts, the author of Colossians did not use them slavishly or mechanically. Instead the author stands out as an independent theologian who thought in a Pauline way and was able to meet new problems using and readjusting Paul's teachings. Indeed the author appears so dependent (and independent) that scholars like C. F. D. Moule and W. G. Kümmel think the author is Paul himself![17]

The manner in which the author of Colossians uses Paul's letters does not indicate that they were regarded as Scripture, but it does presuppose availability of and familiarity with a collection of Paul's letters.

For my part I assume that Colossians was written by a rather independent Pauline disciple (why not the co-author, Timothy?) when Paul was in prison in Rome. I find this idea more natural than to assume that the author cleverly "writes to" a community that does not exist any more — after the earthquake in the Lycus valley in the early sixties — when there would be less chance of being detected![18] Furthermore, we would have to assume that just to sound reliable the author took the trouble to construct a list of salutations, based on the letter to Philemon,[19] and elaborate on it.

Such a view of the authorship of Colossians also corroborates my suggestion that copies of earlier Pauline letters had been kept with Paul or at his "school" and had been read and reread by his disciples. This would be the place where a collection of his letters was available prior to its

---

[14] See, e.g., Schneider 1954, 567, 570-72; Berger 1974, 212-19.

[15] Sanders 1966.

[16] Cf. the simple imitations in the apocryphal Laodicea letter.

[17] Kümmel 1975, 340-46; Moule 1967, 13-14.

[18] Schenk 1983, 140.

[19] Schenke/Fischer 1978a, 167; Vielhauer 1975, 200.

release "on the market". But such an archive and such rereading also intimate that Paul aimed at a wider audience for his letters than we usually assume.[20]

If, on the other hand, one dates Colossians at, say, ca. 70,[21] this usage of other Pauline letters in Colossians must mean at least one thing: its author had a collection of Paul's letters with which he had lived for some time. He may have obtained them like a devoted collector, but it is also possible, indeed probable to my mind, that he obtained them because he had been close to Paul or a member of his "school" during the apostle's lifetime. Thus, also with this dating, the use of Paul's letters in Colossians can support the idea that Paul kept copies of his correspondence. However it may relate to the assumption that he had a wider audience in mind, it hardly speaks against it.

If Paul had in mind a wider circle of readers than the ones mentioned in the letter openings, then the task of interpreting Paul's letters is affected. I therefore turn to some reflections on this problem. In so doing I am consciously entering a jungle. The path I cut through it leaves many philosophical, linguistic, literary, and exegetical problems aside, probably more than I imagine.

This kind of "reading others' letters" is not unique. Many texts formulated in and for given occasions are reread and reused in new situations, at new places, and even in new times. They are reused, then, not simply as charming or revered fossils, but as texts that have something important to tell the new audience. Other examples in antiquity are the OT scriptures (during and after their formation), the classical dramas, Plato's letters, etc.

Different attitudes behind such a rereading of occasional texts can be associated with the three aspects that text-linguistics isolates in a text: the syntactic, semantic, and pragmatic ones. Of these, the last one regards the text as a whole, functioning with its addressees in their situation. It does so not least through its contents, which are considered under the semantic aspect. The content, in its turn, is mediated by the text's network of words, phrases, sentences, etc. (i.e., the text seen from a syntactic point of view).[22]

By focusing on the syntactic aspect of a text, one can use its wording without respect at all to its contents and function. Thus 1 Cor 11:19,

---

[20] The fact that the Pauline letters have not left any certain traces in Acts (von Harnack 1926, 7) is a weak argument against my suggestion. In order to be an argument it must presuppose that Luke had the same theological interest in Paul's letters as modern theologians have. The apocryphal Acts of Paul also disregard them. Cf. the pointed arguments of Jacob Jervell in idem 1979.

[21] Thus, e.g., Schenke 1974-75, 513; Gnilka 1980, 23.

[22] For these three aspects of a text, see Morris 1938/71.

"there must be factions among you", may be cited as nothing more than a somewhat ironic comment on a quarrelsome meeting. Another reader, however, may refer to the same sentence as a decisive scriptural argument against ecumenism. Both interpretations disregard the semantic and pragmatic aspects of the text. The first uses it as a turn of phrase, nothing more; the second one relies on a particular view of scriptural inspiration. This latter view holds that Paul's occasional letter, arguing here against certain abuses at the Lord's supper, is in every detail full of God's eternal word and God's ever valid message, always capable of answering new questions.

Another example of rereading a Pauline text is from Luther's commentary on Galatians. In commenting on 3:23-24 he understands it in this way: "The Law must be laid on those who shall be justified ... not as if they could win justification through the law (that were to misuse the law ...) but so that, after having been terrified and humbled through the Law, they flee to Christ."[23] This understanding of the Galatians passage regards it from a semantic perspective, in a framework of Pauline theology as contained in Galatians and as understood by Luther.[24] But this semantic aspect is not combined with the pragmatic one, which means that the reading largely disregards the precise debate in Galatia.

In a third kind of rereading the text with its expressions and contents is strictly understood as a message in its concrete historical situation. Here it becomes little more than a museum item, insofar as it is taken as a truly occasional text. It could be reused only if the occasion repeated itself. But very often an occasional text deals with an occasional issue by treating it almost as a type of problem, assessing it on a general basis. In this case the pragmatics of the text could be found represented to such an extent in a new situation that the text, in all its three aspects, could be readdressed to it.

A presupposition behind the two latter reusages of (more or less) occasional texts is the assumption that they contain applications of a way of thinking, which then somehow provide basic principles behind the occasional utterance. This is also, of course, what one assumes when construing a Pauline theology or writing a book on Pauline ethics. But the parameters of such reconstructed thought systems are by no means certain. To mention just one glaring example: Is "justification through faith" the heart of Pauline theology, or is it only a *Nebenkrater*, as Albert

---

[23] Imponenda est igitur lex iustificandis, ... non quod per legem iustitiam illam consequantur, hoc enim esset abuti ... lege, sed ut pavefacti et humiliati lege confugiant ad Christum (WA 40. 1, 528).

[24] This interpretation was rightly questioned by Krister Stendahl in his article, "Paul and the Introspective Conscience of the West," in: idem 1976, 86-88.

Schweitzer thought? Furthermore, are the parameters constant through-
out an author's life? What if he changes his mind about some question?
This may well be the case with Paul's view on the law as reflected in
Galatians and Romans.[25]

Even if one wants to be historically fair to the author whose texts are
reused, it is obviously too rigid a position to state that a renewed use of
the letters of, say, Plato, Cicero, Epictetus, or Paul should take place
under the necessary presupposition that the rereading is made within
the framework of the total conception of Plato, Cicero, etc. Let me take
one example from early Christianity. When Clement of Rome urges the
Corinthians to reread Paul's letters to them, he is concerned about their
lack of unity, and more specifically their contempt for the presbyters (1
Clem. 47). This Clement can do without presupposing a common ground
in a total Pauline theology; modern exegetes have even accused him of
not understanding Paul.[26] Instead Clement's application is rather
straightforward: Paul dismissed their dissensions — obey him also
now.[27]

From a semantic perspective, more or less void of a pragmatic one, it
is almost always possible to find ideas and principles mentioned or intimated in a text which in some way or another really belong to the
author's message. They may, however, receive a different importance in
a new situation. Thus, the same Clement in 35.5 apparently uses Rom
1:29-32, a part of Paul's negative description of pagan immorality. But in
1 Clement it turns into a series of admonitions to Christians. It is not contrary to Paul's thinking, but it is not what he intended in Romans 1.

Texts can also be understood as saying things which, by all verisimili-
tude, would not be in harmony with the outlook of the author as reconstructed by the historically interested reader. A Lutheran way of reading
Paul, that equates the Law with God's will, is probably an example of
this.

One may defend this way of rereading Paul by saying that if Paul had
lived in the days of these Lutheran theologians, he would have agreed.
Or one could be tougher and argue that it is with Paul as with Sophocles
and Shakespeare: once their texts have left them, we are free to read
them according to our own minds (cf. H.-G. Gadamer, P. Ricoeur, etc.).
This is how the Christian reading of the Tanakh must appear to a Jew.

---

[26] Goppelt 1954, 239.

[27] In addition, Clement strengthens his reference with an argument *a maiore ad minus:*
Paul attacked divisions based on following apostles of high reputation — now there are a
couple of insignificant people who disturb the unity.

And among the myriads of Christian interpretations of the NT a good proportion probably belongs to the same class.[28]

Let us now return to Paul and his time. Actually, Paul himself provides a few glimpses of how the relevance of an occasional message was widened. One example is the letter to Philemon. Its errand concerns Philemon, and the body of the letter is directly addressing a "thou". But the letter with its truly private message is addressed, in its opening, to the house-church of Philemon. In other words, Paul meant that the assembly should have access to another's letter (possibly at their common worship).[29] I doubt that Paul widens the address in order to put pressure on Philemon; the apostle's personal support of Onesimus would be sufficient. Rather, Paul is of the opinion that the letter pleaded the case of Onesimus in such a way that it had something to say to the larger Christian community.[30]

If this is so with the rather personal Philemon, it is not surprising that according to 1 Cor 1:1-2, Paul writes his letter to the Corinthian church "together with all who call upon the name of our Lord Jesus Christ in every place, theirs and ours". Conzelmann rightly states: "We cannot argue that Paul could not write a greeting to all Christians," in disagreement with Weiß who wanted to delete the words as an addition by the editor of the Pauline letter collection. Nevertheless Conzelmann finds them difficult.[31] In my opinion the difficulty disappears if one posits that although the matters he dealt with in 1 Corinthians were "occasional" and particular, Paul discussed them in such a way that the letter could serve as an apostolic message to other churches as well.

Thus it is possible to assume that the widening of the "occasional" perspective in Philemon and 1 Corinthians was intended by Paul. My suggestion above means that something similar holds true of all his letters.[32] The widening then, on the one hand, meant that the addressees (e.g., the Corinthians) were supposed to return to the letters several times, perhaps even reading them in their services. On the other hand, it also meant that other copies of the Corinthian correspondence were available for rereading in Pauline churches.

Of course one may ask how wide Paul's perspective was in terms of the possible addressees of his "occasional" letters. One possible answer

---

[28] I leave aside the fact that the different Christian Bible interpretations are all coloured by various traditions, whether the interpreters are conscious of them or not.

[29] Gnilka 1982, 17; cf. Hengel 1984, 35.

[30] Cf. Stuhlmacher 1975, 17, 57-58.

[31] Conzelmann 1975, 23; Fascher 1975, 85: "ein Gemeindebrief des Paulus gilt im Grunde allen Gemeinden".

[32] Other passages in the Pauline corpus which in different ways may indicate a wider audience are 2 Cor 1:1; 2 Thess 2:2; 3:17; and Col 4:16.

is that it was not less than the perspective of his apostolic mission. In terms of time no answer is possible. Paul's expectations concerning the imminent parousia underwent change, but already 1 Thessalonians is hardly conceived and composed as if its author seriously doubted that its bearer would arrive in time.[33]

My discussion above is not meant to justify the church's reading of others' letters. But if my suggestion is right, it presents a problem for exegetes trying to say what a text meant historically. Theologians tend to disregard the occasion of a text. In text-linguistic terms, they do not care about its pragmatic aspect. Paul is closer to these theologians than we, historically minded exegetes, would like. To put it in other terms, when asking what the text meant[34] we should ask for two intentions of Paul: the one regarding the specific occasion and, secondly, the one related to more general interest. To turn from the author's side of the communication to the recipient's, we should ask for two understandings of a text: the one in the original letter situation and, secondly, the ones where the letter was reread (e.g., Ephesus).[35]

Thus, it seems to me that Paul wrote his letters to be more than occasional correspondence. He intended them to be read more widely. This raises the hermeneutical question concerning what one is doing when rereading occasional texts. This question concerns not only the one who asks for the conditions of Christian rereading of the Bible, but also the exegete who asks what the text meant in its original situation, for that situation loses something of its singularity. One original situation may have actually meant reading others' letters!

Bibliography

Berger, Kl. 1974: "Apostelbrief und apostolische Rede/Zum Formular frühchrist-licher Briefe", in: *ZNW* 65 (1974) 190-231.

Betz, H. D. 1974-75: "The Literary Composition and Function of Paul's Letter to the Galatians", in: *NTS* 21 (1974-75) 353-79 [= in: idem, *Paulinische Studien*, Tübingen: Mohr (Siebeck) 1994, 63-97].

---

[33] In an Uppsala dissertation to be published in 1987, Bruce C. Johanson deals with the literary, compositional, and rhetorical make-up of 1 Thessalonians. My statement is based on that study.

[34] The attentive reader may hear an echo from Krister Stendahl's often cited article "Biblical Theology, Contemporary" (1962, 419).

[35] To express it in text-linguistic terms: we get a second pragmatic aspect which may modify the semantic one. My taking Ephesus as an example of a wider audience is of course inspired by the discussions concerning Romans 16. Does it contain fragments of an Ephesian letter? See Schenke and Fischer 1978, 136-42; Kümmel 1975, 314-20.

— 1979: *Galatians* (Hermeneia), Philadelphia, PA: Fortress 1979.

Conzelmann, H. 1965-66: "Paulus und die Weisheit", in: *NTS* 12 (1965-66) 231-44 [= in: idem, *Theologie als Schriftauslegung* (BEvTh 65), München: Kaiser 1974, 177-90].

— 1975: *I Corinthians* (Hermeneia), Philadelphia, PA: Fortress 1975.

Dahl, N. A. 1967: "Paul and the Church at Corinth according to I Corinthians 1:10-4:21", in: W. R. Farmer, C. F. D. Moule, and R. R. Niebuhr (eds.), *Christian History and Interpretation. Studies Presented to John Knox*, Cambridge: Cambridge University Press 1967, 313-35 [= in: Dahl, *Studies in Paul*, Minneapolis, MN: Augsburg 1977, 39-61].

Deißmann, A. 1923: *Licht vom Osten*, 4th ed., Tübingen: Mohr (Siebeck) 1923.

Fascher, E. 1975: *Der erste Brief an die Korinther* (ThHK 7.1), Berlin: Evangelische Verlagsanstalt 1975.

Funk, R. W. 1967: "The Apostolic Parousia: Form and Significance", in: W. R. Farmer, C. F. D. Moule, and R. R. Niebuhr (eds.), *Christian History and Interpretation. Studies Presented to John Knox*, Cambridge: Cambridge University Press 1967, 249-68.

Gnilka, J. 1968: *Der Philipperbrief* (HThK 10.3), Freiburg/Basel/Wien: Herder 1968.

— 1980: *Der Kolosserbrief* (HThK 10.1), Freiburg/Basel/Wien: Herder 1980.

— 1982: Der *Philemonbrief* (HThK 10.4), Freiburg/Basel/Wien: Herder 1982.

Goppelt, L. 1954: *Christentum und Judentum im ersten und zweiten Jahrhundert* (BFCTh 2.55), Gütersloh: Bertelsmann 1954.

von Harnack, A. 1926: *Die Briefsammlung des Apostels Paulus und die anderen vorkonstantinischen christlichen Briefsammlungen*, Leipzig: Hinrichs 1926.

Hengel, Martin 1984: *Die Evangelienüberschriften* (SHAW.PH 1984/3), Heidelberg: Winter 1984.

Henshaw, T. 1963: *New Testament Literature*, London: Hodder & Stoughton 1963.

Hübner, H. 1980: *Das Gesetz bei Paulus* (FRLANT 119), 2nd ed., Göttingen: Vandenhoeck & Ruprecht 1980.

Jervell, J. 1979: "Paul in the Acts of the Apostles: Tradition, History, Theology", in: J. Kremer (ed.), *Les Actes des Apôtres*, Gembloux/Leuven: Duculot 1979, 297-306.

Johanson, B. C. 1987: *To All the Brethren. A Text-Linguistic and Rhetorical Approach to I Thessalonians* (CB.NT 16), Stockholm: Almqvist & Wiksell International 1987.

Kümmel, W. G. 1975: *Introduction to the New Testament* (transl. H. C. Kee), Nashville, TN: Abingdon 1975.

Lohse, E. 1971: *Colossians and Philemon* (Hermeneia), Philadelphia, PA: Fortress 1971.

Morris, Ch. W. 1938/71: "Foundations of the Theory of Signs", in: idem, *Writings on the General Theory of Signs* (1938) [reprinted: The Hague: Mouton 1971, 17-71].

Moule, C. F. D. 1967: *The Epistles of Paul the Apostle to the Colossians and to Philemon* (CGTC), Cambridge: Cambridge University Press 1967.

Roller, O. 1933: *Das Formular der paulinischen Briefe* (BWANT 58), Stuttgart: Kohlhammer 1933.

Sanders, E. P. 1966: "Literary Dependence in Colossians", in: *JBL* 85 (1966) 28-45.

Schenk, W. 1983: "Christus, das Geheimnis der Welt, als dogmatisches und ethisches Grundprinzip des Kolosserbriefes", in: *EvTh* 43 (1983) 138-55.

Schenke, H.-M. 1974-75: "Das Weiterwirken des Paulus und die Pflege seines Erbes durch die Paulus-Schule", in: *NTS* 21 (1974-75) 508-14.

Schenke, H.-M./K. M. Fischer 1978a: *Einleitung in die Schriften des Neuen Testaments. Band 1: Die Briefe des Paulus und Schriften des Paulinismus,* Berlin: Evangelische Verlagsanstalt/Gütersloh: Mohn 1978.

— 1978b: *Einleitung in die Schriften des Neuen Testaments. Band 2: Die Evangelien und die anderen neutestamentlichen Schriften,* Berlin: Evangelische Verlagsanstalt/Gütersloh: Mohn 1978.

Schmithals, W. 1964: "Die Thessalonicherbriefe als Brief-Komposition", in: E. Dinkler (ed.), *Zeit und Geschichte. FS Rudolf Bultmann,* Tübingen; Mohr (Siebeck) 1964, 295-315.

Schneider, J. 1954: "Brief", in: *RAC* 2, Stuttgart: Hiersemann 1954, 564-85.

von Soden, H. 1913: *Griechisches Neues Testament,* Göttingen: Vandenhoeck & Ruprecht 1913.

Standaert, B. 1983: "Analyse rhétorique des chapitres 12 à 14 de I Co", in: L. de Lorenzi (ed.), *Charisma und Agape* (Benedictina 7), Rome: S. Paulo fuori le mura 1983, 23-50.

Stendahl, K. 1962: "Biblical Theology, Contemporary", in: *IDB* 1 (1962) 418-32.

— 1976: *Paul Among Jews and Gentiles,* Philadelphia, PA: Fortress 1976.

Stuhlmacher, P. 1975: *Der Brief an Philemon* (EKK), Zürich/Einsiedeln/Köln and Neukirchen-Vluyn: Benziger Verlag and Neukirchener Verlag 1975.

Thraede, Kl. 1970: *Grundzüge griechisch-römischer Brieftopik* (Zetemata 48), München: Beck 1970.

Vielhauer, Ph. 1975: *Geschichte der urchristlichen Literatur,* Berlin-New York: de Gruyter 1975.

White, J. L. 1984: "New Testament Epistolary Literature in the Framework of Ancient Epistolography", in: *ANRW* II. 25. 2, New York-Berlin: de Gruyter 1984, 1730-56.

Wikenhauser, A./J. Schmid 1973: *Einleitung in das Neue Testament*, 6th ed., Freiburg/Basel/Wien: Herder 1973.

Supplement

Berger, Kl.: "Hellenistische Gattungen im Neuen Testament", in: *ANRW* II.25.2 (1984) 1031-1432, 1831-1885.

Malherbe, A.: *Ancient Epistolary Theorists* (SBibSt 19), Atlanta, GA: Scholars Press 1988.

Stowers, S. K.: *Letter Writing in Greco-Roman Antiquity* (LEC), Philadelphia, PA: Westminster Press 1989.

Trobisch, D.: *Die Entstehung der Paulusbriefsammlung. Studien zu den Anfängen christlicher Publizistik* (NTOA 10), Göttingen: Vandenhoeck & Rup-recht/Fribourg: Universitätsverlag 1989.

Taatz, I.: *Frühjüdische Briefe. Die paulinischen Briefe im Rahmen der offiziellen religiösen Briefe des Frühjudentums* (NTOA 16), Göttingen: Vandenhoeck & Ruprecht/Fribourg: Universitätsverlag 1990.

Stirewalt, Jr., M. L.: *Studies in Ancient Greek Epistolography* (SBibSt 27), Atlanta, GA: Scholars Press 1993.

Trobisch, D.: *Die Paulusbriefe und die Anfänge der christlichen Publizistik* (KT 135) Gütersloh: Kaiser 1994.

Gamble, H. Y.: *Books and Readers in the Early Church: a History of Early Christian Texts*, New Haven–London: Yale Univ. Press 1995.

Schmid, U.: *Marcion und sein Apostolos. Rekonstruktion und historische Einordnung der marcionitischen Paulusbriefausgabe* (ANTT 25), Berlin–New York: de Gruyter 1995.

Trobisch, D.: *Die Endredaktion des Neuen Testaments. Eine Untersuchung zur Entstehung der christlichen Bibel* (NTOA 31), Göttingen: Vandenhoeck & Rup-recht/Fribourg: Universitätsverlag 1996.

10. Some Unorthodox Thoughts on the "Household-Code Form"

When professors of New Testament exegesis teach their students about form-criticism and approach New Testament texts outside the Gospels, they discuss confessions, hymns, catalogues of vices and virtues, and the like. If they should be so fortunate as to use Howard Clark Kee's collection *The Origins of Christianity*, they would refer to the lists on pp. 232ff. (Diogenes Laertius, Zeno). Among the parenetic lists, one normally also cites the so-called household codes. Depending on the religious stands of the teachers and on the character of the institutions at which they teach, they may or may not wrestle with questions of the lists' application today, and in such a context would refer to the handbooks that tell that the codes in question are taken over from or inspired by some non-Christian milieus or other.

To the early form critics the sociological perspective of the texts and the implications of this were natural. Such features still play a decisive role when scholars today grapple with the household codes. One sees some relationships between their literary form and certain literary forms to be found in antiquity, and this leads to assumptions concerning the thinking, the life, and the development of the early church.

In this study a little closer look will be taken into the form-critical aspects of the New Testament household codes, concentrating on the oldest one, namely, Col 3:18-4:1. I will conclude with some pessimism as to the strength of some of the positions in this case which are allegedly based on form-criticism. Perhaps they are not sufficiently critical.

It will be necessary to begin with a brief report of some features in the previous scholarly discussion concerning these household codes, paying particular attention to the form-critical assessments and the terminology used in this connection. Then I will apply to Col 3:18-4:1 some analytical tools provided by scholars in text linguistics who have dealt with problems of genres and forms. This will be done in a rather unsophisticated way, but I hope the analysis will suffice to explain the pessimism I just mentioned.

First of all, some features of the scholarly debate concerning the household codes.[1] One of the fathers of form-criticism, Martin Dibelius, devoted a few pages in his commentary on Colossians, Ephesians and Philemon (1st ed., 1913)[2] to dealing with the *Haustafeln*. He suggested that the early church had taken over a "schema" that was originally Stoic. This meant that one organized one's discussion of ethical rules according to a certain pattern. Such rules concerned what was fitting (καθῆκον) "towards the gods, one's parents, brothers, country, and towards foreigners." The quotation is from Epictetus (2.17.31) and is the example Dibelius takes as a point of departure. The Christians took over this scheme, possibly via "Hellenistic Judaism,"[3] and the ἀνῆκεν of Col 3:18 was understood as a variant of the Stoic καθῆκον. The adoption meant that "the early church had started to try to come to grips with the world" and to forget about the imminent end.

Karl Weidinger followed up Dibelius's thesis.[4] He reaffirmed the opinion that the household-code schema had its origin in Stoic-Cynic philosophy. It was used also in Hellenistic Judaism. Colossians 3:18-4:1 not only represented the schema taken over, but also the text itself had been borrowed after having been only slightly revised: one had, for example, added the phrase "in the Lord" to the rule "you wives, be submissive to your husbands, as it is fitting".

Some forty-five years after Weidinger, J. E. Crouch published a study of the Colossian household code.[5] Like Dibelius and Weidinger, he believed that its origin was Hellenistic, but he stressed the influence of Hellenistic Judaism and pointed to a formal feature that Jewish material shared with the New Testament *Haustafeln*, that of reciprocity: people were summoned to fulfil their duties towards one another, wives towards husband and vice versa, children towards parents, etc.[6] Crouch also claimed that Weidinger had been careless in his assessment of the tradition history of the schema: there were differences between "typically Stoic codes and many of the Hellenistic Jewish codes" (p. 23) He had also, according to Crouch, failed "to note the significance of the variations among the Christian *Haustafeln* themselves (ibid.).

In his article in the *Interpreter's Dictionary of the Bible* supplement of 1976, David Schroeder apparently tried to harmonize several of the opinions advanced, including those which assumed a Christian origin of the code.[7] He noted that "formally" the codes were indebted to Old Testa-

---

[1] These discussions are summarized in Crouch 1972, 13-36; Balch 1981, 2-20; Müller 1983.

[2] Dibelius/Greeven 1953, 48-50.

[3] I put the expression within quotation marks since, in a way, all Judaism of the time was Hellenistic. Here it stands for Greek-speaking, largely non-Palestinian Judaism.

[4] Weidinger 1928.

[5] Crouch 1972.

[6] Ibid., 5 and 7.1.

ment apodictic law (address, imperative, motivation) but that "stating the ethic in terms of stations in life is typically Hellenistic, especially Stoic". "The content is drawn basically from the Old Testament, Judaic tradition, although with the addition of certain Greek (what is fitting) and Christian (*agape*) concepts." Furthermore, the "Judaic tradition" represents formal differences from the Stoic lists in two respects: First, "Hellenistic Judaism," especially Philo, mentions the groups in the same order as do the household codes of Colossians and Ephesians — wives, children, slaves. Second, the duties are presented in pairs — wives and husbands, children and parents, slaves and husbands.[8]

After some preliminary moves, new suggestions were advanced around 1980 concerning the issue of the relevant background material behind the household codes in terms of both their "form" and their content. It seems that the men behind them had worked independently, but they all pointed to the *oikonomia* tradition, that is, that of philosophical discussions of how one should manage one's "house". Texts from this tradition appeared to be closer to the household codes than the Stoic-Cynic duty lists.[9] As a matter of fact, some of the passages that had been quoted as examples of the Stoic-Cynic schema belonged to this very tradition, which was represented by texts from Plato and Aristotle, and down through the first centuries CE. The house was, of course, the kernel of society, largely independent, and of fundamental importance to the life of the members of the household and to the community as a whole.

When Klaus Berger in 1984[10] discussed the origin of the household-code form, he combined the two suggestions of the past: certainly the *oikonomia Gattung* must be taken into account when one wants to explain the *Gattung Haustafel*, but the connection with behaviour towards the

---

[7] Schroeder 1976, 546-47. His unpublished Hamburg dissertation from 1959 dealt with the household codes, their origin, and their theological meaning. It has not been available to me. The contributions of E. Lohmeyer and K. H. Rengstorf may be said to deal with the form-critical aspect only indirectly. See Lohmeyer 1953. Lohmeyer held that Col 3:18-4:1 was a pre-Colossian unit of Jewish origin, but he did not ask so much for the "schema", etc., as for the root system of ideas expressed in the code. See also Rengstorf 1953. Rengstorf claimed the household codes were a purely Christian creation that owed to interest in the *oikos* (cf. the more recent adducing of the *oikonomia* treatises as a background).

[8] The two formal issues mentioned last are not in Schroeder 1976 but are in his thesis from 1959 (according to Balch 1981, 6 and Crouch 1972,102). The last item is the same as the one Crouch calls reciprocity. Verner 1983, 83-91 distinguishes between the topos of the household management employed in the *Haustafeln*, and their schema, namely, their literary characteristics.

[9] Lührmann 1975 and 1980-81; Thraede 1977 and 1980; Balch 1981 (after a Yale diss. of 1974); Müller 1983.

[10] Berger 1984.

state and the catalogue form are, he wrote, a remaining heritage from the Stoic catalogues (p. 1081). In addition, he claims, one should not underestimate the influence that the popular gnomic traditions have had on the form (*Gestalt*) of the New Testament household codes (p. 1085).

The scholars who follow the *oikonomia* track have drawn different conclusions from this for the sociolinguistic function of the household codes. Thus, D. Lührmann advanced the thought that this new comparative material indicated that the early church made a latent (not more, though) claim that the Christian house was a model for larger circles of the society (p. 86). D. L. Balch and K. Müller suggest that when the church promoted the morality of the household codes against this sort of background, this meant that it chose a middle course, turning down certain more extreme, "liberal" tendencies.[11]

So much for a review of some features of the scholarly discussion of the household codes. Terms like "schema," "form", "formulas", "typical codes" recur in it. In the latest contribution to the topic that I have come across, the one by Karlheinz Müller, a similar swarm of terms clouds the discussion; thus we hear of "die traditionsgeschichtliche Zuordnung der Haustafeln zum antiken Schrifttum 'Über die Ökonomie'", which is commented upon in a footnote as being a *Gattungsbestimmung* (p. 285); in that literature, we are told, there is also to be found "ein Dreier- bzw. Zweierschema" and certain *Leitmotive* (pp. 285-86). We also learn that knowledge of the *Literaturgattung* περὶ οἴκων, etc., liberates the modern exegete from the old feeling of moral obligation to defend the Christian character of Col 3:18-4:1, a *Literaturgattung* that is also referred to as the "zeitgenössische Textsorte zur Ökonomie" (p. 290).

Thus, in the literature on the household codes one finds a considerable number of analytical terms and classifications that, furthermore, play a role both when the same authors assess features of the history of the early church and its ways of thinking and when they approach the hermeneutics of the household codes.

This means, however, that they are posing the sort of questions to these texts that scholars of linguistics and of literature have treated with considerable refinement. Even to somebody who, like the present writer, has only a shallow acquaintance with these areas, it seems desirable that one try to take advantage of such studies in order to be as fair as possible to the object of our research.[12] I will dare to make a first move, and if there is anything worthwhile in my deliberations, others who are more competent may correct or refine my tentative results.

---

[11] Balch 1981, 109; Müller 1983, 290.

[12] More specialized studies in my scholarly surroundings approach the form-critical issues with linguistics: Hellholm 1980 and 1982 [= revised in idem 1986]; Johanson 1987.

For my purpose, I will apply the approach of Egon Werlich in his *Typologie der Texte*.[13] I will, however, make more explicit the semiotic differentiation between the syntactic, the semantic, and the pragmatic aspects. (The terms will be explained in due course.)

Let me begin with a short description of Werlich's analytical system. After distinguishing the fictional group of texts (*Textgruppe*) from the non-fictional one, he identifies five text types (*Texttypen*), namely, description, narration, exposition, argumentation, and instruction. Speaking of text types means moving on a rather high level of abstraction. Werlich defines them as "ideally typical norms for text structuring, available to the adult speaker as cognitively determined matrices of text-forming elements in linguistic communication concerning things and circumstances".[14]

On a lower level of abstraction we encounter text forms (*Textformen*),[15] defined as "realizations of groups of text constituents, which speakers choose when producing texts according to text-typical invariants on the one hand, and conformably to certain conventions for textual utterances ensuing from history on the other".[16]

As examples of constituents that may be characteristic of a text form, Werlich mentions particular points of view (*Sprecherperspektive*): Is a text personal or impersonal, subjectively or objectively presented? Are present or past tenses used? Other constituents include idiom, style, kind of communication (dialogue, letter, etc.).

A text form can be represented in text-form variants (*Textformvarianten*, pp. 70ff.) Thus, for example, the subjective text form of narrative can cover such text-form variants as anecdote, children's story, and detective novel, all representing different conventions.

Within text-form variants one can use different compositional patterns (*Kompositionsmuster*, pp. 73ff.), which may be established by literary tradition (e.g., the *haiku* or the *tanka*) or by a particular social-rule system (e.g., an abstract, a bibliography, a doctoral thesis). Already the examples just mentioned indicate that one can go on and subdivide the compositional patterns into variants of them (pp. 76-77).

---

[13] Werlich 1979. For a wider discussion, see also Hempfer 1973, 150-91.

[14] "Idealtypische Normen für Textstrukturierung ..., die der erwachsene Sprecher als kognitiv determinierte Matrices textformender Elemente in der sprachlichen Kommunikation über Gegenstände und Sachverhalte generell verfügbar hat" (Werlich 1979, 44).

[15] Werlich prefers this expression to "Textsorte" (ibid., 116 n. 42).

[16] "Aktualisierungen von Gruppen von Textkonstituenten ..., die Sprecher einerseits in Übereinstimmung mit texttypischen Invarianten und andererseits gemäß bestimmten historisch ausgebildeter Konventionen für textliche Äußerungen in der Textproduktion auswählen" (ibid., 44).

Let us now try to apply this classification to the household code of Colossians and, in so doing, approach the task from the syntactic, semantic, and pragmatic angles.

To consider texts as well as text types[17] in their *syntactic* dimension means assessing the texts and text types from a literal point of view. It means taking into account the ways in which their signs (words, phrases, clauses, etc.) are related to one another. The *semantic* dimension has to do with the same signs, and their relationships, as related to that which they designate (the contents, to use a less technical term). The *pragmatic* dimension regards the signs and the contents of the texts in relation to the receiver and the receiver's situation, not least as in some sense shared by the sender and, quite often, as the object of the sender's aims, argument, etc.

There is no doubt that our text[18] belongs to the *text type* of *instruction*. According to Werlich, instruction is characterized by an enumerative construction, and, seen from a syntactic angle, the Colossians passage follows that rule. The text types have different typical "textual bases", that is, real or reconstructed headlines or text openings, out of which the following text is developed. The typically instructive textual basis is a verb in the imperative that forms a predicate to be performed by a subject person.[19] Also in this respect Col 3:18-4:1 presents itself as belonging to the instructive text type, since a reconstructed textual basis could be "Behave in a Christian way in the house".

Regarding our text from the semantic perspective, we can easily see that it displays contents that list certain required attitudes. Thus, also from the semantic perspective, the text qualifies as an exponent of the instructive text type.

With regard to the pragmatic dimension, a discussion on this level of abstraction asks for *typical* communicative external functions of a text type. It is to be expected that texts of the instructive type address human beings in some sort of social situation in order that certain moral and practical goals be achieved. With Col 3:18-4:1 this is certainly true.

Already on this very high level of abstraction we may ask ourselves what happens if we try to pour the parallel material that one normally adduces into these very wide moulds, those of the text types. I dare to try to answer the question by testing a single but frequently adduced text, namely, the Stoic Hierocles' fragments of the second century CE., which were of primary importance for Weidinger's investigation. As far as I can

---

[17] See further Hellholm 1982 and 1986 part 3.

[18] I take the risk of not discussing any "text" definition, nor the delimitation of Col 3:18-4:1.

[19] Werlich 1979, 33.

see, they represent the *expository text type*. This also holds true of the sanctions on household management and marriage. It is characteristic of texts belonging to this text type that statements are related to one another by adverbs such as "namely, for example, in other words" or "similarly, also, not ... either".[20] Their textual basis is a subject (a nominal phrase) followed by a form of "be" or "have" in the present tense as a predicate, and a complement (a nominal phrase). Thus a passage of Hierocles' treatment of marriage is introduced in such a way that the textual basis can be expressed in this way: "Married life is something beautiful" (*Stob.* 4.22.24, 4.505, 5-22 Hense).

As "expositions", texts of this type can have contents (we are using the semantic perspective now) that may be anything that can be explained or that one thinks should be explained. When seen under a pragmatic aspect, Hierocles' treatises may be said to communicate certain concepts of the sender, which are formed through observations in space and time.[21]

Now for the *text form*, beginning from a syntactic point of view. Our Colossians passage has a personal perspective that is visible in the second-person address and in the letter context. Accordingly, its text form is more a set of directions than a series of statutory rules. A text form is often also characterized by a certain idiom. The instructive text idiom can be seen as an application of the textual basis, and accordingly it takes the form of a series of imperatives. The communication is, of course, written — although the written message is to be read out and listened to, the letter replacing the sender — and it takes the form of a monologue.

In a way I have already intimated the semantic and pragmatic dimensions of this text form: it contains directions presented in a personal manner by an authority, and they should be respected by all the receivers.

What about the text form of Hierocles' fragments dealing with household management and marriage? Its exposition is personal, but it has a mixture of subjective and objective presentation and it is held in the present tense. Its text idiom is coloured by the expository textual basis we reconstructed above. The communication is a monologue but receives a seemingly dialogical flavour through rhetorical questions that belong to the conventions of the philosophical treatise of those days. In terms of semantics and pragmatics there is not much to add: the contents exposed should be accepted by the audience.

---

[20] Ibid., 36.

[21] Ibid., 38. Since we have only fragments of the texts, it is difficult to be positive about the text type: possibly it is *argumentative*.

Continuing down the abstraction staircase we arrive at the *text-form variants*. I suggest that Col 3:18-4:1, having the text form of a "set of directions" with the characteristics mentioned above, represents a text-form variant of "set of directions concerning ethical conduct". The contents, then, concern *ethics* and, pragmatically seen, the ethics of the addressees in their present situation.

Hierocles' fragments can be referred to the text-form variant of the expository philosophical treatise. The presentation of such texts had to do with several aspects of human life, often ethics. They addressed those people who could attend the lectures of the philosophers, and should as treatises presumably be held apart from the speeches of the popular philosophers in the street. The latter can hardly be regarded as equal to treatises, even though the contents may have been partly similar in the two cases.

The next step leads to the *compositional patterns*. Syntactically seen, Col 3:18-4:1 is structured according to the diverse stations in life. We may immediately proceed to state that this compositional pattern appears in a variant because of a social convention of the epoch, the "house" pattern (cf. Werlich's *Epochenvariante des Kompositionmusters*, 76). Not surprisingly, this sort of compositional pattern is concomitant with that which one finds when regarding the text's semantic dimension, namely, the way of thinking of the house and its structure of authority and responsibilities. This thought pattern is the "schema" that has played such an important and puzzling role in the form-critical assessments of the household codes from Dibelius on. We should be aware of the fact that it existed independently of household codes and, for that matter, also independently of texts of any sort, because it presented a *social structure*. As such, it would appear to be as natural as biologically conditioned thought structures, such as those in which one combines hunger and thirst, or eyes, ears, nose, and mouth, or such human behaviours as sitting, standing, walking, and lying down (e.g., Ps 139:2-3). In the case of the house pattern, this is also a role pattern of the type that children learn not only by being part of it but also by re-enacting it in their play.[22]

Within this semantic structure an instructive text, having the characteristics we have noted when descending the abstraction steps, gives directions on the ethical conduct of the people of the house. It is also natural that the contents of these rules are structured according to the relevant persons' relationships as defined by the social system inherent in the thought pattern.

---

[22] Cf. Grasberger 1864, 53, 227-35; Groß 1975. See also Plato, *Laws* 1.643C; Aristotle, *Politics* 7.15. 5 (the play prepares the child for the adult life).

It is not totally impossible that the code existed in a literary convention before Col 3:18-4:1. In that case we can safely state that, as to the pragmatic dimension, the function of the compositional pattern in its household-code variant was to instruct people to relate in a moral way to the common social system of the time. If, on the other hand, the first household code to appear was that of Col 3:18-4:1, we can assume with some certainty that it introduced a convention of a pragmatic dimension like the one just sketched.

If we ask for the compositional pattern of Hierocles' treatises on *oikonomia* and marriage, it seems that the former was structured according to the duties to be performed by husband and wife. In the marriage treatise it is not surprising to find traces of the schema in summarizing statements like this one: "We have summarily shown how we ought to conduct ourselves towards our kindred, having before taught how we should act towards ourselves, our parents, and brothers, and, besides these, towards our wife and children" (*Stob.* 4.27.23, 4.672, 11.14 Hense; from Balch 1981, 4). But it is hardly correct to say that the schema has a syntactically structuring function in the same way it had in the case of Col 3:18-4:1. The pattern can work on several levels: on the one hand, in the case of the philosophical treatise, it organizes the chapters in a certain order; on the other, in the household code, there is not only a short set of instructions structured according to it but the instructions also directly address people who represent the different roles in the pattern.

In terms of semantics and pragmatics, it seems that Hierocles' treatises present conventional teaching on social behaviour with the expected effect that a mildly Stoic view on the established society be adopted and carried out.

Above, I expressed a hint of doubt as to whether we could assume that before Col 3:18-4:1 there had existed an instructive text form with a variant following a subdivision of a compositional pattern, namely, the "household code". In other words, did the literary convention "household code" exist? So far nothing of the sort is known — only thought patterns that reappear in different text types, text forms, text-form variants, etc.

On the other hand — and this observation also belongs to the syntactic aspect — Col 3:18-4:1 has a style of its own as compared with the surrounding text: the sentences are built in a more straightforward manner than not only the argumentative parts of the letter but also the preceding parenetic section. But even if Col 3:18-4:1 is a text that, more or less in its present shape, existed before the writing of Colossians, this does not indicate per se that it represented a literary convention, namely, that of the household code. In other words, to pursue the discussion to one or two further levels of abstraction becomes a rather hypothetical undertaking. Instead, I now wish to take the step down to the level of our text itself, from *langue* to *parole*, to use the famous distinction of Saussure. First, we note that it represents some particular features as seen in its syntactic dimension, namely, the composition according to pairs and reciprocity. As mentioned above, Crouch argued that this had counterparts in Jewish but not in Stoic-Cynic material. Balch, however, pointed to the fact that household-management tradition from Plato and Aristotle through Dionysius of Halicarnassus reflected it.[23] Another syntactic particularity is the construction of the individual directions: address, imperative, plus motivation. These compositional structures, of course, also exist outside Col 3:18-4:1. Thus, the last-mentioned construction is that of Jewish apodictic law and of certain sayings in the wisdom tradition: for example, "You children, listen to me, your father, and act in this way in order that you may be saved" (Sir 3:1).[24]

Turning to the semantic dimension of Col 3:18-4:1, we need not worry too much about it. The author remains within the framework of the established social system, although placed under a certain modification through the "in the Lord" theme struck previously in 3:17 and returned to in the repeated references to "the Lord" in 3:18-4:1. This should not conceal the fact that it is possible to find counterparts for the individual directions in other texts in antiquity, both Stoic-Cynic and Jewish. The structure of reciprocity is not least a structure of contents: the duties are mutual.

The pragmatic aspect of Col 3:18-4:1 need not occupy us very much either, since our task is not an exegesis of a text. When one assesses this task, however, one should primarily take into account the context, that is, both the literary one, the letter, and the situational one, which can be imagined behind and around the text. The fact that the passage on the slaves is longer and more detailed has to be accounted for in such an assessment. But one should not discuss the pair structures or the "apodictic law" construction of the directions only as though they were the result of a *Formzwang* — as if the author just slipped into that way of expressing himself because there was a literary setup of conventions that drove him to it. It seems to me that my discussion above and the comparative material brought forward in the scholarly debate indicate that there were no such conventions in terms of the reciprocity and the address-imperative-motivation structures; or more precisely, those syntactic features existed but not as characteristics of a text-form variant fol-

---

[23] Balch 1981, 53ff.

[24] Cf. Gerstenberger 1965, 121; and Gnilka 1980, 214-15. But note that the one addressed in Sirach, in 3:1 as so often elsewhere, is the "son," i.e., the student.

lowing a particular compositional pattern similar to that of a household code. Rather, they can be taken as apt for the situation: the duties were regarded as mutual, in the Lord; the subordinates, wives, children, and slaves were regarded as worthy of being directly addressed and having a moral responsibility, although, of course, one in submission.

The stylistic properties of Col 3:18-4:1 which I touched upon above can suggest that even if there was no wider convention, there were traditions. The parenetic context and its rather close relationships to the preceding argument on the Christian status of the addressees can indicate that the code represents traditional instruction of the Christian community, possibly baptismal instruction (but only possibly).[25] This would, then, mean that one regards the pragmatics of Col 3:18-4:1 from a diachronic point of view.

The considerations above are a rough sketch. In addition, they are mostly made on a synchronic basis. But as we saw in the beginning, most scholars who have discussed the household codes have done so diachronically, explaining the *Gattung*, form, schema, etc. of the different codes as the result of taking over, inheriting, being influenced, etc., from particular literary or cultural circles. Furthermore, those suggestions have led to conclusions of what the adaptation of the form, schema, etc., had to say about the social, religious, or theological situation of the Christian circle in which the form, schema, etc., were taken up.

It seems to me, however, that applying Werlich's analytical model to our material can open our eyes a little to what exegetes have been doing when they have compared the household codes with other literature and drawn conclusions in terms of dependence and interpretation. (I am persuaded that any linguistic analysis dealing with the genre problems would give a similar result; Werlich is not *the* linguist to me.)

The characteristics of a given text can be said to belong to it on different levels of classification. That, for example, an apocalypse normally belongs to the text type of narration is something it shares with a detective story. Both can also be said to represent the story text form, as distinguished from that of a report, but after that they separate. Furthermore, the differentiation between the three semiotic dimensions should receive careful attention. On the one hand, certain syntactic, semantic, or pragmatic characteristics may belong to a piece of text or to a text-form variant, etc.; on the other, those properties may be found in other texts or text-form variants, etc., that are quite different from the first one. In the Book of Susanna, for instance, Daniel demonstrates the innocence of the beautiful and virtuous Susanna in that he examines the two elders and makes them contradict each other. This example of cunning examination

---

[25] E.g., Cannon 1983, chap. 4.

has made some people label the book the first detective story. Of course, this is wrong; the similarity consists of the semantic detail of the intelligent examiner who ensnares the guilty person so as to solve the mystery. But this detail has different functions in the Book of Susanna from those in Dorothy Sayers's *Gaudy Night*. There is a difference both in terms of the function of the motif within the plot and in terms of its role within the different sociolinguistic functions of the stories,[26] that is, the stories regarded from the pragmatic aspect. The first one is admonishing in some way or other,[27] whereas the other is meant to function as entertainment.

With these observations in mind we turn to Col 3:18-4:1 again. Thus, the Stoic καθῆκον lists do not actually belong to the *instructive text type* but summarize or structure the contents of ethical treatises, which can best be referred to in the *expository text type*. Furthermore, the examples adduced often list on an abstraction level not what is "fitting" but the relationships for which the contents of the treatise discuss what is "fitting" for the loyal citizen. The pragmatic aspect is, thus, different from the one we can surmise behind Col 3:18-4:1 Regarded from the syntactic aspect there is a certain similarity between the Stoic lists and Col 3:18-4:1 in that both have an enumerative style. Epictetus (2.17, 31) says he is dealing with "what is fitting towards the gods, one's parents, one's brothers, one's country, and towards foreigners". Enumeration is a widespread phenomenon, however, to be found both in shopping lists and in menus. As the shopping list and the menu are closer to each other than the shopping list and an inventory list of a laboratory — both list food! — so are the Epictetus quotation and Col 3:18-4:1, because both deal with social duties. Note, however, that here we are moving into the area of the semantic aspect. I have already noted that the schema that has played such a role in the scholarly treatment of the household codes is a semantic structure that is not bound to any particular text form or text-form variant, etc. The same thing holds true of the syntactic and semantic characterizations which come into view when one focuses on the "pairs" and on the "apodictic law".

In sum, I think it would be wise to take as wide a perspective as possible when posing form-critical questions to the household codes, to pay attention to the level of abstraction on which one moves, and to remember that it may be fatal not to take all three of the semiotic dimensions into account.

---

[26] Hellholm 1990, §§ 2.1. and 2.2. prefers distinguishing between text-internal and text-external functions.

[27] Cf. MacKenzie 1957.

What I have said so far must not be understood as intimating any desire on my part to deny that the early church was influenced by its contemporary world. Nor am I out to defend New Testament authors against the suspicion of being too indulgent to contemporary social conventions. I do, however, suggest that we cease confusing a socially given thought pattern with conventionally established literary forms, and furthermore, that we cease drawing hasty conclusions in terms of implied content and situation from literary form or literary shape (the former being supraindividual, the latter the formal characteristics of a given text). In brief, the Christians behind the household codes were certainly influenced by their social environment in the normal human way. This influence is also seen in the household codes, but not so much in the fact that they should represent a particular literary convention — a form or *Gattung* — as in their contents. What matters is more *what* is said than *how* it is said because the how in this case is not so well established as a communicative convention that it can be of any real help when assessing the what. (Cf., e.g., the literary convention of the minutes, which already as such indicates that a text that is shaped according to these conventions has normally sprung from a particular kind of situation.)

Thus, even if Col 3:18-4:1 is taken into the letter from elsewhere, the material that should enable us to conjecture the existence of the literary form "household code" is very fragile, and when it comes to drawing conclusions about the history and thinking of the early church from this presumed literary form, the case must be even more fragile. The other Christian passages that are usually labelled household codes hardly corroborate the assumptions. *If* Col 3:18-4:1 could be regarded as bringing a literary form to birth in the church — that of the household code — one would immediately have to conclude that in such a case this form disintegrated very quickly, so quickly, indeed, that one should be reticent in drawing any conclusions from the literary form as such, when appearing in later texts.

Thus, it is my unorthodox contention that New Testament scholars should approach the form-critical problem of the early Christian household codes by applying sharper tools and a stricter analysis. I doubt the validity of the conclusions about early Christian life and thinking which they have drawn from their alleged form-critical analyses. I may be something of a heretic, but is it not true that several heretics have drawn attention to things that have been forgotten or fallen into misuse in orthodox circles?

Bibliography

Balch, D. L. 1981: *Let Wives Be Submissive: The Domestic Code in 1 Peter* (SBLMS 26), Chico, CA: Scholars Press 1981.

Berger, Kl. 1984: "Hellenistische Gattungen im Neuen Testament", in: *ANRW* 2.25.2, New York/Berlin: de Gruyter 1984, 1031-1432.

Cannon, G. E. 1983: *The Use of Traditional Materials in Colossians*, Macon, GA: Mercer Univ. Press 1983.

Crouch, J. E. 1972: *The Origin and Intention of the Colossian Haustafel* (FRLANT 109), Göttingen: Vandenhoeck & Ruprecht 1972.

Dibelius, M./Greeven, H. 1953: *An die Kolosser, Epheser, an Philemon* (HNT 12), 3rd ed., Tübingen: Mohr (Siebeck) 1953.

Gerstenberger, E. 1965: *Wesen und Herkunft des 'apodiktischen Rechts'* (WMANT 20), Neukirchen-Vluyn: Neukirchener Verlag 1965.

Gnilka, J. 1980: *Der Kolosserbrief* (HThK 10/1), Freiburg/Basel/Wien: Herder 1980.

Grasberger, L. 1864: *Erziehung und Unterricht im klassischen Altertum 1/1*, Würzburg: Stahel 1864.

Groß, W. H. 1975: "Spiele", in: *KP* 5 (1975) 310-13.

Hellholm, D. 1980: *Das Visionenbuch des Hermas als Apokalypse: Formgeschichtliche und texttheoretische Studien zu einer literarischen Gattung.* Vol. 1 (CB.NT 13/1), Lund: C. W. K. Gleerup 1980.

— 1982: "The Problem of Apocalyptic Genre and the Apocalypse of John", in: *SBL-Seminar Papers 1982*, Chico, CA 1982, 157-98.

— 1986: "The Problem of Apocalyptic Genre and the Apocalypse of John", in: A. Y. Collins (ed.), *Early Christian Apocalypticism: Genre and Social Setting* (Semeia 36), Decatur, CA 1986, 13-64 [revised version of Hellholm 1982].

— 1990: "The Vision He Saw or: To Encode the Future in Writing. An Analysis of the Prologue of John's Apocalyptic Letter", in: T. Jennings (ed.), *Text and Logos. The Humanistic Interpretation of the New Testament.* FS H. W. Boers (Scholars Press Homage Series), Atlanta, GA 1990, 109-46.

Hempfer, K. W. 1973: *Gattungstheorie. Information und Synthese* (UTB 133), München: Fink 1973.

Johanson, B. C. 1987: *To All the Brethren: A Textlinguistic and Rhetorical Approach to I Thessalonians* (CB.NT 16), Stockholm: Almqvist & Wiksell International 1987.

Kee, H. C. 1973: *The Origins of Christianity. Sources and Documents*, Englewood Cliffs, NJ: Prentice Hall 1973.

Lohmeyer, E./Schmauch, W. 1953: *Die Briefe an die Philipper, an die Kolosser und an Philemon* (KEK 9), 9th ed., Göttingen: Vandenhoeck & Ruprecht 1953 [The 8th ed. was the first written by Lohmeyer and appeared in 1930].

Lührmann, D. 1975: "Wo man nicht mehr Sklave oder Freier ist", in: *WuD* 13 (1975) 53-83.

— 1980-81: "Neutestamentliche Haustafeln und antike Ökonomie", in:*NTS* (1980-81) 83-97.

MacKenzie, R. A. F. 1957: "The Meaning of the Susanna Story", in: *CJT* 3 (1957) 211-18.

Müller, K. 1983: "Die Haustafel des Kolosserbriefes und das antike Frauenthema", in: G. Dautzenberg/H. Merklein/K. Müller, *Die Frau im Urchristentum* (QD 95), Freiburg/Basel/Wien: Herder 1983, 263-319.

Rengstorf, K. H. 1953: "Die neutestamentlichen Mahnungen an die Frau, sich dem Manne unterzuordnen", in: W. Foerster (ed.), *Verbum Dei manet in aeternum.* FS Otto Schmitz, Wittenberg: Luther Verlag 1953, 131-45.

Schroeder, D. 1976: "Lists, Ethical", in: *IDB Sup. Vol.* (1976) 546-47.

Thraede, Kl. 1977: "Ärger mit der Freiheit", in: G. Scharffenorth/K. Thraede, *Freunde in Christus werden ...*, Gelmhausen and Berlin: Burkhardtshaus 1977, 31-182.

— 1980: "Zum historischen Hintergrund der 'Haustafeln' des Neuen Testaments", in: E. Daßmann/K. G. Frank (eds.), *Pietas. FS B. Kötting* (JAC.E 8), Münster: Aschendorff 1980, 359-68.

Verner, D. C. 1983: *The Household of God: The Social World of the Pastoral Epistles* (SBLMS 71), Chico, CA: Scholars Press 1983.

Weidinger, K. 1928: *Die Haustafeln: Ein Stück urchristlicher Paränese* (UNT 14), Leipzig: J. C. Hinrichs 1928.

Werlich, E. 1979: *Typologie der Texte: Entwurf eines textlinguistischen Modells zur Grundlegung einer Textgrammatik* (UTB 450), 2nd ed., Heidelberg: Quelle & Meyer 1979.

Supplement

Fiedler, P.: "Haustafel", in: *RAC* 103 (Stuttgart: Hiersemann 1986), 1063-73.

Balch, D. L.: "Household Codes", in: D. E. Aune (ed.), *Greco-Roman Literature and the New Testament: Selected Forms and Genres,* (SBibSt 21), Atlanta, GA: Scholars Press 1988, 25-50.

Strecker, G.: "Die neutestamentlichen Haustafeln (Kol 3,18 - 4,1 und Eph 5,22 - 6,9)", in: H. Merklein (ed.), *Neues Testament und Ethik. FS R. Schnackenburg,* Freiburg - Basel - Vienna: Herder 1989, 349-75.

Gielen, M.: *Tradition und Theologie neutestamentlicher Haustafelethik. Ein Beitrag zur Frage einer christlichen Auseinandersetzung mit gesellschaftlichen Normen* (Athenäums Monographien: Theologie 75), Frankfurt a. M: Hain 1990.

Yates, R.: "The Christian Way of Life. The Paraenetic Material in Colossians 3:1-4:6", in: *EvQ* 63 (1991) 241-51.

Balch, D. L.: "Neopythagorean Moralists and the New Testament Household Codes", in: *ANRW* II.26.1 (Berlin – New York: de Gruyter 1992) 380-411.

Strecker, G.: *Literaturgeschichte des Neuen Testaments* (UTB 1682), Göttingen: Vandenhoeck & Ruprecht 1992.

Wolter, M.: *Der Brief an die Kolosser. Der Brief an Philemon* (ÖTBK 22), Gütersloh: Gütersloher Mohn/ Würzburg: Echter 1993.

von Lips, H.: "Die Haustafel als 'Topos' im Rahmen der urchristlichen Paränese. Beobachtungen anhand des 1. Petrusbriefes und des Titusbriefes", in: *NTS* 40 (1994) 261-80.

Wagener, U.: *Die Ordnung des "Hauses Gottes". Der Ort von Frauen in der Ekklesiologie und Ethik der Pastoralbriefe* (WUNT II 65), Tübingen: Mohr (Siebeck) 1994.

Seim Karlsen, T.: "A Superior Minority? The Problem of Men's Headship in Ephesians 5", in: D. Hellholm/H. Moxnes/T. Karlsen Seim (eds.), *Mighty Minorities? Minorities in Early Christianity — Positions and Strategies. FS Jacob Jervell* (= StTh 49 [1995]), Oslo – Copenhagen – Stockholm – Boston: Scandinavian University Press 1995, 167-81.

Popkes, W.: *Paränese und Neues Testament* (SBS 168), Stuttgart: Katholisches Bibelwerk 1996.

11. Doing Things With the Words of Colossians

The wording of the headline above was inspired by J. L. Austin's classic work "How to do things with words",[1] in which he dealt with what he termed performative sentences. He defined locutionary, illocutionary, and perlocutionary aspects of speech acts, i.e. he distinguished between, firstly, saying something which has a certain sense and reference, secondly, uttering orders, warnings etc., i.e. sentences with a certain conventional force, and, thirdly, achieving something *by* saying something, e.g., convincing or deterring.[2] I shall not — and, for that matter, I cannot — approach Colossians with the philosophical acumen which characterizes Austin's presentation of his version of a speech act theory, but my way of approaching Colossians in this paper was inspired by his work and also by that of other scholars who ask similar questions. Among these are also those who consider the problems of linguistic communication or study (modern) rhetoric in applying it to NT material.

One way of indicating my problem is as follows. If we compare with each other the outlines of the contents of Colossians which we encounter in a few commentaries on the letter, the variations between the suggestions may appear somewhat bewildering. Take, e.g., Col 2:1-5, which both the Greek New Testament and Nestle-Aland print as one paragraph:

> For I want you to know which struggle I have for you and for those in Laodicea and for all who have not seen my person in the flesh, (2) that their hearts may be encouraged in that they are knit together in love, to (have) all the riches of assured understanding and the knowledge of God's mystery, of Christ, (3) in whom are hid all the treasures of wisdom and knowledge. (4) I say this in order that no one may delude you with persuasive speech. (5) For although I am absent in the flesh, yet I am with you in the spirit, rejoicing to see your orderliness and the firmness of your faith in Christ.

Are these verses part of "the struggle against the heresy" (2:1-19), telling us that "only Christ can grant the fullness of knowledge" (2:1-3) and beginning a call to "hold fast unto the received faith" (2:4-7)? This is

---

[1] Austin 1962.
[2] Austin 1962, 108.

what J. Gnilka says.[3] Or should we think of them in E. Schweizer's manner: as the fourth part of the "foundation" laid in the epistle they deal
with "the apostle's achievement for the community (2:1-15)"?[4] Or is the
passage to be understood as the latter half of the second part of Colossians, dealing with "the authority of the apostle — the binding of salvation to the apostolic message, 1:24-2:5", and does it, within this
framework, deal with "the apostle and the addressees (2:1-5)"? This is
the understanding of P. Pokorný.[5] Or, finally, should we follow F. F.
Bruce, who puts his comments on 1:24-2:7 under the headline "Paul's
Ministry" and within this passage finds that vv. 1-5 deal with "Concern
for the Christians of the Lycus valley"?[6]

These examples vary both as to the suggestions of what the author is
doing with his words and as to the ways of delimiting the smaller units
of the text. Any reader of exegetical commentaries is acquainted with
this kind of variety and is not surprised, nor seriously dismayed by the
seeming discord of the exegetical authorities. I shall not now discuss
whether any of these interpretations are more correct than the others.
Nevertheless I shall spend the rest of this paper on two aspects of Colossians, viz. the structure and the type of contents, respectively, claiming
that the text itself indicates answers to these questions in a way which
implies that, in a historical perspective, some interpretations are better
founded than others.

1. The Structure of Colossians

Normally we receive some help when it comes to finding the organization of a written text, e.g., through its division into chapters, sections and
paragraphs, maybe even introduced by headlines and subtitles. As a rule
we are not conscious of how these details work and how they influence
us when reading; they just work, and we have learnt to handle them. In
spoken texts we rely on such means as pauses, gestures, emphases, etc.
In both written and spoken texts there are such communication-aids as
meta-clauses, e.g., "I will now deal with the problem of ...", and several
other signals which contribute to organizing the text so as to make its
message and its accents understood by its recipient.[7]

As compared with the undisputed Pauline letters Colossians has a
heavier, less lively style, which is relatively poor in particles,[8] and there

---

[3] Gnilka1980, vii.
[4] Schweizer 1976, 7.
[5] Pokorný 1987, viii.
[6] Bruce 1984, 35.
[7] See, e.g., Gülich/Raible 1977, 27f., 42-46.
[8] Bujard 1973, 22-53.

are very few wide-ranging meta-statements, viz. texts on (other parts of) the text. Nevertheless there are markers and features which demarcate phases in the running communication or otherwise contribute to structure it. Some of these are of the following types:[9]

(a) The letter conventions, which to the reader/listener who knows them have the effect that, without further ado, address (1:1-2), report of thanksgiving[10] (1:3ff.), and letter closing (4:7-18) are recognized as natural stages in the text.

(b) Metacommunicative clauses, which, as such, address the reader/ listener concerning the text or parts thereof. One such is 2:4: "I say this in order that no one may delude you with persuasive speech." "This" directly refers to vv. 1-3, but indirectly also to 1:(23c)24-29, and thus binds this partial text together *and* above all explains to the reader the purpose with which it is said and the effect which it should have on him.

(c) Markers in the text which indicate the theme of the context and/or its type. Like Bruce C. Johanson I shall call them Thematic Markers (abbreviated ThM).[11] They often constitute a "metapropositional base" (abbreviated MB) and a "proposition" as E. U. Große describes them,[12] e.g., 1:9ff.: "we do not cease to pray (προσευχόμενοι) and demand", which is the metapropositional base, followed by the "proposition", viz. "that you may be filled with knowledge of his will in all wisdom and spiritual understanding, so that ...". Thus v. 9b characterizes the type of the following text: it contains something concerning which the author prays to God. But at the same time it also introduces a specific theme, viz. the addressees, being filled with knowledge of God's will. Furthermore, the type of theme indicated in the metapropositional base also tells us something of its function vis-à-vis the recipients; in this case, telling people that one prays to God that they shall behave in a certain manner is actually a kind of exhortation. Lastly, the metapropositional base with its proposition has a certain text-delimiting effect: it marks a new step when introduced. Its concluding effect on a partial text may be weaker, but one has passed a limit when the metapropositional base does not fit the text any more, whether this limit be clearly demarcated or not. In our example the limit can be located after v. 12 or v. 13: "so that you walk worthily" etc. of v. 10 clearly belongs to the prayer, and so do "being strengthened" of v. 11 and "giving thanks to the Father" of v. 12. One may get the impression that the participle adjunct to "the Father", viz.

---

[9] Note, however, that I shall not discuss minor details — such an enterprise could easily develop into a study of monograph-size. Cf. Johanson 1987.

[10] This is a better labelling than the usual "thanksgiving"; see Johanson 1987, 67.

[11] Cf. Johanson 1987, 29f., on "thematic markers".

[12] Große 1976, 95ff.; Johanson 1987, 29.

"making you fit for the heritage" is an ending, but this also holds true of the immediately following relative clause "who saved us … to the kingdom of his beloved son" (v. 13). But the relative clause actually introduces a little break in the style, and when "the son" is taken up in v. 14 through a new relative pronoun, the reader realizes that the prayer announced in v. 9 is left behind.

(d) One should not overlook the text-organizing factor which Raible calls "substitution on abstraction level" (abbreviated SAbstr.), i.e., expressions which refer to or replace a partial text or a part of a text in an abstracting, comprehensive way.[13] E.g., in Col 1:9, διὰ τοῦτο refers to 1:3-8.

(e) As mentioned above, Colossians is a rather meagre text in terms of particles and conjunctions. These relate smaller and larger parts of the text to each other, and I call them "relators."[14] One is found in 2:16: "thus (οὖν), no one may judge you in food and drink …". The οὖν indicates that with v. 16 follows a conclusion from the preceding text, viz. from 2:6–15. Reversely, these verses can be regarded as an argument for that which is said in v. 16(ff.).

(f) One further text–organizing factor should be mentioned, viz. the change in the constellation of persons, who are acting, mentioned or addressed in the text (abbreviated ShP). A change of person in a discourse may often have as a consequence that the relation of the text to the reader/listener is changed. Thus, e.g., a change to the second person often means that the addressees and their situation become more directly involved than may be the case in an argument held in the third person. Thus the introduction in 1:23c of "I, Paul" together with the shift in 1:23c and 24 to 1st person singular marks a transition.[15]

Most of the phenomena listed above are to be found on the text surface, or, with a slightly more technical term, on the text–syntactical level. However, they also have text–semantic effects, i.e. pointing to the contents and, also, to which things are done with the words (to allude to Austin again) in relation to the recipients' situation, i.e., the text-pragmatic aspect.[16]

---

[13] Raible 1972, 150f.

[14] Gülich/Raible 1977, 42ff., 138ff. (referring to K. Heger).

[15] In a narrative text it is natural that when a new episode starts, the principal character is introduced by something more than a personal pronoun, e.g., by a repetition of his/her name. Gülich and Raible call it a "renominalization" (1977, 44, 50). But in Col 1:23, the repetition of "Paul" has no such function, already because the text is no narrative. It rather has a more pragmatic than text-delimiting function (see Johanson 1987, 31 and 101, on 1 Thess 2:18).

[16] As to the thematic markers their purely syntactic aspect can, however, be rather weak. See Johanson 1987, 29.

When I now apply these analytic tools to Colossians, the results at which I arrive may resemble shadow boxing; the delimitations will appear to be familiar and rather similar to those which text editors and many commentators present. This should of course not surprise any one, since the text–organizing features to which I devote so much attention are also taken into account by editors and exegetes, although these scholars sometimes let other aspects, e.g., traditio-historical or genetic, guide their organization of the text.[17] It is, however, my hope that my results will emerge from signals of the text itself rather than from my theological interpretation thereof. In terms of contents and pragmatics my analysis may mean not radically new insights, but, hopefully, some new accents to the reading of Colossians.

The epistolary conventions present us with the first features of the organisation of Colossians: the address 1:1-2, the beginning of the reported thanksgiving, 1:3 (signal: εὐχαριστοῦμεν, MB), and the letter closing, 4:7-18 (ShP in 4:7; topics of closing, greetings which begin in v. 10 and are introduced by the ThM ἀσπάζεται, and the signature, v. 18).

For further details indicating the organization of the text as the listener heard it, we are referred to the directives *in* the text. In 1:9, the relator διὰ τοῦτο indicates that the epistolary reported thanksgiving has come to an end and that something new is imminent. On the other hand, τοῦτο is a substitution on the abstraction level and ties a string around 1:3-8, thus making this partial text the starting point or cause of that which follows. Thus, the reported thanksgiving is tied to the argument which begins in 1:9. Above I showed how προσευχόμενοι κτλ. of 1:9 functions as a metapropositional basis under the text through v. 12 or 13. There, without any distinct borderline, a new topic is introduced. It is treated in vv. (13)14-20, which is softly distinguished from its context through the focusing of a new person and a shift in literary style from a relatively heavy prose to a "hymnic" mode.[18]

The καὶ ὑμᾶς ποτε ... νυνὶ δὲ ἀποκατηλλάγητε[19] of 1:21f. has a text-organizing effect: there is a new constellation of persons: from "Christ and the all" to "you and Christ". But ἀποκατηλλάγητε sums up 1:13-20, and particularly its latter part (with ἀποκαταλλάξαι in v. 20) and applies it with the καὶ ὑμᾶς to the recipients. Thus, signals on the textual surface

---

[17] Thus they may, e.g., deal with the "hymn" of 1:15-20 as a separate unit, which, of course, is based on a traditio-historical considerations.

[18] If (13)15-20 is traditional or at least contains traditional material (for which there are good reasons) *and* if it is recognized as traditional by the recipients, they would the more easily keep it together as a unit when listening to/reading the text.

[19] Or, with Cod. Sin etc. ἀποκατήλλαξεν. I prefer the 2nd pers plur passive reading, since it seems to me to be the *lectio difficilior*.

bring 1:(12)13-20 and 1:21-22 together as two partial texts of one partial text on a higher level.

To the listener 1:23c and 1:24 mean a rather marked transition: ἐγὼ Παῦλος of 1:23c re-introduces the author, νῦν is a relator, which, in this case, denotes a shift in the perspective, and the abruptly introduced παθήματα mark a new theme. The τοῦτο of 2:4 introduces the meta-communicative verses 2:4f. ("I say this in order that no one delude you"), and above I showed how they put an end to 1:(23c)24-2:5, thus making it into one partial text. Within this unit the ἡλίκον ἀγῶνα (2:1) is a substitution on the abstraction level which covers 1:24-29 and makes these verses a subunit. θέλω γὰρ ὑμᾶς εἰδέναι is a metapropositional basis and introduces a subunit which is introduced as an explanation (γάρ) of 1:24-29. The sentence also has a metacommunicative function. For the bringing to mind of this ἀγών is connected with the final clause in 2:2: it is done "in order that (ἵνα) your hearts be comforted (παρακληθῶσιν)". This ἵνα-clause indicates the purpose which the information about the sender's situation should have with the recipients. Thus, 1:(23c)24-2:5 is a unit on a higher level, 1:(23c)24-29 is a subunit, followed by two others, viz. 2:1-3 and 2:4-5, the latter of which deals with the whole unit.

With 2:6 the ἐγώ disappears, and the constellation of persons becomes Christ and ὑμεῖς. An οὖν suggests that what follows is the consequence of a παράδοσις· ὡς παρελάβετε τὸν Χριστόν. On the one hand this expression is a substitution on the metalevel, referring to some text-external παράδοσις, but, on the other, it is also an abstract of what was mentioned earlier in the text concerning how the addressees have received Christ (1:5-7, 23, 27; 2:2, 5). Lastly, the 2 pers. plur. imperatives περιπατεῖτε ἐν αὐτῷ (2:6) and βλέπετε μή τις ὑμᾶς ἔσται ὁ συλαγωγῶν (2:8) mark a new phase in the communication; here is direct exhortation concerning the issues which are presented under each imperative. Thus, they function as a kind of thematic markers.

In the constellation "Christ – ὑμεῖς", the ὑμεῖς are focused in 2:6-8, whereas, with 2:9, Christ is the centre of interest. What is said of him in his relationship to ὑμεῖς is introduced with the relator ὅτι, and thus vv. 9ff. are presented as a reason for the imperatives in 2:6-8.

In 2:16 the listener encounters a new οὖν; it puts an end to the argument on Christ's importance to ὑμεῖς in 9-15, but presumably also to 2:6-8, for which 2:9-15 was an argument. Again, this relator suggests that the following is to be regarded as a result of that which precedes. A new constellation of persons, "you" and "somebody," also indicates a new step in the text, and the listener recognizes the "somebody" from the imperative of 2:8 (and from the meta-communicative clause of 2:4). The latter circumstance strengthens the impression that the conclusive effects of 2:16ff. also refer to 2:6-8.

The 3rd pers. sing. imperative sentence of 2:18-19 is asyndetically joined to that of 2:16-17. The conditional sentence of 2:20-23 is also asyndetically introduced, and, as to its semantic function it is but a third imperative, added to the two preceding ones.[20] Given the delimiting features of 3:1, to which I turn in a moment, 2:16-23 is thus kept together as a partial text which draws conclusions from the preceding passage which concern the ὑμεῖς and the "somebody."[21]

To the reader 3:1 (εἰ οὖν συνηγέρθητε) signals the beginning of a new phase in the current communication. οὖν suggests that what follows is a consequence of the preceding text. The συνηγέρθητε summarizes the argument of 2:9-15 on the abstraction level, and preceded by εἰ it makes 2:9-15 the presupposition of the following imperative, τὰ ἄνω ζητεῖτε. In 3:2 follows a second imperative, τὰ ἄνω φρονεῖτε, which is parallel to the first one. The parallelism is strengthened by the fact that it is asyndetically joined to the preceding sentence. This latter imperative too has a presupposition attached to it, viz. the sentence in 3:3, ἀπεθάνετε γὰρ κτλ., which is but another abstraction of the preceding argument in 2:9-15 (cf. 2:12f.). Together the two imperatives function as a thematic marker. If the recipients were accustomed to Pauline epistolary habits, the impression that they were now entering a parenetic section would be strengthened by their knowledge of the common structure of Pauline letters. That the author knew of it we can assume for certain,[22] as to the addressees it is difficult to be positive.

The οὖν of 3:5 indicates that a new step is taken, but the fact that the imperative mood of 3:1-4 is retained indicates that the new imperatives (νεκρώσατε κτλ.) can be regarded as consequences, or further developments of those in 3:1-4. The νεκρώσατε can, in addition, be regarded as a

---

[20] Note the similarity: 2:16f.: "no one may judge you in terms of food and drink ... which is a shadow ..., but Christ is the body"; 2:20 can easily be transformed into a clause which is literally parallel to 2:16f. (the semantic parallelism is there already): "no one may give you rules in terms of what you should touch ... which is perishable, for you died with Christ".

[21] Hartman 1985, 109f. There are, however, some signs that 2:20–23 also have a concluding function. Rhetorical conventions were namely that at the ending of an argument the speaker could make a short enumeration and recapitulate important facts in such a way that the audience was persuaded to agree with him. One could use general terms, and the items could be enumerated asyndetically, polysyndetically, or with a combination thereof. Alliteration and assonances could add to the effect. See Lausberg 1960, § 434, 661-71. All of these phenomena occur in v. 20, where the last colon also contains the alliterations in τιμῇ τινι and πρὸς πλησμονήν and the funny — or scornful — effect of the itacism; the phrase was pronounced in this way: *ouk en timi tini pros plismonin tis sarkos.*

[22] Sanders 1966, 28–45.

Thematic Marker. The οὖν of v. 12 (ἐνδύσασθε οὖν) introduces further consequences, to be related on the one hand to ἀπόθεσθε of v. 8, to ἀπεκ-δυσάμενοι κτλ. of v. 9 and particularly to ἐνδυσάμενοι τὸν νέον (ἄνθρωπον) of v. 10. This makes the motif of the New Man (v. 10) an underlying theme of 3:12 onward. Thus, in v. 12 follow further parenetic consequences, added to those introduced in v. 5. Now the admonitions are positive, whereas the former ones were negative.

The imperatives continue through 4:6, where, as we have noted, the letter closing begins and the shape of the text is influenced by epistolary conventions.

Bringing these observations on the structure to a conclusion we can summarize them as follows:

1. 1:1-2 epistolary address (letter convention).

2. 1:3-4:6 corpus of the argument (letter convention).

    2.1. 1:3-2:23 exhortation with argument.

        2.1.1. 1:3-1:23(b) indirect exhortations with argument.

            2.1.1.1. 1:3-1:23(b) (ShP 1:23c ["I, Paul"]).

                2.1.1.1.1. 1:3-8 reported thanksgiving (letter convention; MB [εὐ-χαριστοῦμεν]).

                2.1.1.1.2. 1:9-12(13) reported prayer (caused by 1:3-8; MB [προσ-ευχόμενοι], putting a limit at 12(13); SAbstr [τοῦτο]; relator [διὰ τοῦτο]).

                2.1.1.1.3. 1:(13)14-23(b) passage in "hymnic" style and application (ShP [Christ – you]).

                    2.1.1.1.3.1. 1:(13)14-20 "hymn" (different style; SAbstr [1:21, ἀποκαταλλάγητε]; ShP [Christ]).

                    2.1.1.1.3.2. 1:21-23(b) application (different style; ShP [you]).

        2.1.2. 1:(23c)24–2:23 direct exhortations with argument.

            2.1.2.1. 1:(23c)24–2:5 reporting on the author in order to explain the exhortative purpose of writing (MC [2:4 ἵνα μηδεὶς ... παρα-λογίζηται]; SAbstr [τοῦτο ... λέγω]; ShP ["I, Paul"]; relator [νῦν]).

                2.1.2.1.1. 1:(23c)24-29 report on author's work for addressees (SAbstr [ἡλίκον ἀγῶνα]; ThM [παθήματα]).

                2.1.2.1.2. 2:1-3 purpose of 1:(23c)24-29 (MB [θέλω ... ὑμᾶς εἰδέναι]; relator [γάρ]).

                2.1.2.1.3. 2:4-5 metacommunicative clauses on 1:24-2:3 (SAbstr [τοῦτο ... λέγω]).

            2.1.2.2. 2:6-2:23 direct exhortation with basic argument (SM [παρε-λάβετε]; ShP [Christ – you]; relator [οὖν]).

2.1.2.2.1.   2:6–8 imperatives (ThM [περιπατεῖτε, βλέπετε]).

2.1.2.2.2.   2:9-15 reason for 6-8 (ShP [Christ vs. you {from 13c; "we"}, powers]; relator [ὅτι]).

2.1.2.2.3.   2:16–23 imperative conclusions concerning "you" and "somebody" from 2:(6)9–15 (relator [οὖν]; ShP ["you", "somebody"]).

2.2.   3:1-4:6 parenesis (Pauline letter convention).

2.2.1.   3:1-4 parenetic conclusions from 2:(6)9–23, and, indirectly, from 1:(23c)24–2:5 (ThM [τὰ ἄνω ζητεῖτε, τὰ ἄνω φρονεῖτε]; SAbstr [συνηγέρθητε, ἀπεθάνετε); relator [οὖν]; Pauline letter convention).

2.2.2.   3:5-4:6 continued, more specific parenesis (relator [οὖν]).

2.2.2.1.   3:5-11 negative commandments (ThM [νεκρώσατε]).

2.2.2.2.   3:12-4:6 positive commandments (ThM [ἐνδύσασθε, the New Man]; relator [οὖν]).

3.   4:7-18 letter closing (letter convention).

3.1.   4:7-9 beginning of letter closing (ShP [from 2nd pers. imperat. to Tychicus]).

3.2.   4:10-17 greetings (ThM [ἀσπάζεται]).

3.3.   4:18 signature.

In a few instances, the borderlines between the sections are not lines but transitory passages, something which is natural in texts written to be spoken. It goes without saying that the detailed hierarchy of the structure is open to discussion.

Let us now return to Col 2:1-5, which in the beginning of this paper served as an example of the different modes of assessing structure and contents. The differences between the commentators' suggestions were, as we remember, considerable. As to the structure of the letter my result above is similar to that of P. Pokorný. But my approach pays more attention to what the author says he is doing. It is a typical difference between us that P. Pokorný finds 2:1-5 to be a part of the unit 1:24-2:5 over which he puts the headline "The authority of the Apostle — the binding of salvation to the apostolic message".[23] In other words, he regards the semantic rather than the pragmatic aspect. That other commentaries differ even more evidently depends on a similar fundamental tendency to read the text as one on theology.[24] But they also pay less regard to the

---

[23] Similarly also Martin 1973; 1:24-2:5 are put under the headline "Paul's Mission and Pastoral Concern".

[24] Typical in this respect are the commentators who refer our passage to a "doctrinal" part of the letter. Thus McDonald 1980, 21; Rogers 1980, xxii; Reumann 1985, 113.

syntactical aspects, letting, as it seems, the contents structure the text more than the signs on the textual surface are allowed to do.

2. Type of Contents and Its Function

In the preceding deliberations one could observe that often the same markers not only had relevance to the surface structure of the text but also concerned the contents or its function within the text or in relationship to the addressees. I now turn to this aspect. What does, then, the author seem to "do with" his "words".

The reported thanksgiving of 1:3-8 describes the addressees' good standing, of which the author has learnt from Epaphras. No doubt it functions as a *captatio benevolentiae*. This *captatio* is then said to be the cause (διὰ τοῦτο, v. 9) of that which follows, viz. the reported prayer of 1:9-12(13). I have already stated, above, that telling people that one prays that they may have certain virtues actually has the semantic function of gently exhorting them to evince these virtues. The strength of the indirect exhortation is of course augmented through the preceding praise of the addresses' moral standard. The virtues sought are rather generally expressed: knowing God's will in spiritual wisdom, a life worthy of the Lord, steady endurance, being thankful for the heritage among the saints. Nevertheless they apparently stand in opposition to the so-called philosophy which claims to represent better morals and a higher, divine wisdom (see 2:8, 16, 18, 21, 23).

We encounter a similar exhortative function in 1:21–23. The passage applies the preceding "hymn" (1:(13)14-20) to the addressees. In the context the author also presents the purpose of the reconciliation of the ὑμεῖς, viz. they should be holy and blameless (1:22). To state such a purpose of the addressees' participation in the reconciliation is already a mild exhortation, although it is held in general terms. It becomes more precise, when immediately the author adds a condition: the holiness etc. can be realized, insofar as (εἴ γε) they remain steadfast and are not shaken from the hope of the gospel. This refers to the situation of the letter, viz. the risk that the addressees will yield to the "philosophy". In the "hymn" the authorities of the "philosophy" were ranked under Christ. Thus the "hymn" forms a Christological base under the indirect exhortation of 1:21-23.[25] It performs two functions, albeit indirectly: to defame the "philosophy" and its authorities; the mysterious powers, lordships etc., whose authority the "philosophy" cites, are all dependent on Christ.

---

[25] If the addressees recognized the "hymn" as a (semi)quotation, it naturally stood out as a unit. But nevertheless it is well fused with its context. It should also be noted that its argumentative weight may be greater if a recipient identifies it as traditional.

Secondly it provides a reason why the recipients should not yield to the "philosophy"; they already have what they need with Christ (the body), forgiveness of sins, reconciliation with the all.

Thus, 1:3-23 proves to be more exhortative than the commentaries generally lead us to believe. 1:3-8 will predispose the listeners favourably to receive the exhortation in 1:9-12(13), 1:(13)14-20 is an awe-inspiring, Christological foundation under the exhortation in 1:22-23, indirectly also casting a shadow over the powers to which the addressees should not submit.

The next partial text on a relatively high level is 1:(23c)24–2:5. Some features of the passage function as a new *captatio benevolentiae*, particularly in 1:(23c)24-29, which describes how the author disinterestedly devotes himself to his task for the benefit of the addressees. Thus, in the sentence on the apostle's struggles the ὑμεῖς are introduced as a favoured part three times in a somewhat astonishing way (v. 24, "my sufferings for your sake"; v. 25, "to fill God's word to you"; v. 27, "the mystery among the Gentiles, Christ in you"). In addition, at the end of the passage (2:5), the author expresses his joy over their order and steadfastness. The reason why (γάρ) the author so describes his struggle is, however, its purpose, presented in 2:1-3: the addressees shall be exhorted or comforted (παρακληθῶσιν) in that they are held together in love and knowledge of God's mystery in Christ (2:2).[26] Furthermore, according to 2:4 the purpose of what the author "says" (i.e., in 1:24-2:3) is that no one shall deceive them through πιθανολογία. Of course the overall effect of both praise and purpose declaration is also indirectly exhortative: keep to the Christian religion you have learnt.

Against the background of the latter *captatio*, the second subunit, 2:6-8, introduces two thematic imperatives (2:6 περιπατεῖτε, 2:8 βλέπετε ...). With regard to the addressees' situation they are more outspoken than the preceding indirect exhortations. Now the addressees are explicitly enjoined to remain at that which they have received, and are warned not to pay any regard to the "philosophy". In other words, the difference in terms of what is "done with" the "words" is rather one of mood than of contents.

Above I suggested that the "hymn" in 1:(13)14-20 forms a Christological foundation under the indirectly exhortative 1:21-23. It appears that 2:9-15 has a similar function over against 2:16-23, where the recipients are admonished not to allow "somebody", i.e. representatives of the

---

[26] The combination of *captatio* and indirect exhortation is particularly striking in 2:2-5: "I say this — i e., I tell about my struggle for your knowing about the treasures of wisdom hid in Christ — *in order that no one deceive you*; because (γάρ) ... in my spirit *I am with you*, *rejoicing when I see your order* ...."

"philosophy", to be an ethical authority over them. This "somebody" is of course the same as in 2:4 and 2:8. Thus the Christological passage 2:9-15 is closely related both to the imperatives in 2:6-8, giving the reason for them (ὅτι) and to the admonitory triple conclusions in 2:16-23. As was the case with 1:(13)14-20, 2:9-15 also denigrates the status of the powers and lordships (Christ is their head [v. 10] and has triumphed over them [v. 15]), and other motifs serve the pragmatic purpose too, viz. the indwelling in Christ of the πλήρωμα τῆς θεότητος (v. 9), the elimination of the δόγματα (v. 14; cf. v. 20 τί ... δογματίζεσθε). In other words, although certainly essential parts of 2:9-15 may be traditional,[27] in its context the passage serves the admonitory purpose of 2:6-23, indeed, its being traditional can strengthen its effect.

Thus we have seen how also the partial text 1:(23c)24-2:23 is borne throughout by an exhortative purpose which, furthermore, is decisive for the role of the theological (or, rather, Christological) elements. They are there to serve the exhortation. But it also turns out that its structure is parallel[28] to that of 1:3-23b(c). Both begin with a *captatio benevolentiae*, both continue with a Christological passage which forms the basis of an exhortation. However, in 1:3-23b(c) the exhortation is milder, more indirect and held in less specific terms, whereas in 1:(23c)24-2:23 it is much more outspoken, in 2:16-23 culminating in citations of (and derogation of) actual rules and claims on the part of the "philosophy".

So far, we have seen that the "theological" part of Colossians seems to aim not so much at theology from which some practical consequences are drawn, as at exhortation for which theological arguments are adduced. This exhortation has a negative and a positive side, which are closely interrelated. Thus, the addressees must not yield to the demands of the "philosophy" concerning what to revere and how to behave. Instead, they must keep to what they have learnt, both in belief and in morality. In matters of belief the first two chapters were explicit, whereas the exhortations were rather general; the readers are summoned, e.g., to be filled with knowledge of God's will (1:9), or to "live in him, rooted and built up in him" (2:7). Only the references to the rules of the "philosophy", which the addresses must not respect, are specific (2:16-23).

What, then, of the parenesis, 3:1-4:6? How far, if at all, do the pragmatic aspects, which are so important in 1:3-2:23, colour this part of the letter? Reflecting upon a possible answer to such a question, we should begin by asking, why a parenesis at all? The author does not mention any reason why he writes these lines, nor does he refer to any particular

[27] See Cannon 1983, 37-49.
[28] Note, in addition, that each of them refers to a teacher of the community, viz. Epaphras in 1:7 and Paul in 1:23f., 2:1.

problems to which they are directed. Instead, we are to think of Pauline letter convention: this is how Paul wrote letters.[29] But Paul was not alone in such a practice: in the NT 1 Peter, James and Hebrews follow a similar pattern, and it seems that among the Jews there was a convention to the same effect; thus, e.g., The Epistle of Baruch (2 *Apoc.Bar.* 78-86) is an example of an epistle which, at its end, contains instructions to keep to the Law.

Thus, there are no direct indications in 3:1-4:6 as to what the author is doing with his words — except that he summons his addressees. There might be details which aim at the addressees' concrete situation, i.e. especially the intruding "philosophy"; but then we cannot but surmise which they are in assuming hidden polemic against the "philosophy". As a matter of fact this is also done by commentators, and some random examples of such possible polemics are the following: over against the ascetic morality of the "philosophy" the author presents traditional lists of vices and virtues, which are an adaptation of God's own Law, the Decalogue,[30] furthermore, against the so-called humility of the "philosophers" (2:18) he puts the mildness and mercy of the list of virtues (3:12), and over against the "philosophers'" angelic service (2:18), sabbaths, etc. (2:16) he refers his readers to the word of Christ (3:16). Above all, the central position of Christ may have meant such a hidden contrast. As the New Man, whom the readers shall put on (3:12), he is the fundamental pattern of the whole parenesis,[31] and also in the "household code" he is a key figure to whom the particular rules are related. This dominant position is in line with what we learn in 2:14f. concerning his victory and supremacy over the cosmic powers.

When we regard the parenesis in this way, the very fact that it uses traditional material can also be an indirect address to the recipients, viz. telling them that they must hold fast to the well established "good old religion", instead of yielding to the novelties and exclusive things which the "philosophy" favours.

It is also worthwhile to examine the list of greetings, asking what the author is doing to his addressees. One point is so obvious that we may not even perceive it, viz. that again and again the writer relates himself to the recipients. Thus, e.g., "my" situation is reported to "you" (4:7), "you" shall remember "my" chains (4:18), Onesimus is "my" brother and one among "you". Thus, the author binds his audience to himself, and so these may be more inclined to accept what he tells them.

---

[29] Schnider/Stenger 1987, 76-107.
[30] Gnilka 1980, 185; Hartman 1987.
[31] Gnilka 1980, 187, 192.

To the greeting from Epaphras (4:12) is added some positive words on him: he is Christ's slave and worries about the addressees, praying that they will "stand mature and assured in all God's will". Indirectly this urges the readers to be steadfast against the "philosophy".

Finally, in the very last line of Colossians, we may surmise a last cautious admonition; "Paul" prays: "remember my chains" (4:18). This wish should be understood in the light of 1:24-29, where the readers have learnt about the apostle's struggle and sufferings in his mission for their sake. Here he seems to tell them: if you do not remain steadfast, you cause pain to somebody who is already suffering.

Approaching Colossians as I do in this paper does not mean forgetting that its author is a theologian. But I believe that this theologian has formulated himself in such a way that he stands forward as a pastor who uses theological reasons for an argument, the purpose of which is mainly pastoral and exhortative. If this is so, it should have consequences for scholars who seek a historical understanding of which things he did with the words of Colossians.

Bibliography

Austin, J. L. 1962: *How to Do Things with Words*. The William James Lectures delivered at Harvard University in 1955, Oxford: Oxford University Press 1962.

Bruce, F. F. 1984: *The Epistles to the Colossians, to Philemon, and to the Ephesians* (NICNT), Grand Rapids, MI: Eerdmans 1984.

Bujard, W. 1973: *Stilanalytische Untersuchungen zum Kolosserbrief als Beitrag zur Methodik von Sprachvergleichen* (StUNT 11), Göttingen: Vandenhoeck & Ruprecht 1973.

Cannon, G. E. 1983: *The Use of Traditional Materials in Colossians*, Macon, GA: Mercer University Press 1983.

Gnilka, J. 1980: *Der Kolosserbrief* (HThK X:1), Freiburg–Basel–Vienna: Herder 1980.

Große, E. U. 1976: *Text und Kommunikation. Eine lingvistische Einführung in die Funktionen der Texte*, Stuttgart etc.: Kohlhammer 1976.

Gülich, E./Raible, W. 1977: *Lingvistische Textmodelle* (UTB 130), Munich: Fink 1977.

Hartman, L. 1985: *Kolosserbrevet* (KNT 12), Uppsala: EFS-förlaget 1985.

— 1987: "Code and Context: A Few Reflections on the Parenesis of Col 3:6-4:1", in: G. F. Hawthorne/O. Betz (eds.), *Tradition and Interpretation in the New Testament, Essays in Honour of E. E. Ellis*, Grand Rapids, MI: Eerdmans (Tübingen: Mohr (Siebeck) 1987, 237-47.

Johanson, B. C. 1987: *To all the Brethren. A Text–Linguistic and Rhetorical Approach to 1 Thessalonians* (CB.NT 16), Stockholm: Almqvist & Wiksell International 1987.

Lausberg, H. 1960: *Handbuch der literarischen Rhetorik,* Munich: Hueber Verlag, 1960.

Martin, R. P. 1973: *Colossians. The Church's Lord and the Christian's Liberty,* Grand Rapids, MI: Zondervan 1973.

McDonald, H. D. 1980: *Commentary on Colossians & Philemon* (WBC 44), Waco, TX: Word 1980.

Pokorný, P. 1987: *Der Brief des Paulus an die Kolosser* (ThHK X:1), Berlin: Evangelische Verlagsanstalt 1987.

Raible, W. 1972: *Satz und Text* (BZRPh 132), Tübingen: Niemeyer 1972.

Reumann, J. H. P. 1985: *Colossians* (Augsburg Commentary on the NT), Minneapolis, MN: Augsburg 1985.

Rogers, P. V. 1980: *Colossians* (NT Message 15), Wilmington, DL: Glazier 1980.

Sanders, E. P. 1966: "Literary Dependence in Colossians", in: *JBL* 85 (1966) 28–45.

Schnider, F. S./Stenger, W. 1987: *Studien zum neutestamentlichen Briefformular* (NT TS 11), Leiden: Brill 1987.

Schweizer, E. 1976: *Der Brief an die Kolosser* (EKK XII), Neukirchen-Vluyn: Neukirchener/Zürich, Einsiedeln etc.: Benziger 1976.

Supplement

Wright, N. T.: *The Epstles of Paul to the Colossians and to Philemon* (TNTC), Grand Rapids, MI: Eerdmans 1986.

Aletti, J.-N.: *Saint Paul Épître aux Colossiens* (EtB), Paris: Gabalda 1993.

Wolter, M.: *Der Brief an die Kolosser. Der Brief an Philemon* (ÖTBK 12), Gütersloh: Mohn/Würzburg: Echter 1993.

Barth, M./ Blanke, H.: *Colossians* (AncB 34B), New York etc.: Doubleday 1994.

Betz, H. D.: "Paul's 'Second Presence' in Colossians", in: T. Fornberg/D. Hellholm (eds.), *Texts and Contexts. Biblical Texts in Their Textual and Situational Contexts. Essays in Honor of Lars Hartman,* Oslo – Copenhagen – Stockholm – Boston: Scandinavian University Press 1995, 507-18.

Drake, A. E.: "The Riddle of Colossians: *Quaerendo invenietis*", in: *NTS* 41 (1995) 123-44.

Dunn, J. D. G.: *The Epistles to the Colossians and to Philemon* (NIGTC), Grand Rapids, MI: Eerdmans / Carlisle: Paternoster 1996.

12. 1 Cor 14:1-25
Argument and Some Problems

Asked to deliver a paper on 1 Cor 14:1-25, and notably an exegetical one, I have chosen to approach my topic in the following manner. Firstly, I will try to unravel the argument of the passage, as I think such an undertaking may be of some importance for an exegesis of it. Secondly, I will discuss a few particular issues in the text. This means that I am not going to comment on the whole text and thus will disregard many details and aspects which certainly could be treated, but for which I refer to the standard commentaries.

1. The Structure of the Argument

1.1. The Literary Context

Our passage is part of 1 Cor 12-14, the contents of which are introduced in 12:1, "concerning the spiritual things ..." (περὶ δὲ τῶν πνευματικῶν).[1] Paul was probably induced to deal with the topic by a letter from the Corinthians concerning this and other problems.[2] In the Corinthian church the common Christian experience of the Holy Spirit had turned into an enthusiasm that Paul found necessary to temper, not least because of the disorder it caused at the worship. Some people, notably the ones who spoke in tongues, thought that they were better equipped with spiritual gifts than others, and this seems to have coloured their behaviour at the common worship.[3] They may even have called themselves πνευματικοί.[4]

---

[1] Reasons can be advanced in favour of reading the masc. plur. (see, e.g., Weiß 1910/70, 294 and Schmithals 1971, 172), but the χαρίσματα in the context and τὰ πνευματικά of 15:1 make me prefer reading the neutr. Cf. note 4.

[2] See 1 Cor 7:1.

[3] For attempts to fit these details into a wider framework see, e.g., Hurd 1965/83, 186ff.; Barrett 1971, 1ff.; Conzelmann 1975, 14ff.; Horsley 1980-81.

[4] That could explain the differentiation between prophets and πνευματικοί in 14:37. Although Paul, then, would accept their usage, he widens its reference by pointing to all the gifts of the πνεῦμα.

Paul has dealt with disorder at the worship already in chapter 11, and his argument there concerning the Lord's Supper is not dissimilar to some fundamental lines of thought in chapters 12-14, such as the concept of the one body and of the mutuality of its members in chapter 12, the stress on love in chapter 13, and the principle of the edification of the church in chapter 14.

The topic of "the spiritual things" is first dealt with in a general way in chapter 12: there are different gifts but one spirit, who distributes them on the whole community. This is developed through the imagery of the body, vv. 12-27, which is followed, in 12:28, by a list of spiritual gifts, viz., apostles, prophets, teachers, etc. It is probably not by chance that "kinds of tongues" come last. Also the appended series of rhetorical questions — "are all apostles?", etc. — puts the glossolalia last: "do all speak in tongues, do all interpret?" (12:30). The implicit answer should be: "no, only some are apostles, some prophets, etc., only some speak in tongues and only some interpret".

The next sentence starts a new line of thought: "but strive for the greater gifts". Read — or, rather, heard — together with the preceding sentences it says: "given the differentiation of the gifts — a lesser one of which is glossolalia — you need not stay at the bottom. To want to become an apostle may be too much,[5] but why not a prophet or a teacher, who come next?".

So everything is prepared for an argument in favour of these greater gifts, but instead chapter 13 comes in. On the one hand, the chapter apparently lies there like an island between 12:31a and 14:1b,[6] but on the other, its content fits in well with the context, both details (e.g., the tongues of men and angels [v. 1], prophecy [vv. 2:8f.], tongues [v. 8], childish talk [v. 11]) and the general theme of love.

So much for the context that precedes 14:1-25. As to 14:26-40, in which "the spiritual things" are still dealt with, I will say a few words on that passage below apropos of the organization of chapter 14 and its content. One can also question whether one should delimit 14:1-25 as one passage, in differentiation from 14:26-40, and not, rather, draw the line between v. 19 and v. 20. I will return to that question also, when dealing with the organization of the chapter.

---

[5] Holmberg 1980, 198 points to Paul's putting himself as a apostle in power over the prophets.

[6] The awkwardness of the bridge in 14:1a from chap. 13 to 14:1b strengthens this impression. See the comm., e.g., those of Weiß 1910/70, Barrett 1971, and Conzelmann 1975.

1.2. *The Argumentative Structure of 14:1-25*

1.2.1. *Introductory Considerations*

My presentation below of the argument of 14:1-25 may suggest that I disagree violently with Dr Conzelmann, who comments on the argument of 1 Cor 14 in this way: "However sharply outlined the *theme* of chap. 14, the *argument* is loose".[7] I may not think that it is so loose as Dr Conzelmann does, but my presentation is misunderstood, if anyone should think that I am suggesting that the argument of chapter 14 is actually very strict and logical. What I *am* doing, is to try to trace how elements of the text itself organize it, and thereby possibly also reveal something of its argumentative structure.[8] I regard my analysis mainly as an attempt to articulate a little more exactly what any reader unconsciously does when he reads a text and lets it organize its message to him. The figures in the table below that indicate an hierarchy between the elements in the text are there to make my suggestions clear, but these are precisely suggestions, not firm conclusions. Not least they should be taken together with my attempts to describe the function of the textual elements in question (in the fourth column of my display).

The features of the text that organize its argument are of different kinds. First, there are expressions that function like guides to the reader as to the core of the message. Such are the imperatives in the beginning and the end of the chapter, echoed in vv. 5 and 12. Another organizing factor, but less salient, is the repetition of a word or the recurrence of words belonging to a particular word field (e.g., the terms having to do with clearness in 14:5ff.). One might call such expressions and factors "paradigmatic".[9] Details of another type that organize the text are "relators" such as adverbs, particles, and conjunctions,[10] but also phrases on a meta-level in relation to other parts of the text (τί οὖν ἐστίν, 14:5, 26, and οὕτως καὶ ὑμεῖς, 14:9, 12, could be deemed such.[11] Further organizing details are renewed allocutions ("brothers") and transitions, e.g., from 1st person to 3rd. These latter phenomena tend to create caesuras in the text.[12] In my display I do not differentiate between the elements of the latter types, but present them in one column superscribed "relators

---

[7] Conzelmann 1975, 233.

[8] My approach is inspired by the text-linguistics, but I want to state clearly that my knowledge in that field is, at the most, superficial. The literature is hopelessly vast, but for this paper I have, i.a., consulted Stock 1974, 28ff.; Schmidt 1976, and Gülich/Raible 1977.

[9] See, e.g., Stock 1974, 30ff.

[10] See, e.g., Stock 1974, 33ff., and Gülich/Raible 1977, 42ff., 138ff. (referring to Heger) on "relators".

[11] Cf. Gülich/Raible 1977, 27f.

etc.". As to the first, topic-deciding factor (the "paradigmatic" type), I consider that in the introductory paragraphs of 1.2.2.

1.2.2. A Display of the Argumentative Structure of 14:1-25

Chap. 14 has a practical message. That that is so, is seen from the conclusions in vv. 39f.; "thus (ὥστε), brothers, strive after prophecy and do not prevent the glossolalia. But let everything be done decently and in good order". This message is to be understood in direct relation to the concrete worship situation in Corinth.[13] Paul wants a corrected practice and the correction means a promotion of prophecy at the cost of glossolalia, which, however, should not disappear. The corrected practice Paul wants the Corinthians to assume is described in vv. 26ff., and the preparation for that message on church order is made in vv. 1-25.

If, then, vv. 26-40 are mainly practical advice, and vv. 1-25 are an argumentative background for that, nonetheless the practical viewpoints play a decisive role also in the first half of the chapter. So the practical aim comes to the surface of the text in the passages where the author expresses his will as to the desired practice. Thus, the reader enters the chapter with 12:31 in his mind, "strive (ζηλοῦτε[14]) for the greater gifts". This is reinforced by the imperatives of the introduction in 14:1, which form a transition in three steps from chapter 13 and set the topic: "Pursue love, and strive (ζηλοῦτε) for the spiritual gifts, but especially that you may prophesy". The same practical theme reappears in 14:5: "I want you all to speak in tongues, but more that you prophesy". In 14:12f. the argument has advanced further, so that the apostle can be more precise in his practical advice: "since you are men who strive for spirits,[15] be eager to be rich for the edification of the church. Therefore, he who speaks in tongues should pray that he may interpret".

The imperative of v. 20 is a little less practical: "Brothers, do not be children in discernment, but be babes in evil, yet be mature in discernment". Nonetheless, in the context this exhortation is almost as practical

---

[12] Certainly the style of 1-25 stands close to that of the diatribe, characterized by short sentences, pictorial language, shifts of person, etc., but this cultural background does not, of course, exclude that the stylistic features have the communicative effects mentioned. — Dautzenberg (1975, 27) takes as "strukturbildend" only some elements that are characterized by their type of expression, such as imperatives and questions.

[13] Not only the fact that prophecy and glossolalia belonged to the worship must lead the readers' thoughts to the worship, but also the way in which Paul uses the word ἐκκλησία in the chapter (vv. 4, 5, 12, etc.). Cf. Cerfaux 1959, 189ff.

[14] I take it as an imperative, not as an indicative. Cf. Iber 1963.

[15] The expression is enigmatic: is it only another way of saying "spiritual gifts" (so, e.g., Conzelmann 1975, *ad loc.*), or is there some idea of indwelling spirits behind (so, e.g., Héring 1962, *ad loc.*; Ellis 1973-74, 134f.)?

as the preceding ones, for obviously it says to the Corinthians: "be mature in that you balance rightly prophecy and glossolalia".

These imperatives (or equivalents to such) should have an organizing effect on the argument. Where they appear, viz., in vv. 1, 5, 12f., and 20, they can give the argument a push or a new turn, or they can sum it up. But they are only one factor, a "paradigmatic" one, and one that interplays with others, to be considered later on. The deliberations so far of their role form, however, the background of the following detailed suggestions as to the argumentative structure that especially take into account the elements of the other types.

Vv.	Relators etc.	Organization	Function	Argument
1b-4	Asynd.[a]	1	Practical main rule, with argument	Community-internal argument for main rule
1 bc		1.1	Main rule	Prophecy preferred among the spiritual gifts
2-4	γάρ	1.2	Explicative arguments in two steps	Prophecy edifies the church, glossolalia does not
2-3		1.2.1	Step one, more general	Characterizing glossolalia and prophecy
2		1.2.1.1	Depreciation of glossolalia	
2a		1.2.1.1.1	Negative statement	Glossolalia not addressed to men
2b	ἀλλά	1.2.1.1.2	Positive statement	Glossolalia addressed to God
2c	γάρ	1.2.1.1.3	Reason	Nobody hears; "mysteries"
3	δέ	1.2.1.2	Appreciation of prophecy	Prophecy addressed to men, edification, exhortation, etc.
4	Asynd.	1.2.2	Step two, more specific	Characterizing glossolalia and prophecy with regard to edification
4a		1.2.2.1	Depreciation of glossolalia	Speaker in tongues edifies himself

Vv.	*Relators etc.*	*Organization*	*Function*	*Argument*
4b	δέ	1.2.2.2	Appreciation of prophecy	Prophet edifies the church
5-19	δέ	2	Presentation of an exception to main rule, with argument and explanations	Glossolalia, if made understood, edifies the church
5a	Trans. to 1st[b] pers. sing.	2.1	Repetition of main rule	Prophecy preferred to glossolalia (because of edification)
5bc	δέ, trans. to 3rd pers.	2.2	Presentation of exception	If interpreted, glossolalia is as good as prophecy
5b		2.2.1	Statement of normal situation	Prophecy is better than glossolalia
5c	ἐκτὸς εἰ μή	2.2.2	Statement of exception	Glossolalia is interpreted
6-12	νῦν δέ, alloc.	2.3	Argument for exception	Clearness promotes edification
6	ἐάν, trans. to 1st pers. sing.	2.3.1	Personal example	What is useful and not useful
6a		2.3.1.1	Negatively	Glossolalia is not useful
6b	τί... ἐὰν μή	2.3.1.2	Positively	Speaking in revelation, knowledge, prophecy, teaching, is useful[c]
7-12	Trans. to 3rd pers.	2.3.2	Demonstration through examples with applications, in two steps	Only distinct language has desired communicative effect, i.e., edification
7-9		2.3.2.1	First step	Importance of clearness of that which is to be understood
7-8	ὅμως[d]	2.3.2.1.1	Three[e] examples	Examples from musical instruments

Vv.	Relators etc.	Organiza-tion	Function	Argument
7		2.3.2.1.1.1	Example one and two	Κιθάρα and αὐλός: one understands (γνω-) only if there is distinction (διαστολή)
8	καὶ γάρ	2.3.2.1.1.2	Example three	Trumpet: one obeys the signal only if it is not unclear (ἄδηλος)
9	οὕτως καί, trans. to 2nd pers. plur.	2.3.2.1.2	Preliminary appli-cation to address-ees	The "tongues" should produce clear (εὔσημος) speech so that one under-stands (γνω-)
10-12	Asynd., trans. to 3rd pers.	2.3.2.2	Second step	Only distinct speech can edify the church
10-11		2.3.2.2.1	Example	Example from language
10		2.3.2.2.1.1	Basic statement	Point of departure: lan-guages have meaning
11	ἐὰν οὖν, trans. to [1st pers. sing.]	2.3.2.2.1.2	The example itself	If I do not know the meaning (δύναμις), I am a βάρβαρος to the other, and he is a βάρβαρος to me
12	οὕτως καί, trans. to 2nd pers. plur.	2.3.2.2.2	Application, gener-ally held, to addressees	Striving for "spirits" they should promote edifica-tion (through clearness)
12a	ἐπεί	2.3.2.2.2.1	Restatement of the position of addressees	They strive for "spirits"
12b		2.3.2.2.2.2	Advice	They should seek the edi-fication of the church
13-19	διό	2.4	Practical conclu-sion concerning exception, and explanation	Speaker in tongues needs interpretation so that oth-ers are edified
13	Trans. to 3rd pers. sing.	2.4.1	Conclusion	Speaker in tongues should pray for interpre-tation

Vv.	*Relators etc.*	*Organiza-tion*	*Function*	*Argument*
14-19	γάρ (?)[f] (asynd.?)	2.4.2	Explanations	Reason for 2.4.1: If νοῦς is involved in prayer, others are edified
14-15	Trans. to 1st pers. sing.	2.4.2.1	Explanation, positive, in 1st pers.	
14	ἐάν	2.4.2.1.1	Possible negative background	In glossolalia only the spirit is active, not νοῦς
15	τί οὖν ἐστιν	2.4.2.1.2	Positive corrective statement	How it really should be: prayer in spirit and νοῦς
16-17	ἐπεί, trans. to 2nd pers. sing.	2.4.2.2	Further (negative) explanation in form of assumed Cor situation	Prayer in spirit prevents the uninitiated from understanding and from edification
16a	ἐάν	2.4.2.2.1	Possible situation	Eulogy in spirit is not understood
16b		2.4.2.2.2	First negative consequence	Uninitiated cannot say "amen"
16c	ἐπειδή	2.4.2.2.3	Reason why	Uninitiated does not understand
17	γάρ	2.4.2.2.4	A further negative consequence	The other member is not edified
18-19	Trans. to 1st pers. sing.	2.4.2.3	Final personal argument for the exception and for the explanation	Paul's example: although more gifted with tongues than the Cor, he prefers to speak even a few words with νοῦς in the assembly to instruct others
20-25	Alloc., trans. to 2nd pers. plur.	3	Further argument for main rule	Community-external argument for main rule: a mature mind realizes that prophecy is superior to glossolalia when unbelievers are exposed to them
20		3.1	Exhortation	Be mature, not childish, in mind

Vv.	Relators etc.	Organiza-tion	Function	Argument
21-25	Asynd.	3.2	Argument	Glossolalia does not give faith, prophecy convinces of God's presence
21	Trans. to 3rd pers.	3.2.1	Scripture quotation	Isa 28:11f. Not even strange tongues will be heeded
22	ὥστε	3.2.2	Conclusion from quote	
22a		3.2.2.1	Conclusion on glossolalia	Glossolalia is a sign for unbelievers, not for believers
22b	δέ	3.2.2.2	(Indirect) conclu-sion on prophecy	Prophecy is not for[g] unbe-lievers, but for believers
23-25	οὖν	3.2.3	Application in two assumed cases	
23	ἐάν	3.2.3.1	Case one	Glossolalia
23a		3.2.3.1.1	Assumed situation	"All" (!) speak in tongues, unbeliever enters
23b		3.2.3.1.2	Consequence of sit-uation	Unbeliever says: "you are possessed"
24-25	ἐὰν δέ	3.2.3.2	Case two	Prophecy
24a		3.2.3.2.1	Assumed situation	"All" (!) prophesy, unbe-liever enters
24b-25	καὶ οὕτως	3.2.3.2.2	Consequence of sit-uation	Unbeliever is convinced, worships God: "God is verily among you"
26ff.	τί οὖν ἐστιν, trans. to 2nd pers. plur., alloc.	4	Practical ruling	Advice concerning the worship, prophecy and glossolalia included

a. For v. 1a see below, 1.2.3.
b. This shift to 1st pers. sing. is a bit different from, e.g., that in v. 6, as, in fact, it rather becomes a means of expressing an imperative.

   c. Actually the logic of v. 6 is not totally clear. Weiß 1910/70, *ad loc.* wants to supply an "instead of that" to its second half, so that we get: "if I come to you speaking in tongues, what good will I do to you, if I do not, instead of that, speak to you with revelation, etc." In the light of v. 19 I would prefer to add a "rather" (Barrett 1971, *ad loc.* "in addition").

   d. The ὅμως is problematic, but I choose (with Blaß/Debrunner/Rehkopf 1976, § 450, and Barrett 1971, *ad loc.*) to read it as meaning "in the same way", similar to ὁμοίως.

   e. The γάρ of v. 8 helps to bring the three together, and so does, of course, the οὕτως καί of v. 9.

   f. The γάρ is missing in p⁴⁶ B G etc., and, although it would fit in very well, this is precisely the reason why it may be secondary.

   g. Many (like Barrett 1971, *ad loc.*, Conzelmann 1975, *ad loc.*, Bruce 1971, *ad loc.* and others) want to supply "a sign". E.g., Weiß 1910/70, *ad loc.* thinks that is causing an unnecessary difficulty.

1.2.3. *Some Comments on the Display of the Argument*

As indicated under 1.2.1. above, there are several factors, elements and aspects of the text that go together organizing it in conveying its message to the reader. In the first paragraphs of 1.2.2., I mentioned the imperatives (and their equivalents). In combination with other elements, especially those listed in the second column, they become sign-posts in the text and play an important role for its organization. So they all occur at major transitions, except for the one in v. 12. But there a phrase on a meta-level, οὕτως καὶ ὑμεῖς, determines its function.

Looking briefly at some other paradigmatic features, we note that the passage 6-12 is held together by the "understanding" motif (γνῶσις, διδαχή [v. 6], γινώσκειν [vv. 7, 9], εἰδέναι [v. 11]) and by the occurrence of several words referring to clearness or its contrast (ἀποκάλυψις [v. 6], διαστολή [v. 7], ἄδηλος [v. 8], εὔσημος [v. 9], δύναμις [v. 11], βάρβαρος [v. 11]). Similarly νοῦς plays a particular role for the coherence of 14-19 (vv. 14, 15 bis, 19).[16]

Furthermore, the idea of the οἰκοδομή is important in 1-19, vv. 1-4 directly dealing with it, 5-12 and 13-19 leading their argument up to it (vv. 12, and 17). As a matter of fact the place of this concept may suggest that the transitional and introductory "pursue love" (14:1a) should be brought together with the idea of edification. Then chapter 13 gives a general perspective to the argument of chapter 14, as seen especially in the argument for edification. (Cf. 8:1: "love edifies".)[17]

One may wonder why, in distinction from both Nestle-Aland and GNT, I have brought vv. 1-4 together, referring v. 5 to the following block.

---

[16] Certainly ἀκούειν and μυστήρια appear in vv. 1-14, but nonetheless vv. 6-12 are more dominated by the motif of understanding and clearness.

[17] See Johansson 1973, 42ff.

This depends on my combining the data of my second column with the considerations of the function of each phase in the argument (col. 4). V. 5 introduces the new theme to be dealt with through v. 19. On the other hand, we should remember that the text was written to be listened to. In such texts it seems that transitional passages can summarize the past and introduce a new phase in a way that may confuse a modern reader, when he wants to divide the text into "paragraphs".

In vv. 6-12 we come across two instances of comparison, one referring to musical instruments (7-8), one to language (10-11). In both cases the examples are applied to the Corinthians via a οὕτως καὶ ὑμεῖς (vv. 9 and 12). In the second case, however, the linkage between the comparison and the wording of the application is a bit loose.[18] Obviously Paul lets the practical aim of the argument prevail over its strictness, and it is also natural that the concluding v. 12 takes into account that which has been going on since v. 5b. Making the implicit explicit we get: "so it is also with you: you are eager for spiritual gifts, (but it happens that you and your neighbours do not know the meaning of what you speak in the spirit); therefore strive that you be rich (in such gifts that are good) for the οἰκοδομή of the church (through understandable language)".

When dealing with the context I indicated that there could be some hesitation concerning the place of vv. 20-25 in the argument. Thus Dr Conzelmann, for example, takes vv. 20-40 as the second section of the chapter. The markers on the textual surface turn out to be of no help for a decision, being similar in v. 20 and v. 26, viz., a renewed allocution and a transition to 2nd person. But the style of 20-25 is of the same arguing type as the one in 1-19, including the use of more or less hypothetical examples (note all cases of ἐάν !), whereas 26-40 is a set of practical instructions. The τί οὖν ἐστιν of v. 26 indicates this transition from argument to practical advice (cf. v. 15). This speaks against taking 20-25 as the first part of the practical section. On the other hand, 20-25 stand out as relatively independent from 1-19, which deal with the spiritual gifts as regarded *within* the church, whereas 20-25 relate them to people from outside.

In the preceding paragraphs I have touched upon the "relators etc." now and then. It is now time to discuss them a bit more in detail. My observations can only be very tentative. As for more ascertained results, one should have to analyse and consider much more material.

The γάρ brings two parts of the text together, viz., an explanation and that which is explained. By receiving the explanative function that which follows after the γάρ is held together as far as the explanation goes. Thus,

---

[18] So, e.g., Weiß 1910/70, *ad loc.* and Dautzenberg 1975, 226f. let a new section begin with v. 12.

e.g., the γάρ of v. 2 creates the expectation that that which follows will explain why the Corinthians should rather prophesy, and so vv. 2-4 are brought together. A similar, more wide-embracing function can also be given to the γάρ of v. 8, and to that of v. 14, if original.

The two cases of οὕτως καί (vv. 9 and 12) have a rather clear function: they tie a string around the preceding examples (vv. 7-8, and 10-11) and introduce the application.

The οὖν (vv. 11, 15, 23) has an effect similar to that of γάρ: it gathers into a unit a preceding passage (vv. 10, 14, and 21-22, respectively) and introduces a conclusion or an application of it. (The result becomes that vv. 10-11, 14-15, and 21-25 become units of the text.)

As expected, shifts of person create caesuras in the text, and so do renewed allocutions.[19]

These and other "relators etc." sometimes appear together, and that can reinforce their effect. Of course they also function together with the paradigmatic features as I have intimated above.

In retrospect we now regard the larger sections of our text and state which organizing factors we have considered as being at work in each case:

Vv. 1-4 (1.): Introductory, thematic imperatives; the γάρ of v. 2 holds vv. 2-4 together, and, secondarily, vv. 1-4.

Vv. 5-19 (2.): Repetition of thematic imperative, δέ, shift of person, in v. 6 followed by νῦν δέ and allocution; within the section vv. 6-12 (= 2.3.) is permeated by the understanding and clearness motifs and vv. 14-19 (= 2.4.2.) by the νοῦς concept.

Vv. 20-25 (3.): Imperative, allocution; the οὖν of v. 23 brings vv. 21-25 (= 3.2.) together.

Vv. 26ff. (4.): Shift of person, τί οὖν ἐστιν, allocution; change from argument into ruling.

To round up: 1 Cor 14 has two parts, one practical (26-40) and one that argues for the corrected practice (1-25). The arguing part has two passages that speak in favour of prophecy and against glossolalia. The first (1-4) argues from an internal perspective of mutual edifications as the decisive criterion, the second (20-25) evaluates prophecy and glossolalia with outsiders in view.

Between these passages come vv. 5-19, which argue an exception to the main rule of the superiority of prophecy over against glossolalia, namely if the glossolalia is interpreted. I have termed it an exception because of the wording in v. 5, ἐκτὸς εἰ μή. But, as a matter of fact, so

---

[19] As to a couple of *asyndetha* it has been astonishing to see that in both vv. 4 and 10 a second step of a two-step argument starts with an *asyndethon*. Could possibly the one in v. 21 be regarded in a similar may, viz., that vv. 20 and 21 stand side by side in the argument?

much energy is spent on arguing this exception that one may prefer to call it a plea for an alternative, viz., an alternative way of fitting glossolalia into the assembly worship, so that it is as edifying as prophecy and neither dominates nor disappears as compared to it. So, according to 14:27-29 two or three speakers in tongues may appear plus an interpreter and also two or three prophets, whose message is to be submitted to διά-κρισις. The argument for this exception — or alternative — is introduced first (5b), then an argument for it follows (6-12) and then a conclusion (v. 13). One could think that this would suffice, but vv. 14-19 explain how the reasonable mind has to be involved in order that all can be edified. Interpretation is not explicitly mentioned in vv. 14-19, and the noetic εὐ-λογεῖν, the ψάλλειν and εὐχαριστεῖν may be such as mentioned in v. 26 ("when you assemble, each has a hymn ...") and not necessarily interpreted pieces of glossolalia.[20] But considered within the argument structure, it seems that, instead of only contrasting pneumatic and noetic praise, the passage rather elucidates further the need for interpreting the glossolalia, i.e., the precondition that it must edify the church.

2. Aspects of Some Issues

2.1. The Cultic Perspective

The fact that the issues at stake in chapter 14 belong to the worship gives them a frame of reference which I believe is worthy of consideration.[21]

A basic feature in such worship is that divine acts and salvific events, including divine revelation, are made present. They are represented in such a way that the worshipping community shares the benefit of them. These acts belong mostly to the past, but sometimes the promised future, or the ἔσχατον, is also brought into this *Vergegenwärtigung*.[22] The representation or the application to the community can take place through a rite or through the reciting of a text.

Not only divine acts are made present — the cultic language is filled by phrases that express a belief or a hope that the god himself be present: one prays "before the face" of the god, that he may "come" or "be among" his worshippers. Thus the application can also be regarded as a divine action in the worship.

Worship, then, is normally a common affair, because it takes place within the relationship between the god(s) and the community which is of fundamental importance to the community.[23]

---

[20] Allo 1956, *ad loc.*, seems, however, to suggest such an understanding.

[21] See for the following, van der Leeuw 1956, part 3; Eliade 1955 and 1958, chaps. 10-11.

[22] Cf. for Qumran Kuhn 1966, part C.

[23] Cf. Schmaus 1975.

Furthermore, one can speak of different "directions" in worship, both in actions and words.[24] They are most easily seen in the different addressees of cultic texts, e.g., "hear our prayer", and "hear the word of God", respectively. In thus differentiating between "God-directed" and "man-directed" elements in worship one should not, however, forget that both types are ruled by the overall principle of the re-presentation of the divine acts, the bringing near of the divinity itself, and the community's participation in the effects thereof, i.e., one may very well think that one's god is the first actor or giver or inspirator also of God-directed worship.

These few remarks have something to say concerning some items in chapter 14. The divine presence, confessed by the visitor (vv. 24f.) and experienced by the pneumatics, is a presence within the cult, and the conviction (v. 24) is in a way a divine act. Furthermore, one can combine Paul's criterion of the common οἰκοδομή with the feature that worship is a community affair. The different "directions" apply to prophecy and glossolalia, as prophecy can be seen as principally man-directed,[25] whereas glossolalia, also when interpreted, speaks towards God, both, however, being for the good of the church, its οἰκοδομή. But at the same time, the glossolalia is a divine gift. Finally, if there has been an "overrealized eschatology" at Corinth,[26] such a phenomenon is also quite thinkable within a cultic framework with its possibilities of blurring the time perspectives.

Against this background I will now return to some of the issues of 1 Cor 14.

2.2. Glossolalia — οἰκοδομή

1 Corinthians is the only place in which Paul openly mentions glossolalia. The Book of Acts indicates, though, that it was not a phenomenon that occurred only in Corinth,[27] and, in addition, 14:18 can hardly mean that Paul himself had and used the gift only when visiting Corinth.

I need not discuss the phenomenological background of glossolalia — others have done that sufficiently.[28] Instead I will pick up a few aspects from their investigations. First, this ecstatic babbling was regarded as the result of the indwelling of God's spirit, i.e., the divine promises of the

---

[24] Cf. Martimort 1961.

[25] One should not, however, be too firm in terms of "directions" — cf. 11Q5 (11QPs[a]) col. 27, where David's 4050 songs and psalms — which should be "God-directed"! — are said to be spoken by him "through prophecy" — and "from the Most High".

[26] See lately Thiselton 1977-78.

[27] Cf. Mark 16:17 and Rom 8:26 (Käsemann 1973, *ad loc.*).

[28] Dautzenberg 1981 (+ lit.).

eschatological blessings were being fulfilled and experienced in the worship. One such promise was Ezek 36:27: "I will put my spirit within you". So glossolalia — and Paul was eager to add other, and better, gifts as well — was the result of God's own presence in the community, described in the age-old imagery of the breath: invisible, effective, life-giving, "inspiring". However, to people in the Hellenistic age the idea of a divine madness was not unfamiliar, be they Jews like Philo, or not.[29] The reaction in 14:23, "you are mad", should be seen also in such a context: it can mean: "you are in a divine frenzy" — which ever its origin may be.

Furthermore, however, one has compared 13:2, where, it seems, glossolalia is labelled "tongues of angels", with a passage in the *Testament of Job* (48ff.), according to which Job's daughters receive the gift of speaking the languages of different classes of angels, thereby praising the mighty acts of God (cf. Acts 10:46).[30] Now, lauding God is typical of angels (cf. Luke 2:13f., Rev 5:11, etc.). The Corinthians, especially the ones speaking in tongues, may have meant that they, somehow, took part in that heavenly liturgy, or even possibly that angels took part in their own worship.[31]

At any rate the lauding of God by angels forms a reasonable background for the statements on the glossolalia in chapter 14. It is directed to God: its practitioner speaks mysteries to God,[32] not men (v. 2), and in vv. 14ff. we read: "I pray (προσεύχωμαι) in a tongue ... I will play the harp (ψαλῶ) with the spirit ... you bless (εὐλογῆς) in (or with) the spirit ... you praise (εὐχαριστεῖς)", i.e., all "God-directed" cultic actions. There is no sign indicating that Paul would like to change this direction.

But now 5b-19 argue as an exception — or alternative — that glossolalia can be edifying for the church, viz., by interpretation. Does not interpretation change the "direction" of glossolalia? I should say not: even the interpreted glossolalia addresses God, but the fellow Christian can say his "amen", and thus he receives οἰκοδομή. The "amen" means, namely, that he makes the prayer his own,[33] and in this way the praise becomes part of the *common* worship. When somebody in that *common* worship

---

[29] See further, e.g., Conzelmann 1975, *ad* vv. 1, 11, and 23-24.

[30] See further Dautzenberg 1979, 611.

[31] Cf. 1 Cor 11:10 (Fitzmyer 1957-58; Dautzenberg 1975, 267). For Qumran see Kuhn 1966, 46f., 66ff., et passim.

[32] Possibly the "mysteries" mean "things not understood", but it is tempting to take into account the usage according to which it means "things belonging to God's hidden counsel" (Dautzenberg 1975, 234ff.). Such things might very well be brought into an eulogy. Eph 1:4ff. is an example, several hymnic passages of Rev are others.

[33] Cf. the Rabbinic regulations and discussions which point to the importance fastened to the amen answer (see [Strack-]Billerbeck III 1926, 456ff., and also Harder 1936, 79ff.).

lauds God, this means praising Him for what He is in relationship to the world of the community. This is "edifying" without necessarily being instructive as in the case of a teaching.

2.3. Prophecy

Sometimes prophecy and interpreted glossolalia are almost equated by commentators. Thus, e.g., C. K. Barrett says: "Interpretation ... had the effect of turning tongues into prophecy".[34] Certainly, the two are closely related. Both are gifts of the Spirit, both belong to the enthusiastic side of the worship, both should "edify", and both are somehow related to the divine secrets — the prophet may come to know some of them (13:2), and the speaker in tongues praises God for them.[35]

Nevertheless Paul distinguishes rather neatly between them (12:30; 14:23f.), and I think it is justified to stick to the principal difference between the "directions" of the two, prophecy being a means by which God speaks to man.[36] Variants of the phenomenon were of course to be found outside of Judaism and Christianity.[37]

I now disregard much of what is said on prophecy in vv. 26ff. and concentrate on vv. 1-4 and 20-25. In vv. 1-4 the argument takes the advantages of prophecy as a point of departure in order to show the deficiency of (uninterpreted) glossolalia. It gives οἰκοδομή to the church, παράκλησις and παραμυθία. It seems to me that these terms are too imprecise to permit any firm conclusion as to what prophecy really was like in Corinth. They can cover instruction, comfort, exhortation, parenesis, eschatological promises or threats, foretellings, revealing convictions. Vv. 24f. certainly describe a case of the last-mentioned type: the prophet proclaims God's judgement on behalf of Him who knows everyone's heart.[38] This uncovering of a stranger's thought is of course a marvellous sign to him that "God is among you", that divine knowledge has been "revealed" (cf. v. 31!) to the prophet. But to the believers other expressions of the prophetic gift, though maybe less spectacular, were also the result of divine "revelation".[39] This is to say that the conviction case of vv. 24f. may have been chosen — or construed — for the sake of the argument,

---

[34] Barrett 1971, *ad* 14:5.

[35] See Dautzenberg 1979, 610, and note 32 above.

[36] See for the following Müller 1975, part 1 (+ lit.); Dunn 1975, 227ff.; Dautzenberg 1975, §§ 1-6, 32-37 (+ lit.).

[37] A returning problem is how to know whether the alleged divine messenger is trustworthy or not. In some contexts ecstasy could be regarded as a kind of legitimation, and it has been suggested that people in Corinth understood the glossolalia in that way (Gillespie 1978). However that may be, Paul does not himself interpret it so, and he does not seem to need to defend his rule that there had to be a διάκρισις of the prophecy.

[38] See further Dautzenberg 1975, 246ff.

not because that was the form of prophecy. It was certainly one,[40] and also an "edifying" one, but the way Paul argues elsewhere in the chapter seems to indicate other accents. In v. 6 prophecy appears in the following enumeration: "if I talk to you in a revelation, in knowledge, in prophecy or (in a) teaching."[41] And the effect of the appearance of the prophets in v. 31 is that "all learn (μανθάνωσιν)" and "all are comforted (παρακαλῶνται)." That is, in the common worship the prophets teach, instruct and comfort the community from God, so making God, His revelation and acts for His people topical for them.

2.4. Interpretation

It seems that the "tongues" spoken in Corinth were not regarded as one or several existing languages like, e.g., Coptic or Latin.[42] Rather the ecstatic babbling was called a tongue of angels of this or that order. But in order to "edify" the church it had to be "interpreted".

The verb behind (διερμηνεύειν) has several meanings. The scene as described in vv. 27f. seems to preclude the one according to which an interpreter translated words and sentences of one (angelic!) language into words and sentences of another (human). Dr Thiselton has argued that we should render the verb by "articulate", "put into words", and, as far as I understand his argument, that Paul rules that there be no ecstatic babbling at all; instead it should be put directly into understandable words.[43] But as I read the instructions of vv. 26ff., I find it difficult to go along with this suggestion — then there would actually be no "tongue" to "have" (v. 26).[44]

Thus, it seems to me that the best way to understand the "interpretation" of the tongues is that the one who is equipped with the gift of interpretation puts into understandable words what the speaker in tongues "said", not through "translating" in the ordinary sense of the word, but by "interpreting" it in a less precise way. I then use the verb as we do when saying, for example, that a president "interprets" the opinions expressed at a meeting when he summarizes them.

---

[39] After proper διάκρισις, whatever it might mean. Cf. Dautzenberg 1975, 122ff., Dunn 1975, 233ff., and Grudem 1978.

[40] Cf. Hahn 1972; Hartman 1980, esp. 142ff.

[41] There is no ἐν in the best mss. So "prophecy" and "teaching" are brought closer together. Cf. Barrett 1971, *ad loc.*

[42] See Stendahl 1976, 116ff.; Thiselton 1979, 22ff.

[43] Thiselton 1979.

[44] I also find certain difficulties in understanding v. 28 with Dr Thiselton's reading (not to mention the fact that the verse is a bit unclear anyway — see, e.g., Conzelmann 1975, *ad loc.*).

2.5. The Sign for Unbelievers

The logic of vv. 21-25 has puzzled many expositors, and nor am I so clear on it as I would like to be.[45] The quotation from Isa 28:11f.[46] and the assumed examples of how outsiders would react, if the "whole" assembly spoke in tongues or prophesied, fit reasonably well together. But the conclusion in v. 22 of the Scriptural quotation raises questions: how is glossolalia a sign for unbelievers who think that its practitioners are possessed, and how is prophecy for believers,[47] when unbelievers' thoughts are revealed and they are brought to confess God's presence? Does "sign" have a positive or negative meaning?[48] Does "believer" also mean "believer to be"?

The over-all message of Paul in vv. 20-25 is relatively clear. But how does he say it? My way of understanding him is like this:[49] once more Paul is derogating glossolalia, now by relating it to outsiders' reactions in two rather artificial situations. He argues: be not childish (cf. 3:1ff.; 13:11) in your appreciation of it (v. 20), for Scripture says that people will not listen when God speaks to them in glossolalia (v. 21). Thus, it is in accordance with Scripture that unbelievers do not "listen" and only see a frenzy in the glossolalia (v. 23). This is an application (οὖν) of v. 22, which says that glossolalia is a sign to them. I take that as saying: it is a mere sign,[50] not understood. Concerning prophecy Paul says: a mature discernment keeps prophecy in a high esteem (v. 20). The Scripture quotation of v. 21 says something on prophecy indirectly. Glossolalia and prophecy being under discussion, the first is rejected; there remains the second, and to that they "will listen", and this is well demonstrated by the example of vv. 24f. Then, somehow, this example should be an application of v. 22b ("prophecy is not for the unbelievers but for the believers"). With some reluctance and finding it the least unsatisfactory

---

[45] See the commentaries, and the monographs by Dautzenberg (1975, 243ff.), Dunn (1975, 230ff.), and Stendahl (1976, 113ff.). In addition, the passage has lately been dealt with in several articles: Roberts 1978-79; Grudem 1978-79; Johanson 1978-79. Also Gillespie 1978. These articles refer amply to previous discussions.

[46] On its relation to known versions see, e.g., Dautzenberg 1975, 243ff.

[47] Then I have not (as, e.g., Barrett 1971, *ad loc.* and Conzelmann 1975, *ad loc.*) supplied an εἰς σημεῖον in v. 22b, so that prophecy becomes "a sign for believers". Nor do Weiß 1910/70, *ad loc.* or Stendahl (1976, 116). With such a supplement one also gets the problem whether "sign" has a constant meaning or not.

[48] One can complicate matters even more by assuming that Paul is using a slogan of the Corinthian pneumatics (J. M. Robinson, J. P. M. Sweet, Th. W. Gillespie — see idem 1978, 81f.). But how would one explain their use of the semitizing εἶναι εἰς?

[49] Johanson 1978-79 cuts the Gordian knot by suggesting that one read the ὥστε-clause as a question. It is a witty solution, but as for me, I would like to have the Greek look different in order to have such a meaning.

[50] So also Stendahl 1976, 115.

solution, I am driven into taking v. 22b as meaning: prophecy promotes belief.[51]

The argument on how glossolalia is received by uninitiated people brings us back to where we began the second half of this paper, viz., to the cultic perspective. I mentioned that the worship is basically an affair of the community and is placed within its fundamental relationship to its God. This was applied to the way Paul argues for the common edification through prophecy and interpreted glossolalia. But vv. 20-25 widen the concept of the community affected by the worship. The world concerned by the Corinthian Christians' relationship to God was not delimited to the circle of the believers. Already the mixed families mentioned in chapter 7 are a reminder. The application in the worship of the basic salvific events and of the divine revelation thus had a wider reference than that of the small flock. If this is so, one should not understand Paul's argument in vv. 20-25 as one based on missionary tactics. Rather it says that a mature discernment of what is going on at a Christian worship realizes that it must be edifying or constructive also for outsiders, because actually they also belong to the ones concerned by it. This should be all the more natural as the prime salvific event represented at their worship must have been the Christ event, which was the content of the gospel which Paul had preached to them (15:1) and for which he was commissioned to win the obedience of belief among all the Gentiles (Rom 1:5).

Bibliography

Allo, E.-B. 1956: *Saint Paul. Première Épître aux Corinthiens* (EtB), 2nd ed., Paris: LeCoffre 1956.

Barrett, C. K. 1971: *A Commentary on the First Epistle to the Corinthians* (BNTC), 2nd ed., London: Black/New York: Harper 1971.

Billerbeck, P. [-Strack, H. L.] 1926: *Kommentar zum Neuen Testament aus Talmud und Midrasch, Dritter Band: Die Briefe des Neuen Testaments und die Offenbarung Johannis*, München: Beck 1926.

Blaß, F./Debrunner, A./Rehkopf, F. 1976: *Grammatik des neutestamentlichen Griechisch*, 14. Aufl., Göttingen: Vandenhoeck & Ruprecht 1976.

Bruce, F. F. 1971: *1 and 2 Corinthians* (NCBC), Grand Rapids, MI: Eerdmans 1971.

Cerfaux, L. 1959: *The Church in the Theology of St. Paul*, New York: Herder & Herder 1959.

---

[51] Stendahl (1976, 116) paraphrases: "Prophecy ... is toward faith and not toward the hardening of unbelief."

Conzelmann, H. 1975: *1 Corinthians* (Hermeneia), Philadelphia, PA 1975.

Dautzenberg, G. 1975: *Urchristliche Prophetie. Ihre Erforschung, ihre Voraussetzungen im Judentum und ihre Struktur im ersten Korintherbrief* (BWANT VI:4), Stuttgart: Kohlhammer 1975.

— 1979: "Glossa", in: *EWNT* I (Stuttgart: Kohlhammer 1979), 604-14.

— 1981: "Glossolalie", in: *RAC* 11 (Stuttgart: Hiersemann 1981), 225-46.

Dunn, J. D. G. 1975: *Jesus and the Spirit. A Study of the Religious and Charismatic Experience of Jesus and the First Christians as Reflected in the New Testament*, London: SCM 1975.

Eliade, M. 1955: *The Myth of the Eternal Return*, London/New York: Routledge & Kegan 1955.

— 1958: *Patterns in Comparative Religion*, London/New York: Sheed & Ward 1958.

Ellis, E. E. 1973-74: "'Spiritual' Gifts in the Pauline Communities", in: *NTS* 20 (1973-74) 128-44.

Fitzmyer, J. A. 1957-58: "A Feature of Qumran Angelology and the Angels of 1 Cor xi.10", in: *NTS* 4 (1957-58) 48-58.

Gillespie, Th. W. 1978: "A Pattern of Prophetic Speech in First Corinthians", in: *JBL* (1978) 74-95.

Grudem, W. A. 1978: "A Response to Gerhard Dautzenberg on 1 Cor. 12.10", in: *BZ* 22 (1978) 253-70.

— 1978-79: "I Corinthians 14:20-25: Prophecy and Tongues as Signs of God's Attitude", in: *WThJ* 41 (1978-79) 381-96.

Gülich, E./Raible, W. 1977: *Linguistische Textmodelle. Grundlagen und Möglichkeiten* (UTB 130), München: Fink 1977.

Hahn, F. 1972: "Die Sendschreiben in der Johannesapokalypse. Ein Beitrag zur Bestimmung prophetischer Redeformen", in: G. Jeremias/H.-W. Kuhn/H. Stegemann (eds.), *Tradition und Glaube. Das frühe Christentum in seiner Umwelt. Festgabe Karl Georg Kuhn*, Göttingen: Vandenhoeck & Ruprecht 1972, 357-94.

Harder, G. 1936: *Paulus und das Gebet* (NTF 1, 10), Gütersloh: Bertelsmann 1936.

Hartman, L. 1980: "Form and Message. A Preliminary Discussion of 'Partial Texts' in Rev 1-3 and 22,6ff.", in: J. Lambrecht (ed.), *L'Apocalypse johannique et l'Apocalyptique dans le Nouveau Testament* (BEThL 53), Gembloux: Duculot & Leuven Univ. Press 1980, 129-49 [No. 7 in this volume].

Héring, J. 1962: *The First Epistle of Saint Paul to the Corinthians*, London: Epworth 1962.

Holmberg, B. 1980: "Sociological versus Theological Analysis of the Question Concerning a Pauline Church Order", in: S. Pedersen (ed.), *Die Paulinische Literatur und Theologie. The Pauline Literature and Theology* (Teologiske Studier 7), Århus: Aros/Göttingen: Vandenhoeck & Ruprecht 1980, 187-200.

Horsley, R. 1980-81: "Gnosis in Corinth: 1 Corinthians 8.1-6", in: *NTS* 27 (1980-81) 32-51.

Hurd, J. C. 1965/83: *The Origin of 1 Corinthians*, London: S.P.C.K. 1965 [new ed. Macon, GA: Mercer Univ. Press 1983].

Iber, G. 1963: "Zum Verständnis von 1 Cor 12,31", in: *ZNW* 54 (1963) 43-52.

Johanson, B. C. 1978-79: "Tongues, a Sign for Unbelievers?: A Structural and Exegetical Study of I Corinthians xiv. 20-25", in: *NTS* 25 (1978-79) 180-203.

Johansson, N. 1973: *Women and the Church's Ministry. An Exegetical Study of I Corinthians 11-14*, Uppsala: Pro veritate 1973.

Käsemann, E. 1973: *An die Römer* (HNT 8a), Tübingen: Mohr (Siebeck) 1973.

Kuhn, H.-W. 1966: *Enderwartung und gegenwärtiges Heil. Untersuchungen zu den Gemeindeliedern von Qumran mit einem Anhang über Eschatologie und Gegenwart in der Verkündigung Jesu* (StUNT 4), Göttingen: Vandenhoeck & Ruprecht 1966.

van der Leeuw, G. 1956: *Phänomenologie der Religion,* 2. Aufl., Tübingen: Mohr (Siebeck) 1956.

Martimort, A.-G. 1961: "Le double mouvement de la liturgie: culte de Dieu et sanctification des hommes", in: idem (ed.), *L'église en prière*, Paris etc.: Desclée 1961, 187-97.

Müller, U. B. 1975: *Prophetie und Predigt im Neuen Testament* (StNT 10), Gütersloh: Gerd Mohn 1975.

Roberts, P. 1978-79: "A Sign – Christian or Pagan?", in: *ET* 90 (1978-79) 199-203.

Schmaus, M. 1975: "Worship", in: *Encyclopedia of Theology*, London: Burns & Oates 1975, 1838-41.

Schmidt, S. J. 1976: *Texttheorie. Probleme einer Linguistik der sprachlichen Kommunikation* (UTB 202), 2nd ed., München: Fink 1976.

Schmithals, W. 1971: *Gnosticism in Corinth*, New York/Nashville: Abingdon 1971.

Stendahl, K. 1976: *Paul among Jews and Gentiles*, Philadelphia, PA: Fortress 1976.

Stock, A. 1974: *Umgang mit theologischen Texten. Methoden, Analysen, Vorschläge* (Arbeits und Studienbücher Theologie), Zürich/Einsiedeln/Köln: Benziger 1974.

Thiselton, A. C. 1977-78: "Realized Eschatology at Corinth", in: *NTS* 24 (1977-78) 510-26.

— 1979: "The 'Interpretation' of Tongue: A New Suggestion in the Light of Greek Usage in Philo and Josephus", in: *JThS* 30 (1979) 15-36.

Weiß, J. 1910/70: *Der erste Korintherbrief* (KEK 5), Göttingen: Vandenhoeck & Ruprecht 1910 [reprinted 1970].

Supplement

Baker, D. L.: "The Interpretation of 1 Corinthians 12-14", in: *EvQ* 46 (1974) 224-34.

Hill, D.: *New Testament Prophecy*, London: Marshall, Morgan and Scott 1979.

Grudem, W. A.: *The Gift of Prophecy in 1 Corinthians*, Washington: Washington Univ. Press 1982.

Wolff, Chr.: *Der erste Brief des Paulus an die Korinther. Kap. 8-16* (ThHK 7/2), Berlin: Evangelische Verlagsanstalt 1982.

Aune, D. E.: *Prophecy in Early Christianity and the Ancient Mediterranean World*, Grand Rapids, MI: Eerdmans 1983.

Martin, R. P.: *The Spirit and the Congregation. Studies in 1 Corinthians 12-15*, Grand Rapids, MI: Eerdmans 1984.

Callan, T.: "Prophecy and Ecstasy in Greco-Roman Religion and in 1 Corinthians," in: *NT* 27 (1985) 125-40.

Siegert, F.: *Argumentation bei Paulus gezeigt an Röm 9-11* (WUNT 34), Tübingen: Mohr (Siebeck) 1985.

Forbes, C.: "Early Christian Inspired Speech and Hellenistic Popular Religion", in: *NT* 28 (1986) 257-70.

Lang, F.: *Die Briefe an die Korinther* (NTD 7), Göttingen: Vandenhoeck & Ruprecht 1986.

Richardson, W.: "Liturgical Order and Glossolalia in 1 Corinthians 14:26c-33a", in: *NTS* 32 (1986) 144-53.

Fee, G. D.: *The First Epistle to the Corinthians* (NIC) Grand Rapids, MI: Eerdmans 1987 [repr. 1988].

Strobel, A.: *Der erste Brief an die Korinther* (ZBK), Zürich: Theologischer Verlag 1989.

Wire, A. Clark: *The Corinthian Women Prophets. A Reconstruction through Paul's Rhetoric*, Minneapolis, MN: Fortress 1990.

Mitchell, M. M.: *Paul and the Rhetoric of Reconciliation. An Exegetical Investigation of the Language and Composition of 1 Corinthians* (HUTh 28), Tübingen: Mohr (Siebeck) 1991/Nashville, TN: Knox/Westminster 1992.

Martin, D. B.: "Tongues of Angels and Other Status Indicators", in: *JAAR* 59 (1991) 563-69.

Pogoloff, S. M.: *Logos and Sophia. The Rhetorical Situation of 1 Corinthians* (SBL.DS 134), Atlanta GA: Scholars Press 1992.

Smit, J.: "Argument and Genre of 1 Corinthians 12-14", in: S. E. Porter/Th. H. Olbricht (eds.), *Rhetoric and the New Testament. Essays from the 1992 Heidelberg Conference* (JSNTS 90), Sheffield: Sheffield AP 1993, 211-30.

Witherington III, B.: *Conflict and Community in Corinth. A Socio-Rhetorical Commentary on 1 and 2 Corinthians*, Grand Rapids, MI: Eerdmans 1994.

Smit, J. F. M.: "Tongues and Prophecy: Deciphering 1 Cor 14,22", in: *Bib.* 75 (1994) 175-90.

13. A Sketch of the Argument of 2 Cor 10-13

Second Corinthians 10-13 is a coherent piece of text, the place of which within the present 2 Corinthians is a matter of discussion among the commentators on the Letter. Is it, e.g., the larger piece of the so-called Letter of tears (Bultmann[1] and others), and, if it was originally (part of) a separate letter, how is it to be dated in relation to the other parts of 2 Corinthians? I need not take a stand on these questions here, although I sympathize with the theory that the chapters have come to belong to their present context through the work of an editor within the Pauline school. But notwithstanding that Paul's language in these chapters is rather confusing in places, many exegetes feel like F. Lang who states that this part of 2 Corinthians is "in sich klar gegliedert".

The following text-linguistically inspired analysis confirms this impression, albeit in this respect I arrive at other results than both Lang and others. The reason why I embarked on such an analysis is, however, not primarily that I want to test earlier results as to the overall structure of these chapters. Rather it should refine them somewhat and, hopefully, enable us to see the larger structures and how the elements of the argument are interrelated.

As to the text-linguistic technical terms, I refer to other articles in this volume, particularly those on Colossians ("Doing Things with the Words of Colossians" [No. 11 in this volume]) and Galatians ("Gal 3:15-4:11 as Part of a Theological Argument on a Practical Issue" [No. 14 in this volume]). After some hesitation I have decided to present my investigation, not as a ready-made analysis, but rather as an advancing procedure. In consequence the presentation may now and then become repetitious.

In recent decades several forms of "structuralism" have played important roles in Biblical exegesis, and the word "structure" has also been understood in several ways. When I arrive at results concerning the

---

[1] Bultmann 1976. — I have also consulted the following commentaries on 2 Cor (I shall, however, seldom refer to the views expressed in them): Barrett 1973 (repr. 1976); Carrez 1986; Furnish 1984; Klauck 1986; Lang 1986; Martin 1986; Schlatter 1969; Talbert 1987; Windisch 1924/70.

Special attention to 2 Cor 10-13 pay Aejmelaeus 1987; Betz 1972; Fitzgerald 1990, 190-200; Lohse (ed.) 1992; Zmijewski 1978.

structure of 2 Cor 10-13 which differ from those of other scholars, this
does not mean that the others are wrong. As a matter of fact, they have
seen other structures. The decisive difference between my suggestions
and those of my colleagues is the importance I attach to the signals on
the surface of the text. For example, I wish to take it seriously that in 10:7
Paul asks the addressees to regard what is before their eyes (τὰ κατὰ
πρόσωπον); accordingly I should look for something in the text which fits
the description of being before the addressees' eyes and which functions
as an argument vis à vis them. This wish of mine is not simply a whim,
but builds on the normal phenomenon that statements of a communication which deal with (parts of) the same communication determine how
an addressee understands the contents, the relationships between textual
elements and their contents, and, in addition, how all these factors relate
to the addressee. Thus, I believe that an approach according to such linguistic principles may enable us to achieve an improved understanding
of the original communication.

Paul himself organizes 2 Cor 10-13 in a few large pieces. He does so
by telling his addressees what he is going to do or what he is doing or
has done in a passage, etc. This means that he says things about what he
says, thus signalling that the passages of which he speaks can be
regarded as textual units. Such comments can be called metacommunicative statements. In 2 Cor 10-13 we easily recognize that at least the following statements have this function:

10:1   what follows is a paraclesis (παρακαλῶ)
11:1   what follows is ἀφροσύνη
11:21   what is going on is ἀφροσύνη
12:1   what follows deals with ὀπτασίαι καὶ ἀποκαλύψεις
12:11   what precedes is by an ἄφρων
12:19   what precedes is not apology but τὰ πάντα is for οἰκοδομή
13:10   what precedes (ταῦτα) is written so that Paul will not have
        to use ἐξουσία when present.

In addition, 10:7a appears to have a metacommunicative function. Paul
invites his audience to reflect on their own: "regard τὰ κατὰ πρόσωπον".[2]
But it soon appears that he actually means, "I am going to argue concerning τὰ κατὰ πρόσωπον".

Considering these metacommunicative statements, we note that *13:10*
indicates that the text from 10:1 onward is a unit. In *10:1* Paul summons
(παρακαλῶ) the Corinthians, praying that he will not have to be harsh

---

[2] Most commentators mention the possibility of understanding the βλέπετε as an indicative, but as a rule they prefer the imperative option. In my view, the running argument
links well up with the latter understanding.

when with them; this is taken up again in 13:10, where the ταῦτα refers to the whole text from 10:1.[3]

The caesura of *10:7a* sets off 10:1-6 as an introduction to the whole of 10:1-13:10. The argument on τὰ κατὰ πρόσωπον, introduced in 10:7a, continues until *11:1*, where a new metacommunicative statement signals a new partial text, dealing with "foolish things". It lasts until *12:11*, which marks the end of the treatment of this topic. The character of the contents is re-stated in *11:21*.

12:1 introduces the following topic, viz. visions and revelations. Obviously it is a part of the treatment of the foolish things, which, as we have seen, goes from 11:1 to 12:11. The vision topic is explicitly left behind by 12:7ff.: "in order that I be not elated by the loftiness of the revelations, a σκόλοψ was given unto me."

12:19 characterizes what Paul writes as a non-apology; instead τὰ πάντα is for the οἰκοδομή of the Corinthians. How much of the text is covered by the πάντα? Apparently it should be a text which could be understood as an apology. Since this holds true for most of the deliberations from the first reference to what people say of Paul or accuse him of in 10:1ff. onward, the πάντα should refer to the whole text so far.

Thus, the text is organized as follows (disregarding for the moment how to assess the text-delimiting effect of 12:19):

10:1-13:10 a *paraclesis*
    10:1-6 introduction
    10:7-18 τὰ κατὰ πρόσωπον
    11:1-12:10 ἀφροσύνη
        11:1-33
        12:1-6 visions
        12:7-10 σκόλοψ

We now turn to 12:11-21. The commentators differ considerably from each other when they describe the contents of these verses. To mention only a few examples:

Windisch: 12:14-13:13 Schluß des Briefteils C. Das Programm des neuen Besuchs und Abschluß der Auseinandersetzung mit der Gemeinde. a) 12:14-21 Erste Ankündigung eines neuen Besuchs. b) 13:1-10 Zweite Ankündigung des bevorstehenden Besuchs, daran angeschlossen letzte Drohungen und Vermahnungen.

Bultmann: 2. 10:12-12:18 Die τόλμα des Paulus bzw. der Vergleich mit den Gegnern. a) 10:12-18… b) 11:1-21… c) 11:22-12:18… α) 11:22-33… β) 12:1-

---

[3] This metacommunicative signal is astonishingly seldom taken seriously by commentators. One exception is Fitzgerald 1990, who characterizes the chapters as an "appeal", also referring to a παρακλητική type of letter, discussed by Ps.-Libanius.

10... γ) 12:11-18 Der Schluß des καυχᾶσθαι. 3. 12:19-13:10 Drohung mit der δοκιμή beim dritten Besuch.

Barrett: 12:11-18 Answering Objections. 12:19-13:10 The Apostle and the Church: the Truth.

Furnish: 12:11-13 Epilogue (viz. of the "fool's speech"). 12:14-21 Expressions of Concern. 13:1-10 Warning and Admonition.

Klauck: 12:14-13:10 Besuchspläne.

The differences are obvious, and evidently depend on different manners of understanding what the text is about or at least where the accents lie. My continued analysis will show that a text-linguistically inspired reading leads to results, which are partly similar to these, partly different. A basic difference, though, is that it starts at the level of the text-syntactical signals, and not, as the authorities quoted, with an assessment of the contents.

Unlike the preceding metacommunicative statements, that of 12:11a looks backwards, characterizing that which precedes: "I have been foolish, but you forced me into it". 12:11b-13 develop the reasons why (γάρ, *ter*), viz. that Paul has done so because of the superapostles' denigrating him, and because of the criticism of his refusal to receive support from the Corinthians. In other words, 12:11-13 deals with the preceding part of the text with regard to the communicative situation.

In 12:14 the reader is informed of something, which has hitherto been put forward only as an hypothesis, viz. that Paul plans to visit Corinth a third time (cf. 10:2, 8, 11). It is introduced by an appeal for attention, viz. the particle ἰδού, and linked up with the accusations, mentioned in the immediately preceding verse, of not receiving support: as little as Paul has "burdened" the Corinthians before, he will "burden" them at this new visit. The topic of not burdening remains through 12:18.

This introduction of the visit theme on the one hand, and the continuation of the "burdening" theme on the other, have apparently caused the separate judgments concerning how to organize the text, and concerning what is going on in it; some commentators do not draw any borderline at 12:14, others do.

Also 12:19 refers to the preceding text — it has been for οἰκοδομή. But at the same time 12:19f. introduce a more general parenesis, which, however, is given with Paul's visit in view. So the reason, or need, for the οἰκοδομή is explained (γάρ) by a reference to the coming visit: "because I am afraid that, upon my arrival I will find you such as I would not want, and that I will be found by you such as you would not want" (12:20). The failure to be as Paul wishes is exemplified in a catalogue of vices in 12:20, which has no evident links to the critical situation. All of the vices listed are, however, such as to disturb or destroy interpersonal relationships through quarrels, disputes, slander etc. One may imagine that this represents a generalization of the specific problem treated earlier. 12:21 again makes the visit the background of a possible correction: may Paul then not have to correct those who have not repented. Thus, the perspective of Paul's future visit is retained, and its function becomes a sharpening of the warnings. In other words, Paul tells the Corinthians that what was intimated as a possibility in the introduction might very well become a reality: "I pray that I need not be bold when (if) present" (10:2). These connections backwards and forwards of 12:19-21 are evidently the reason why they have been linked to the text-structure in different ways by different authors *and* why they have been differently understood as to what they are about: do they deal with "l'édification, but de l'action apostolique" (Carrez), are they part of 12:19-13:10 which contains "Drohung mit der δοκιμή beim dritten Besuch" (Bultmann; similarly R. P. Martin: "Warnings and a Third Visit Promised"), or are they the conclusion of 12:14-21, "Erste Ankündigung eines neuen Besuchs" (Windisch)?

The distribution of the contents is undeniably somewhat confusing. The "burdening" is at stake in 12:11-13 and in 12:14-18, the visit in 12:14-18 and 12:19-21, as well as in 13:1-4(10), the threat that the visit will mean a confrontation in 12:19-21 and in 13:1-4. But a closer inspection reveals that the visit is never dealt with *as such*. Rather it is introduced as the presupposition of how Paul will act towards the rebellious people in Corinth, viz. that he will stubbornly insist on not being served by the congregation, and that he is prepared to act with every apostolic authority against those who have not repented.

The confusing impression just mentioned should remind us that a "structuring" of the text in clear-cut units, sub-units, etc., might very well be only an unrealistic construct, particularly if we bear in mind that the text is written to function as an piece of oral communication. Transitions from one element or one theme to another may therefore be made in softer ways than through blanks between paragraphs etc. What matters is not so much the spatial organization of the written text in paragraphs, enabling us to insert headlines, subtitles etc., but how the contents are structured and where the accents lie. But normally such organization of the contents is communicated to the reader through signals on the text surface.

It is now time to sum up our assessment of the metacommunicative statements of 12:11-21 and their effects. *12:11-13* conclude the part on ἀφροσύνη in excusing it by reference to the critics. Simultaneously they lead to *12:14-18*, which introduce the perspective of Paul's third visit to Corinth; in this capacity these verses confirm Paul's stand on the issue of "burdening" — he will not refrain from it at the new visit. At the same time, vv. 14-18 become the conclusion of the text characterized in 12:19 as being for οἰκοδομή. The general warnings of *12:19-21* (and of 13:1-4) are voiced in the same perspective of Paul's visit: hopefully it will not be a traumatic experience for writer and addressees. Actually, the function of the message is: repent, or...! Thus, 12:11-18 seem, on the one hand, to conclude two preceding partial texts, on the other, to be a transition in two steps from the part on ἀφροσύνη to one of warnings in view of the future visit, introduced in 12:19f. In this transition the pragmatic perspective of the four chapters is allowed to dominate the contents. Actually 12:19ff. make it clear that Paul has now finished the argument and applies it to the fact that he is about to return to Corinth and is prepared to put things straight there; i.e., another feature of the text's pragmatic aspect comes to the fore.

Thus, so far 12:11-21 appear to be organized in this way:

12:11-18:   end of 10:(1)7-12:18; transition in two steps
          12:11-13:   ending of part on ἀφροσύνη; reason for it: defence,
                   inter alia, for not "burdening"
          12:14-18:   introducing new perspective: the third visit; continued and finished topical argument on "burdening"
12:19-21:   characterizing 10:(1)7-12:18; reason for it: οἰκοδομή to assure moral standard before visit to come; ethical warnings.

We now turn our attention to 13:1-10. The passage is not distinguished from the preceding context by such a major dividing signal as a metacommunicative statement. But there is a caesura, viz. the fact that Paul explicitly thematizes the planned visit which forms the background of his warnings. The thematization is strengthened by a Biblical quotation, which accentuates the gravity of the future confrontation. Vv. 2-4 are tightly bound together: προείρηκα καὶ προλέγω ... ὅτι ... ἐπεὶ ... ὅς ... καὶ γὰρ ... ἀλλὰ ... καὶ γάρ ... The solemn προείρηκα καὶ προλέγω is a metapropositional basis which presents the proposition of the ὅτι-clause with its continuation in the ἐπεί- and ὅς-clauses. This proposition becomes a marker of the theme treated, i.e., "if I come again, I will not spare them". Thus, the third visit is not the main topic of the passage, only its presupposition. Positively this means that the textual surface favors a judgement like that of Bultmann, who puts 12:19-13:4 under the headline "Drohung mit der δοκιμή beim dritten Besuch".

From 13:5 we notice a certain difference in style. We encounter a second person imperative — hitherto the text has not contained any imperatives with an admonitory function.[4] It is followed by a few more utterances which also have an exhortatory function: v. 5b "or do you not know that ..." , which equals "be certain that ...", furthermore v. 6: "I

hope you know ...", meaning "remember that ...", and v. 7 "we pray that
..." which gives to the subordinate clause the effect of an imperative.
Something similar is, finally, encountered in v. 9b: "we pray for your
being straightened", which, of course, equals "please, by God, straighten
up".

Thus, 13:5-9 is clearly a concluding admonitory passage: this is seen
from its very style and from its imperatives which aim at the pragmatic
function of the text.

Finally, as we noted in the beginning, 13:10 marks the end of this piece
of text, begun at 10:1. It restates briefly the topic indicated in the introduction and some of its aspects which have been treated along the way,
viz. Paul's attitude as present and as absent, his readiness to exert his
apostolic power when present, although the opponents have questioned
it. In this power he has also written the present text for the οἰκοδομή of
the community.

Almost without exception the commentators agree that a — or maybe
even, the — principal aim of 2 Cor 10-13 is apology. Paul claims instead
that he is doing something else: admonition (10:1; παρακαλῶ) and edification (οἰκοδομή: 13:10; 12:19; cf. 10:8).[5] In 12:20 he presents a reason why
that which has every appearance of an apology should function rather as
something which builds up the Church, namely, that its purpose is to
make the opponents repent and the community return to loyalty to Paul.
One may think that this is a fairly Paul-centered idea of building up a
church, and that he is far from the irenic position which he seems to have
in Phil 1:18 — "yet Christ is proclaimed". But for some reason, in 2 Cor,
the whole well-being of the Corinthian Church seems to hang on its
acceptance of Paul, the apostle of Christ.

Be that as it may, by now 2 Cor 10:1-13:10 presents itself as having the
following organization:[6]

---

[4] Except the metacommunicative statements in 10:7 and 11:1 (which is no imperative
from a grammatical point of view, but has the function of one).

[5] Chevallier 1990 argues something similar, maintaining that the goal of the chapters is
a pastoral one.

[6] Talbert 1987 finds an A B A' pattern to be the overarching literary structure of 10-13
(10:1-11 + 10:12-12:13 + 12:14-13:10). As so many others, this structuring depends totally on
the semantic dimension of the text, and pays as little attention to the signals on the text-
syntactical level as other commentaries. Chevallier 1990, also sees a concentric organization
(A B C B' C') in the chapters. Certainly such a structure is there, particularly when one
regards the text in its semantic dimension as Chevallier does. Marguerat 1988 follows a
slightly different track, inspired as he is by Palo Alto to approach the text as regarded from
a communicative-rhetorical angle, which means that he adds the pragmatic dimension to
the semantic one.

1.   10:1-13:10 a paraclesis.
  1.1.   10:1-6 introduction.
  1.2.   10:7-12:18 arguments in order to perform οἰκοδομή.
    1.2.1.   10:7-18 τὰ κατὰ πρόσωπον.
    1.2.2.   11:1-12:10 ἀφροσύνη.
      1.2.2.1.   11:1-33.
      1.2.2.2.   12:1-6 visions.
      1.2.2.3.   12:7-10 σκόλοψ.
    1.2.3.   12:11-18: ending of 10:(1)7-12:18; transition in two steps.
      1.2.3.1.   12:11-13 ending of part on ἀφροσύνη; reason for it: defence, *inter alia*, for not "burdening".
      1.2.3.2.   12:14-18 introducing new perspective: the third visit; continued and finished topical argument on "burdening".
  1.3.   12:19-13:9 warnings and exhortations in view of the visit.
    1.3.1.   12:19-21 characterizing 10:(1)7-12:18; reason for it: οἰκοδομή to assure moral standard before visit to come; ethical warnings.
    1.3.2.   13:1-4 continued warnings in view of the visit.
    1.3.3.   13:5-9 concluding imperatives.
  1.4.   13:10 conclusion of paraclesis.

So far, I have only treated 11:1-12:10 as a unit delimited by the metacommunicative statements at its beginning and its end. But it must be analysed further. Thus, 11:1 introduces the foolish character of what follows, but it is not until 11:5 that the theme which is the reason for the foolishness (γάρ) becomes visible. The theme is introduced by a metapropositional basis, λογίζομαι, followed by the proposition "I am not inferior to the superapostles in anything" (μηδὲν ὑστερηκέναι τῶν ὑπερλίαν ἀποστόλων). The metacommunicative statement of 12:11 ("you forced me into being foolish ... I am not inferior to the superapostles in any respect") makes it clear that the argument of the theme continues through 12:10.

The lines between the metacommunicative statement of 11:1 and the theme presentation in 11:5 become an introduction which will prepare the listener/reader to accept the speech.

11:6 briefly mentions a first item in which Paul is not inferior to the superapostles, viz. knowledge, but he does not argue it. Instead, he continues hastily to the topic of non-support, which appears to be more painful. The superapostles have questioned Paul's practice and thereby also his legitimacy as an apostle. It is first treated in vv. 7-11, which are delimited by the substitution on the abstraction level in v. 12, "what I do". This little clause covers the argument of the preceding verses. The γάρ of v. 13 hangs the invectives of vv. 13-15 directly on vv. 7-11. So vv. 7-

15 are a unit, which claims that the non-support practice does not make Paul inferior to the superapostles.

11:16-21 contain several remarks on the text which Paul is writing, i.e. they are on some kind of meta-level to it. Thus, v. 16 a is a metapropositional basis (πάλιν λέγω) with a proposition ("no one may think I am a fool"), and the "what I am saying" (ὃ λαλῶ) of v. 17 is a substitution on the abstraction level, referring to what is going on and, particularly, to what is to come: καύχησις on Paul's part. Vv. 19-21a explain (γάρ, *bis*) why the Corinthians should accept this foolish boasting of Paul. Thus, vv. 16-21a make a pause in the fool's speech; they refer partly to what has been going on in it so far, partly they introduce its next step.

11:21b (ἐν ἀφροσύνῃ λέγω) is a metacommunicative statement which restates the mode of the fool's speech. It also becomes a metapropositional basis for the theme in the next phase of the speech, in that its proposition is "whatever anyone dares to boast of, I also dare to boast of" (ἐν ᾧ ... ἄν τις τολμᾷ, ... τολμῶ κἀγώ). Thus also ἐν ᾧ becomes a substitution for the contents of vv. 22-29 (or 22-33), i.e. for the list of Paul's merits as a Jew and as a servant of Christ, as compared with the superapostles.

Vv. 30-33 mean a change in style. V. 30f. on the one hand states once more the mode of vv. 22-29, i.e. they represent a reflection in the rearview mirror. On the other hand, 12:1-10 show the reader that vv. 30f. also holds true of that which follows. Thus, the passage becomes a transition passage, which stands on a metalevel in relation to its context.

Thus, if we also fit 11:1-33 into its context,[7] it turns out to be built in this way:

1.2.2.   11:1-12:10 ἀφροσύνη speech.
    1.2.2.1.   11:1-4 introduction: may the readers accept.
    1.2.2.2.   11:5 theme: not inferior to superapostles.
    1.2.2.3.   11:6-12:10 defending theme of 11:5.
      1.2.2.3.1.   11:6 argument: not in gnosis.
      1.2.2.3.2.   11:7-15 next argument: not because of non-support.
        1.2.2.3.2.1.   11:7-11 defending practice.
        1.2.2.3.2.2.   11:12-15 explaining defence with regard to opponents, who are attacked.
      1.2.2.3.3.   11:16-21a petition for acceptance, transition.
      1.2.2.3.4.   11:21b-29 listing Paul's merits as a boastful servant of Christ.

---

[7] For the integration of this textdelimitation into the overall hierarchical structure of the text-sequence 10:1-13:10, see the structural delimitation above page 242f. and below page 249f.

Let us now scrutinize the different stages of the argument and see how Paul performs his paraclesis, or his οἰκοδομή.

In the introduction 10:1-6, Paul does three things in the first verse: (1) he introduces the following as a paraclesis, (2) draws Christ into this paraclesis as being meek and mild, and (3), introduces himself as having the features his opponents hold against him: he is weak when present and harsh when absent. Against this background a metapropositional basis in v. 2 ("I pray") introduces a precision of what the paraclesis is about, i.e. its main topic: the addressees shall see to it that the one who has been meek when present will not be forced, when visiting them, to be harsh towards "some who hold the opinion that we are weak according to the flesh". In v. 3 such harshness is explained (γάρ): first through a flat denial of Paul's carnality: he lives *in* the flesh, but not according to it. At the same time, through changing "walking" (περιπατοῦντας) of v. 2 into "fighting" (στρατευόντας), the further explanation of vv. 4ff. is prepared, in which the war imagery is applied to the apostle's work: his weapons are not carnal but powerful to (through) God (δυνατὰ τῷ θεῷ). In other words, the addressees should know that the opponents are mocking a person with this divine power, and that, if needed, he will use this power. In the light of our preceding discussions we realize that this is a real introduction: it presents Paul's attitude and the apostolic position which he is about to defend and from which he intends to argue, and indicates the main topic of these chapters, viz. that the opposition had better dissolve before Paul appears in Corinth. This "defence" is after all not for Paul's sake but for that of the Corinthians. The argument has a practical touch, in that its ultimate purpose is not so much: "realize that I am a real apostle", as "change your attitude versus the opponents and versus me, and do this for your own good". We should also note that the theme of weakness has been forced upon Paul by the opponents, and a cynical reader may even suggest that Paul skilfully makes a virtue out of the necessity, when he turns the weakness into something which speaks in his favor as Christ's envoy.

The first argument why the opposition should dissolve is in 10:7-18. In these verses the addressees are summoned to consider the outward appearance and καύχησις of Paul and of the τις of v. 7 as well as of the τινὲς λογιζόμενοι of v. 2. This argument is indicated by the metacommunicative statement of v. 7a: τὰ κατὰ πρόσωπον βλέπετε. Its first phase is introduced by the metapropositional basis in v. 7b: λογιζέσθω ..., the proposition of which is: "(also) we are Christ's". This proposition contains a comparison with "somebody" who "has the confidence" (πέποιθεν) to regard himself as Christ's. Verse 8 explains (γάρ) the proposition by silently equating being Christ's with having an ἐξουσία from the Lord and claiming that Paul will not be afraid of relying upon this power. This in turn is illustrated in vv. 9-11. ἵνα μὴ δόξω etc. is equal to: "concerning the fact that I will not be ashamed of boasting of my ἐξουσία, do not think that I only threaten — as (v. 10) some say that I am strong when absent and weak when present." A concluding metapropositional base (λογιζέσθω) applies Paul's self-confidence to such people, i.e. the text's pragmatic perspective comes to the fore: he may very well exert his ἐξουσία also when present. In other words, the topic "(also) we are Christ's" has been elaborated in vv. 8-11 but has hardly been logically argued, only proclaimed.

Thus, as yet only the proposition of v. 7b has been aired: Paul *has* an authority from Christ and he is proud of it and prepared to use it. But the argument τὰ κατὰ πρόσωπον βλέπετε has not yet come to the fore. The commentators normally expect v. 7a to refer to something in vv. 7-11. But the claim of being Christ's (envoy) is hardly convincing as a visible proof — on the contrary, this seems rather to be questioned in Corinth. The same holds true of Paul's authority. Some commentaries refer to Paul's presence, mentioned in v. 1 (e.g., Schlatter, R. P. Martin), others to the signs Paul had shown (Bultmann). But it seems to me that the fact which can really serve as a basis for a judgment from eyesight is what is cited in vv.12-18. viz. that Paul reached Corinth as an apostle. These verses elaborate (γάρ) on the pride, i.e. a pride κατὰ τὸ μέτρον. In an ironic comparison Paul begins by pretending that he dare not compare himself with such persons as justify themselves (συνιστάνειν) and use their own measures (αὐτοὶ ἐν ἑαυτοῖς ἑαυτοὺς μετροῦντες). But of course he does! For in v. 13 he contrasts himself to them: *our* preaching of the Gospel to you was according to *God's* μέτρον, and so *we* do not boast εἰς τὰ ἄμετρα. The μέτρον is that which was decided at the division of the mission areas between Paul and the other apostles (Gal 2:9) and which conformed to Paul's divine commission to the Gentiles. So, in vv. 12-16 "our" legitimation and μέτρον are contrasted to those of "others", either of the opponents or of those persons to whom they refer. As Paul was the Corinthians' missionary, they could judge for themselves: regarding τὰ κατὰ πρόσωπον Paul has reason to boast κατὰ τὸ μέτρον, the others do not.

In vv. 17f. the passage concludes with a generalization in the form of an Old Testament quotation followed by an explanation of its relevance: a valid legitimation (of apostles) comes only from the Lord, and such a legitimation alone justifies pride. This is the case with Paul, not with the "somebody", and with "some people".

In 11:1-5 the fool's speech begins, and we have seen its theme introduced in 11:5. The introduction 11:1-4 will prepare the listener/reader to accept the speech. This is what Paul asks in v. 1, and vv. 2-4 argue in different ways why the Corinthians should do so. First he adduces a positive reason (γάρ), which may bring them into a positive mood: he has a divine zeal for them (v. 2a). Then, in v. 3, follows a negative argument. Paul fears that nevertheless (φοβοῦμαι δέ) they will be seduced, i.e., (γάρ) by the superapostles, whom Paul introduces ironically in v. 4: they are certainly accepted by the Corinthians, despite the fact that they proclaim another gospel. As a matter of fact, this may shed some light on the way Paul presents his "apology": we noticed above that he regards it as a building-up of the Corinthians. His zeal, when eager to make them return to loyalty to him, is God's zeal. Is this only rhetoric? Hardly "only". Apparently Paul sincerely means that to turn away from God's envoy is to turn away from God.

So Paul will argue the theme, "I am not inferior to the superapostles". Very briefly he mentions a first item in which he is not their inferior, viz. knowledge. Then, in vv. 7-15, he deals with an issue which is more delicate, viz. that he has not — as the superapostles — made use of an apostle's right to be served by the community. After explaining his practice in view of his regard, indeed, his love, for the Corinthians (vv. 7b-11), he sums up his way of action as described and defended in the preceding verses in v. 12: ὃ δὲ ποιῶ. So v. 12 contains a more direct application to the theme "I am not inferior ..." concerning precisely this issue: he will pursue his practice because of the superapostles. He expresses himself in such a way that their being false apostles of Christ is a reason why (γάρ) he will continue his practice of supporting himself. It is not clear which effects he thinks his continued practice will have vis-à-vis them, but for some reason he is of the opinion that it will. Then, he heaps invectives upon them in vv. 13-15.[8]

11:16-21 introduce a new part of the fool's speech and we have already seen that they are on some kind of meta-level to it. V. 16a ("no one may think I am a fool") and the following sentence twist the foolishness theme, but are in harmony with the inverted tendencies of this language of folly. V. 17 also refers to what is going on, and, particularly, to what is to come: Paul intends to boast, and, indeed to boast κατὰ σάρκα (καυχήσομαι, v. 16c and v. 18; ἐν ταύτῃ τῇ ὑποστάσει τῆς καυχήσεως, v.

17c). Vv. 19-21 explain (γάρ, *bis*) why the Corinthians should accept this foolish boasting: they accept the boasting superapostles who eat them out of house and home, which Paul — to his shame — has been too weak to do; i.e. he argues according to what he seems to hope will be an *a minore ad maius* approach.

After this introduction which has — with many reservations and ironic turns and twists — set the tone for the following part of the fool's speech, Paul begins it in v. 22. We have seen that its theme is "whatever anyone dares to boast of, I also dare to boast of". V. 23 forms a certain borderline within the partial text of vv. 22-29. For in vv. 22-23a Paul boasts of the same things as do the opponents, but the continuation of the list stands under some sort of headline in v. 23b: they may be Christ's servants, but so is Paul, only far more so: ὑπὲρ ἐγώ. In addition, this headline is softly underlined through a brief statement on the metalevel: παραφρονῶν λέγω.

As to vv. 30-33, one may ask for their possible prehistory, particularly of vv. 32f., viz. the notice of Paul's flight from Damascus. Why are they here? Bultmann mentions some possible answers: maybe they are an "einfacher Nachtrag"; but, if so, why? Or they might be an interpolation, say, by an amanuensis. (This was what Windisch suggested.) If we consider the other side of the communication process, we have noted above that vv. 30f. is a transition passage, which stands on a metalevel in relation to its context. As for the Damascus episode, vv. 32f., to a reader/listener it stands out as a single, concrete, narrative element among all the generalizations and abstractions of these chapters. This stylistic property is a simple fact. As for its communicative effect, we may note that not only modern propagandists and polemicists know that a concrete detail in a flow of abstract, general speech is effective; it catches the interest of

---

[8] For once in this article, allow me at this point to illustrate the difference between my results in terms of structure and those of other scholars. According to Martin 1986, "a major decision awaits the interpreter of 11:1-15." Is it "an interlude in which Paul turns aside from his chief theme of missionary service and the dispute of territoriality (in 10:12-18), only to revert to that topic in 11:16 ..."? Or is "10:13-18 a digression, albeit related to the main theme. Then, at 11:1 the reader is confronted with the beginning of a new topic" (328). Prof. Martin himself prefers the former option. — It seems to me that my analysis proves helpful in the dilemma which Prof. Martin describes. Thus, it has indicated that "the missionary service and the dispute of territoriality" is the chief theme, neither of 10:12-18, nor of 11:16 onward. Rather, it is only an argument concerning τὰ κατὰ πρόσωπον to support the claim which is signalled in 10:7, namely "also we are Christ's". As to 11:1-15, the metacommunicative statements and the metapropositional bases with their propositions suggest that the introduction of the fool's speech is in vv. 1-6 and presents its main theme, "I am not inferior to the superapostles" (v. 5). Vv. 6-15 contain the first arguments for the legitimacy of this claim. If this is correct, "the major decision" which the interpreter has to make, need not be made at all, and the accents of the argument place themselves elsewhere.

the audience and sometimes arouses its sympathy. The rhetors of Antiquity also knew this, e.g., (Pseudo-) Aristotle and Pseudo-Longinus.[9]

12:1b is a metacommunicative statement which presents the next topic to be discussed as an item of καύχησις in the current explanation how Paul is not inferior to the superapostles, viz. visions and revelations, (ἐλεύσομαι εἰς) ὀπτασίας καὶ ἀποκαλύψεις κυρίου. This becomes the theme of 12:1-6. The visions and revelations are narrated in vv. 2-4 as being those of another person. According to v. 5. Paul will boast of "this kind of person" (ὑπὲρ τοῦ τοιούτου) instead of himself; this τοιοῦτος is a substitution on the abstraction level which holds vv. 2-4 together. Furthermore, v. 6 contains two comments on the metalevel. They deal with vv. 2-5a: first, if Paul would pride himself on this, he would speak the truth. Second, he indirectly labels the ecstatic phenomena "things one cannot see or hear from me". The phrase ὑπερβολὴ τῶν ἀποκαλύψεων (v. 7) is also a substitution on the abstraction level, referring to vv. 2-4. Thus, vv. 5-7a move to a great extent on a metalevel in relation to vv. 2-4, commenting on them; their contents are taken as something meritorious, but, although Paul could boast of these merits, he does not want to.

So vv. 5-7a become a first piece which deals directly with the topic introduced in v. 1b, visions and revelations. As a negative pendant to this part come vv. 7b-10, on the σκόλοψ. Implicitly, with regard to v. 6c, these verses must be said to deal with "things one can see or hear from me", i.e. things which represent Paul's weakness, and of which Paul is prepared to boast (9b); we could add: as a real apostle and follower of Christ.

As for 12:11-18 and 12:19-13:10 the discussion above may suffice, and so my second walk through 2 Cor 10-13 has come to an end.

If we combine the different tables of the analysis above with each other, we obtain the following result. Let me emphasize that the aim of the table is not to make Paul appear as a man with a computer mind. It is rather a condensed summary of the above discussion of the organization of the argument structure in 2 Cor 10-13. Certainly one can discuss the indentation here and there, but hoping that the table will not be overinterpreted I venture to present it.

---

[9] (Pseudo-) Aristotle, *Rhet. ad Alex.* 8 (1429a), 32 (1439a); *Ps-Longinus*, 15,1. Talbert 1987, 123 can think of three reasons for vv. 30-33, a) they are an illustration of the dangers in the city (v. 26), b) they constitute a rest for author and reader, a solution proposed already by S. Augustine (*Doctr. Christ.* 4.7.12), c) they represent a persuasive trick, recommended by Plutarch, that one should mention some personal flaws to temper a eulogy. As is evident from the suggestions above, the second option seems to me to be the best.

1.   10:1-13:10 a paraclesis.
 1.1.   10:1-6 introduction.
 1.2.   10:7-12:18 arguments in order to perform οἰκοδομή.
  1.2.1.   10:7-18 argument: τὰ κατὰ πρόσωπον.
  1.2.2.   11:1-12:10 ἀφροσύνη speech.
   1.2.2.1.   11:1-4 introduction: may the readers accept.
   1.2.2.2.   11:5 theme: not inferior to superapostles.
   1.2.2.3.   11:6-12:10 defending theme of 11:5.
    1.2.2.3.1.   11:6 argument: not in gnosis.
    1.2.2.3.2.   11:7-15 argument: not because of non-support.
     1.2.2.3.2.1.   11:7-11 defending practice.
     1.2.2.3.2.2.   11:12-15 explaining defence with regard to opponents, who are attacked.
    1.2.2.3.3.   11:16-21a petition for acceptance, transition.
    1.2.2.3.4.   11:21b-29 listing of Paul's merits as a boastful servant of Christ.
     1.2.2.3.4.1.   11:21b-23a equal to superapostles.
     1.2.2.3.4.2.   11:23b-29 superior to superapostles.
    1.2.2.3.5.   11:30-33 re-stating of mode; a final example of hard service.
    1.2.2.3.6.   12:1-10 argument: visions and revelations.
     1.2.2.3.6.1.   12:1-6 visions and revelations.
     1.2.2.3.6.2.   12:7-10 σκόλοψ.
  1.2.3.   12:11-18: ending of 10:(1)7-12:18; transition in two steps.
   1.2.3.1.   12:11-13 ending of part on ἀφροσύνη; reason for it: defence, *inter alia*, for not "burdening".
   1.2.3.2.   12:14-18 introducing new perspective: the third visit; continued and finished topical argument on "burdening".
 1.3.   12:19-13:9 warnings and exhortations in view of the visit
  1.3.1.   12:19-21 characterizing 10:(1)7-12:18; reason for it: οἰκοδομή to assure moral standard before visit to come; ethical warnings.
  1.3.2.   13:1-4 continued warnings in view of the visit.
  1.3.3.   13:5-9 concluding imperatives.
 1.4.   13:10 conclusion of paraclesis.

In this paper I have concentrated on the structure of the arguments. It is something other than an exegetical assessment of the individual clauses and groups of clauses which constitute the argument. It is possible that if I were to present an exegesis of the details and the whole of the contents

in 2 Cor 10-13, my interpretation thereof would resemble what one normally finds in the commentaries. But there would also be differences,
depending on how my analysis suggests that several details of the contents function within the chain of the argument. Furthermore, other differences could be caused by an attempt on my part to take seriously
Paul's own statements on what he is doing. Thus, for example, he says
that he is writing a paraclesis and that his aim is *oikodome*, which makes
his stated aim practical and pastoral. Moreover the situation in Corinth
and the opponents there have the upper hand and dictate the problems;
so the theology becomes subservient to Paul's handling of these pastoral
problems.[10] This should also have some effect on attempts at a historical
interpretation of 2 Cor 10-13. But so far these concluding remarks are
mainly speculations on the basis of what is only a sketch.

Bibliography

1. Commentaries

Barrett, C. K. 1973: *A Commentary on the Second Epistle to the Corinthians* (BNTC),
London: Black 1973 [reprint 1976].

Bultmann, R. 1976: *Der zweite Brief an die Korinther* (KEK Sonderband), Göttingen:
Vandenhoeck & Ruprecht 1976.

Carrez, M. 1986: *La deuxième épître de saint Paul aux Corinthiens* (CNTN[N] II.8), Ge-
nève: Labor et fides 1986.

Furnish, V. P. 1984: *II Corinthians* (AncB 32 A), Garden City, N.Y.: Doubleday 1984.

Klauck, H.-J. 1986: *2. Korintherbrief* (NEB.NT 8), Würzburg: Echter 1986.

Lang, F. 1986: *Die Briefe an die Korinther* (NTD 7), Göttingen & Zürich: Vandenhoeck & Ruprecht 1986.

Martin, R. P. 1986: *2 Corinthians* (WBC 40), Waco, TX: Word Books 1986.

Schlatter, A. 1969: *Paulus, der Bote Jesu. Eine Deutung seiner Briefe an die Korinther*,
4th ed., Stuttgart: Calver 1969.

Talbert, C. H. 1987: *Reading Corinthians. A Literary and Theological Commentary on 1
and 2 Corinthians*, New York, N.Y.: Crossroad 1987.

Windisch, H. 1924/70: *Der zweite Korintherbrief* [reprint from 1924, ed. G. Strecker],
Göttingen: Vandenhoeck & Ruprecht 1970.

---

[10] As for the theological features Chevallier 1990, 13f. correctly denies the importance of
a *theologia crucis* for the argument of these chapters.

2. Special Studies on 2 Cor 10-13

Aejmelaeus, L. 1987: *Streit und Versöhnung. Das Problem der Zusammensetzung des 2. Korintherbriefes* (Schriften der finnischen exegetischen Gesellschaft 46), Helsinki: Die Finnische Exegetische Gesellschaft 1987.

Betz, H. D. 1972: *Der Apostel Paulus und die sokratische Tradition. Eine exegetische Untersuchung zu seiner "Apologie" 2 Korinther 10-13* (BHTh 45), Tübingen: Mohr (Siebeck) 1972.

Chevallier, M.-A. 1990: "L'argumentation de Paul dans II Corinthiens 10 à 13", in: *RHPhR* 70 (1990) 3-16.

Fitzgerald, J. T. 1990: "Paul, the Ancient Epistolary Theorists, and 2 Corinthians 10-13. The Purpose and Literary Genre of a Pauline Letter", in: D. L. Balch etc. (eds.), *Greeks, Romans, and Christians. Essays in Honor of A. J. Malherbe*, Minneapolis, MN: Fortress 1990, 190-200.

Lohse, E. (ed.) 1992: *Verteidigung und Begründung des apostolischen Amtes (2 Kor 10-13)* (Monogr. Reihe "Benedictina", Bibl.-ökum. Abteilung 11), Rome: S. Paulo f. le mura 1992.

Marguerat, D. 1988: "2 Corinthiens 10-13. Paul et l'expérience de Dieu", in: *ETR* 63 (1988) 497-519.

Zmijewski, J. 1978: *Der Stil der paulinischen "Narrenrede". Analyse der Sprachgestaltung in 2 Kor 11,1-12,10 als Beitrag zur Methodik von Stiluntersuchungen neutestamentlicher Texte* (BBB 52), Bonn: Hanstein 1978.

Supplement

1. Commentaries

Wolff, Chr.: *Der zweite Brief des Paulus an die Korinther* (ThHK 8), Berlin: Evanglische Verlagsanstalt 1989.

Hughes, Ph. E.: *Paul's Second Epistle to the Corinthians*. (NIC), Grand Rapids, MI: Eerdmans 1962 [reprint 1992].

2. Other Literature

Watson, F.: "2 Cor. x-xiii and Paul's Painlful Letter to the Corinthians", in: *JThS* 35 (1984) 324-46

Forbes, C.: "Comparison, Self-Praise and Irony: Paul's Boasting and the Conventions of Hellenistic Rhetoric", in: *NTS* 32 (1986) 1-30.

Aejmelaeus, L.: *Streit und Versöhnung. Das Problem der Zusammensetzung des 2. Korintherbriefes* (SESJ 46), Helsinki: Finnische Exeg. Gesellschaft 1987.

Fitzgerald, J. T.: "Paul, the Ancient Epistolary Theorists, and 2 Corinthians 10-13", in: D. L. Balch/E. Ferguson/W. A. Meeks (eds.), *Greeks, Romans, and Christians*, Minneapolis, MN: Fortress 1990, 190-200.

Hafemann, S.: "'Self-Commendation' and Apostolic Legitimacy in 2 Corinthians: a Pauline Dialectic?", in: *NTS* 36 (1990) 66-88.

Crafton, J. A.: *The Agency of the Apostle. A Dramatistic Analysis of Paul's Responses to Conflict in 2 Corinthians*, Sheffield: Sheffield Academic Press 1991.

Loubser, J. A.: "A New Look at Paradox and Irony in 2 Corinthians 10-13", in:*Neotest.* 26 (1992) 507-21.

Strecker, G.: "Die Legitimität des paulinischen Apostolates nach 2 Korintherbrief 10-13", in: *NTS* 38 (1992) 566-86.

Holland, G.: "Speaking like a Fool: Irony in 2 Corinthians 10-13", in: S. E. Porter/ Th. H. Olbricht (eds.), *Rhetoric and the New Testament. Essays from the 1992 Heidelberg Conference* (JSNT.S 90), Sheffield: Sheffield Academic Press 1993, 250-64.

Witherington III, B.: *Conflict and Community in Corinth. A Socio-Rhetorical Commentary on 1 and 2 Corinthians*, Grand Rapids, MI: Eerdmans 1994.

14. Gal 3:15-4:11 as Part of a Theological Argument on a Practical Issue

1. Introduction

Theologians are tempted to regard Bible texts as boxes full of theology. This can lead them to isolating sentences from their literary context without paying regard to the text's actual surface organisation. Furthermore, and more often, they may forget the fact that the text was meant to say something and, indeed, to achieve something in the historical situation of the text. Thus, the main purpose of the text might have been practical. In such a case, the interpreter should be conscious of the serious possibility that this purpose determines the choice of theological statements to such an extent that one should be cautious when using them for a reconstruction of the writer's theology.

In any communicative situation the reader/listener lets details on the textual surface organize the structure of the contents. The results of the interrelation between these two aspects of the text function over against the reader. But the communication also has an external context, in which the author is doing something to his reader in order to achieve something. Or to shift the perspective to that of the recipients: in the context the communication is supposed to have certain results, emerging from what is going on on the textual surface and on the level of contents.[1]

In the following, I will try to resist the temptation at which I hinted above. In accordance with the task given to me for this paper, I will try to deal with the text allotted to me in regarding it as a piece of communica-

---

[1] To express the same things with a text-linguistic terminology: the mentioned surface organisation stands for the syntactic aspect (dealing with the relation between sign and sign); the contents, which is understood as theological statements correspond to the semantic aspect (concerning the relation between signs and designata); lastly, the historical situation and the function of the text over against its addressees are ways of speaking of the pragmatic aspect (regarding the relation between signs, designata and sign-users). Of these aspects the pragmatic one includes the two others, of which the semantic one, in its turn, includes the syntactic aspect (see Plett 1979, 52). Actually one has not rendered justice to a textual communication, unless one takes into regard all these text dimensions. On the other hand, as soon as one begins to reconstruct details of the supposed situation of an ancient text, one gets into troubles; see for Galatians, Barclay 1987.

tion in the way just intimated. As a matter of fact, this means that I am going to apply some analytic tools which are taken from the field of text-linguistics.

Without going too much into technicalities, these are the types of textual features which are instrumental for my analysis.

(a) Meta-communicative clauses: such clauses are clauses about the communication at hand. E.g., the first statement of the letter: "Paul ... to the churches of Galatia".

(b) In an arguing text there are different ways of signalling the theme dealt with or topic to be dealt with. Following B. C. Johanson,[2] who refers to E. U. Große,[3] I have called them Thematic Markers (abbreviated ThM). They can introduce larger or smaller sections or subsections of the argument. Often they are introduced by an expression on meta-level as related to the clause indicating the theme. Such an expression can be labelled a "meta-propositional base" (abbreviated MB). Here are a few examples from Galatians:

1:11: "I announce to you brethren, (concerning) the gospel preached by me, that it is not from men". Here "I announce to you" is the meta-propositional base which stands on a meta-level over against the following expression which mentions the theme to be dealt with, viz. that Paul's gospel is not from men.

Furthermore 3:2: "this one thing I want to know from you: did you receive the Spirit by works of the law, or by hearing in faith?" Likewise 3:15: "Brethren, I speak in human terms: no one annuls even a man's will or adds to it, once it has been ratified". All these Thematic Markers are introduced by a meta-propositional base; this is, however, not the case in the Thematic Marker of 3:19: "What is the law?" (although one might make the question-form imply a "I ask, what ...").

The thematic markers may introduce a theme to be dealt with at length as well as one that is only the subject of a subsection. Such sections and subsections can be delimited in different ways. Thus, when the aim for which the author set out is reached, a conclusion can be explicitly introduced, e.g., by ἄρα or ὥστε. E.g., in 4:7: "Thus, you are no longer a slave, but a son." In an arguing text such markers seem to me to be rather important when it comes to organizing the text.

Furthermore, a certain means of delimitation can be the indication of the ultimate purpose or (divine) aim of a circumstance or something argued for. This is, e.g., the case in 3:22 "in order that, out of belief in Jesus Christ, the promise might be given to those who believe".

In yet other cases the reader realizes that the discussion of a topic has come to an end, in that a new one is introduced. This can be done abruptly as in 3:1; there the reader quickly realizes that the speech, formally directed to Peter, is finished by 2:21, because then Paul bursts out: "Oh, foolish Galatians".

In 3:14, 3:22, and 3:29 we encounter a feature that goes together with other signs which indicate that the discussion of a theme is over. In all these instances a

---

[2] Johanson 1987, 29f.
[3] Große 1976.

new theme is introduced in the sentence that concludes the treatment of the former. E.g., 3:29: "if you are Christ's, then (ἄρα) you are Abraham's seed, heirs according to the promise"; here, the treatment of the promise to Abraham comes to an end and the motif of the heir is introduced.

(c) When an author turns directly to his addressees he can be doing several things to them. Of course the whole of the letter is an address to the readers. But in certain passages Paul turns to the Galatians in a more intensive way, i.e., in such passages where they are directly addressed or when Paul applies the results of an argument to them.[4] It is to be expected that the readers/listeners get the impression that such passages are especially important and that the author is here at kernel points of the things concerning which he wishes to influence them. In other words, seen from a pragmatic point of view, when an author argues that the addressee should take a practical stand or make a practical move, and he pursues this argument in a theoretical key in 3rd person, and then returns to 2nd person, this latter move has a certain text-delimiting, text-organizing effect, of which we should be aware. In these instances Paul often adds a direct appeal to them, "brethren".

(d) Shifts of person can also mean changes of style, and, in general, shifts of style may have text-organizing effects. E.g. the series of (rhetorical) questions directed to 2nd person plural in 3:1-5.[5]

(e) Temporal and/or spatial markers often indicate a new step, especially in narrative texts, e.g., in 2:1: "then, after 14 years, I went up again to Jerusalem.

(f) The "connectors"[6] are conjunctions, particles etc. (such as δέ, ἵνα, ἀλλά), which relate clauses in different ways to each other. They function mainly within the text and do not alone mark the beginning of a new passage, but may cooperate with other, weightier markers, as, e.g., in 3:23: "but (δέ) before the faith came ..." (the other markers being the shift to first person plural and the return to the topic of faith, introduced in the concluding ἵνα-clause of 3:22b). Other connectors, as οὖν, γάρ, εἰ, do deserve the designation, as they connect clauses with each other, often in a logical relationship. I have already maintained that in an arguing text such as ours, connectors like ἄρα and ὥστε deserve extra attention, because they mark logical structures of the text, often introducing the result of the argument of a preceding passage.

2. The Context Preceding Gal 3:15-4:11

I have been asked to deal with Gal 3:15-4:11. But because the passage is tightly bound to the preceding argument, I feel obliged briefly to regard this context.

In 1:6ff. the reader/listener is confronted with the theme which will dominate Galatians throughout. The language of 1:6ff. however, sets the

---

[4] See Lategan 1989, 173f.
[5] See Lategan 1989, 176.
[6] See Johanson 1987, 32, referring to Gülich/Raible 1977 and Hellholm 1980 and 1986.

theme only indirectly. But the phrase "I am surprised that" is actually a
reproachful way of saying "I urge you not to", viz. "not to turn away
from him who called you in Christ's grace to another gospel ..." Again,
this is but a negative way of saying: "return to (or: in case one had not
given in to the propagators: hold on to) the one who called you in Christ
and do so through keeping to my gospel." The theme returns in varied
forms in 4:9(-20), 5:1(-12), 6:11-17. Accordingly, within the whole of Galatians, the theme introduced in 1:6 is dealt with through to 6:17; Gal 1:6-
6:17, then, forms one big partial text.

The meta-propositional base "I am surprised that"/"I urge you (not)
to" is an indicator that the theme is not directly a theoretical, theological
one, but one concerning behaviour. Thus, we should remind ourselves of
the differentiation between theoretical and practical argumentation. The
former aims at bringing home a cognitive point, the latter has the purpose of making the addressee accept a given obligation or evaluation.[7]
Quite often, however, the two types are not exclusive of each other. Thus,
although Paul certainly uses theoretical arguments in Galatians, there is
hardly any doubt that his argument is mainly a practical one in the sense
just indicated.

Already my paraphrase of 1:6f., above, intimated that it is reasonable
to assume "a double reader" of Galatians,[8] i.e., both those who had
accepted the "other gospel" and those who did not or had not yet done
so. As a consequence, the behaviour for which Paul argues is not simply
to turn away from the propagators of the other gospel, but can — and
does, as a matter of fact — also develop what it means to stay with Paul's
gospel, also in terms of ethical standards. This gives a natural function to
the parenesis from 5:13 and on.

The next thematic marker appears in 1:11. It introduces the first argument as to why the Galatians should keep to Paul's gospel: "I announce
to you:[9] my gospel is not a human thing." The report of significant episodes will support this argument, and the treatment of this comes to an
end in 2:10.[10]

---

[7] Kopperschmidt 1985, 161.

[8] See Lategan 1989, esp. 177.

[9] A meta-propositional base.

[10] In a way, the treatment of the theme that the gospel is not a human thing seems to be
finished in 1:19. For after the mention of the fortnight in Jerusalem something like a period
is put into the text, in that Paul comments on the preceding data: "Before God, what I write
to you is the truth". (One may discuss how far back this statement reaches. A fair assumption is that it covers the text from 1:16c and on, thus beginning with the first denial of any
contacts with other thinkable sources of the gospel than Christ.) But with v. 21 Paul continues the history of his gospel and adds new episodes. Thus it is not until 2:10 that the treatment of the theme "my gospel is not a human thing" is finished.

With 2:11ff. we are, on the one hand, still in a narrative style. But at the same time the reader should sense that something different is coming up. A crisis is signalled with the introduction of the new episode: "but when (ὅτε δέ, linking up with Peter's giving his right hand to Paul in Jerusalem, 2:9) Cephas arrived in Antioch, I stood up against him because he stood condemned". The first sentence of the speech in v. 14b signals the issue, both as regarded within the narrative world of the Antioch episode, and in the world of the Galatian addressees. Thus, the words to Peter, "How can you compel the Gentiles to live like Jews?," are also directed at the representatives of "the other gospel" in Galatia.[11] This plea joins the one in 1:6ff., as well as those in 3:1ff. and 4:8ff.

The theological items which are brought up in the speech support the plea and point to essential elements of the gospel to which the address-ees should remain faithful. These deliberations on "the truth of the gos-pel" (2:14) concern the Galatian situation much more than the former one in Antioch.[12]

Thus, 2:11-21 forms the second argument for 1:6ff., spelling out from what gospel the Galatians should not deviate.[13] 2:11-13 is its introduc-tion, 14-21 its main piece. Here it is marked out as a unit also by the fact that it is a speech, although formally it is a part of the narrative in the Antioch episode. When Paul, in 2:14-21, presents the truth of the gospel, this means that he takes up the feature in the presentation of the main theme in 1:6ff., which contrasts "the gospel of Christ" and "the grace of Christ" to "another gospel — which there is none". The speech intro-duces the principle of being justified through faith in Christ and not by doing the law. We should note that this principle is presented as some-thing on which Paul and his adversary (Peter and the other Jewish Chris-tians) agree; hopefully the opponents in Galatia should also agree: "*we know*" (2:16).

---

[11] Cf. Kieffer 1982, 33-36.

[12] See also Kieffer 1982, 15 (+ literature).

[13] Betz 1979 is of the opinion that Paul followed certain rhetorical patterns when deal-ing with the Galatians. To my mind Betz attaches too much importance to the rhetorical pattern as such, as if the rhetorical patterns of the handbooks were relatively strict rules. This has got the consequence that he presents 3:1-4:31 as the "probatio" of the "propositio" in 2:15 (sic!)-21. But there is no dividing line whatsoever between 2:14 and 15 in Paul's "speech" to Peter (see Kieffer 1982, 27). If we assume that the text — as a rhetorical piece of work! — should be understood as a means of communication, the text surface (its syntacti-cal aspect) should indicate what the author was doing in these lines, viz. introducing the thing he wanted to bring home with his audience. I find it hard to believe that the receivers of Galatians heard the text tell them that this part of Paul's speech presented the thing to be demonstrated in the following. To take 2:15-21 as a propositio also prepares the way for a view of Galatians which, I think, a bit too quickly finds the text expressing theological opinions. See also the remarks by Kraftchick 1990.

The subunit of the Antioch episode receives a clear-cut end by the abrupt new beginning in 3:1. There we encounter a renewed direct address ("Oh, foolish Galatians"), a series of direct, theme-setting questions in second person plural, and a shift of style (direct reproaches). The first question picks up and actually re-states the main theme of Galatians in a circumscription: "who has bewitched you, before whose eyes Christ, the crucified, was painted?" (3:1). This is the same as saying something like: "do not pay attention to him who deludes you in leading you away from the gospel of Christ, viz. from the gospel I proclaimed to you."

Since the only possible answer to the questions in 3:2-5 is one in the affirmative, they are equal to statements. As such they launch the new argument: the gift of the Spirit depends on listening to the gospel in faith, not on works of the law.[14] The introduction, "this one thing I want to know from you," functions as a meta-propositional base and can be re-written as: "this is a thing we agree on, and I want you to take it seriously".

The argumentative topic thus indicated has three components. Paul must deal with each of them and relate them to each other. The first one, the Spirit, is no problem but the circumstances of its giving — on which the parties agree — can shed light on the other two, viz. the importance of faith and the role of the law.

When is this complex argument brought to an end? The Spirit does not play any salient role in the discussion: it appears as belonging to the concept of the promise in 3:14: "in order that we should receive (the gift contained in) the promise of the Spirit". Thus it is probably also hidden behind the treatment of the promise in 3:15-22, as well as behind 3:29, "heirs according to the promise (viz. of the Spirit you have received)".[15] But no doubt the argument from the gift of the Spirit reaches its conclusion in 4:6f. "because you are sons, God sent the Spirit of his Son into our hearts, crying, Abba, Father. Thus you are no longer a slave but a son; and if you are a son, then you are also an heir, through God."[16]

---

[14] Cf. Lategan 1989, 173f.

[15] When Paul explicitly says in 3:14b that the promise concerned the Spirit, he does so as if the interpretation was self-evident. Either this actually is self-evident to Paul and to his addressees, or it is another example of Paul's attempts to persuade his audience through an exegetical *coup*. The coherence of the chapter becomes greater if we take "promise" as meaning every time "promise of the Spirit" as in 3:14; thus Williams 1988. The idea is attractive and is supported by my way of analysing 3:1-4:11, but should not be applied exclusively: in 3:15-29 the concept may well stand for the promise of the Spirit, but, in addition, is also open to other implications.

[16] 4:6f. is also the ending of the arguments on sonship in contrast to slavery, and on being an heir.

The Spirit-argument is, however, one in support of the re-stated, practical, main theme, indicated in 3:1. Gal 4:8-11 contains reproaches and indirect admonitions to remain with (or: return to) Paul's gospel, and this obtains the result that these verses round off the unit 3:1-4:11, by returning to the main, practical theme. The upshot is a ring-composition.[17]

Thus, in 3:6f. the argument begins concerning the faith principle, the validity of which is indicated by the gift of the Spirit. Whereas the Spirit argument in 3:2-5 was presented in an address in second person plural, the argument itself is held in third person. Paul also shifts his style into an argumentative one. This makes it proceed at a certain distance from the audience.[18]

The argument begins with a sub-thesis (3:6f.), based on an analogy from Scripture and is introduced by a meta-propositional clause: "just as (καθώς) Abraham believed God and it was reckoned to him for righteousness, so you should know (ἄρα γινώσκετε) that those of faith are the sons of Abraham." Although the linguistic borderline between verses 5 and 6 is very thin,[19] the meta-propositional base of v. 7a ("you should know") intimates that the following sentence (in 7b) is the theme do be dealt with in support of the argument put forward in 3:2-5.[20] The argument for this sub-thesis on the son-ship goes on through 3:29, where we encounter the conclusion: "if you belong to Christ, then (ἄρα) you are the seed (σπέρμα) of Abraham, heirs according to the promise."

On his way to this conclusion Paul also airs other themes which are adduced to clarify the complex cluster of elements in 3:2-5. The argument structure is a bit complicated, but if we analyse its beginning in 3:6-9 the links of the chain seem to be the following ones:[21]

(1a) Abraham believed [< Gen 15:6; *3:6*]
(1b) So Abraham was justified [< Gen 15:6; *3:6*]
(2) "In" Abraham all Gentiles were to be blessed [< Gen 12:3; *3:8*]
(3) Gentiles believe [< Paul's mission]

---

[17] Cf. Johanson 1987, chapter 5.

[18] Lategan, *ibid.*

[19] Rohde 1989, 135: the connection through καθώς is "nur lose".

[20] The ἄρα indicates that the thesis can be implied from the analogy. I have indicated the relationship between the two by "just as – so". — Of course, one could interpunctuate 3:5-6 differently: "the bestower of the Spirit ... (did he bestow it) because of works of the law or because of listening in faith, as Abraham believed God? Accordingly, you (must) realize that those of faith are Abraham's sons?" This interpunctuation is chosen by, i.a., NEB and by Bruce 1982. The same reading as the one I have preferred is found in JerB, NRSV, and the *Einheitsübersetzung*. However one reads these verses, their function in the argument seems to be the same.

[21] For the logical structure cf. also Hübner 1984, 17.

(4) The believing Gentiles are "in" Abraham [< 1a, 2 and 3; *3:8*]
(5) God justifies the Gentiles by faith [< 1b, 2 and 4; *3:8*]
(6) Those of faith are blessed with the believing Abraham [< 1a, 2, 3, 4; *3:9*]

It may be noted that the thesis of v. 7 does not form a link in this chain, and we have seen that it takes 3:8-29 to argue it. But item 6 (3:9) above is, on the one hand, the conclusion (ὥστε) of 3:6-9. On the other, in bringing in the concept of blessing, it introduces a sub-sub-theme, viz. that believers/Gentiles receive Abraham's *blessing*. The treatment of this sub-sub-theme becomes the first step of the argument for the sub-theme of 3:7, "those of faith are Abraham's sons".

3:10-14 present themselves as an argument (γάρ) why Abraham's blessing belongs to those of faith. V. 14 sums up the argument from 3:8 and on: "in order that (ἵνα) Abraham's blessing would come to the Gentiles through (in) Christ Jesus, so that (ἵνα) through faith we would receive (the fulfilment of) the promise of the Spirit".

Leaving aside for the moment the latter of the two ἵνα-clauses, we may analyse the web of statements contained in these verses:

(1) Those of the works of the law are under a curse [< Deut 27:26; *3:10*]
(2) The just shall live of faith [< Hab 2:4; *3:11b*]
(3) The one who does the commandments shall live in them [< Lev 18:5; *3:12*]
(4) The law is not of faith [< 3; *3:12*]
(5) No one is just through the law [< 2, 3, 4; *3:11a*]
(6) Christ became a curse [< Deut 21:23; *3:13c*]
(7) "We" were under curse (really or potentially) [< 1]
(8) Christ died "for us" [< tradition; *3:13b*]
(9) Christ liberated "us" from the curse [< 6, 7, 8; *3:13a*]
(10) Those of faith (including the Gentiles) will be blessed with the believing Abraham [< 3:8-9 = items 4–6 of the preceding table]
(11) Through Christ Abraham's blessing comes to the Gentiles [< 8, 9, 10; *3:14*]

A basic new feature in this sequence is the introduction of the Christ-event and its relevance to the Gentile believers who are blessed with Abraham. The impact of this element is increased through its being presented in terms of "we" and "us" in vv. 13f.

3:10-14a has argued the claim raised by the Genesis quotation in 3:8, understood by Paul (in 3:9) as supporting a conclusion that those of faith will be blessed with the believing Abraham. Through and in Christ this blessing was to be (ἵνα!) available to the Gentiles (14a). V. 14b, however, adds a goal or a consequence (ἵνα again) of this blessing and of Christ's taking away the curse of the law (13), namely, that "we", i.e., Paul, other Jewish Christians, and the Gentile Christians, were to receive the (fulfilment of the) promise of the Spirit through faith. Apparently Paul

assumes that the blessing of the Gentiles is contained in God's promise.[22]

Regarded in its context, 3:14b also means introducing the next step of
the argument for the sub-thesis that believers are Abraham's sons (and
heirs). As a matter of fact, it presents another sub-sub-theme, viz. that the
promise (of the Spirit) is available *through faith*. In other words, the faith/
Spirit combination in 3:2-5 is combined with the promise to Abraham
and his seed.

Regarded in this way, the context which precedes Gal 3:15-4:11 represents the first steps of an argumentation in which the caesura after 3:14 is
only a minor one.

3. The Argument Structure of 3:15-4:11[23]

3.1. Gal 3:15-29

A PRELIMINARY SURVEY

We noticed that the last ἵνα-clause of 3:14 actually introduced the next
step of the argument, viz. that the *promise* (of the Spirit given to Abraham
and to his seed) is valid for *those of faith*.

One may ask when this argument concerning the promise is finished.
The concept is first introduced in 3:14b and last appears in 3:29. On the
other hand, there is no direct discussion of it after 3:22. But from 3:2-5
and on the goal of the main argument is not only to prove why the Spirit
was given because of faith, but also that it was not by doing the law. So,
when Paul introduces the topic of the promise in 3:14b, he does so, it
appears, in order to prove that the promise (of the Spirit!)[24] is older than
the law and cannot be surpassed by it. Thus, the promise cannot be thoroughly dealt with without finding a place and function for the law. This
is done from 3:19.

If, then, the priority of the promise over against the law is treated as a
sub-sub-theme from 3:(14b)15 and on, the topic of the law becomes a
sub-sub-sub-theme, introduced in 3:19. First, Paul deals with it on a principal level through 3:22; thereafter, in 3:23-24, he returns to speaking in
the first person as in the formulation of the thesis in 14b. He states the
role of the law in "our" past, ending up with a conclusion "thus (ὥστε)
the law was our custodian until Christ ...".

---

[22] Betz 1979, 152f.; Bruce 1982, 168.

[23] Barrett 1985, ch. 3 contains an insightful discussion of the passage, from which I have
learnt a good deal.

[24] See note 15.

But the argument on the promise to Abraham — and to his seed = Christ — in 3:15-18 has not yet reached all the way to what Paul claimed in 3:14 b, viz. that "we" were to receive the Spirit through faith. Nor has that happened in 3:19-22, although in 22b the concept of the promise reappears. The missing link between the realization of the claim in 14b and the element concerning the promise/will to be received by the seed = Christ is provided in 3:25-29: faith goes together with baptism "into" Christ, the seed. So, in 3:29, Paul can arrive almost triumphantly at the concluding application to his addressees: "because you are Christ's, you are the seed of Abraham, heirs according to the promise"! Thus, the argument introduced by 3:14b and begun in 3:15 reaches its goal in 3:29.

THE ARGUMENT LINKAGE

Thus, in 3:15 the argument begins for the sub-sub-theme that the promise is for those of faith. The new phase of the argument is signalled by the newly introduced concept ("promise," 3:14b), and also by a couple of other demarcating features, viz. by a renewed address (ἀδελφοί) and a shift from the concluding "we"-style of 3:13-14 to third person. Furthermore a meta-clause presents the type of argument to be used: "I speak in human terms" (15a).

Apparently Paul here identifies promise and will. We have also noted that Paul seems to assume that the blessing to the Gentiles was included in the promise (3:14), and we remember that his aim is to prove why the Gentiles through faith can receive the (fulfilment of the) promise of the Spirit. In other words, he now has to demonstrate that the believing Gentiles could belong to the heirs envisaged in this promise/will. In the Bible the inheritance which was contained in the promise/will, was the land (Gen 12:7; 17:7f.). But its contents had since long been spiritualised and understood as standing for (eschatological) salvation and the like.[25] Thus Paul must show that the believing Gentiles are sons (3:7), or can be reckoned among Abraham's seed.

By 3:15-18 a first step is taken towards a proof. Paul submits two presuppositions: (a) a human analogy of the validity of a ratified will,[26] and, (b) as an intermediate phase on his way towards his goal he infers that the promise "also" concerned the "seed" (3:15-16; καὶ τῷ σπέρματι αὐτοῦ, referring to Gen 13:15; 17:8). The human analogy (15a) is described on a meta-level: κατὰ ἄνθρωπον λέγω. But ὅμως ἀνθρώπου already indicates the

---

[25] This did not, however, exclude a literal understanding. See, e.g., Foerster 1938, esp. 779ff.

[26] There are some problems in terms of the detailed legal background to this analogy; see Betz 1979, 155f. Cosgrove 1988, suggests, with good reasons, that these problems demonstrate that Paul consciously argues *ad hominem*, and therefore also can allow himself to be inexact.

coming of *a minore* conclusion.[27] To the second presupposition Paul adds an interpretation: "the seed is Christ", obviously assuming that his addressees will accept his manner of dealing with Scripture, although one may feel that it is rather an instance of exegetical wizardry. With v. 17 Paul applies his analogy. A meta-propositional base introduces the appli- cation — and the theme now argued: "this is what I mean: much less than a human testament can God's promise be invalidated by anything," viz. the law, which, according to Exod 12:40 (LXX) was given 430 years later. As a matter of fact Paul's statements fly in the face of any decent Judaism of those days,[28] and should be shocking also to the opponents. But by isolating the Abraham covenant from the others, Paul succeeds in driving a wedge between law and promise.[29]

Then, in verse 18 Paul gives the wedge an additional blow. When the verse is presented as an explanation (γάρ), not all commentators regard it as a real explanation.[30] The sentence *can*, however, be regarded as a real explanation if one sees a point in the fact that the inheritance is now mentioned for the first time: "the law ... does not invalidate the promise, for when it comes to the inheritance, if this were given because of the law, then it were not because of the promise." Then also that which fol- lows does not sound like a meaningless repetition: "but (as a matter of fact) to Abraham God is proven gracious by promise" (18a).

As we have noted, the contrast between faith and law is inherent in the theme indicated in 14b-15. Thus in 3:19 we encounter the question, "what, then, is the law?". We found, above, that it becomes a theme-set- ting question, and that in relation to the sub-sub-theme on the promise (as contrasted with the law!) it becomes a sub-sub-sub-theme. This rela- tionship can be illustrated by taking the definite article (and the οὖν) seri- ously and translating "why, then, this law?". The theme so raised is dealt with through 3:24 with an application to "us" in 23-24.[31] There the end-

---

[27] Mußner 1974, 240, rightly sees the contrast between ἀνθρώπου in v. 15 and ὑπὸ θεοῦ in v. 17. He also labels it a *a minore ad maius*-conclusion.

[28] Betz 1979, 159. In Judaism promise and law belonged together and the covenant between God and Israel was regarded as an expression of God's grace over against his peo- ple and included, actually as a token of grace, that the commandments should be respected (Sanders 1977, 84-125, 364-74, 419ff.). In addition, although Scripture knew about several covenant-makings, be it with Noah, Abraham, on Sinai or in Moab, they were all regarded as representations of the one covenant with its mutual promises and obligations (Sanders 1977, e.g., 97f., 367, 370f.).

[29] He also disregards the Jewish tradition that Abraham actually followed the law; see, e.g., the material in [Strack-]Billerbeck III 1926, 204ff.

[30] Betz 1979, 159 rather understands the verse as a summary. Similarly Lührmann 1978, 62.; Mußner 1974, 242 labels it "explikativ" rather than "begründend".

[31] The delimitation at v. 24 is a bit unclear, as v. 25 seems to function as a transition.

ing of the elaboration is marked by a conclusion, "thus (ὥστε), the law was our custodian until Christ (came)".

In 19b-20, Paul gives a condensed, fundamental answer to the theme-setting question: the law was added by angels, handed over by a mediator, for the sake of transgressions, until the coming of the seed. The "adding" of the law echoes the preceding analogy of adding and not-adding to a ratified will (3:15-17). The time limit of its sway becomes, according to 3:16, the appearing of Christ. These references to the preceding 3:15-18 mark the position of this subsection within 3:15-24.

The appearing of angels and Moses' role as a mediator both belong to Jewish tradition. In v. 20 Paul adds that the mediator (Moses) serves more than one, which is put into contrast with God's being one. The logic of ὁ δὲ μεσίτης ἑνὸς οὐκ ἔστιν, ὁ δὲ θεὸς εἷς ἐστιν may not be too lucid, but anyway Paul makes use of these traditions for the part of his own interpretation in which he denigrates the law by attributing only an indirectly divine origin to it. The element that its function was to define sins as transgressions, or, maybe, even to provoke sins,[32] must have seemed hard to accept for Paul's opponents, and the claim that it was to function only a limited time must have appeared horrendous to them.[33]

3:21 engages the addressees in a dubious conclusion (οὖν): "is, then, the law against God's promises?". Again, the deliberations on the law are subordinated to 15-18 and ranged within the whole of 15-24. Paul has certainly argued for a split between law and promise, but nevertheless he is not willing to accept such a conclusion and rejects it off-hand: μὴ γένοιτο. The explanation (γάρ), in 3:21c-22, of this rejection begins with what Paul deems an unreal condition: "if a law had been given that was able to make alive, then righteousness would indeed come from law". The presuppositions behind this are: righteousness does *not* come from law (that has been "proven" above in 3:11) and, furthermore, being justified and having life are the same thing. Then the conclusion is this: although not life-giving and not justifying, the law had a function, compatible with the promises (since it is not against them!). Repeating in pictorial language what he said in the basic definition of 19a, Paul presents this function in the positive part of the answer which begins in v. 22. It stands in a certain contrast (ἀλλά) to the unreal condition assumed in v.

---

[32] In this respect Hübner 1984 is of the same opinion as most of his colleagues, but not when he differentiates between the law as intended by its (hostile) angelic givers, and the law as willed by God (26-30). At any rate the receivers of Paul's letter hardly were able to learn such a distinction from the text. Cf. Sanders 1983, 67f.

[33] One might, for example, compare Paul's attitude with a statement like the one in Bar 4:1, which by no means stands isolated: "This is the book of the commandments of God, the law that stands for ever; those who keep her live, those who desert her die." See further Davies 1952.

21c: Scripture locked everything up under sin. This is where the question of v. 19 receives its topical answer. It is notable that now Paul says "Scripture". There may be a point in not equalling this concept with the law.[34] It is rather to be taken as a wider concept, although including the law.

The following ἵνα-clause (v. 22b) is similar to the one of 14b, i.e., it gives a certain interpretation of what has been said on the locking up — it had a purpose; but it also returns to the main line of the argument: that which was promised (3:14-18) was to be given out of faith in Jesus Christ to those who believe (3:6-14).[35] Thus, in v. 22 Paul has gathered some of the threads from 3:6-14 (faith, Christ) and 3:14-18 (promise). But the result is not yet applied to "us", and much less to "you". The first of these steps is taken in 23-24.

In the same way as in 3:13f. (Christ redeemed us),[36] Paul passes in 3:23 from third person singular to first person plural. Also here the effect is that the contents come closer to the people involved in the communication and that a certain concluding effect is achieved.

Thus, as I see it, 3:23-24 belongs to the explanation begun in 3:21b.[37] With a slightly changed imagery the verses repeat what was said about law's task in 19a and 22a, but applying it to "our" past — as contrasted to the present situation, which was mentioned as a goal in v. 22b: ἵνα ... δοθῇ τοῖς πιστεύουσιν. In the past, "we" were imprisoned (23) and to "us" the law was a custodian (παιδαγωγός).[38] So 23-24 is the concluding part of 19-24 with an explicit conclusion in 24 (ὥστε). In this verse the following items from the preceding 19-22 are gathered: law, custodian, "until", Christ, faith, justification; this adds to the conclusive character of the verse.

---

[34] This is done by Barrett 1985, 34. Otherwise Betz 1979, 175; Bruce 1982, 136.

[35] Somebody would maybe argue that this way of reading v. 22, is contradicted by v. 24: "law is become (γέγονεν — I prefer this reading to the ἐγένετο) our custodian, in order that we might be justified by faith". Law did not intend "our" justification! But I suggest that "is become" is so passive in its contents, that the agent behind both "is become" and "might be justified" is God.

[36] And in 4:3-5: we were slaves; we might receive adoption as sons.

[37] Betz 1979, 175. Others (as, e.g., Bruce 1982, Lührmann 1978), as also the edition of Nestle-Aland, begin a new paragraph with 3:23. That the verses continue the preceding explanation is indicated by the δέ, which is fitted into this sequence: ἀλλὰ συνέκλεισεν ... ἵνα ἡ ἐπαγγελία ἐκ πίστεως ... δοθῇ ... πρὸ τοῦ δὲ ἐλθεῖν .... Thus the πρὸ ... δέ links up with the preceding ἵνα-clause: the latter directs the attention to the future, the πρὸ δέ returns to the past.

[38] Gordon 1989 argues that the law — παιδαγωγός — had, above all, a protective task until the people of God came to age. I tend to read the term in the more negative light of 4:1-3.

This is not the place to discuss the salvation-historical periodization behind Paul's argument. What matters in the communication of Galatians is that Paul has argued that the age of the fulfilment of the promise to the seed (3:16, 19) has dawned because Christ has come. This implies that the custody-function of the law has come to an end as far as "we" are concerned. Does this mean that to Paul's mind also the Christians from the Gentiles were once locked up under custody?[39] Demanding an answer to such a question probably means trying to press something out of the text that it can hardly produce, given its rhetorical situation and practical aim. The shift to "we" language has the rhetorical effect of engaging the listeners, and of bringing speaker and hearer on the same footing. From the point of view of the actual past, only Paul and the Jewish Christians among the Galatians could look back to a time with the *halakhoth*; but that which is at stake now is that the age of liberty has dawned so that believers who take on the yoke of the law would adopt a form of life which is not only outdated but also against God's will, now and as far as they are concerned. Thus, I suggest that there is much less theology than rhetorics behind the "we" of v. 23.

In the concluding verse 24, the abstract "(period of) faith" is replaced by "Christ": his coming fulfilled the divine plan as to how "we" would be "justified". The effect of the return of this term[40] is, I believe, rather one in terms of rhetoric than of contents, in that the upshot is a ring composition.[41] As far as the contents go, we have seen how Paul in this chapter tends to use justification, blessing, contents of the promise, and life-giving rather indiscriminately. He can do so, because the overarching argument of the chapter has more weight than the usage of the individual terms.

The borderline in 3:25-26 is not very sharp. There is a change from the look into the past to the new situation, marked by the connectors δέ– οὐκέτι; furthermore, there is a transition from 1st person plural to second person plural, i.e., the argument gets closer to the addressees. As 3:29 sets a period (ἄρα) to a couple of other themes, which we have already observed, so it also marks the end of this unit. This effect is strengthened by the fact that 4:1 signals a new partial text through, i.a., the meta-propositional clause "I mean" (λέγω δέ).

---

[39] Betz 1979, 176 suggests caution. Bruce 1982, 167 answers in the affirmative in dealing with the problem in his comments on 3:13. He reads the passage in the light of Rom 2:14f., which may raise questions of methodology. But at least if one asks for what probable effect Galatians had with its Galatian readers/listeners, the validity of such a reference is far from granted. Beker 1980, 49 assumes that Paul's unclear position is due to his fierce anti-Jewish argument.

[40] It has been used earlier in 3:6, 11, and 21.

[41] See Johanson 1987, chap. 5 (where more literature is also cited).

V. 25 is a transition. On the one hand, it joins the ἵνα-clause of v. 24: the foreseen has now come true — note the present tense; on the other hand, the result thereof, viz. that "we" are no longer "under the παιδα-γωγός", actually remains to be applied in a binding manner to the addressees who have been the target of the argument since they were last directly addressed in the introductory theme-setting reproaches of 3:1-5.

In a somewhat surprising manner Paul introduces a new motif when beginning to speak directly to and about the Galatians: "you are God's sons" (3:26). This is adduced as a reason why (γάρ) "we are no longer under any custodian". In a way the sonship seems to be relatively unimportant to the chain of arguments Paul is just about to complete. It is not totally unrelated to it, however. For "it is Christ as the 'Son of God' who makes adoption as 'sons' available" and in 4:4-6 the gift of the Spirit is the gift of the Spirit of the Son.[42] On the other hand, when arriving in 4:1-7 the reader/listener realizes that the theme dealt with there was anticipated in 3:26. Here, in 3:26-29, being "in Christ" is the crucial point for the applications.

The weight of the argument is on faith and on "in Christ".[43] Paul takes the Galatian Christians back to the time of their conversion, when they listened to the gospel and believed. This coming to faith also meant entering into the life-giving community with Christ.[44] In v. 27 Paul explains (γάρ) how that can be by referring to another fact from the Galatians' initiation, viz. baptism.[45] Faith and baptism are closely related: we might express it as baptism being the visible aspect and faith the invisible aspect of the one entry into the Christ community. Baptism, the sacrament of faith, meant getting "into Christ".[46] The meaning of this is then described with the picture of putting on Christ, i.e., he and his work have become the basic life conditions of the addressees.[47] To be baptized "into Christ" led to being "in Christ", and to this fact Paul refers in 28c; it is the basis not only for Christians being united with Christ, but also for their being one among themselves. So 28a is a solemn, rhythmically con-

---

[42] Betz 1979, 186; similarly, Bruce 1982, 183; Lührmann 1978, 65; Mußner 1974, 261.

[43] ἐν Χριστῷ Ἰησοῦ is hardly to be taken as an attribute of πίστις. Elsewhere in Galatians this relationship is expressed with a genitive (2:16 [bis], 20; 3:22) and, on the other hand, the ἐν Χριστῷ formula is encountered in 1:22; 2:4, 17; 3:14, 28.

[44] "Community of Christ" or "Christ community" also has a church dimension, which, however, is not salient here.

[45] In Hartman 1992, 55-59 I have dealt with these verses as dealing with baptism.

[46] In Hartman 1992 I have discussed the background of this expression in an old baptism formula, "into the name of ...". As a phrase it became capable of several meanings, a circumstance which Paul makes use of here.

[47] Thus, e.g., Mußner 1974, 263; Betz 1979, 187ff.

strued statement.[48] What matters in it in this context — revolutionary as it is — is the element which mentions Jews and Greeks, and possibly also the one concerning male and female (only males were circumcised!). The rhetorical finesse adds to the weight of the sentence.

The protasis in 3:29 sums up 3:26-28:[49] "if you are Christ's" is apparently more or less the same as "if you are in Christ". The apodosis in 29b draws the conclusion (ἄρα): "then you are Abraham's seed, heirs according to the promise". This picks up the thesis of 3:6 (Abraham's sons) and suggests that it is now proven. Then the consequence is drawn that the Galatians belong to the ones to whom the promise is applicable: accordingly they are also heirs, i.e. the inheritance in its transferred meaning of salvation, etc., is also theirs.

3.2. Gal 4:1-7

A PRELIMINARY SURVEY

We found that 3:29 concluded the discussion that started in 3:6. Although this conclusion certainly applies the preceding argument to the Galatians, we have not yet arrived at a follow-up on the opening and theme-setting questions concerning faith and Spirit. Also, although the παιδαγωγός imagery only indirectly concerned the Gentile Christians — they should not let themselves be brought under such a one or be locked up — , the conclusions of 3:6-29 need to be brought into still closer relationship to the Galatians and their situation.

In 4:1 Paul suspends the second person plural address and returns for a moment to the argumentative third person. The meta-propositional clause of 4:1, "I mean" refers to the human analogy of the young heir in 4:1-2, and picks up the imagery of 3:29. The "thus also we" (οὕτως καὶ ἡμεῖς) in the beginning of 4:3 actually functions as a new meta-propositional expression; through the καί it takes up the thread from 4:1. It is equal to "the following is an application to us of my analogy". There is no explicit thematic marker, but the meta-propositional expressions call the reader's/listener's attention to the analogy and its application, including the contrast past – present. In 4:3-5 Paul makes precisely this application. Just as in 3:23-25 and 3:26-29, the "we"-passage is followed by one in second person plural, which applies the argument to the addressees (4:6-7). In verse 7, a conclusion is drawn: "thus (ὥστε), you (sing.!) are no longer a slave but a son ...". Thus, we have come to an end of the discussion of the true inheritance from Abraham, including the

---

[48] It may, or may not, have been recognized by the Galatians. Cf. Betz 1979, 189-200; Bruce 1982, 187ff.

[49] Thus Betz 1979, 201. Similarly Mußner 1974, 266.

gift of the Spirit, which was the point of departure in 3:2-5. We can say that 4:1-7 sets a period to the argument started in 3:2.

THE ARGUMENT LINKAGE

The analogy in 4:1-2 has a temporal contrast as its focal point, viz. the one between the child and the heir-come-of-age. So in the application, "our" former slavery is contrasted with the present "fulfilment of time" (v. 4), when Christ "redeemed those under the law" (4:5). "We" were once slaves, viz. under "the elements of the world" (τὰ στοιχεῖα τοῦ κόσμου). This is not simply another way of speaking of the law, but the "we" and the immediate context make it clear that somehow the law is included in the term, in that it contrasts this past slavery with the new situation. In 4:8 these στοιχεῖα are, however, also equated with "gods who are not by nature gods". The expression thus refers to the past of both Paul and of his addressees, i.e., to both Jewish and Gentile Christians. The law of the Jews and the divine authorities to whom the former Gentiles had turned their backs were brought together into one category.

Since this seeming equating of law and pagan deities has been the point of departure of much theologizing,[50] it is imperative that regardless of the problem of what one may or may not do with a text, we listen carefully to what Paul is doing to his addressees with his text.

One elementary thing is clear: once more the solidarity between Paul (and other Jewish Christians) and the Gentile Christians is expressed: there is no principal difference between them. Furthermore, we shall keep in mind that the aim of the argument is to convince the Galatians to live up to their being adult heirs and not to give in to the propagators of the law. Thus Paul is forced to put Jewish Christians and Gentile Christian heirs on the same footing: both have a past of bondage.[51] But in the argument the detailed character of this past bondage — including the philosophical assessment of how to relate the law to gods who really are no gods — is only of secondary importance. It is but a detail which fits into an argument that says: you come from slavery, as I do as a Jew; if you take up what I have left (cf. 2:18), you deny that you are free heirs.

One should also take into account that στοιχεῖα is a term the meaning of which is very uncertain.[52] If one, e.g., assumes a meaning "mundane fundamentals" this need not be offensive to a Jew as referring to the law. But, also, to several Gentiles the same term might tell something of the

---

[50] See Sanders 1983, 68ff. (with referenses).

[51] Sanders even states; "The common denominator is bondage and the equation of law and *stoicheia* is material" (1983, 69). Rohde 1989, 169, suggests that the combination of the two services is made on the basis of the fact that both Gentiles and Jews had to observe the celebration of certain feasts. In his discussion of 4:9, Rohde comes rather close to Sanders' point of view: turning to the law meant turning to a slavery like the Gentile one (180f.).

divine powers holding sway over the world. Considerations like these suggest to me that one should beware of using this detail as an important stone in a reconstruction of Paul's theology.

After the first (negative) part of the analogy has thus been applied, the application of the second part is introduced as a contrast (ὅτε ... ὅτε δέ). The time when the young heir has come of age is the one when the fullness of time has come (v. 4a) and God has sent His Son.[53] That the Son was put "under the law" (4c) is important in the flow of the argument and reminds of 3:13 (Christ becoming a curse to redeem [ἐξηγόρασεν — cf. ἵνα ἐξαγοράσῃ v. 5a] those under the law). That the two passages do not totally cover each other[54] is apparently not allowed to disturb the argument; in the rhetorical situation the latter actually functions as a reference to the former, adapting it to the present phase of the argument regarding those who were once serving masters of different kinds.

With v. 5 the purposes of the fundamental action of God at the appointed time are spelled out with reference to "us". But as the text goes, the details of the line of thought are not totally harmonized: *we* (you and me/we Jewish Christians) were enslaved, but ... God sent his Son in order that he might redeem *those under the law*, in order that "*we* might receive status as sons*". Nonetheless, Paul obviously does not regard Christ's redemption of those under the law (= Jews) as being of no effect to the others. The explanation is, I suggest, that Paul to such a large extent concentrates on his practical purpose that he can leave aside the specification of the dark past of both Jewish and Gentile Christians. What matters is that, being in Christ, or being Christ's (3:26-29), they need not yield to the law-propagators.

At any rate, "our" sonship appears as the ultimate purpose of God's sending (5c). Thus Paul picks up the result of faith and baptism he men-

---

[52] Among the more recent contributions is Schweizer 1988, 455-468. After a review of the textual material, Schweizer finds the expression to refer to man's being enslaved "in the ceaseless rotation of the four elements". Rusam 1992 has had access to more material and votes for a similar understanding: "the elements of the world" refers to the four (five) elements. But his example from Sextus Empiricus (*Pyrr. Hyp.* 3,152) indicates to my mind the possibility of a meaning like the one in my text above (the numbers, οἱ ἀριθμοί, are the cosmic fundamentals).

[53] The language of sending is traditional (also in pagan religions — Betz 1979, 206) and should be recognized by the addressees. Here it adds to the weight of the ἵνα-clauses in v. 5: God's sending intended redemption and "our" sonship.

The detail that the sending meant or implied that the Son was born from a woman does not seem to play any significant role in the argument. Maybe it belongs to traditional language (cf. Rom 1:3). In its cultural context the expression distinguishes this sending from how other divine messengers were pictured, like Hermes or the chtonian Hecate.

[54] Cf. Betz 1979, 207.

tioned in 3:26, now however, also loaded with the implication that the son is an heir (4:1ff.).

In 4:6-7 next application to the addressees comes up, marked by the direct address in second person plural. The Galatians' participation in "our" sonship is taken for granted ("as you are sons") and is the reason why they have received the Son's Spirit. Thus the text again takes up the fact brought to the fore in 3:2-5: the Galatians received the Spirit when they accepted Paul's gospel, believed and were baptized, and this without doing the law.[55] The attempts of theologians to decide on the relationship between sonship and gift of the Spirit[56] are certainly worthy of respect: which one is the presupposition of the other? But, again I would maintain that the text as it stands[57] is part of a discussion and asserts a specific understanding of the fact that all agree on, the gift of the Spirit.[58] How it functions as an element of this discussion is, I believe, best seen in a paraphrase like this one: you got the Spirit — as you know — in your capacity as sons — as you also know; what this sonship implies, I have just demonstrated: you became God's sons through God's Son, the seed, who redeemed "us" from the curse of the law; furthermore, it has been made clear that this gift is in accordance with the promise given to Abraham and his "seed" as a token of the blessing which, through Abraham, out of faith, should be bestowed on all Gentiles.

V. 7 brings the argument to a conclusion, signalled by ὥστε. It stresses some aspects which are of importance to the practical issue, with which Paul is dealing. The phrase "you are no longer slaves" (v. 7a) rubs in that the past is past, as maintained from 3:23 and onwards as well as in the analogy in 4:1-2 (ἐφ᾽ ὅσον ... ἄχρι); instead (ἀλλά) you are a son, as demonstrated in 3:26-28, and as restated in 4:5f. Verse 7b, finally, drives the argument home: as son "you are a heir", i.e., the gifts of the Spirit, connected as they are with your sonship, tell you that you belong to the

---

[55] The somewhat strange to-and-fro movement is notable: "because *you* are sons, God sent his Son's Spirit in *our* hearts, crying, Abba ...". Again I would suggest that the rhetorical aims can be adduced as an explanation — or, if we regard it from the receivers' end, the rhetorical effect. The "we" is inclusive, the "you" prodding.

[56] See Betz 1979, 209, and Bruce 1982, 198.

[57] Betz 1979, 210, suggests that it may reflect traditional usage.

[58] One may wonder which is the point of the notice that the Spirit cries, "Abba, Father" (6c). Paul presupposes that the Galatians are acquainted with the Aramaic term, and the suggestion may very well be correct that we already encounter with St. Augustine (*PL* 35, 2126f.; Betz 1979, 211), viz. that the Aramaic and the Greek addresses to God stand for the two-fold nature of the Church, consisting of Jews and Gentiles. I.e., it is an expression of the same basic fact as the one described in the sentence of 3:28, "not Jew nor Greek". That the Spirit shouts or cries (κράζων) from the heart of the believer, *may* refer to enthusiastic phenomena and some sort of spiritual rage, also hinted at in 3:1-5 (the Galatians have experienced so much from the Spirit, mighty works included).

divine race, for which the promised heritage is meant, the salvation "from the present evil age" (1:4) and this without doing the law.[59]

3.3. Gal 4:8-11

A PRELIMINARY SURVEY

The conclusion in v. 7 of the argument concerning the faith as the cause of the gift of the Spirit contained a "no longer", which put the contents of the conclusion into a contrast with a situation of past slavery (4:1). 4:8 takes up the same contrast between past and present. But the contrast is also qualified: the slavery "at that time" (τότε μέν) meant not to know God, the present, however (νῦν δέ, v. 9), to know him. If Paul had expressed himself symmetrically, the contrast between the situations would have looked like this: "(you [second pers. sing.] are a son and heir) but at that time, not knowing God you (second pers. plur.) were slaves; now, however, knowing God ... you are free." However, Paul does not explicitly mention the present liberty, but instead combines the new situation of God-knowledge with a reproaching question: "how can you return to the weak and poor *stoicheia* ...?" 4:8-9a form the background of this reproach. So the question becomes the theme of the unit.[60] Of course the question is but another way of saying: "do not return". Thus, 4:8-11 returns to the main topic of the letter, last touched upon in 3:1-5, especially in 3:1. It is done on the basis of the concluding results of 4:1-7.

THE ARGUMENT LINKAGE

The characterization of past and present in 4:8-9a would certainly be acceptable to the Galatians,[61] both to the adherents of the other gospel and to others; they are traditional Jewish ways of describing paganism and Jewish religion. Thus, the negative background is, "formerly, when you did not know God,[62] you were enslaved to the gods who by nature are no gods".[63] To this negative part of the background, in its turn, the positive one is contrasted: "now, when you have come to know God, or, rather, to be known by God" (τότε μέν ... μὴ εἰδότες ... νῦν δὲ ... γνόντες ...); in other words, now, after they have accepted Paul's gospel, they have entered the favoured group of people who can boast of being

---

[59] I.e., Paul is here of the same opinion as in 2 Cor 1:22; 5:5: the Spirit is the guarantee of the eschatological life.

[60] If one is looking for a meta-propositional expression, this may be said to be inherent in the question-form, equalling "I ask you". See Johanson 1987, 30.

[61] Betz 1979, 213, 216.

[62] See, e.g., Jer 10:25; Ps 79:6; Wis 13:1.

[63] Cf., e.g., Deut 32:21; Wis 13:2f.

enlightened. From the point of view of his communication with the Galatians Paul seems to advance a bit further than the spokesmen of the other gospel might be prepared to follow him; for of the Gentile Christians he uses the language of God-knowledge, which actually had its established usage in contexts dealing with people who were enlightened through God's law and living according to it,[64] i.e., precisely what Paul so eagerly was attempting to prevent.

After "you have come to know God" Paul inserts a "correction", "rather to be known by God".[65] I suggest that the turn of phrase represents a subtle innuendo: according to the Bible (Ps 1:6; 37:18, etc.) God "knows" the just, his people, etc. The moment at which (aorist aspect) the Galatians became known by God was when they came to know him, viz. when they received Paul's gospel in faith. Then they entered this community of the just, etc.

In this context of subtle inducing, Paul takes a few additional steps down the same road. The first one represents a persuasive trick: "how can you return again to the weak and poor elements whom you want to serve again?". We found that the question is a way of formulating the theme of the passage. On the basis of the preceding identification of slavery (etc.) under the law (3:22-25) with one under the *stoicheia* (4:3), Paul pretends that that argument has been accepted. For this is the presupposition behind his calling it a falling back when former idolaters tend to turn to law-observance![66]

By rubbing in the ("practical"!) message of the theme, Paul describes what the addressees are tending to do:[67] "you observe days and months and seasons and years" (v. 10). The line is best understood as irony. Both pagan religion, astrology included, and Judaism observed certain calendar rules. But to focus on them in this way is, as far as the Torah goes, a misrepresentation. Actually Paul ridicules the adherents to "another gospel" as being silly, scrupulous people, victims of superstition, *deisidaimonia*.[68]

A last ironic, or bitter, remark concludes this passage, in which Paul has worked more with insinuations and irony than with intellectual

---

[64] See, e.g., Isa 1:3; Jer 31:34; Hos 8:2.

[65] Several authors assume that behind the theme are Pauline reservations over against gnostic tendencies (Bultmann 1933, 709; see also Betz 1979, 215f.; Bruce 1982, 202).

[66] Also in this case I tend to assume that Paul is more engaged in persuasion than in analytic theology.

[67] I follow Betz (1979, 217) who maintains that the sentence does not describe something that is a reality — yet. Cf. Bruce 1982, 205. Of course P[45] has a reading which gives an easier text: the participle παρατηροῦντες instead of the affirmative; but this smoothness is of course the reason which speaks against it.

[68] Bultmann 1910, 103; Betz 1979, 217f.

arguments and logic: "I am afraid for you, lest I might have laboured over you in vain" (4:11). Once more the addressees are reminded of the time when they received the gospel from Paul in faith. Did they enter the people to be saved, only now to fall back? Thus Paul finishes this part of his argument by intimating that he sees an extreme danger lurking behind the demands of the spokesmen of the other gospel.[69]

Thus, 4:8-11 returns to the practical argumentation of the letter, delivering another attempt to reinforce the request of 1:6ff. It is worthy of notice that to support it Paul does not adduce any more theoretical arguments, although he stands on the basis of 3:2-4:7.

With 4:12-20 Paul adds still other arguments in favour of his demand that the Galatians keep to his gospel, the only one. Now, however, he does so by turning to sentimental reasons — Schlier speaks of "an argument of the heart", and Betz has pointed to conventions of arguing from friendship.[70]

So, what has come out of this analysis of the argument and its line of thought? The myopic observation of details on the textual surface has been the main instrument in an attempt to find a structural whole in Gal 3:1-4:11, and partly, also in Gal 1-2. This kind of centering the interest on the text has, however, been connected to a conviction that this is also an important way (among others) to study the way the author handles his addressees for his purposes, using mainly theoretical arguments for a practical argumentation.

4. A Few Reflections of an Interpreter

The text which I have dealt with can raise several questions which might be aired at an encounter of a group of exegetes from different Christian communities.[71] I will now briefly deal with a couple of these.

I have intimated that "theologians" may deal a bit frivolously with the historical meaning of NT texts. I have also argued that in Galatians Paul is primarily pursuing a polemic concerning a matter of behaviour rather than writing a treatise in theology. Nevertheless, I am of the opin-

---

[69] We can also note a compositional finesse: not only does 4:8-11 return to the style of the introductory 3:1-5, and lead the thoughts of the addressees to the same initial phase of their Christian existence, but also it reinforces the effect of the ring composition through a word repetition, viz. of the adverb "in vain" (εἰκῇ), which appears in 4:11 and twice in 3:4.

[70] Schlier 1971, 208; Betz 1979, 221.

[71] Issues which have been topical in the confrontation between Churches and for which passages from Gal 3-4 have been adduced are, e.g., baptism as related to faith (3:26-27), the role of "external" rites (4:1), the problem of who interprets Scripture (the magisterium or ...? — cf. Paul's somewhat daring exegesis), criteria of Christian unity and intercommunion (3:26-28), the Spirit as personal experience and as the soul of the Church, can a Jewish Jew be saved?, anthropology: how pessimistic is Paul after all?

ion that Paul produced his letters to be more than occasional writings; after the critical situation for which they were written they were to be read by (and to) new audiences in new situations — and so they were.[72]

Then a question of principle transpires: if already Paul intended that his letters were capable of a more generalized meaning, what role can (could) or should the historical meaning of the text and of its elements play?[73] One simple example is the term "law". In the Galatian situation it refers to Torah. But in much Christian usage it has come to mean "God's moral demands".[74]

Another example is the interpretation of Gal 3:24 which appears in Lutheran tradition from Confessio Augustana and onwards: God's commandments, including the ones given by Jesus, shall press man to despair about his own capacity and so make him flee to redemption (*sola fide*) in Christ. Indeed, generally, it is held as characteristic of the divine commandments that man cannot fulfil them. This interpretation of Gal 3:24 is wrong, historically seen. But should a Church care? An answer to the question should be given only after much deliberation, but all in all, I would say yes, it should care, simply because the Church is rooted in history. Therefore she should not base important positions on interpretations which sound exegesis has demonstrated to be incorrect as far as the historical meaning of the text is concerned.[75]

There are other ways of generalizing Paul's argument against his Galatian opponents. Is the fundamental reason, already with Paul, why righteousness from law and righteousness by faith exclude each other (Gal 3:11-13) that "man's desire to win salvation by doing the law, already is *the* sin"?[76] And is the function of the law that "seine (i.e.,

---

[72] Hartman 1986 [No. 9 in this volume]. In other words, it was not so that, a generation or so after Paul's death, one or two devoted disciples came upon the idea to collect his letters and have them spread and used in the Churches.

[73] Already when the Pauline disciple behind the Pastorals interpreted Paul, he reinterpreted Paul's position so that, instead, he spoke of "works of the law" (i.e. such demanded by the Torah) as signifying "works of righteousness that we do" (Tit 3:5).

[74] In that sense the term was used, when Roman Catholics and Lutherans, in the 16th century, began their debates concerning the role of good works (*CA Apol IV, De dilectione et impletione legis*). On the whole, those differences are now regarded as something belonging only to the past, but "law" is still used with this wider reference, e.g., in the declaration of the Second Vatican Council on Religious Freedom (*Dignitatis Humanae*), 3.

[75] Another example: let us, e.g., assume that I am right in my way of understanding that Paul's gathering the law and the idols under the same concept of *stoicheia* is to be understood as rhetorical technique rather than as a reflected statement on what the Torah really meant (and means!) to the Jews and/or to the Christians. A discussion with Jews would perhaps be easier if this is so, but to which extent are readers of later times generally obliged to respect what probably is the original meaning?

[76] Bultmann 1968, 264f.

man's) Verlorenheit und nichts anderes macht das Gesetz offenbar".[77] It would be in harmony with this way of reading Paul to bring in Gal 4:10, pretending that Paul actually means that it is an expression of man's will to feel secure and to master his existence, when he devotes himself to ritual observations, demanded by this or that religious law.[78]

Readings like these assume a specific anthropology and theology on Paul's part, which are supposed to be the source out of which arguments like the one in Galatians flow. But perhaps such theological reconstructions have a skeleton which is less Pauline than, let us say, a Lutheran reading of Heidegger? Paul is, however, made to provide the flesh — and its authority. Is such a freedom vis à vis the historical meaning permissible? If so, why? Or, if not, why?

I would think that it is good scholarship to be prepared to question both scholarly, historical results and Church interpretations, giving reasons for one's questioning. It is also good theology to do so.

5. Appendix: A Table of the Argument of Gal 3:1-4:11

The following table may give the impression that I suggest that the text is incredibly neatly organized. This is, however not my intention. Rather the table shall be regarded as a summarizing survey, which, as such, also includes certain simplifications.

1.   3:1-4:11 A third argument

   1.1.   3:1 Restatement of practical theme (ThM; renewed 2nd pers. address, shift of style; return/keep to the gospel)

   1.2.   3:2-4:7 Argument in favour of 3:1

      1.2.1.   3:2-5 Thematizing questions (ThM; Spirit given from faith, not law)

      1.2.2.   3:6-4:7 Discussion because of 3:1-5 (believers receive, as heirs, Abraham's promise of the Spirit)

         1.2.2.1.   3:6-29 Sub-theme (believers are sons of Abraham and heirs)

           1.2.2.1.1.   3:6-7 Thesis of 6-29 (MB, ThM; from 3rd to 2nd pers.; Scriptural quote; believers are Abraham's sons)

           1.2.2.1.2.   3:8-14 Arguing of sub-sub-theme (shift to 3rd pers.; δέ; believers/Gentiles receive Abraham's blessing)

              1.2.2.1.2.1.   3:8 Introductory Scriptural quote

              1.2.2.1.2.2.   3:9 Theme-setting conclusion (ThM; ὥστε)

---

[77] Bornkamm 1969, 134.

[78] Cf. Käsemann 1973, 351-55, on, i.a., Rom 14:5. See also Barclay's criticism of Koester's (1965, 309 [= 1971, 147]) interpretation of the passage (1987, 81).

1.2.2.1.2.3.   3:10-14 Argument (γάρ; through Christ blessing is given to believers)

1.2.2.1.2.3.1.   3:10-12 Argument from contrast (law brings curse, but faith brings justification)

1.2.2.1.2.3.2.   3:13-14 Christological argument (Christ's redemption mediates blessing)

1.2.2.1.2.3.2.1.   3:13 Basis (shift to 1st pers. sing.; Christ's redemption of "us")

1.2.2.1.2.3.2.2.   3:14 Consequences

1.2.2.1.2.3.2.2.1.   3:14a Consequence (ἵνα) with regard to 3:8-9 (in Christ, Abraham's blessing is given to the Gentiles)

1.2.2.1.2.3.2.2.2.   3:14b Consequence (ἵνα) and anticipation of new theme ("we" receive the fulfilment of the promise of the Spirit through faith)

1.2.2.1.3.   3:15-29 New sub-sub-theme (ThM; address; shift to 3rd pers.; promise/will concerns believers without their doing the law)

1.2.2.1.3.1.   3:15-24 Arguing of sub-sub-theme

1.2.2.1.3.1.1.   3:15-22 Principal deliberations

1.2.2.1.3.1.1.1.   3:15-18 Positive argument (promise is valid in spite of the law)

1.2.2.1.3.1.1.1.1.   3:15-16 Arguments from analogy and from Christology (promise concerns the seed)

1.2.2.1.3.1.1.1.1.1.   3:15 Human analogy (MB; on will)

1.2.2.1.3.1.1.1.1.2.   3:16a Statement on range of coming application (Abraham *and* seed)

1.2.2.1.3.1.1.1.1.3.   3:16b Christological clue (seed = Christ)

1.2.2.1.3.1.1.1.2.   3:17-18 Application (ThM, MB; law cannot interfere)

1.2.2.1.3.1.1.2.   3:19-22 Sub-sub-sub-theme (the role of the law)

1.2.2.1.3.1.1.2.1.   3:19-20 Basic statements

1.2.2.1.3.1.1.2.1.1.   3:19a Theme-setting question (ThM; what is ...?)

1.2.2.1.3.1.1.2.1.2.   3:19b-20 Basic answer to 19a (for the sake of transgression, etc.)

1.2.2.1.3.2.2.2.2.3.2.   3:28b Reason for 28a (γάρ; one in Christ)

1.2.2.1.3.2.3.   3:29 Conclusion (ἄρα)

1.2.2.1.3.2.3.1.   3:29a Protasis, summing up 26-28

1.2.2.1.3.2.3.2.   3:29b Apodosis, applying results of 6-28 (Abraham's seed, heirs according to promise)

1.2.2.2.   4:1-7 Application to addressees' situation (ThM [?]; heirs, gift of the Spirit)

1.2.2.2.1.   4:1-2 Analogy (MB, shift of person to 3rd person; heir's situation)

1.2.2.2.2.   4:3-5 Application of analogy to "us" (shift of person to 1st pers. plur.)

1.2.2.2.2.1.   4:3a Application formula (MB)

1.2.2.2.2.2.   4:3b First part of analogy applied (ὅτε; past in slavery)

1.2.2.2.2.3.   4:4-5 Second part of analogy applied (ὅτε δέ; new situation, redemption)

1.2.2.2.2.3.1.   4:4 Basic event (God sent His Son)

1.2.2.2.2.3.2.   4:5 Purpose of 4:4

1.2.2.2.2.3.2.1.   4:5a Vague purpose (ἵνα; redemption)

1.2.2.2.2.3.2.2.   4:5b Specific purpose (ἵνα; "our" sonship)

1.2.2.2.3.   4:6-7 Application to "you" (δέ; shift to 2nd pers.)

1.2.2.2.3.1.   4:6 Consequence of 4:3-5

1.2.2.2.3.1.1.   4:6a Basis (ὅτι; being sons = 4:5b)

1.2.2.2.3.1.2.   4:6b Consequences (Son's Spirit)

1.2.2.2.3.2.   4:7 Conclusion (ὥστε; no slave, heir)

1.3.   4:8-11 Final reproaches and innuendos (contrasted to 3:6-4:7: ἀλλά; ThM; how can you return to slavery?)

1.3.1.   4:8-9 Setting the theme

1.3.1.1.   4:8-9a Background

1.3.1.1.1.   4:8 First part, pejorative (τότε μέν; slavery under στοιχεῖα)

1.3.1.1.2.   4:9a Second part, positive (νῦν δέ; knowledge of God)

1.3.1.2.   4:9b Theme (ThM; how can you turn back?)

1.3.2.   4:10 (Ironic) description of consequences (scrupulosity)

1.3.3.   4:11 (Ironic) despair over addressees (in vain?)

Bibliography

Barclay, J. M. G. 1987: "Mirror-Reading a Polemical Letter: Galatians as a Test Case", in: *JSNT* 31 (1987) 73-93.

Barrett, C. K. 1985: *Freedom and Obligation. A Study of the Epistle to the Galatians,* Philadelphia, PA: Westminster/London: SPCK 1985.

Beker, J. C. 1980: *Paul the Apostle. The Triumph of God in Life and Thought.* Philadelphia, PA: Fortress/Edinburgh: T. & T. Clark 1980.

Betz, H. D. 1979: *Galatians* (Hermeneia), Philadelphia, PA: Fortress 1979.

Billerbeck, P. [-Strack, H. L.] 1926: *Kommentar zum Neuen Testament aus Talmud und Midrasch, Dritter Band: Die Briefe des Neuen Testaments und die Offenbarung Johannis,* München: Beck 1926.

Bornkamm, G. 1969: Paulus (UB 119), Stuttgart: Kohlhammer 1969.

Bruce, F. F. 1982: *The Epistle to the Galatians* (NIGTC) , Grand Rapids, MI: Eerdmans/Exeter: Paternoster 1982.

Bultmann, R. 1910: *Der Stil der paulinischen Predigt und die kynisch-stoische Diatribe* (FRLANT 13), Göttingen: Vandenhoeck & Ruprecht 1910.

— 1933: "γιγνώσκειν", in: *ThWNT* 1 (Stuttgart: Kohlhammer 1933), 688-719.

— 1968: *Theologie des Neuen Testaments,* 6th ed., Tübingen: Mohr (Siebeck) 1968.

Cosgrove, C. H. 1988: "Arguing like a Mere Human Being: Galatians 3.15-18 in Rhetorical Perspective", in: *NTS* 34 (1988) 536-49.

Davies, W. D. 1952: *Torah in the Messianic Age and/or the Age to Come* (SBL.MS 7), Philadelphia, PA: SBL 1952.

Foerster, W. 1938: "κληρονόμος C–E", in: *ThWNT* 3 (Stuttgart: Kohlhammer 1938), 776-85.

Gordon, T. D. 1989: "A Note on ΠΑΙΔΑΓΩΓΟΣ in Galatians 3.24-25", in: *NTS* 35 (1989) 150-54.

Große, E. U. 1976: *Text und Kommunikation. Eine lingvistische Einführung in die Funktionen der Texte,* Stuttgart etc.: Kohlhammer 1976.

Gülich, E./Raible, W. 1977: "Überlegungen zu einer makrostrukturellen Textanalyse: J. Thurber, The Lover and His Lass", in: T. van Dijk /J. S. Petöfi (eds.), *Grammars and Descriptions. Studies in Text Theory and Text Analysis* (Research in Texttheory 1), Berlin – New York: de Gruyter 1977, 132-75.

Hartman, L. 1986: "On Reading Others' Letters", in: G. W. E. Nickelsburg/G. W. MacRae, SJ (eds.), *Christians Among Jews and Gentiles. Essays in Honor of Krister Stendahl,* Philadelphia, PA: Fortress 1986 [= *HThR* 79 (1986)], 137-46 [No. 9 in this volume].

— 1992: "*Auf den Namen des Herrn Jesus*". *Die Taufe in den neutestamentlichen Schriften* (SBS 148), Stuttgart: Katholisches Bibelwerk 1992 [Engl. edition forthcoming 1997: Edinburgh: T. & T. Clark].

Hellholm, D. 1980: *Das Visionenbuch des Hermas als Apokalypse. Formgeschichtliche und texttheoretische Studien zu einer literarischen Gattung* (CB.NT 13:1), Lund: Gleerup 1980.

Hübner, H. 1984: *Law in Paul's Thought*, Edinburgh: T. & T. Clark 1984.

Johanson, B. C. 1987: *To All the Brethren. A Textlinguistic and Rhetorical Approach to I Thessalonians* (CB.NT 16] , Stockholm: Almqvist & Wiksell 1987.

Käsemann, E. 1973: *An die Römer* (HNT 8), Tübingen: Mohr (Siebeck) 1973.

Kieffer, R. 1982: *Foi et justification à Antioche* (LeDiv 111), Paris 1982.

Koester, H. 1965: "ΓΝΩΜΑΙ ΔΙΑΦΟΡΟΙ. The Origin and Nature of Diversification in the History of Early Christianity", in: *HThR* 58 (1965) 279-318 [reprint in: J. M. Robinson/H. Koester, *Trajectories through Early Christianity*, Philadelphia, PA: Fortress 1971, 114-57].

Kopperschmidt, J. 1985: "An Analysis of Argumentation", in: T. A. van Dijk (ed.), *Handbook of Discourse Analysis, Vol. 2: Dimensions of Discourse,* London etc.: Academic Press 1985, 159-68.

Kraftchick, S. J. 1990: "Why Do the Rhetoricians Rage?", in: R. W. Jennings, Jr. (ed.), *Text and Logos. The Humanistic Interpretation of the New Testament. FS H. W. Boers* (Scholars Press Homage Series), Atlanta, GA: Scholars Press 1990, 55-79.

Lategan, B. 1989: "Levels of Reader Instructions in the Text of Galatians," in: *Semeia* 48 (1989) 171-84.

Lührmann, D. 1978: *Der Brief an die Galater* (ZBK.NT 7), Zürich: Theologischer Verlag 1978.

Mußner, F. 1974: *Der Galaterbrief* (HThK 9), Freiburg–Basel–Wien: Herder 1974.

Plett, H. F. 1979: *Textwissenschaft und Textanalyse* (UTB 328), 2nd ed., Heidelberg: Quelle & Meyer 1979.

Rohde, J. 1989: *Der Brief des Paulus an die Galater* (ThHK 9), Berlin: Evangelische Verlagsanstalt 1989.

Rusam, D. 1992: "Neue Belege zu den στοιχεῖα τοῦ κόσμου (Gal 4,3. 9; Kol 2,8. 20)", in: *ZNW* 83 (1992) 119-25.

Sanders, E. P. 1977: *Paul and Palestinian Judaism*, London: SCM/Philadelphia, PA: Fortress 1977.

— 1983: *Paul, the Law, and the Jewish People*, Philadelphia, PA: Fortress Press 1983.

Schlier, H. 1971: *Der Brief an die Galater* (KEK 7), 14th ed., Göttingen: Vandenhoeck & Ruprecht 1971.

Schweizer, E. 1988: "Slaves of the Elements and Worshipers of Angels: Gal 4:3, 9 and Col 2:8, 18, 20", in: *JBL* 107 (1988) 455-68.

Williams, S. K. 1988: "*Promise* in Galatians: a Reading of Paul's Reading of Scripture", in: *JBL* 107 (1988) 709-20.

Supplement

Longenecker, R. N.: *Galatians* (WBC 41), Dallas, TX: Word 1990.

Vos, J. S.: "Die hermeneutische Antinomie bei Paulus (Galater 3.11-12; Römer 10.5-10)", in: *NTS* 38 (1992) 254-70.

Boyarin, D.: "Was Paul an 'Antisemite'? A Reading of Galatians 3 - 4", in: *USQR* 47 (1993) 47-80.

Dunn, J. D. G.: *The Epistle to the Galatians* (BNTC), London: Black 1993.

Fairweather, J.: "The Epistle to the Galatians and Classical Rhetoric: Parts 1&2", in: *TynB* 45 (1994) 1-38.

— : "The Epistle to the Galatians and Classical Rhetoric: Part 3", in: *TynB* 45 (1994) 213-43.

Geonget, B.: "Galates III", in: *SémBib* 76 (1994) 49-59.

Hong, I.-G.: "Does Paul Misrepresent the Jewish Law? Law and Covenant in Gal. 3:1-14", in: *NT* 36 (1994) 164-82.

Boers, H. W.: "A Context for Interpreting Paul", in: T. Fornberg/D. Hellholm (eds.), *Texts and Contexts. Biblical Texts in Their Textual and Situational Contexts. FS L. Hartman,* Oslo – Copenhagen – Stockholm – Boston: Scandinavian University Press 1995, 429-53.

Dunn, J. D. G.: "Was Paul Against the Law? The Law in Galatians and Romans: A Test-Case of Text in Context", in: T. Fornberg/D. Hellholm (eds.), *Texts and Contexts. Biblical Texts in Their Textual and Situational Contexts. FS L. Hartman,* Oslo – Copenhagen – Stockholm – Boston: Scandinavian University Press 1995, 455-75.

15. The Eschatology of 2 Thessalonians
as Included in a Communication

There are several ways in which one can deal with the topic of the eschatology of 2 Thessalonians. For example, one can relate it to Pauline theology and ask theological questions.[1] Or one can concentrate on historical problems, either by investigating the origin and prehistory of motifs and constellations of motifs and traditions[2] or by asking for a place in Early Christianity in which to locate this eschatology.[3] I do not deny the legitimacy of such work. In fact, I will pose similar questions in a couple of instances in this paper. However, I will try above all to regard the eschatology of 2 Thessalonians as a message included in the communication which is constituted by the letter.

In principle such an approach means that we take the text as something by which someone, using specific linguistic means, says something to someone else in a certain situation in order to achieve a goal. I use such terms, because as theologians we sometimes focus our interest on details of the contents to such an extent that we neglect not only the linguistic organization, but in particular the situation and the practical purpose of the text with regard to its receivers.

My concern can also be expressed in text-linguistic terms: I suggest that we do not concentrate on the semantic aspect[4] of the text to such an extent that we forget about its syntactic and, in particular, its pragmatic aspects. It is, moreover, to be expected that the contents of the text are structured by those organising features that pertain to its syntactic aspect. Markers such as meta-expressions, adverbs, and conjunctions determine the text's semantic dimensions.[5] And references to or echoes

---

[1] E.g., Beker 1980, 160-62; Lindemann 1977; Bailey 1978/79.

[2] E.g., Aus 1976; idem 1977. Aus' Yale dissertation from 1971 was not available to me. Bailey 1978-79, 144-45; Gundry 1987. According to *Dissertation Abstracts* 37 (1976) no 1/287C Stephens 1976, deals with the topic.

[3] Koester 1982, 242-46. Quite different (i.e., assuming a Pauline authorship of 2 Thess) is Mearns 1980/81. Such problems are also dealt with in Littleton, Jr. 1973.

[4] Morris1938/53; Plett 1979, 52.

[5] Gülich/Raible 1977.

from the social context, in which the communication is intended to work, must be allowed to qualify how it is to be understood.

It is only fair that at this point I should begin by declaring my position in terms of authorship and other introductory matters. I accept the arguments of those scholars who think that 2 Thessalonians was not written or dictated by Paul.[6] Instead, the letter was produced within the Pauline school[7] as a complement to the Pauline letters,[8] which at the time of 2 Thessalonians were on their way to becoming a letter-collection. This collection, however, was not yet fixed as to its extent. In Christian communities of Pauline tradition they were read and re-read,[9] so that they now were related to different situations and different readers from the first ones. 2 Thessalonians is a complement insofar as it takes up an issue which has not really been dealt with in the Pauline letters to which the readers had access. Formally the author directs it to the Thessalonian church but I think it is written for a wider group of Pauline churches.[10] The Thessalonian address is explained by the fact that 1 Thessalonians deals with problems which remind of those treated in 2 Thessalonians. In fact, the author has borrowed quite a lot from 1 Thessalonians.[11] However, although I take this sort of position in terms of authorship and addressees, I nonetheless believe that the letter gives evidence of being written for rather specific circumstances, which troubled the addressees, namely persecutions and sufferings inflicted by an unbelieving majority.[12]

I will argue that in a situation of this kind the author is less a theologian who tries to come to grips with a theological problem, that is, the delay of the *parousia*, than he is a pastor who wants to strengthen the faithful in their afflictions. In doing so, he assesses their situation by putting it into an eschatological framework and corrects one suggested eschatological interpretation of it, one which says that the Day of the Lord is at hand.[13]

Let me begin by going through the text and asking what the author is doing *versus* his addressees. In the reported thanksgiving (1:3ff.) he makes the addressees favourably disposed[14] by praising them for their virtues, not least for their steadfastness (ὑπομονή) and faithfulness (πί-

---

[6] Especially Trilling 1972, and Bailey 1978/79. See also Collins 1988, 209-26.

[7] Schenke/Fischer 1978, 243-44.

[8] Trilling 1980, 25.

[9] Cf. Schenke/Fischer 1978, 192; Hartman 1986 [In this volume no. 9].

[10] Schenke/Fischer 1978, 190. Cf. Trilling 1980, 26-27.

[11] Wrede 1908, 9-10; Trilling 1972, 95, 156-57.

[12] See also Schenke/Fischer 1978, 190.

[13] Trilling 1980, 25, believes 2 Thess was "eine als notwendig empfundene *weiterführende Unterweisung*", although he plays down the importance of the persecutions (p. 26).

στις) in all the afflictions they endure. Thus their problematic situation is drawn into the text already in its first sentence after the epistolary address. The continuation indicates, however, that the praise for steadfastness in 1:3ff. is actually a gentle admonition.

1:5-10 sheds eschatological light on the afflictions of the audience: they are suffering for the sake of the Kingdom, of which God will find them worthy at the parousia of Christ. On the other hand, God will inflict vengeance on their persecutors, the unbelievers.[15] All this, of course, strengthens the self-esteem of the community. With regard to this perspective (εἰς ὅ; 1:11) the author ends the introductory part by binding the addressees by subtle means to the duty he is laying before them: he reports praying for them that God may make them worthy of his call, so that Christ may be glorified and they be glorified in him, namely at the parousia (v. 11; cf. v. 10).

At the beginning of chapter 2 the author turns directly to his audience with a renewed address and a verb of request. The request concerns a specific issue in the situation on which the author has shed eschatological light in chapter one. They were not to be deceived into thinking that the Day was at hand.[16] The following argument for this, he says, is based on what the addressees already know, namely, that before the day the man of lawlessness must appear (2:7). In concentrating on the communication aspect of the text, we need not decide whether the author is stating the truth or not, when he says that they were told about this at Paul's visit (2:5). Because of the way it is presented here the item must have been new to the readers in any case; otherwise they would already have drawn the conclusions the author wanted them to draw. At any rate, in this way he intimates that his argument should be anchored in their own knowledge.

The appeal to their knowledge concerning "that which restrains" also invites the audience to reflect, or even suggests that they have already reflected (2:6), on the matter. The knowledge of the past calls, namely, for an inference concerning the present;[17] to paraphrase: "so you also know, as to the present,[18] what is keeping the lawless one back until his time".

---

[14] That sender and receiver will share the coming release (v. 7) also brings them closer to each other, as also does the reference to the addressees' reception of the author's testimony in v. 10.

[15] See Meeks 1983, 689.

[16] The meaning of ἐνέστηκεν is disputed; see Trilling 1972, 124-25; idem 1980, 78 (with further references); Schenke/Fischer 1978, 192; Stephenson 1968.

[17] Relatively similar is Best 1972, 290-91. Cf. Giblin 1967, 159-66.

[18] For this way of understanding the νῦν see Frame 1912, 262-63; Best 1972, 290-91; Rigaux 1956, 663-64.

After having engaged his addressees in the argument in this way, the author describes the unbelievers' apostasy, deception, and unrighteousness connected with the appearance of the lawless one (2:7-12). But he also locates something of this lawlessness in the present time of his audience: it is already at work, although secretly (2:7). Then he addresses them again: by way of contradistinction to the activity of Satan and to the activity of delusion sent by God upon the unbelievers, he must thank God for what he has done and is doing for the addressees: they are loved, called through the gospel, elected for salvation, and living in sanctification and faith (2:13-14). On every point this puts them in contrast to the wicked unbelievers. This way of describing them would strengthen their group identity, not least by reminding them again of the larger perspective of their being Christians.[19] In this way the author prepares for the conclusion of the argumentation he started at 2:3,[20] where he told them not to be shaken in mind: "Thus, brethren, stand firm and hold to the traditions which you have been taught by us, either orally or by letter" (2:14). The "stand firm" motif has been shown by Selwyn to belong to a persecution catechism.[21] Thus, in other words the author says, "continue to stand firm in your afflictions, and do not loose your mind when people say the Day is at hand; now you know what is true Pauline teaching on the matter." Finally, a wish-prayer (2:15) includes the concluding imperatives in a framework of divine caring for the addressees: "may the Lord and God our Father comfort and strengthen your hearts." This would appeal for a favourable mind to the preceding argument.

This survey of the text as directed to its addressees indicates to me that, although a matter of eschatological teaching is at stake in chapter two, the framing situation in which this communication functions is not primarily a discussion of the time of the parousia, but rather it is the strained situation of persecution in which the audience could be tempted to fall away.[22]

Our next step will be to consider more closely the argumentative structure of the two eschatological passages. I will pay attention to markers which have a structuring function, such as meta-expressions, deictic pronouns, adverbs, and so forth. I will, however, avoid using the advanced analytic terminology of text-linguistics, although such a method lies behind my remarks.

---

[19] Meeks 1983, 690.

[20] Many commentators fail to see the role of v. 15 in the total argument of chapter two; thus Best 1972, 316-17; Rigaux 1956, 686; Trilling 1980, 127. On the other hand, see von Dobschütz 1909/74, 301; Giblin 1967, 41-49, 241-49; Friedrich 1976, 269; Marshall 1983, 209.

[21] Selwyn 1955, 454-58.

[22] Cf. Rigaux 1956, 645.

1:3-12 is rather clear: the praised steadfastness and faith(fulness) in afflictions (vv. 3-4) are characterised as an "evidence of God's righteous judgement" (5a), which is then described in vv. 5b-10. This description (or possibly only the part of it which concerns the addressees) is then referred to by a pronoun and made the object of a reported prayer for the audience (εἰς ὃ καὶ προσευχόμεθα ... περὶ ὑμῶν, v. 11f.). It has a mild exhortative function.

The argumentative structure of chapter 2 is less clear. V. 1-2 define the specific problem (ὑπὲρ τῆς παρουσίας τοῦ κυρίου) as the object of a request (ἐρωτῶμεν). For this request the author then argues (ὅτι, v. 3b) in vv. 3b-12. "First" (πρῶτον) in v. 3b is related to "is at hand" (ἐνέστηκεν) in v. 2b. This prior appearance of the lawless one and the characteristics given in v. 3b and 4 are referred to by the ταῦτα of v. 5 as the object of a teaching dated to ἔτι ὢν πρὸς ὑμᾶς. From this past, remembered in the present, the author moves to the present in v. 6 (νῦν; cf. ἤδη v. 7). It is, however, not totally evident how to fit v. 6 into the argument, as the καὶ νῦν causes problems.[23] As mentioned above, the author intimates that the readers should infer a knowledge about the restrainer from the information they have previously received about the lawless one. This knowledge of the restrainer is relevant for the present (νῦν), and this, as well as the fact of the restraining, is then explained in v. 7 (γάρ): in spite of the present (ἄρτι) restraining the lawlessness is namely (γάρ) already (ἤδη) at work until "it is let out".[24] Thus, the explanation regarding the present activity of lawlessness stands, so to speak, in the middle: it relates a present lawlessness to a subsequent, worse one, and via the role of the restrainer the two expressions of lawlessness go back to one Satanic source. The τότε of the revelation (v. 8) of the lawless one relates to the preceding expressions for the time of appearance (v. 6b ἐν τῷ ἑαυτοῦ καιρῷ; v. 7b ἕως ἐκ μέσου γένηται).[25] The description of the parousia of the lawless one (vv. 8-9) shifts to deal with those who perish and are deceived, vv. 10-12. The logic of vv. 10-12 is, however, not clear. The

---

[23] It is hardly admissible to take καὶ νῦν as introducing a contrast (cf. Trilling 1980, 88: "jetzt *aber*," and Marshall 1983, 193), which would require a νῦν δέ. Furthermore, the degree of temporality in νῦν has been discussed, and, if such a sense is assumed, whether it, together with οἴδατε, is contrasted to the past time of Paul's visit (ἔτι), or, together with *katechon*, it stands over against the time of the revelation of the lawless one (ἐν τῷ ἑαυτοῦ καιρῷ), or, finally, whether it is related to ἔτι without being connected to the οἴδατε or the κατέχων. See Rigaux 1956, 663, and note 18 above.

[24] For this understanding of the Greek text, see Barnouin 1976/77.

[25] Thus the text does not represent much of an "apocalyptic time-table". Cf. Beker 1980, 161, and Koester 1982, 245. There is, by the way, much scholarly tradition on such "time-tables", which needs correction through a careful reading of the texts themselves. Cf. Hartman 1975-76 [In this volume no. 6].

parousia of the lawless one is said to take place, *inter alia*, "in every deceit of wickedness for those who perish" (τοῖς ἀπολλυμένοις). ἀνθ᾽ ὧν in v. 10b probably introduces the reason why they perish:[26] they did not accept the truth. A consecutive understanding of εἰς τό in v. 10c is also probable:[27] they will thus not be saved. The deceit in question should belong to the future. Likewise their perishing, although this would be the consequence of their life, including their non-acceptance of the gospel.[28] One should probably assume that the latter precedes the situation of 2 Thessalonians. V. 11 is worse: "therefore (διὰ τοῦτο) God sends (πέμπει) upon them a work of delusion (ἐνέργειαν πλάνης), so that (or: in order that, εἰς τό) they believe in the lie, in order that (ἵνα) all the non-believers ... may be condemned". Does διὰ τοῦτο point backwards, to their non-acceptance, or forwards, that is, to ἵνα, introducing the purpose of their condemnation? Linguistically seen, the former understanding seems preferable,[29] although the contents turn out a bit harsh. (It is normal that διὰ τοῦτο functions in this way in Pauline texts, and the author is imitating Paul's style. Above all, however, the distance to ἵνα is a little too great.) Furthermore, how is the God-sent work of delusion (ἐνέργεια πλάνης v. 11) related to the "deceit of wickedness" (ἀπάτη ἀδικίας) in v. 10? It seems a reasonable assumption that the former somehow covers the latter, and in this way it can include both past, present, and future.[30] Thus, "being deceived" as well as "unbelief" become both cause and aim, and are included in an all-embracing divine will.

As to the conclusion of the argument, we have already noted how in vv. 13-14 the addressees are contrasted with the condemned ones as being on the right side in the supra-human tension between God and the evil forces. We have also seen how v. 15 is the exhortative conclusion (ἄρα οὖν) of the argument.

These observations confirm the results of the preceding survey of how the author handles his audience. Although he certainly deals with a mysterious future, in so doing he interprets the present[31] and essential parts of the argument deal directly with the problematic situation of the present.

I have already touched upon the relationship between chapters 1 and 2. There are evident differences: the eschatology of chapter one is deter-

---

[26] E.g., Frame 1912, 270-71; Best 1972, 307.

[27] von Dobschütz 1909/74, 289; Best 1972, 308.

[28] Trilling 1980, 109.

[29] von Dobschütz 1909/74, 290; Best 1972, 308; Marshall 1983, 204; Frame 1912, 271. Trilling 1980, 112, can be interpreted as supporting the former alternative. Cf. Blass/Debrunner/Funk 1961, § 290.8.

[30] Cf. Trilling 1980, 111-12; Marshall 1983, *loc.cit.*

[31] Trilling 1980, 116.

mined by the stated problem — the accounts of the persecuted and the persecutors will be balanced to the benefit of the former. In chapter two we encounter the lawless one and the *katechon*, whose activities are to precede the balancing of accounts dealt with in chapter one. But two items appear in both chapters, namely, the Day of the Lord and the evil-doers.

That the Day of the Lord with the parousia of Christ is mentioned in both is not surprising. Yet, it may be worth noticing that the unbelievers play such prominent roles not only in chapter one, where their hostility makes it natural, but also in chapter two. As I see it, their presence in chapter two is also to be connected with the situation of the text. For in that context the ones "who did not believe in the truth but had pleasure in wickedness" (2:12) are placed on the eschatological map: they are among those who will adhere to the blasphemous and deceiving lawless one. But this activity of lawlessness is already going on secretly (2:7), that is among the unbelievers, and, with their doom in view, the delusion is already sent by God upon them (2:11-12).[32] I have already pointed to the strengthening effect these lines would have on the addressees who suffered under such pressure from the unbelievers.

It is not explicitly stated that the ones who perish according to 2:10 are the same people as the persecutors of chapter one. The two groups are, however, given the same attributes[33] except that in chapter two nothing is said about their carrying out affliction or persecution; they only "have pleasure in wickedness" (τῇ ἀδικίᾳ). It seems, nonetheless, a reasonable assumption that although the persecutors (1:4, 6) are not identified with "those who perish" (2:10), they are nevertheless included in the latter group. Such a view is supported not only by the allusions to the present deceptive activity (2:7, 11), but also by the way in which unbelievers and addressees are contrasted in both passages (1:6-12; 2:13-14).[34]

The question of the relationship between chapters 1 and 2 should also be posed as one concerning the rhetorical[35] organization of the letter. Several studies have lately shown how, for example, the so-called thanksgivings of NT letters function as rhetorical *prooimia*.[36] It seems to me that such observations are also applicable to 2 Thessalonians.[37] According to practice a *prooimion* should arouse the desired attitude in the audience, as a rule one that is favourable towards the speaker. Fur-

---

[32] Trilling 1980, 111-12.

[33] In chapter one the persecutors "do not know God" and "do not obey the gospel" (1:8); they will have to pay for their attitude with affliction (1:6) and perennial destruction (1:9) according to God's just judgement (1:5-6). In chapter two "the ones who perish" (τοῖς ἀπολλυμένοις, 2:10) have "not received the love of the truth so as to be saved" (2:10); instead. "God sends them the work of delusion so as to believe in the deception in order that they who do not believe in the truth be condemned" (2:12).

thermore, and of importance, it should indicate the subject. In this capacity it could contain blame, exhortation or appeals to the audience (Aristotle, *Rhet*. 3.14.4). It seems to me that this is precisely what happens in 2 Thessalonians. Chapter one prepares for chapter two. It introduces the general subject of the present tribulations regarded in an eschatological perspective, and it does so in a subtly admonishing manner. As such it also functions as a *philophronesis* or a *captatio benevolentiae*. After this preparation chapter two presents the specific problem[38] and an argument for its solution is given.[39] The conclusion is in 2:15: "stand firm", and the wish-prayer of 2:16-17, has the same function as a *peroratio*, a last attempt in the discussion to turn the addressees favourably to what has been argued.

This rhetorical perspective could certainly be applied in much more detail. What I have already touched upon supports the suggestions that the two chapters should be held together[40] and that the basic situation is one of afflictions and persecutions. The message is given in this situation

---

[34] Above I mentioned Selwyn's views on the "stand firm" parenesis. The author's use of 1 Thess in this context (see also Trilling 1980, 127) may also support the assumption that the situation addressed in 2 Thess was one of afflictions. In 2 Thess 2:15-17 we encounter "Thus *stand firm* (στήκετε) and hold on to the traditions ... And the Lord ... may *comfort and strengthen your hearts* (παρακαλέσαι ὑμῶν τὰς καρδίας καὶ στηρίξαι) in every good work and word". The terminology is clearly coloured by 1 Thess 3: "I sent Timothy ... to *strengthen* (στηρίξαι) and *comfort* (παρακαλέσαι) you ... in order that you be not shaken in these afflictions" (1 Thess 3:2). Timothy's report was that "you *stand firm* (στήκετε) in the Lord (v. 8). Finally, in Paul's wish-prayer in the same context: "May the Lord make you abound in love ... so that he may *establish your hearts* (στηρίξαι ὑμῶν τὰς καρδίας) unblamable...." (1 Thess 3:12-13). As in so many other instances our author twists the expressions he takes over (cf. the material in Rigaux 1956, 133-34, and in Trilling 1980, *passim*). In general, however, the expressions thus taken over from 1 Thess are used in 2 Thess with references which are relatively similar to those they have in 1 Thess. Thus, the fact that afflictions are the situation in which the addressees of 1 Thess are summoned to stand firm, etc., intimates that a similar situation is behind the echoes of the same language used in 2 Thess.

[35] "Rhetoric", "rhetorical", etc., are used with several meanings by NT scholars these days. See the useful survey by Wuellner 1987. In the following paragraphs I consider 2 Thess 1-2 from the aspect of the *dispositio* often discussed in the rhetorics of Antiquity, and of the functions of the *partes* over against the audience.

[36] Betz 1974-75, 359-62; Wuellner 1976, 335-37.

[37] According to *Dissertation Abstracts* 45 (1984/85) 3669-70 A, Hughes 1984 finds the *partes* spoken of in classical rhetoric represented in 2 Thess. Without knowing whether my hesitation applies to Dr Hughes' work, I am generally a bit skeptical towards the recent not uncommon manner of laying schemes of classical rhetoric on texts without combining the study with a careful analysis of the text's semantic and pragmatic features and aspects. One should remember the freedom of the old rhetoricians and their respect for the exigencies of the situation. See Johanson 1987, 42-43.

[38] Perhaps someone would want to compare it to a *narratio*.

[39] Applying the technical terminology, one could label it an *argumentatio*.

in order to achieve a goal (recall our initial definition of a communication!). It is therefore a reasonable assumption that the cause of the specific problem of chapter two — people thinking that the Day was at hand — was that they interpreted their sufferings as being those of the end.[41] If such an interpretation was presented as a spiritual revelation (2:2), it could also easily find support in other early Christian prophecies (cf., e.g., Matt 24/Mark 13; Rev 2:10). However, it could even possibly be squeezed out of turns of phrase in the Pauline letters, such as Gal 1:4, "he gave himself up to deliver us from the present evil age".[42]

Of course, one wishes that the author had told us explicitly that the background of chapter two is also that of persecution, and that the present persecutors of the Christians are also among the unbelievers who are to perish. Although *we* may desire such information, I submit that the addressees did not need to be reminded once more of their situation.

I now turn to the contents, and ask what is new to the addressees in 2 Thessalonians as compared to other Pauline letters they may have known.[43] The answer is easy: the motifs of apostasy,[44] the lawless one, and the *katechon*. This does not mean that we can assume that the author is not serious when, for example, in chapter one he writes about the parousia. The features of this event largely represent the picture one gets when reading Romans, First and Second Corinthians and First Thessalonians; its consequences of triumph for the afflicted are certainly of weight in the circumstances of the letter. As for the lack of any reference to resurrection this does not mean that the author was secretly against the idea. I suggest that the topic simply would not have been of any use for the purpose of the letter.

The man of lawlessness is so thoroughly described that one may doubt whether the addressees knew of him before, as the writer pretends they do. At least they hardly knew about him in the form the author presents him. The idea has of course deep mythological roots, and the inter-

---

[40] The close connection between the two chapters is also strengthened by the fact that the concluding wish-prayer 2:16-17 largely takes up the same concepts as those found in the reported prayer of 1:11-12: *pistis, klesis, doxa, agatha erga.*

[41] Thus also Schenke/Fischer 1978, 191.

[42] Schenke/Fischer 1978 refer to 1 Thess 5:1-11.

[43] I disregard Col, Eph, and the Pastorals. The overall communication perspective in which I regard 2 Thess, and which I believe is fair to history, makes me doubt the thesis of Hughes, which, according to the abstract (see above, note 37), is that 2 Thess is an argument against Col – Eph.

[44] Apostasy or lack of morality is often regarded as a sign of the end, not only in Early Jewish and Christian religion, but also in, e.g., Orphicism, Stoicism, and Nordic Religion. In the Pauline letter-collection it only appears here and in 1 Tim 4:1; 2 Tim 3:19.

Argumentative Texts

pretation of Antiochus Epiphanes in the Book of Daniel has influenced Christian conceptions of Antichrist.[45] Often a blasphemous figure of this kind is more than human. In Jewish texts Beliar may play a similar role, but there is no Jewish fixed or generally accepted expectation of such a phenomenon. In 2 Thessalonians he is human; and the combination of features in our text has no precedents.[46] In spite of what an authority like Bousset maintains,[47] the appearance of Beliar, and so forth, is only rarely connected with seducing signs and wonders, namely, in two instances in the *Sibylline Oracles* (2:165ff.; 3:63ff.). Instead, the motif of seducing signs is rooted in the idea of false prophets who so legitimate their message.[48] Deuteronomy 13, which deals with the problem, has influenced many Jewish texts of NT times which deal with apostasy, and, sometimes, with eschatological expectations.

As a matter of fact, there is one text which contains so many of the features of the appearance of the man of lawlessness that I find it plausible to assume that our author is drawing on a version of it, namely, the synoptic apocalypse.[49] In its Matthean form we read how the abomination of desolation, spoken of by Daniel, stands in the holy place (24:15), and how during this time of affliction (24:21, 29) false Christs and false prophets will appear, "working mighty signs and wonders so as to lead astray, if possible, even the elect" (24:24). Then comes: "immediately, after the tribulation of those days" the Son of Man will appear (24:29-31). It seems to me that the author of 2 Thessalonians has combined the motifs of the abomination of desolation and that of the sign-working false Christs and prophets and added other features from the Danielic texts of the evil king[50] as well as from a few other OT texts. The result is the lawless one, who is to appear "first", that is before the parousia. In Matthew the parousia comes "immediately, after the tribulation".

To the addressees the traditio-historical background was probably of minor importance. If they had any ideas similar to those of the synoptic apocalypse in this matter, the author has now reinterpreted them with Pauline authority, and his presentation of the blasphemous figure told them that the parousia was not at hand. But, on the other hand, the

---

[45] See Bousset 1895; Rigaux 1932; Lohmeyer 1950-51; Maag 1961.

[46] Trilling 1980, 87.

[47] Bousset 1895, 115ff.

[48] I have discussed the combination Antichrist – miracles in Hartman 1967.

[49] Mearns 1980-81, 153. In Hartman 1966, chapter 6, I analysed the relationship between the Synoptic Apocalypse and 2 Thess, assuming a pauline authorship of 2 Thess. Although I have changed my mind concerning the authorship of 2 Thess, the analysis still contains, I think, some relevant observations. Cf. also Gundry 1987.

[50] In Rev 13:13-14 the figure of the Second Beast is painted in Danielic colours, and is working deceiving signs.

Satanic wickedness he was going to embody, once it appeared on the stage of history,[51] was already active in their situation. Also the work of seducing was going on, namely among the unbelievers, the adversaries who were actually seduced (and at that by God!),[52] when they refused to accept the gospel. The triumph of the faithful was certain, if only they stood firm.

As to the *katechon*,[53] I do not pretend to have any new solution. But I find Professor Barnouin's analysis of the Greek[54] to the point, and thus I read "so you know, as for the present, what holds *him* (i.e., the lawless one) back...only that he who now holds *him* back *will do so* until he (i.e., the lawless one) comes forth". The *katechon* seems to be something/someone controlling history. Perhaps not God himself, but something included in his plan, or something like the Philonic Logos, who holds the reins of the chariot of the world and of history (*Fuga* 101; *Heres* 301), and in due time lets the man of lawlessness enter the arena.

In terms of communication the *katechon*, as we noted above, is something the author says the readers know about or could infer from earlier knowledge. We can have our doubts. In any case the introduction of the *katechon* does not simply delay the final crisis. The concept also goes together with the identification of the present evil as being of the same sort as that still withheld. The present tribulations of the addressees are not the end, but nonetheless, they are eschatological. Thus the author calms down an expectation and keeps it alive at the same time.[55] (In this connection we may remember that both the author and the addressees are assumed to take part in the triumph at Christ's *parousia*; 1:7; 2:1.)

A few words on how God is presented in 2 Thessalonians 1-2. Throughout he is a God on the side of the addressees: he has called them through the Pauline gospel (2:14), which meant an election[56] to be saved, that is, in the salvation at the eschaton (2:13). All this means that he loves

---

[51] He is thus not appearing from a hidden preexistence (I admit, though, that the word is imprecise!); thus Rigaux 1956, 666. The expression means that persons and phenomena are "revealed" when they appear in history according to God's plan, whether they are "preexistent" or not. It is used of the Son of Man (*1 Enoch* 52:9; 62:7; 69:29), of the Messiah (*4 Ezra* 7:28; 12:32; *2 Apoc. Bar.* 29:3; 39:7), of the Behemoth (*2 Apoc. Bar.* 29:4), of the hostile nations (*2 Apoc. Bar.* 70:7), of the great joy in the new age (*2 Apoc. Bar.* 73:1), etc. See Hartman 1966, 37.

[52] This present-time aspect is rightly stressed by Trilling 1980, 111-12.

[53] The discussion has seen many suggestions. See the surveys in Best 1972, 295-301; Trilling 1980, 89-102; and, of course, the deliberations in Giblin 1967, 167-242.

[54] Barnouin 1976-77.

[55] Cf. Trilling 1980, 116-17.

[56] I prefer reading ἀπαρχήν in 2:13, not ἀπ᾽ ἀρχῆς. Cf. Rigaux 1956, 682; Best 1972, 312-13; Trilling 1980, 120-21.

the addressees (2:13, 16) and has given them a hope of taking part in his kingdom (1:5; 2:16).

The other side of God's engagement in the faithful is his attitude to the adversaries. His righteous judgment will repay them with affliction and eternal destruction (1:5-7, 9; 2:12), a thought otherwise not well represented in Paul, nonetheless a biblical idea.[57] The unbelievers have refused to accept the truth (2:10), and therein lies a Satanic deception once to be revealed (2:9-10). But, in addition, their unbelief is also embraced in God's work; he sends the activity of delusion upon people in order that they be condemned (2:11-12). (In this very context it may also be of some interest to note that in Deuteronomium 13 [the chapter on false prophets working signs] such deceptive things are ascribed to God: "The Lord your God is testing you..." [Deut 13:3].) The upshot is a view of God as one who is so much on the side of the addressees that we come close to the idea of a God who causes absolutely everything — election, deception, unbelief and condemnation. At the same time the author nevertheless ascribes an activity and a responsibility to humans: they have believed (1:10) or not believed (2:12), and they are urged to stand firm (2:15).

We may have some difficulties with a theo-logy of this sort,[58] but, again, I think it is fair to the author that we consider the context. What the writer says about God is meant to comfort afflicted people, whose expectation of an imminent release he puts to shame. Consequently, everything, even the deception, is placed in the hands of the Almighty. We may not think very highly of such a comfort,[59] but, at any rate, neither the theo-logy nor the comfort are foreign to biblical thought (which does not necessarily mean that all of it should be regarded as good Christian theology).[60]

Before summarizing my discussion of the eschatology of Second Thessalonians as related to the audience, I will briefly return to the question of the texts and traditions used by the author. To begin with, I think there are reasons to believe that Christians of different traditions learned from each other. In any case, this appears to be so at the time of Second Thessalonians (say in the late 70's).[61] I have already mentioned that the synoptic apocalypse seems to represent a close parallel to 2 Thessalonians 2. There, the abomination, standing in the holy place,[62] and the

---

[57] Cf. Rom 1:18ff.; 2:6ff.; 12:19; 13:4f.; Phil 1:28. See Schenke/Fischer 1978, 195; Friedrich 1976, 255; Braun 1952-53/1967.

[58] Cf., e.g., Trilling 1980, 112-13.

[59] Cf. Trilling 1980, 67.

[60] A more complete discussion of the view of God of 2 Thess would require an examination also of the christology. The author goes, e.g., considerably farther than Paul in deifying Christ; see, e.g., Trilling 1972, 128-32; idem 1980, 64-65; Friedrich 1976, 255.

fatal deception of false Christs and prophets precede the parousia. There are more links: the ἐπισυναγωγή of 2:1 is a *hapax* of the NT, and the picture does not appear elsewhere in Paul. Thus, the author knows of other eschatological imageries than those represented in Paul, and, since he does not work out any details, he seems to presuppose that the addressees do the same. Of course the picture has OT roots,[63] but when it is coupled with the technical term "parousia", it is natural to take into account that in the synoptic apocalypse the parousia[64] (the word is explicitly used in Matt 24:3) means that the angels will "gather" (ἐπισυνάξουσιν) the elect[65] to the Son of Man.

Furthermore, in 2 Thess 2:2 the addressees are requested not to be alarmed (μηδὲ θροεῖσθαι) by people who thought that the Day was at hand: "let no one lead you astray" 2:3: (μή τις ὑμᾶς πλανήσῃ). Compare Matt 24:4ff. "take heed, let no one lead you astray (μή τις ὑμᾶς πλανήσῃ), for many will come in my name saying 'I am the Christ' and they will lead many astray. And you will hear of wars and rumours of wars. See that you are not alarmed (μὴ θροεῖσθε)". The references of the similar clauses concerning not going astray are compatible,[66] but the two θροεῖσθαι refer to different rumours, one of wars, the other of the presence of the Day.[67] But this way of using words and phrases from other texts, and of twisting their references a bit, is something which we encounter over and over again in this author's use of the Pauline epistles, not least First Thessalonians.[68] Accordingly, it is not astonishing to find him doing the same thing in relation to a version of the synoptic apocalypse.

---

[61] Trilling 1981, 154 wants to distance the epistle even more from Paul (also in 1980, 28: from 80 and on into the 2nd century). Hengel 1984, 29, on the other hand, dates it to a time before 70, because of 2:4. Trilling's late dating seems less plausible to me considering the fact that the epistle apparently has belonged to the Pauline collection very early. As to 2:4, I take it as so traditional, and thus pictorial, that the fate of the Jerusalem temple did not form any obstacle for its use here.

[62] Dan 9:27, LXX and Theod., reads ἐπὶ τὸ ἱερὸν βδέλυγμα τῶν ἐρημώσεων.

[63] See the material in Hartman 1966, 156-58.

[64] Trilling 1980, 74 admits "apokalyptische Einfärbung ... von Mk 13:27/Mt 24:31."

[65] In Mark the Son of Man will send his angels and gather (sing.).

[66] Best 1972, 280, is open to their belonging "to the apocalyptic tradition." Cf. Koester 1982, 245; Marshall 1983, 189.

[67] von Dobschütz 1909/74, 265 (an echo of a Jesus-saying). Cf. Best 1972, 275; Marshall 1983, 186.

[68] Some examples: 1 Thess 1:6-8 – 2 Thess 1:5 (cf. 2 Cor 7:4, 14; 9:23); 1 Thess 2:12 – 2 Thess 1:11; 1 Thess 4:7-8 – 2 Thess 2:13-14; 1 Thess 5:25 – 2 Thess 3:1; 1 Thess 5:23-24 – 2 Thess 3:3; 1 Thess 4:9-10 – 2 Thess 3:4; 1 Thess 1:6; 2:1,9 – 2 Thess 3:7-8; 1 Thess 4:11 – 2 Thess 3:10-12; 1 Thess 5:14 – 2 Thess 3:14-15. See further the material in Rigaux 1956, 133-34.

Thus I find reasons for assuming that our author has known and used a version of the synoptic apocalypse[69] when assessing the eschatological interpretation of the situation of the addressees. That he also makes use of the OT[70] and of Pauline epistles, especially of First Thessalonians, is a trivial complement to this short discussion of the sources behind our text.

Thus, in this paper I have argued that if we listen carefully to what the author of 2 Thessalonians is saying, his eschatological passages appear to be determined by a situation, that is, persecution of the communities addressed. I suggest that our usual reading of them as mainly represent- ing an effort to calm down an outburst of enthusiastic eschatological expectation (*Naherwartung*) should be modified. The basic situation in which the author takes up the question of the parousia is one in which Christian minorities have been harassed by their neighbours. The pur- pose of his writing is only partly to add a couple of eschatological ideas to the ones they already have. This is only one means among others to achieve his main purpose, namely to encourage steadfastness.[71]

Afflictions of such a kind were nothing new in Pauline churches. First Thessalonians is a witness to that (2:14; 3:3-4). But it seems that during the time, say, between Nero and Domitian, local harassment was a com- mon experience in several Christian churches. The Gospel of Mark reflects this (4:17; 10:30), as do Matthew (10:17-19), Acts (14:22),[72] First Peter (4:12-19), and Hebrews (10:32-39). In some of these texts the adver- sities are interpreted in an eschatological key (e.g., Matt 24:9; 1 Pet 4:13). The same thing occurred, I believe, in some communities of Pauline tra- dition, and so our author felt that an authoritative word from Paul was needed. He used existing eschatological ideas, possibly partly known by the addressees, and interpreted them to correct the misunderstanding *and* to shed another eschatological light on their situation. First Thessalo- nians, known by him and by his addressees, formed a suitable basis, when he, not without talent, put Paul's mask on and set out to frustrate some of his addressees, and above all to strengthen them all for contin- ued struggle and continued hope.

---

[69] Cf. Hartman 1966, 195-205 and see also Orchard 1938; Rigaux 1956, 95-105; Pesch 1968, 120, 214; Wenham 1984, 176-79.

[70] Rigaux 1956, 94-95; Aus 1976.

[71] It has commonly been assumed that the admonition not to live "unorderly" (ἀτάκτως, 3:6-15) but to "work quietly and to earn their own living", is directed against apocalyptic *Schwärmgeister* who have abandoned work in view of the approaching end (Rigaux 1956, 519-21; Best 1972, 176-78, 334-35; Friedrich 1976, 272-75). But if I have assessed the situation of the letter correctly, this is an overinterpretation. See also Russell 1988; Trilling 1980, 150-52. Cf. Marshall 1983,218-19.

[72] See also Conzelmann 1971, 110: persecution in Acts reflects the times of the book.

Bibliography

Aus, R. D. 1971: *Comfort in Judgement. The Use of the Day of the Lord and Theophany Traditions in Second Thessalonians 1*, Diss. Yale 1971.

— 1976: "The Relevance of Isaiah 66,7 to Revelation 12 and 2 Thessalonians 1", in: *ZNW* 67 (1976) 252-68.

— 1977: "God's Plan and God's Power: Isaiah 66 and the Restraining Factor of 2 Thess 2:6-7", in: *JBL* 96 (1977) 537-53.

Bailey, J. A. 1978-79: "Who Wrote II Thessalonians?", in: *NTS* 25 (1978-79) 131-45.

Barnouin, M. 1976-77: "Les problèmes de traduction concernant II Thess. II.6-7", in: *NTS* 23 (1976-77) 482-98.

Beker, J. C. 1980: *Paul the Apostle. The Triumph of God in Life and Thought*, Edinburgh: T. & T. Clark 1980.

Best, E. 1972: *A Commentary on the First and Second Epistles to the Thessalonians* (BNTC), London: Black 1972.

Betz, H. D. 1974-75: "The Literary Composition and Function of Paul's Letter to the Galatians", in: *NTS* 21 (1974-75) 353-79.

Blass, F./Debrunner, A./Funk, R. W. 1961: *A Greek Grammar of the New Testament and Other Early Christian Literature*, Chicago, IL: Chicago University Press 1961.

Bousset, W. 1895: *Der Antichrist in der Überlieferung des Judentums, des Neuen Testaments und der alten Kirche*, Göttingen: Vandenhoeck & Ruprecht 1895.

Braun, H. 1952-53/1967: "Zur nachpaulinischen Herkunft des zweiten Thessalonicherbriefes", in: *ZNW* 44 (1952/53) 152-56 [reprinted in: idem, *Gesammelte Studien zum Neuen Testament und seiner Umwelt*, 2nd ed., Tübingen: Mohr (Siebeck) 1967, 205-09].

Collins, R. F.: *Letters That Paul Did Not Write: The Letter to the Hebrews and the Pauline Pseudepigraha* (GNS 28) Wilmington, DE: Glazier 1988.

Conzelmann, H. 1971: *Geschichte des Urchristentums* (GNT 5), 2nd. ed., Göttingen: Vandenhoeck & Ruprecht 1971.

von Dobschütz, E. 1909/74: *Die Thessalonicher-Briefe* (KEK 10), Göttingen: Vandenhoeck & Ruprecht 1909 [= reprint Göttingen 1974].

Frame, J. E. 1912: *A Critical and Exegetical Commentary on the Epistles of St. Paul to the Thessalonians* (ICC), Edinburgh: T. & T. Clark 1912.

Friedrich, G. 1976: *Der zweite Brief an die Thessalonicher*, in: J. Becker/H. Conzelmann/G. Friedrich, *Die Briefe an die Galater, Epheser, Thessalonicher und Philemon* (NTD 8), Göttingen: Vandenhoeck & Ruprecht 1976, 252-76.

Giblin, C. H. 1967: *The Threat to Faith. An Exegetical and Theological Re-Examination of 2 Thessalonians 2* (AnBib 31), Rome: Pontifical Biblical Institute 1967.

Gülich E./Raible, W. 1977: "Überlegungen zu einer makrostrukturellen Textana-lyse: J. Thurber, The Lover and His Lass", in: T. A. van Dijk,/J. S. Petöfi (eds.), *Grammars and Descriptions* (Research in Text Theory 1), Berlin – New York: de Gruyter 1977, 132-75.

Gundry, R. H. 1987: "The Hellenization of Dominical Tradition and Christianiza-tion of Jewish Traditions in the Eschatology of 1 – 2 Thessalonians", in:*NTS* 33 (1987) 161-78.

Hartman, L. 1966: *Prophecy Interpreted. The Formation of Some Jewish Apocalyptic Texts and of the Eschatological Discourse Mark 13 Par.* (CB.NT 1), Lund: Gleerup 1966.

— 1967: "Antikrists mirakler", in: *RoB* 26 (1967) 37-63.

— 1975-76: "The Functions of Some So-Called Apocalyptic Time-Tables", in:*NTS* 22 (1975-76) 1-14 [In this volume no. 6].

— 1986: "On Reading Others' Letters", in: G. W. E. Nickelsburg/G. W. MacRae (eds.), *Christians Among Jews and Gentiles. FS K. Stendahl*, Philadelphia, PA: Fortress 1986, 137-46 [In this volume no. 9].

Hengel, M. 1984: "Entstehungszeit und Situation des Markusevangeliums", in: H. Cancik (ed.), *Markus-Philologie* (WUNT 33), Tübingen: Mohr (Siebeck) 1984, 1-45.

Hughes, F. W. 1984: *Second Thessalonians as a Document of Early Christian Rhetoric.* Diss. Northwestern University 1984; see *Dissertation Abstracts* 45 (1984/85), 3669-70 A.

Johanson, B. C. 1987: *To All the Brethren. A Text-Linguistic and Rhetorical Approach to I Thessalonians* (CB.NT 16), Stockholm: Almqvist & Wiksell International 1987.

Koester, H. 1982: *Introduction to the New Testament, Vol. 2,* Philadelphia, PA: Fort-ress/Berlin – New York: de Gruyter 1982.

Lindemann, A. 1977: "Zum Abfassungszweck des Zweiten Thessalonicherbrie-fes", in: *ZNW* 68 (1977) 35-47.

Littleton, H. E., Jr. 1973: *The Function of Apocalyptic in 2 Thessalonians as a Criterion for its Authorship.* Diss. Vanderbilt 1973; see *Dissertation Abstracts* 34 (1974) 4395 C.

Lohmeyer, E. 1950-51: "Antichrist", in: *RAC* 1 (1950-51) 450-57.

Maag, W. 1961: "Der Antichrist als Symbol des Bösen", in: *Das Böse.* Mit Beiträgen von M.-L. von Franz u. a. Vortragszyklus des Winters 1959 bis 1960 (SJI 13), Zürich – Stuttgart: Rascher 1961, 63-89.

Marshall, I. H. 1983: *1 and 2 Thessalonians* (NCB), Grand Rapids: Eerdmans/Lon-don: Marshall, Morgan & Scott 1983.

Mearns, C. L. 1980-81: *Early Eschatological Development in Paul: the Evidence of I and II Thessalonians*, in: *NTS* 27 (1980-81) 137-57.

Meeks, W. A. 1983: "Social Functions of Apocalyptic Language in Pauline Christianity", in: D. Hellholm (ed.), *Apocalypticism in the Mediterranean World and the Near East*, Tübingen: Mohr (Siebeck) 1983, 687-705.

Morris, Ch. W. 1938/53: *Foundations of the Theory of Signs* (International Encyclopedia of Unified Sciences, 1:2), Chicago, IL: Chicago University Press 1938 [repr. 1953].

Orchard, J. B. 1938: "Thessalonians and the Synoptic Gospels", in: *Bib.* 19 (1938) 19-42.

Pesch, R. 1968: *Naherwartungen. Tradition und Redaktion in Mk 13* (KBANT), Düsseldorf: Patmos 1968.

Plett, H. F. 1979: *Textwissenschaft und Textanalyse. Semiotik, Linguistik, Rhetorik* (UTB 328), 2nd ed., Heidelberg: Quelle & Meyer 1979.

Rigaux, B. 1932: *L'Antéchrist et l'opposition au royaume messianique dans l'Ancien et le Nouveau Testament* (Universitas Lovaniensis, Dissertationes ad gradum magistri, Facultas Theologica II.24), Paris – Gembloux: Duculot 1932.

— 1956: *Saint Paul. Les épîtres aux Thessaloniciens* (EtB), Paris: Gabalda/Gembloux: Duculot 1956.

Russell, R. 1988: "The Idle in 2 Thess 3.6-12: an Eschatological or a Social Problem?", in: *NTS* 34 (1988) 105-19.

Schenke H.-M./Fischer K. M. 1978: *Einleitung in die Schriften des Neuen Testaments, Band 1: Die Briefe des Paulus und Schriften des Paulinismus*, Berlin: Evangelische Verlagsanstalt/Gütersloh: Mohn 1978.

Selwyn, E. G. 1955: *The First Epistle of St. Peter*, London: Macmillan 1955.

Stephens, D. J. 1974: *Eschatological Themes in II Thessalonians 2:1-12*, Diss. St. Andrews, UK 1974; see *Dissertation Abstracts. International, C: European Abstracts* 37 (1976)1/287C.

Stephenson, A. M. G. 1968: "On the Meaning of ἐνέστηκεν ἡ ἡμέρα τοῦ κυρίου in 2 Thessalonians 2,2", in: F. L. Cross (ed.), *Studia Evangelica IV* (= TU 102), Berlin: Akademie-Verlag 1968, 442-51.

Trilling, W. 1972: *Untersuchungen zum 2. Thessalonicherbrief* (EThS 27), Leipzig: St. Benno 1972.

— 1980: *Der zweite Brief an die Thessalonicher* (EKK 14), Zürich – Einsiedeln – Köln: Benzinger Verlag/Neukirchen-Vluyn: Neukirchener Verlag 1980.

— 1981: "Literarische Paulus-Imitation im 2. Thessalonicherbrief", in: K. Kertelge (ed.), *Paulus in den neutestamentlichen Spätschriften: Zur Paulusrezeption im Neuen Testament* (QD 89), Freiburg – Basel – Wien: Herder 1981, 146-56.

Wenham, D. 1984: *The Rediscovery of Jesus' Eschatological Discourse* (Gospel Perspectives 4), Sheffield: JSOT Press 1984.

Wrede, W. 1908: *Die Echtheit des zweiten Thessalonicherbriefs untersucht* (TU NF 9:2), Leipzig: Hinrichs 1908.

Wuellner, W. 1976: "Paul's Rhetoric of Argumentation in Romans: An Alternative to the Donfried – Karris Debate Over Romans", in: *CBQ* 38 (1976) 330-51.

— 1987: "Where Is Rhetorical Criticism Taking Us?", in: *CBQ* 49 (1987) 448-63.

Supplement

Jewett, R.: *The Thessalonian Correspondence. Paul, the Rhetoric and Millenarian Piety* (Foundations and Facets. NT), Philadelphia, PA: Fortress 1986.

Holland, G. L.: *The Tradition that You Received from Us: 2 Thessalonians in the Pauline Tradition* (HUTh 24), Tübingen: Mohr (Siebeck) 1988.

Hughes, F. W.: *Early Christian Rhetoric and 2 Thessalonians* (JSNT.S 30), Sheffield: Sheffield Academic Press 1989.

Koester, H.: "From Paul's Eschatology to the Apocalyptic Schemata of 2 Thessalonians", in: R. F. Collins (ed.), *The Thessalonian Correspondence* (BEThL 87), Leuven: Leuven Univ. Press / Peeters 1990, 441-58.

Sunney, J. L.: "The Bearing of a Pauline Rhetorical Pattern on the Integrity of 2 Thessalonians", in: *ZNW* 81 (1990) 192-204.

Menken, M. J. J.: "Paradise Regained or Still Lost? Eschatology and Disorderly Behaviour in 2 Thessalonians", in: *NTS* 38 (1992) 271-89.

Schmidt, A.: "Erwägungen zur Eschatologie des 2 Thessaloniker und des 2 Johannes", in: *NTS* 38 (1992) 477-80.

Acknowledgements

The articles of this volume originally appeared in the following publications:

1. "Till frågan om evangeliernas litterära genre", in: AnASU 21(1978) 5-22. (Translated for this volume.)

2. "Das Markusevangelium, 'für die lectio sollemnis im Gottesdienst abgefaßt'?", in: H. Cancik/H. Lichtenberger/P. Schäfer (eds.), *Geschichte — Tradition — Reflexion. Festschrift für Martin Hengel zum 70. Geburtstag, Band III: Frühes Christentum*, Tübingen: Mohr (Siebeck) 1996, 147-171.

3. "Reading Luke 17:20-37", in: F. van Segbroeck et alii (eds.), *The Four Gospels 1992. Festschrift Frans Neirynck* (BEThL 100), Leuven: University Press/Peeters 1992, 1663-1675.

4. "An Attempt at a Text-Centered Exegesis of John 21", in: *StTh* 38 (1984) 29-45 [Oslo – Copenhagen – Stockholm – Boston: Scandinavian University Press].

5. "Survey of the Problem of Apocalyptic Genre", in: D. Hellholm (ed.), *Apocalypticism in the Mediterranean World and the Near East*, Tübingen: Mohr (Siebeck) 1983 (= 2nd ed. 1989), 329-343.

6. "The Functions of Some So-Called Apocalyptic Timetables", in *NTS* 22 (1975/76) 1-14 [Cambridge: Cambridge University Press].

7. "Form and Message. A Preliminary Discussion of 'Partial Texts' in Rev 1-3 and 22,6ff.", in: J. Lambrecht (ed.), *L'Apocalypse johannique et l'Apocalyptique dans le Nouveau Testament* (BEThL 53), Gembloux: Duculot / Leuven: Leuven University Press 1980, 129-149.

8. "Vad säger Sibyllan? Byggnad och budskap i de sibyllinska oraklens fjärde bok", in: P. W. Böckman, R. E. Kristiansen (eds.), *Context: Essays in Honour of Peder Johan Borgen*, Trondheim: Tapir 1987, 61-74. (Translated for this volume.)

9. "On Reading Others' Letters", in: G. Nickelsburg/G. MacRae (eds.), *Christians Among Jews and Gentiles. Essays in Honor of Krister Stendahl*, Philadelphia, PA: Fortress 1986, 137-146.

10. "Some Unorthodox Thoughts on the 'Household-Code Form'", in: J. Neusner et alii (eds.), *The Social World of Formative Christianity and Judaism. Essays in Tribute to Howard Clark Kee*, Philadelphia, PA: Fortress 1988, 219-232.

11. "Doing Things with the Words of Colossians", previously unpublished.

12. "1 Co 14,1-25: Argument and Some Problems", in: L. De Lorenzi (ed.), *Charisma und Agape (1 Ko 12-14)* (SMBen.BE 7), Rome: Benedictina 1983, 149-169.

13. "A Sketch of the Argument of 2 Cor 10-13", previously unpublished.

14. "Galatians 3:15-4:11 as Part of a Theological Argument on a Practical Issue", in: J. Lambrecht (ed.), *The Truth of the Gospel (Galatians 1:1-4:11)* (SMBen.BE 12), Rome: Benedictina 1993, 127-158.

15. "The Eschatology of 2 Thessalonians as Included in a Communication", in: R. Collins (ed.), *The Thessalonian Correspondence* (BEThL 87), Leuven: Leuven University Press/Peeters 1990, 470-485.

Index of Passages

(Selective)

1. Old Testament

2. OT Apocrypha, Pseudepigrapha and Other Early Jewish Texts

3. Qumran Texts

4. Rabbinic Texts

5. New Testament

6. Apostolic Fathers and Other Early Christian Texts

7. Classical Texts

Index of Modern Authors

Index of Subjects

Wissenschaftliche Untersuchungen zum Neuen Testament

Alphabetical Index of the First and Second Series

Forbes, Christopher Brian: Prophecy and Inspired Speech in Early Christianity and its Hellenistic Environment. 1995. *Volume II/75.*

Fornberg, Tord: see *Fridrichsen, Anton.*

Fossum, Jarl E.: The Name of God and the Angel of the Lord. 1985. *Volume 36.*

Frenschkowski, Marco: Offenbarung und Epiphanie. Volume 1 1995. *Volume II/79* – Volume 2 1997. *Volume II/80.*

Frey, Jörg: Eugen Drewermann und die biblische Exegese. 1995. *Volume II/71.*

– Die johanneische Eschatologie. Volume I. 1997. *Volume 96.*

Fridrichsen, Anton: Exegetical Writings. Ed. by C.C. Caragounis and T. Fornberg. 1994. *Volume 76.*

Garlington, Don B.: ›The Obedience of Faith‹. 1991. *Volume II/38.*

– Faith, Obedience, and Perseverance. 1994. *Volume 79.*

Garnet, Paul: Salvation and Atonement in the Qumran Scrolls. 1977. *Volume II/3.*

Gräßer, Erich: Der Alte Bund im Neuen. 1985. *Volume 35.*

Green, Joel B.: The Death of Jesus. 1988. *Volume II/33.*

Gundry Volf, Judith M.: Paul and Perseverance. 1990. *Volume II/37.*

Hafemann, Scott J.: Suffering and the Spirit. 1986. *Volume II/19.*

– Paul, Moses, and the History of Israel. 1995. *Volume 81.*

Hartman, Lars: Text-Centered New Testament Studies. Ed. by D. Hellholm. 1997. *Volume 102.*

Heckel, Theo K.: Der Innere Mensch. 1993. *Volume II/53.*

Heckel, Ulrich: Kraft in Schwachheit. 1993. *Volume II/56.*

– see *Feldmeier, Reinhard.*

– see *Hengel, Martin.*

Heiligenthal, Roman: Werke als Zeichen. 1983. *Volume II/9.*

Hellholm, D.: see *Hartman, Lars.*

Hemer, Colin J.: The Book of Acts in the Setting of Hellenistic History. 1989. *Volume 49.*

Hengel, Martin: Judentum und Hellenismus. 1969, ³1988. *Volume 10.*

– Die johanneische Frage. 1993. *Volume 67.*

– Judaica et Hellenistica. Volume 1. 1996. *Volume 90.*

Hengel, Martin und *Ulrich Heckel* (Ed.): Paulus und das antike Judentum. 1991. *Volume 58.*

Hengel, Martin und *Hermut Löhr* (Ed.): Schriftauslegung im antiken Judentum und im Urchristentum. 1994. *Volume 73.*

Hengel, Martin und *Anna Maria Schwemer* (Ed.): Königsherrschaft Gottes und himmlischer Kult. 1991. *Volume 55.*

– Die Septuaginta. 1994. *Volume 72.*

Herrenbrück, Fritz: Jesus und die Zöllner. 1990. *Volume II/41.*

Hoegen-Rohls, Christina: Der nachösterliche Johannes. 1996. *Volume II/84.*

Hofius, Otfried: Katapausis. 1970. *Volume 11.*

– Der Vorhang vor dem Thron Gottes. 1972. *Volume 14.*

– Der Christushymnus Philipper 2,6-11. 1976, ²1991. *Volume 17.*

– Paulusstudien. 1989, ²1994. *Volume 51.*

Hofius, Otfried und *Hans-Christian Kammler:* Johannesstudien. 1996. *Volume 88.*

Holtz, Traugott: Geschichte und Theologie des Urchristentums. 1991. *Volume 57.*

Hommel, Hildebrecht: Sebasmata. Volume 1 1983. *Volume 31* – Volume 2 1984. *Volume 32.*

Hvalvik, Reidar: The Struggle of Scripture and Convenant. 1996. *Volume II/82.*

Kähler, Christoph: Jesu Gleichnisse als Poesie und Therapie. 1995. *Volume 78.*

Kammler, Hans-Christian: see *Hofius, Otfried.*

Kamlah, Ehrhard: Die Form der katalogischen Paränese im Neuen Testament. 1964. *Volume 7.*

Kieffer, René und *Jan Bergman (Ed.):* La Main de Dieu / Die Hand Gottes. 1997. *Volume 94.*

Kim, Seyoon: The Origin of Paul's Gospel. 1981, ²1984. *Volume II/4.*

– »The ›Son of Man‹« as the Son of God. 1983. *Volume 30.*

Kleinknecht, Karl Th.: Der leidende Gerechtfertigte. 1984, ²1988. *Volume II/13.*

Klinghardt, Matthias: Gesetz und Volk Gottes. 1988. *Volume II/32.*

Köhler, Wolf-Dietrich: Rezeption des Matthäusevangeliums in der Zeit vor Irenäus. 1987. *Volume II/24.*

Korn, Manfred: Die Geschichte Jesu in veränderter Zeit. 1993. *Volume II/51.*

Koskenniemi, Erkki: Apollonios von Tyana in der neutestamentlichen Exegese. 1994.
    Volume II/61.
Kraus, Wolfgang: Das Volk Gottes. 1996. *Volume 85.*
– see *Walter, Nikolaus.*
Kuhn, Karl G.: Achtzehngebet und Vaterunser und der Reim. 1950. *Volume 1.*
Laansma, Jon: I Will Give You Rest. 1997. *Volume II/97.*
Lampe, Peter: Die stadtrömischen Christen in den ersten beiden Jahrhunderten. 1987, ²1989.
    Volume II/18.
Lau, Andrew: Manifest in Flesh. 1996. *Volume II/86.*
Lichtenberger, Hermann: see *Avemarie, Friedrich.*
Lieu, Samuel N.C.: Manichaeism in the Later Roman Empire and Medieval China. 1992.
    Volume 63.
Loader, William R.G.: Jesus' Attitude Towards the Law. 1997. *Volume II/96.*
Löhr, Gebhard: Verherrlichung Gottes durch Philosophie. 1997. *Volume 97.*
Löhr, Hermut: see *Hengel, Martin.*
Löhr, Winrich Alfried: Basilides und seine Schule. 1995. *Volume 83.*
Maier, Gerhard: Mensch und freier Wille. 1971. *Volume 12.*
– Die Johannesoffenbarung und die Kirche. 1981. *Volume 25.*
Markschies, Christoph: Valentinus Gnosticus? 1992. *Volume 65.*
Marshall, Peter: Enmity in Corinth: Social Conventions in Paul's Relations with
    the Corinthians. 1987. *Volume II/23.*
Meade, David G.: Pseudonymity and Canon. 1986. *Volume 39.*
Meadors, Edward P.: Jesus the Messianic Herald of Salvation. 1995. *Volume II/72.*
Meißner, Stefan: Die Heimholung des Ketzers. 1996. *Volume II/87.*
Mell, Ulrich: Die »anderen« Winzer. 1994. *Volume 77.*
Mengel, Berthold: Studien zum Philipperbrief. 1982. *Volume II/8.*
Merkel, Helmut: Die Widersprüche zwischen den Evangelien. 1971. *Volume 13.*
Merklein, Helmut: Studien zu Jesus und Paulus. 1987. *Volume 43.*
Metzler, Karin: Der griechische Begriff des Verzeihens. 1991. *Volume II/44.*
Metzner, Rainer: Die Rezeption des Matthäusevangeliums im 1. Petrusbrief. 1995. *Volume II/74.*
Mittmann-Richert, Ulrike: Magnifikat und Benediktus. 1996. *Volume II/90.*
Niebuhr, Karl-Wilhelm: Gesetz und Paränese. 1987. *Volume II/28.*
– Heidenapostel aus Israel. 1992. *Volume 62.*
Nissen, Andreas: Gott und der Nächste im antiken Judentum. 1974. *Volume 15.*
Noormann, Rolf: Irenäus als Paulusinterpret. 1994. *Volume II/66.*
Obermann, Andreas: Die christologische Erfüllung der Schrift im Johannesevangelium. 1996.
    Volume II/83.
Okure, Teresa: The Johannine Approach to Mission. 1988. *Volume II/31.*
Park, Eung Chun: The Mission Discourse in Matthew's Interpretation. 1995. *Volume II/81.*
Philonenko, Marc (Ed.): Le Trône de Dieu. 1993. *Volume 69.*
Pilhofer, Peter: Presbyteron Kreitton. 1990. *Volume II/39.*
– Philippi. Volume 1 1995. *Volume 87.*
Pöhlmann, Wolfgang: Der Verlorene Sohn und das Haus. 1993. *Volume 68.*
Pokorný, Petr und *Josef B. Souček:* Bibelauslegung als Theologie. 1997. *Volume 100.*
Prieur, Alexander: Die Verkündigung der Gottesherrschaft. 1996. *Volume II/89.*
Probst, Hermann: Paulus und der Brief. 1991. *Volume II/45.*
Räisänen, Heikki: Paul and the Law. 1983, ²1987. *Volume 29.*
Rehkopf, Friedrich: Die lukanische Sonderquelle. 1959. *Volume 5.*
Rein, Matthias: Die Heilung des Blindgeborenen (Joh 9). 1995. *Volume II/73.*
Reinmuth, Eckart: Pseudo-Philo und Lukas. 1994. *Volume 74.*
Reiser, Marius: Syntax und Stil des Markusevangeliums. 1984. *Volume II/11.*
Richards, E. Randolph: The Secretary in the Letters of Paul. 1991. *Volume II/42.*
Riesner, Rainer: Jesus als Lehrer. 1981, ³1988. *Volume II/7.*
– Die Frühzeit des Apostels Paulus. 1994. *Volume 71.*
Rissi, Mathias: Die Theologie des Hebräerbriefs. 1987. *Volume 41.*
Röhser, Günter: Metaphorik und Personifikation der Sünde. 1987. *Volume II/25.*

Rose, Christian: Die Wolke der Zeugen. 1994. *Volume II/60.*
Rüger, Hans Peter: Die Weisheitsschrift aus der Kairoer Geniza. 1991. *Volume 53.*
Sänger, Dieter: Antikes Judentum und die Mysterien. 1980. *Volume II/5.*
– Die Verkündigung des Gekreuzigten und Israel. 1994. *Volume 75.*
Salzmann, Jorg Christian: Lehren und Ermahnen. 1994. *Volume II/59.*
Sandnes, Karl Olav: Paul – One of the Prophets? 1991. *Volume II/43.*
Sato, Migaku: Q und Prophetie. 1988. *Volume II/29.*
Schaper, Joachim: Eschatology in the Greek Psalter. 1995. *Volume II/76.*
Schimanowski, Gottfried: Weisheit und Messias. 1985. *Volume II/17.*
Schlichting, Günter: Ein jüdisches Leben Jesu. 1982. *Volume 24.*
Schnabel, Eckhard J.: Law and Wisdom from Ben Sira to Paul. 1985. *Volume II/16.*
Schutter, William L.: Hermeneutic and Composition in I Peter. 1989. *Volume II/30.*
Schwartz, Daniel R.: Studies in the Jewish Background of Christianity. 1992. *Volume 60.*
Schwemer, Anna Maria: see *Hengel, Martin*
Scott, James M.: Adoption as Sons of God. 1992. *Volume II/48.*
– Paul and the Nations. 1995. *Volume 84.*
Siegert, Folker: Drei hellenistisch-jüdische Predigten. Teil I 1980. *Volume 20* – Teil II 1992.
    Volume 61.
– Nag-Hammadi-Register. 1982. *Volume 26.*
– Argumentation bei Paulus. 1985. *Volume 34.*
– Philon von Alexandrien. 1988. *Volume 46.*
Simon, Marcel: Le christianisme antique et son contexte religieux I/II. 1981. *Volume 23.*
Snodgrass, Klyne: The Parable of the Wicked Tenants. 1983. *Volume 27.*
Söding, Thomas: Das Wort vom Kreuz. 1997. *Volume 93.*
– see *Thüsing, Wilhelm.*
Sommer, Urs: Die Passionsgeschichte des Markusevangeliums. 1993. *Volume II/58.*
Souček, Josef B.: see *Pokorný, Petr.*
Spangenberg, Volker: Herrlichkeit des Neuen Bundes. 1993. *Volume II/55.*
Speyer, Wolfgang: Frühes Christentum im antiken Strahlungsfeld. 1989. *Volume 50.*
Stadelmann, Helge: Ben Sira als Schriftgelehrter. 1980. *Volume II/6.*
Strobel, August: Die Stunde der Wahrheit. 1980. *Volume 21.*
Stuckenbruck, Loren T.: Angel Veneration and Christology. 1995. *Volume II/70.*
Stuhlmacher, Peter (Ed.): Das Evangelium und die Evangelien. 1983. *Volume 28.*
Sung, Chong-Hyon: Vergebung der Sünden. 1993. *Volume II/57.*
Tajra, Harry W.: The Trial of St. Paul. 1989. *Volume II/35.*
– The Martyrdom of St.Paul. 1994. *Volume II/67.*
Theißen, Gerd: Studien zur Soziologie des Urchristentums. 1979, [3]1989. *Volume 19.*
Thornton, Claus-Jürgen: Der Zeuge des Zeugen. 1991. *Volume 56.*
Thüsing, Wilhelm: Studien zur neutestamentlichen Theologie. Ed. by Thomas Söding. 1995.
    Volume 82.
Tsuji, Manabu: Glaube zwischen Vollkommenheit und Verweltlichung. 1997. *Volume II/93*
Twelftree, Graham H.: Jesus the Exorcist. 1993. *Volume II/54.*
Visotzky, Burton L.: Fathers of the World. 1995. *Volume 80.*
Wagener, Ulrike: Die Ordnung des »Hauses Gottes«. 1994. *Volume II/65.*
Walter, Nikolaus: Praeparatio Evangelica. Ed. by Wolfgang Kraus and Florian Wilk.
    1997. *Volume 98.*
Watts, Rikki: Isaiah's New Exodus and Mark. 1997. *Volume II/88.*
Wedderburn, A.J.M.: Baptism and Resurrection. 1987. *Volume 44.*
Wegner, Uwe: Der Hauptmann von Kafarnaum. 1985. *Volume II/14.*
Welck, Christian: Erzählte ›Zeichen‹. 1994. *Volume II/69.*
Wilk, Florian: see *Walter, Nikolaus.*
Wilson, Walter T.: Love without Pretense. 1991. *Volume II/46.*
Zimmermann, Alfred E.: Die urchristlichen Lehrer. 1984, [2]1988. *Volume II/12.*

For a complete catalogue please write to the publisher
Mohr Siebeck, P.O.Box 2040, D–72010 Tübingen.